THE FAR WEST
AND THE GREAT PLAINS
IN TRANSITION
1859–1900

The

New American Nation Series

EDITED BY

HENRY STEELE COMMAGER

AND

RICHARD B. MORRIS

THE FAR WEST
AND THE GREAT PLAINS
IN TRANSITION
1859 ★ 1900

RODMAN W. PAUL

ILLUSTRATED

1817

HARPER & ROW, PUBLISHERS, New York
Cambridge, Philadelphia, San Francisco, Washington
London, Mexico City, São Paulo, Singapore, Sydney

Editor's Note

Professor Rodman W. Paul died before the completion of the editorial work on this book. Professor Martin Ridge saw the work through the press.

THE FAR WEST AND THE GREAT PLAINS IN TRANSITION. Copyright © 1988 by N.T. Paul. All rights reserved. Printed in the United States of America. No part of this book may be used or reproduced in any manner whatsoever without written permission except in the case of brief quotations embodied in critical articles and reviews. For information address Harper & Row, Publishers. 10 East 53rd Street, New York, N.Y. 10022. Published simultaneously in Canada by Fitzhenry & Whiteside Limited, Toronto.

FIRST EDITION

Designer: Sidney Feinberg

Copy editor: Rick Hermann

Indexer: Carol Pearson

Map by George Colbert

Library of Congress Cataloging-in-Publication Data

Paul, Rodman W. (Rodman Wilson), 1912–1987
   The far west and the great plains in transition,
1859–1900.

(The New American Nation series)
   Bibliography: p.
   Includes index.
   1. West (U.S.)—History—1848–1950. 2. Mines and mineral resources—West
(U.S.)—History—19th century. 3. Ranch life—West (U.S.)—History—19th century.
I. Title. II. Series.
F595.P27   1988   978'.02   87-17666
ISBN 0-06-015836-0   88 89 90 91 HC 10 9 8 7 6 5 4 3 2 1
ISBN 0-06-091448-3 (pbk.)   88 89 90 91 HC 10 9 8 7 6 5 4 3 2 1

To
Anne especially,
and to the whole family for
patience and loyalty

Contents

Illustrations appear following page 238.

Acknowledgments

TWO institutions have helped me greatly: the California Institute of Technology, which has paid me, provided secretarial services, and granted research support; and the Henry E. Huntington Library, which supplied most of the raw materials out of which this book has been written. But more than that, the Huntington has proved a friendly and inspiring environment for scholarship. At the Huntington I wish particularly to thank the Director, Robert Middlekauff, and Martin Ridge, who has general charge of research.

Huntington staff members were wonderful. Virginia Renner, head of Readers' Services, was unfailing in her patience. Brita Mack and Susan Naulty searched through the Huntington's rich collections to find most of the illustrations. At Caltech Joy Hansen taught me how to use a word processor and rescued the resulting copy when I got into trouble. Edith Tayler typed the early part; Maxine Fredericksen ran the discs after I entered the modern age.

The California State Library's California Section, the Denver Public Library's Western History Department, and the Montana Historical Society all contributed pictures. Judy Austin saw to it that the Idaho Historical Society provided pictures with admirable celerity and discrimination.

This volume has been finished under difficulties that would have been insurmountable without the support of my wife and the morale-boosting visits of our children.

—RODMAN W. PAUL

Pasadena

xi

Editors' Introduction

As the late Rodman W. Paul informs us in his superb overview of the Far West and the Great Plains in transition between 1860 and 1900, an area so enormous in its reach and so complex in its natural resources, peoples, and occupations could not be fully comprehended by any single early visitor, whether a crotchety if redoubtable Horace Greeley or the author of *Roughing It*. If Mark Twain graphically described the "flush times" of Virginia City, with its saloons, gambling dens, brothels, police courts, and jails, which he regarded as an "unfailing sign of high prosperity" in a mining region, Rodman Paul's richly detailed book paints on a broader canvas. It reaches far beyond the cowboy and Indian stereotype and the striking landscapes associated with Albert Bierstadt and Frederic Remington and portrays a complex society of varied occupations.

The time span of this book covers an area rapidly settled by a people, restless, expansionist, resourceful, if not too attentive to the niceties of the law, and harboring ill-concealed prejudices toward various ethnic groups. Each area posed a diversity of challenges, and they were met by the creation of ingenious methods of transportation, communication, and farming and lumbering technology. The reader moves by mule team, then by pony express, and finally travels by railroad and communicates by telegraph. If the opportunities enriched the luckier among the early miners, the greater wealth and power were to be acquired by merchants and bankers in major cities like San Francisco and Denver, and even in Brigham Young's Mormon land, where traders, particularly non-Mormons, were denounced.

The many people Rodman Paul introduces us to were opportunists and expansion-minded, in some cases with New York origins and connections. They employed every conceivable legal device, heavy lobbying, and the arts of chicanery to create such giant combinations as Wells Fargo, and the Union Pacific and Central Pacific Railroads, among other combines, and to acquire mining rights and farming and pasture lands. Herein we meet Collis Huntington, Charles Crocker, Levi Strauss, and Lloyd Tevis, among other astute men of business.

The story of the transition of the Far West and the Great Plains during these years is one of epic proportions. On the Northern extremities, from Washington to Oregon (on both sides of the Cascades) and the late developing Montana down to Texas on the Southern rim, from the start of the arid zone around 100°NL on the East and then westward to the Pacific slope, the reader gains insights into a vast region of enormous contrasts. Settled by fits and starts, it would be peopled from many lands, including non-Anglos—Hispanics, Scots, Irish, Germans, Chinese, and, of course, the first Americans, the Indians. For the latter, herded on reservations, often cheated of their lands, the author reports total economic collapse and lasting sullen resentment. He condemns the treatment of the Indians as riddled by politics and corruption and cites with approval Clark Wissler's characterization of them as "prisoners in a concentration camp."

Exploitation was not confined to the Indians, however. The Chinese by working for lower wages infuriated the poorer whites, while the Hispanic population of New Mexico and Texas found so much of their land claims to have disappeared in a maze of legal transactions. When mining technology of the base metals assumed the character of the factory system, miners organized and staged strikes. These conflicts of class and ethnic differences occurred in years of sensational development for an area which expanded at an exceptional rate both in population and wealth.

Rodman Paul sees much of that prosperity coming as a result of the ruthless pursuit of private gain, tempered somewhat by conservationists who attacked the heavy-handed exhaustion of the natural resources of the area. Vigilantism and railroad scandals, mining frauds, lack of concern for the safety and welfare of underground miners—these were all part of the larger picture of unbridled acquisitiveness. By 1900 the Far West and a large part of the Great Plains had undergone a transformation to modern times. Where in the past were scattered hamlets of tents, hovels, and cottonwood-log cabins, stood planned metropolises operating under a rule of law. Horace Greeley's advice to a young man to "Go West" seems to have been prophetic. Greeley's West had come a long way. It had helped forge a union from sea to sea and had contributed much substantiation to the myth of America as a land of rags to riches.

Rodman Paul's is the third of the four volumes devoted in the New American Nation Series to the history of the West. Francis S. Philbrick's initial volume covers the early West, 1754–1830; Ray A. Billington continues the story of *The Far Western Frontier, 1830–1860;* and in a forthcoming volume, Earl Pomeroy will relate the development of the area in the twentieth century. This volume, and the others mentioned, are part of the New American Nation Series, a comprehensive, cooperative history of the area now embraced in the United States from the days of discovery to our own times.

HENRY STEELE COMMAGER
RICHARD B. MORRIS

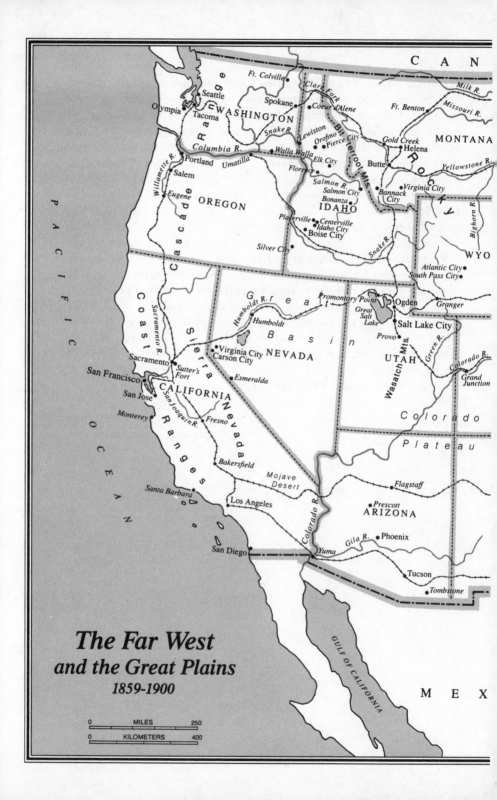

The Far West
and the Great Plains
1859–1900

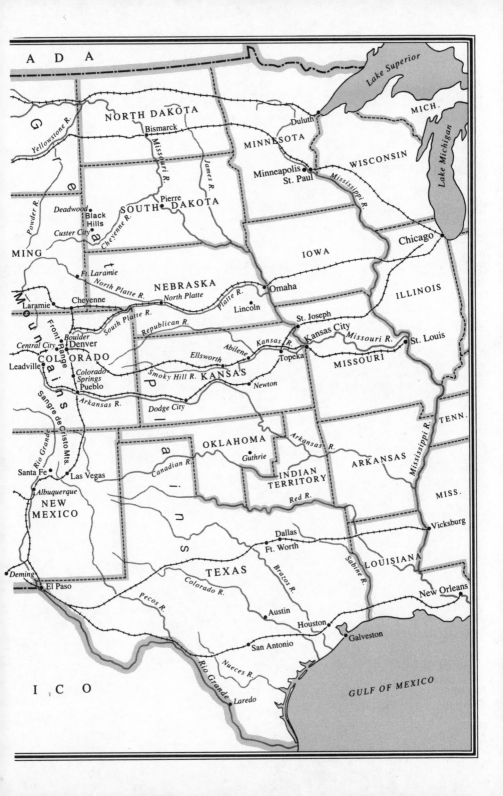

A Varied People in a Varied Land in an Era of Rapid Change

FOR the Far West and the Great Plains the forty years between the eve of the Civil War and the opening of the new century were at once a period of climax, when long-developing pioneer ways reached their final expression, and also a time of rapid transition, in which parts of the west imitated the nation as a whole by moving quickly into a capitalized, industrialized economy that spread its rewards very unevenly between entrepreneurs and workers. In the 1870s, for example, the west had notable mining rushes, Indian fights, and cowboy drives that grew directly out of the attitudes and practices of earlier years, and yet the 1870s had also factory-like absentee-owned mines whose angry workers organized into militant, violence-prone unions, while at San Francisco, which was the principal mercantile and industrial center of the west, the insecurity, unemployment, and poverty of the workers inspired a class warfare and a racist violence that mocked the legend of California as the golden land of opportunity.

Of the two wests, it has been the simpler one—the cowboy, prospector, Indian-fighting one—that has traditionally attracted the world's attention. The sheer color, drama, and uniqueness of that type of west has enabled novelists, artists, and moviemakers to reach huge audiences. Emerson Hough, one of the most successful writers of fictionalized history of his day, declared in 1897 that "the story of the West is a story of the time of heroes."[1] And in fact there were heroes, villains, and picturesque people and events sufficient to fill

1

any book. The cast of characters included Frederic Remington's blue-shirted soldiers fighting fierce mounted Indians, bearded gold rushers en route to Pike's Peak or the Boise Basin, cowboys pushing longhorns northward on the Long Drive from Texas, greenhorns and miners heading for the Black Hills and Tombstone, and land seekers stampeding into Oklahoma. All of this is indeed a part of the story.

But there is much more besides. Nor is it merely a need to tell of class warfare in the mines and at San Francisco, nor of the accumulation of great wealth and power by the few. Henry George has already covered much of that ground in the west's most famous economic tract, *Progress and Poverty* (1879). Henry George did not have available to him the insights suggested by modern social scientists. The present book could well have been entitled "Men in Motion," to borrow a phrase from a well-known modern scholar.[2] One of the major achievements of present-day students has been to use quantitative methods and computers to reveal to us how incredibly mobile were nineteenth-century Americans—in both east and west.

Men and women were moving restlessly from east to west in covered wagons, stagecoaches, and railroad cars, as tradition has so long told us, but also, less dramatically, they were moving in and out of both eastern and western cities, in and out of whole states and territories. As recently as 1963 the present writer thought that he was describing something exceptional when he pointed out that a contemporary observer had "expressed the belief that a hundred thousand people had lived in Colorado for varying periods between 1858 and 1870, even though there had rarely been more than a third of that number in the territory at any one time."[3] With the preliminary insights that recent research is offering us, such a rate of turnover in an unstable new mining territory appears to have been not that much greater than in a reasonably well-established western city like San Francisco, and perhaps not even dramatically higher than in a really well-established eastern center like Boston.

Throughout the book an attempt will be made to identify the origins and geographical and occupational changes of some of the leaders who directed the transformation of the western country. A similar attempt to explain whence came the simpler folk—the bulk of the western population—is much more difficult. It requires evidence concerning not only the poorer native-born, English-speaking whites, who left few records, but also information about the masses of almost anonymous immigrants from Ireland, from the several German-speaking regions, from England, Cornwall, Scotland, and Wales, and from France, Italy, Yugoslavia, Scandinavia, and China. The census frequently reported western states and territories in which from 20 to 40 percent of the population was foreign born, and occasionally the figure was even higher.

Comparable problems arise when we seek to know more about the three native-born ethnic minorities: the Native American Indians, Hispano-Americans, and blacks, all of whom the lords of the land reduced to a subordinate status that did little to encourage record keeping. Only within recent years have we begun to recognize meaningful evidence concerning the fate of these three.

Then there is the question of failures. For a full understanding of these forty years we would like to know the life stories not only of those who achieved "upward mobility" (i.e., success), but also of those who never moved up from humble beginnings or who rose and fell, never to recover. Only rarely are we fortunate enough to inherit the life story of a failure, as happened with the discovery of the seventy-nine volumes of diaries faithfully kept for more than half a century by Alf Doten, a New Englander who started as a Forty-Niner in the California gold rush, worked as a journalist on the Comstock Lode, and became for a brief moment a successful newspaper publisher on the Comstock before he began his long, dreary slide down into uncontrollable alcoholism, social and economic uselessness, and pathetic dependency on the erratic charity of those who had known him in his better days.[4]

This book, then, will be in considerable part a tale of "men in motion," and of the surprisingly large minority of women and children who had the courage to accompany them and make new homes in a new land. The men opened routes for wagon trains, stagecoaches, railroads, and steamboats; they built major regional centers like San Francisco, Denver, Salt Lake City, and Portland, or lesser ones like Boise and Phoenix; they promoted mines or worked in them; they seized unoccupied ranges and ran cattle or sheep on them; they tried farming in a land of precariously little rain; and they cut down the forests and hauled them to sawmills. In other words, promoters, bosses, the self-employed, and hired workers joined in an incredibly rapid, often extravagantly wasteful exploitation of the west and its natural resources. Notable achievements, ingenuity, courage, and generous actions loomed up side by side with petty intrigues and sheer greed, as good men and bad schemed for material success. Yet for all the unevenness and instability thus implied, out of the efforts of this mixed population there emerged by the turn of the century a new society, one that copied extensively from eastern models and yet added enough of its own to create something that was fresh and exciting and distinctive.

But what of the land itself? The land wherein such great changes took place within so short a time? That it was huge—nearly half the United States—is obvious. That it was as varied and uneven as the people who exploited it is equally obvious, for everyone knows of its massive mountain ranges, such as the Rockies, Sierra Nevada, and Cascades, its vast deserts, its high semiarid plains and intermontane plateaus, its oases of rich irrigated farm districts, its occasional stands of valuable timber, and its underground wealth in minerals and oil. To describe such a land in a single generalization is impossible.

The most nearly universal characteristic of the west is inadequate precipitation. Traditionally twenty inches per year has been regarded as the minimum for agriculture without irrigation or special dry-farming practices or carefully selected drought-resistant crops. Government charts of "mean annual precipitation" and "annual average precipitation" show that the twenty-inch line begins and ends at the ninety-eighth meridian, on the Canadian border and the Gulf Coast of Texas respectively, but for most of its distance follows the hundredth meridian. To allow for difference in temperature and rate of evaporation, a true "line of semiaridity," as it is termed, should be bent somewhat westward in North Dakota and somewhat eastward in Texas.[5]

Seasonally the Pacific Coast's rainfall comes in winter, the southwest's in summer (save for winter snow and rain in the mountains and higher plateaus), while the area from Utah northward receives its precipitation in winter and early spring; in the Great Plains, however, "the drought hazard is greatest in winter and least in late spring and early summer."[6] Everywhere the west's abundant sunshine promotes plant growth and yet also snatches away water by evaporation.

While the inadequate and highly seasonal precipitation is a generalizing characteristic, an obvious exception must be made in favor of the Pacific Northwest (west of the Cascades) and northwestern California, for there the rainfall is ample, anywhere from two to three times the twenty-inch figure. Farther south in California, precipitation shades off from adequacy to semiaridity to true aridity.

But even the northwestern exception does not alter the circumstance that for former eastern, middle western, or immigrant farmers and stock raisers who were accustomed to forty or fifty inches distributed throughout the year, the climate of most of the western half of the United States demanded a severe and puzzling adjustment. The climate, in turn, meant that lumber, the universal American building material, was abundant in the Pacific Northwest and northwestern California, but was available elsewhere only in mountainous locations and under conditions that made lumbering costly. For farmers, stockmen, miners, railroad builders, and city promoters alike, this was a sobering consideration.

To climatologists the Pacific Coast west of the Sierra Nevada–Cascades was a region of "summer-dry climates" and mild if wet winters,[7] while to soil scientists much of it was a land that had the deep, nitrogen-rich, humus-poor soils so characteristic of dry regions.[8] To pioneers of the 1840s and 1850s such subtleties were unknown, but their instincts told them that the Pacific Coast was far preferable to the unappealing semiarid Great Plains or the huge "arid region [which] comprises a broad belt of mountain, valley, and desert . . . between the western margins of the Great Plains and the crests of the Sierra Nevada–Cascade barrier."[9] Only the Mormons disagreed. By 1860 the census credited California with nearly 380,000 inhabitants, Oregon with 52,000, and Utah with 40,000.

CHAPTER 1

Horace Greeley Goes West

A LL too often the public's most definite recollection of a notable man centers around some remark that he is alleged to have made—Washington's youthful discourse on the unwisdom of logging his father's cherry orchard, Franklin's Poor Richard homily on the importance of saving a penny. Horace Greeley did indeed urge a clergyman friend to "Go West, young man, go West," although killjoys among the historical profession now claim that when Greeley said this in 1853 he was merely echoing a phrase employed earlier by an Indiana editor. Be that as it may, the pity is that so many modern people can remember nothing else about Greeley save this one famous bit of advice.

In fact, Greeley was one of the striking figures of his generation. His very appearance and manner were so bizarre as to be unforgettable: a pink baby face fringed with throat whiskers, a squeaky voice, acute absentmindedness, illegible handwriting, and the careless costume that became his trademark—white overcoat and socks, shapeless trousers and crooked cravat, a broad-brimmed hat. Yet the readers of the highly influential newspaper that he created, the New York *Tribune*, followed his crusades and his sometimes eccentric enthusiasms with intense interest. The *Tribune* circulated throughout the north and west and was quoted more and argued about more than any journal of its day. Nowhere was this more true than in the west. As his biographer has remarked, "The West loved Horace Greeley,"[1] and the west was delighted when it learned that

7

the famous editor was going to make a journey of observation through the Far West and Great Plains in the spring and summer of 1859. Having urged his young friend to go west, he was now going to follow his own advice.

Greeley's visit became a western classic, forever preserved in popular memory by the hopeless anecdote of what Hank Monk, the stage driver, said to Greeley while the stagecoach was jolting and swaying on its clattering way over the Sierra Nevada to Placerville. Mark Twain claimed that on his own later stagecoach rides he had to listen to that story either 481 or 482 times, he wasn't sure which, and that the one occasion when he refused to endure the tale once more was fatal to the frustrated raconteur: "In trying to retain the anecdote in his system he strained himself and died in our arms."[2]

Although he was only forty-eight at the time, Greeley found the trip an exhausting experience, characterized by endless hours of physical discomfort in lurching, banging coaches and wagons, not to mention primitive accommodations at wayside stations, together with the psychological depression that came from gazing upon arid, dust-blown landscapes once he had entered the farther west. The Great Plains he termed a "land of starvation," a "treeless desert," a region whose "terrible" climate alternated between daytime's baking heat "in the sun's unsoftened glare" and nighttime's "chill and piercing" cold. But when his coach reached the Humboldt Sink of Nevada, he concluded that the Great Plains had been green by comparison. "Here, on the Humboldt," he exclaimed, "famine sits enthroned, and waves his scepter over a dominion expressly made for him."[3]

Greeley's adventures had started in more civilized fashion when he took the railroad from New York City via Chicago to Quincy, Illinois, on the Mississippi, then crossed the state of Missouri on the brand-new Hannibal and St. Joseph Railroad, so that he could board a river steamer to go down the muddy Missouri ("its color and consistency are those of thick milk porridge," he reported) to the frontier outfitting hamlet of Atchison, Kansas. At Atchison the Missouri conveniently makes a sharp bend to the west, well past the ninety-fifth meridian of longitude, and there Greeley found wagon trains making up for the Mormon settlements at Salt Lake; for the overland-trail posts at Laramie and Fort Hall; for Green River, made famous by the old fur traders; and even, he heard, for fabled

Santa Fe. Would-be miners, about to start on the gold rush to Pike's Peak, were everywhere; their wagons and tents dotted the prairie around Atchison. With deep satisfaction Greeley reported: "I have long been looking for the West, and here it is at last" (p. 19).

Greeley's first travel letter to the *Tribune* was dated at Atchison, May 15, 1859; his last at San Francisco, September 4–5. In the less than four months between these two dates he managed to see an astonishingly good sampling of the types of human beings that dwelt in the Far West and Great Plains, and an equally representative selection of the climatic and physical settings. An excellent reporter who not only observed but interpreted, Greeley sent back travel letters that in their totality constituted a perceptive inventory of the farther west as it was in that year 1859.

Especially notable among Greeley's findings was his recognition that however new the west of 1859 might seem to be, nevertheless its population was a complex blending of old and new elements, some of them almost legendary in the west by then, others as recently arrived as the greenhorns among the crowd bound for Pike's Peak. In a letter written after he had reached Denver, which was just coming into being as a gold-rush camp built of cottonwood logs cut in the Platte River bottom, Greeley remarked on the "vagrant instincts and habits" that had so suddenly brought together at the foot of the Rockies a motley assortment of natives of all parts of the United States plus some Europeans. "But," he continued, "worse than this; you cannot enter a circle of a dozen persons of whom at least three will not have spent some years in California, two or three have made claims and built cabins in Kansas or Nebraska, and at least one spent a year or so in Texas (p. 157).

All these, blended with veteran Mountain men, Indians of all grades from the tamest to the wildest, half-breeds, French trappers and *voyageurs* (who have generally two or three Indian wives apiece) and an occasional negro, compose a medley such as hardly another region can parallel. (p. 158)

The former occupations were as varied as the prior geographical experiences. Greeley spoke of his stagecoach's stopping at a way station whose proprietor had been a lawyer practicing in Cincinnati, while the ex-lawyer's wife, who was the cook, had been an actress performing at theaters in the Bowery in New York City. Lest that sound excessively urban, soon afterward Greeley encountered a family caravan of six or seven wagons that was moving from Missouri to California under conditions that reminded Greeley of Abraham and Lot: taking with them their oxen, horses, milk cows, and young cattle, the family had the girls assigned to do the milking, the women the cooking and washing, the men the herding and driving, and the small children the playing.

It's obvious that some of the varied types seen by Greeley were picturesque survivals that would have only a limited role in the future of the west. The mountain men, in particular, had done well to persist even this long, which was years after the dwindling of the fur trade. Resourcefully they had exploited their unrivaled knowledge of the country and its aboriginal inhabitants to seize every opportunity to hunt, trade, raise livestock, and serve as overland guides. They, with their Indian women and half-breed children, formed a separate caste, Greeley reported, but one of their latter-day activities, however unintentionally, had already pioneered the way for cattle raising in the northern half of the mountain west.

Having discovered that livestock could be carried through the winter on the natural pasture offered in the more sheltered, better-watered mountain valleys, they had developed a lucrative business of exchanging cattle with the westward movers over the California and Oregon trails. By the time that his wagon train reached the Rockies, the average emigrant was in acute need of fresh animals. The mountain men would take worn-out oxen and emaciated steers off the emigrant's hands at practically their own terms, and in exchange swap a few head of rested and fattened work stock.

The mountain men were a tiny, if colorful, group. The Indians with whom they had traded, lived, and interbred for decades were vastly more numerous, though in areas where Indians had been in too intimate contact with large numbers of whites, as in California, Greeley discovered that the aborigines were dying so rapidly from disease, poverty, liquor, and battles with both each other and whites that they seemed headed for extinction.

Greeley observed Indian bands and tribes under two quite different conditions. When he arrived at the Missouri River outfitting towns of Atchison and Leavenworth, he was at the point where white advance had stopped for a generation. Instead of pushing into the treeless prairies and the arid plains that lay beyond, white settlers had jumped clear to Oregon, California, and Texas, while in the vacant land left behind them the Federal government sought to create a new Indian frontier located, roughly speaking, west and north of Missouri and Arkansas. Into this were to be packed all the Indians that could be persuaded or compelled to abandon their ancestral homes east of the Mississippi or in the first tier of states west of that river.

In view of Greeley's record as a reformer, one might have expected sympathy for these so-called intruded Indians who had lost their old eastern homes to white land hunger, but central to Greeley's thinking were his Jeffersonian belief in the superiority of farming as a way of life and his thoroughly American belief that everyone must earn his living. It hurt Greeley to see good prairie land sitting idle while Indians did "nothing," in his opinion, save hunt and accept government supplies. As he traveled through Kansas, past the Sac and Fox reserve, then the Potawatomie and Delaware, and then a reserve held by half-breeds, Greeley was moved to comment:

I give the good-for-nothing rascals credit for admirable judgment in selecting their land. . . . I begin to comprehend, though I do not excuse, the covetous impatience wherewith Indian reservations are regarded by their white neighbors. (p. 53)

When he continued his journey westward, Greeley encountered Indians who had not yet been uprooted, Indians who were still approximately in their accustomed homelands. Always indefatigable in pressing his favorite theme—the virtues of agrarian life in Colorado—Greeley hunted up an Arapaho chief, Left-Hand, who understood enough English to follow Greeley's argument. But the protagonist for agriculture failed. With unexpected humor he concluded:

Left-Hand, though shrewd in his way, is an Indian, and every whit as conservative as Boston's Beacon street or our Fifth Avenue. He knows that there is a certain way in which his people have lived from time immemorial, and in which they are content still to live, knowing and seeking no better. (p. 152)

Greeley's general conclusion about Indians—he made little attempt to discriminate between different bands and their varying cultures—was unfavorable. He saw no prospects for them unless they could learn what white men regarded as useful arts, but attempts in that direction were sure to be frustrated by Indian restlessness, he pointed out. Therefore, he concluded:

I have learned to appreciate better than hitherto, and to make allowance for, the dislike, aversion, contempt, wherewith Indians are usually regarded by their white neighbors, and have been since the days of the Puritans. It needs but little familiarity with the actual, palpable aborigines to convince any one that the poetic Indian—the Indian of Cooper and Longfellow—is only visible to the poet's eye. (pp. 151–52)

If the Indians, like the mountain men, had no great future in the west, with whom did the future lie? A partial answer rose dramatically before Greeley's eyes as he approached Leavenworth, on the Missouri River:

As we neared the California trail, the white coverings of the many emigrant and transport wagons dotted the landscape, giving the trail the appearance of a river running through great meadows, with many ships sailing on its bosom. (p. 23)

Later, as Greeley continued south from Leavenworth, he had a similar experience when he crossed the head of the Santa Fe Trail. This time it was the big contract wagons of the professional freighters that dominated the scene, and near Leavenworth itself he visited the huge depot of Russell, Majors and Waddell, where that famous firm had in reserve literally acres of extra wagons, pyramids of extra axletrees, large herds of oxen, and regiments of drivers.

Here were two of the dynamic forces that were opening the west. The settlers had begun moving to Oregon and California in the 1840s even before the California gold rush, and since that cataclysmic event had gone west in such a flood that now the trail was said to be an unbroken succession of canvas-topped wagons, strung out in a thin line that plodded westward throughout the spring and summer of each year, with literally thousands of prospective settlers on the road at any one moment. By 1859 the movement had gone on long enough that a backwash was evident. Greeley reported meeting caravans, as he called them, that had tried California, hadn't liked it, and were now on their way back to the Missouri River frontier.

The professional freighters were something else again. They were the lifeline that maintained Santa Fe, Tucson, Salt Lake City, the Army posts, the Indian reservations, and the supply points along the California and Oregon trails. Now with the Pikes Peak rush beginning, they would have a new destination at Denver.

That gold-rush crowd, as Greeley encountered it at Denver and at Gregory's Diggings in the Rockies above Denver, was a new and irresistible element in opening the interior. Greeley became exhausted as he rode muleback up Clear Creek to Gregory's Diggings, with a "wilderness of mountains" and forests towering above him. At his destination he found a setting that had been untouched wilderness six weeks earlier but now had, he guessed, a hundred log cabins, many tents and crude shelters, and a population of four thousand, including "five white women and seven squaws living with white men" (pp. 121–22). Here, where disappointed greenhorns had already given up in disgust, veteran gold seekers from California, Georgia, and even Australia were quietly prospecting and opening claims.

Greeley was right in pessimistically concluding that out of the immense expenditure of effort and capital represented by this sudden rush into the Rockies,

[a] few will be amply and suddenly enriched by finding "leads" and selling "claims;" some by washing those "claims;" other[s,] some by supplying the mountains with the four apparent necessaries of mining life—whisky, coffee, flour, and bacon; others by robbing the miners of their hard earnings through the instrumentality of cards, roulette, and the "little joker;" but ten will come out here for gold for every one who carries back so much as he left home with, and thousands who hasten hither . . . will lay down to their long rest beneath the shadows of the mountains. (pp. 143–44)

From the new Colorado diggings Greeley went north to old Fort Bridger, famous as a trading post and supply point, and thence south to Salt Lake City and the Mormons, to inspect there still another major force that was opening the west. At Salt Lake he was well received, being granted the privilege of nearly two hours with the all-powerful Brigham Young, whom Greeley described as "a portly, frank, good-natured, rather thick-set man of fifty-five, seeming to enjoy life, and to be in no particular hurry to get to heaven" (p. 216). Greeley's views about the Mormons were mixed. He recognized that most of them were "in the main an industrious, frugal, hard-working people" who meant to be honest, just, and humane

(p. 234). He admired their neat little adobe-brick houses, the well-cultivated and fenced farmlands, and the universal evidence of irrigation.

But Greeley feared the Mormons' fanaticism against those who opposed them. He doubted that "the plural-wife system can long endure," and he pointed out that the subordination of women implicit in polygamy carried over to a more general attitude that relegated women to childbearing and household drudgery. "No Mormon," he declared, "has ever cited to me his wife's or any woman's opinion on any subject" (pp. 217, 238).

Life in Utah was hard, Greeley felt; it took more days of labor to support a family there than in Kansas or the states farther east. The Mormons had made a mistake, he said, in trying to introduce new industries such as iron making, sugar refining, and cotton growing and spinning. Furthermore, he was convinced that out of the unquestionably constructive effort in Utah had emerged a perceptible economic inequality, by which the leaders had become well-to-do while the "saints" as a whole remained poor.

Greeley's report on the only substantial English-speaking colony between the Missouri River frontier and the Pacific Coast was thus a qualified one. When he reached California in July, his reactions there, too, were varied. Like many an easterner he suffered an environmental shock when his stagecoach, as it crossed the Sierras, rattled down from an idyllic setting of lofty coniferous forests, lush mountain meadows, and delicate wild flowers to the "all but universal deadness" of the valleys and lower foothills in midsummer. "Some hardy weeds, a little sour, coarse grass along the still living water-courses, some small, far between gardens and orchards rendered green and thrifty by irrigation, from striking exceptions to the general paralysis" at that time of year (p. 324).

Clearly, California had serious climatic problems to overcome, and yet Greeley was impressed by what had been accomplished. The state had grown enormously in population. The Federal census to be taken in the next year, under conditions that made accuracy unlikely, would at least demonstrate how disproportionately big— indeed, huge—California had become as compared to the remainder of the west beyond the Missouri. California's population in that year was recorded as just under 380,000, whereas Oregon's was 52,000, Utah's 40,000, and the boom region of Colorado 34,000.

The faraway territory that included Washington, Idaho, and parts of Montana and Wyoming showed only 11,000, while Nevada, just beginning its boom, was credited with only 7,000.

New Mexico, because of its large, long-settled Hispanic population, and the unusual inclusion in the census of 10,500 "civilized" Indians (presumably the Pueblo groups), was recorded as second to California with a total of 93,500, a figure that included the small population of what is now Arizona. This total may be too small. Texas, again because of its Spanish-Mexican origins, had significant population centers in the western counties, such as Bexar County, where San Antonio is located, with 15,000, and El Paso with 4,000.[4]

If California was big by 1860 western standards, it was also most unevenly developed. Mining was going through a difficult transition. Throughout the foothills Greeley saw evidence that once there had been extensive placer mining, for everywhere he noticed unsightly heaps of debris and found polluted streams, where bands of Chinese, who would work for less than whites, were patiently reworking diggings abandoned by the whites. The new forms of mining for white men, Greeley noted, were quartz (also known as lode, vein, or hard-rock mining); hydraulicking, which meant disintegrating a gold-bearing hillside with a stream of water under high pressure; and drift mining, which meant sinking a shaft and from the base of it driving a small tunnel along the "lead" (the promising streak of gold-bearing material).

With his usual skepticism Greeley wondered if even one out of four quartz mines had as yet paid expenses, but he recognized that hydraulicking was potentially a very efficient process that would make possible the handling of masses of low-grade material, especially since elaborate water systems had been built, with aqueducts to span deep canyons and with many miles of canals to deliver the water to a point above the mine that needed it.

Agriculture and stock raising aroused both praise and censure. Greeley saw enough well-tended gardens, orchards, and vineyards in the central part of California to become convinced that California had immense possibilities, especially for fruit, despite a pay scale for farm labor that was twice Atlantic Coast rates. Greeley correctly guessed that probably less irrigation was going to be needed in the center of the state—that is, in the latitude of San Francisco—than had been supposed. Wheat, for human food, and barley, for draft animals, were already great successes and always grown without irrigation. All in all, he concluded, "[n]o part of the union is making more rapid strides in building, fencing, opening farms, setting fruit-trees, breeding stock, etc." (p. 355).

Yet Greeley saw serious potential dangers. There were too many undeveloped cattle ranches, where few improvements other than an occasional corral could be seen. Barns and the cultivation of feed crops for cattle were unknown. His love of good agricultural practices offended by what he was seeing, Greeley burst out:

[A]n honest, straight-out barn has not blessed my eyes in connection with any farm since I left civilized Kansas—if even there. A Californian would as soon think of cutting hay for the sustenance of his family as for that of his herd. (p. 327)

Sooner or later, he prophesied correctly, California ranchers would discover that they were overgrazing their lands, and in the meantime the pattern of dispersed settlement that was growing up had social implications. The huge tracts facilitated by the land grants inherited from Spain and Mexico, and "this cattle ranching, with long intervals between ranches, is destined to half barbarize many thousands of the next generation, whom schools can scarcely reach, and to whom the 'sound of the church-going bell' will be a stranger" (p. 298).

Greeley's western adventure closed at San Francisco, which he noted as having the largest trade of any city on the Pacific. He might have added that with a recorded population of 56,802 in 1860, San Francisco was the only community west of the Missouri River frontier that clearly deserved to be called a city; its nearest rival, Sacramento, had only 13,785. "San Francisco has some fine buildings, but is not a well-built city—, as indeed, how could she be?" being hardly ten years old and having been burned down several times. Nor, after her first five years, he thought, had she grown as rapidly as other new urban centers such as Chicago, Liverpool, or St. Louis.

California, he concluded, had a uniquely varied population. The Indians were dwindling rapidly because of harsh treatment by whites and their own idleness and depravity. "The native or Spanish Californians are already reduced in number since 1849, and are now mainly confined to the southern agricultural counties" (p. 354). "The Chinese are hardly used here. . . . 'John' does not seem to be a very bad fellow, but he is treated worse than though he were" (p. 288).

Greeley's travels missed two significant areas of settlement, the Spanish-speaking southwest and the Pacific northwest. He had intended to return east from Los Angeles via the new road that had just been opened from Fort Yuma through Tucson to El Paso. This would have given him an insight into at least the southernmost strip of the southwest, just above the Mexican border. But the return of an old ailment, boils, forced Greeley to abandon the strenuous overland journey in favor of taking the steamship from San Francisco—even though this meant the certainty of seasickness, which Greeley dreaded almost as much as boils. Travel was never easy for Horace Greeley.[5]

His failure to consider visiting Oregon and Washington was understandable, because in 1859 few places were more remote or isolated. Settlement in Oregon had increased annually during the 1840s, as what Leslie M. Scott called "the oxteam pioneers" plodded in from the Missouri River frontier to occupy the fertile and pleasant Willamette Valley, which is on the well-watered western side of the Cascade mountains.[6] The California gold rush had brought a boom in 1849 and the early 1850s by giving Oregon's pioneer farmers, millers, and lumbermen—most of whom were small-scale operators—an outlet for their produce at San Francisco, but as California developed its own resources, that market became less certain, and in the late 1850s the Willamette settlers appeared unimaginative in devising ways to sell their surplus profitably. Scott, a loyal Oregonian and the son of Oregon's most famous pioneer newspaper editor, referred to the Willamette Valley as "a district proverbial for retarded growth."[7]

Surely a reason for lethargy was the Willamette's remoteness from the rest of the United States, including even its nearest neighbor, California. When Oregon was granted statehood in 1859, the good news took more than a month to reach Portland, since it had to come via overland stage to California and thence north by steamer from San Francisco. As the indirect nature of this route suggests, Portland was to a large degree dependent on San Francisco for communications and supplies from the outer world. Although already the metropolis of Oregon, strategically situated near the junction of the Columbia and Willamette rivers, Portland was in fact little more than a town, with a population of only 2,874 in 1860. As a modern historian has remarked, "compared to San Francisco, Portland in the 1860s was a mere village."[8]

Just as the Willamette is the principal tributary west of the Cascades that flows into the Columbia from the south, so the Cowlitz flows into the Columbia from the north, and the Cowlitz serves also as part of a trough that runs from the Columbia northward to Puget Sound to provide a natural route for land travel. A scattering of former Hudson's Bay Company employees, some of them French Canadians, had long been established north of the Columbia. Americans began to join them early in the 1850s, only to have their number sharply reduced by Indian wars that broke out in the middle of that decade. Resettlement hardly began before 1859.

Meantime California's gold rush had inspired a development of quite a different kind. Mining and city building require immense amounts of lumber, and California itself could offer only a limited amount of good timber that was close enough to navigable water to be commercially feasible. Initially lumber was imported via Cape Horn all the way from Maine and New York, where lumber and the related shipping industry were well established and aggressively alert for new markets.

To veteran lumbermen and sea captains from northeastern America, it was apparent that there was no sense in this exceedingly long voyage, and in the early 1850s men with experience in Maine, New York, Nova Scotia, and other northeastern regions cruised the Pacific shoreline from San Francisco northward. Of the possible forest sites that they discovered in California, Oregon, and Washington, the most appealing was Puget Sound, where magnificent, dense stands of Douglas fir grew right down to the edge of navigable water, and where inlets and coves offered promising locations for wharves and mills.

Here was the right combination, and throughout the 1850s companies were establishing sawmills at isolated points around the spacious shores of Puget Sound. Their market and their business headquarters were at San Francisco, and when they overproduced for the California market, as they did frequently, they exported their surplus to the Hawaiian Islands, to Australia, which was then enjoying one of the biggest gold rushes in history, and even to China. There were always two aspects to the Puget Sound operations: the market and financial anxieties of the company officers in San Francisco, and the operational difficulties and loneliness of the men in the woods at Puget Sound. The latter's troubles were well indicated by an erratically punctuated and imaginatively spelled report from an expatriate New Englander who had brought his ships, mill hands, and machinery around the Horn from East Machias, Maine:

You may well imagine that it requires much labor, time and money to carry on this concern with much trouble and some losses; being in a wilderness far from men and things costs us much . . . [we have] troubles of Indians, war, && so on.

Many of [these] things no man can know without being present . . . [including the] trouble of this concern situated in this vast wilderness, where we cannot hear of the Ellection of a President of the United States [for] 55 to 60 days.[9]

If white population was scant and thick wilderness plentiful west of the Cascades, on the dry, eastern side of the Cascades, Indians were the dominant force throughout eastern Oregon and Washington until just before 1859, when the outcome of a series of Indian wars opened a few preferred sites to settlement, especially at Walla Walla, near Marcus Whitman's onetime mission.[10] Still farther east, beyond the boundaries of present-day Oregon and Washington, lay the mountains and forests of the northern Rockies, an area that would soon become known as Idaho and western Montana, as yet the domain of Indians and of those few mountain men that Greeley met when they came down to trade along the California Trail.

Had Greeley carried out his plan to return east via stagecoach, through the southern strip of the Spanish-speaking southwest, he would have encountered not only exceeding discomfort but also danger. Raphael Pumpelly, a mining engineer who took the stage west through El Paso and Tucson to reach a silver mine in 1860, described the experience in alarming terms. By the time he reached El Paso, after lurching across a "desolate and barren region" behind half-wild horses, he was delirious from lack of sleep, and by the time he reached Tucson, he collapsed on the floor of the first room he entered, there to sleep unmolested for twelve hours, until awakened by an exchange of pistol shots between gamblers who were plying their trade in that same room.[11]

If that sounds melodramatic, his description of life in southern Arizona sounds even more so.

Murder was the order of the day among a total white and peon population of a few thousand souls; it was daily committed by Americans upon Americans, Mexicans, and Indians; by Mexicans upon Americans; and the hand of the Apache was, not without much reason, against both of the intruding races.

If it is said that the Indians are treacherous and cruel, scalping and torturing their prisoners, it may be answered that there is no treachery and no cruelty left unemployed by the whites.[12]

· Southern Arizona was but the outer, lawless edge of the Spanish-speaking region. The center, where by far the greater part of the total Hispanic population of the southwest lived, was in the Rio Grande settlements of upper New Mexico. There, since the seventeenth century, the people of Hispanic descent, who were mostly "*mestizo*" (mixed blood), had lived close by the well-established communities of the Pueblo Indians, whose town life, intricately organized society, and agrarian economy had fitted so well into Spanish thinking as to be a major factor in the original Spanish decision to make this area their headquarters north of Mexico.

By 1860 small colonies of New Mexicans had thrust still farther northward into southern Colorado, while far down on the southern Rio Grande, north of El Paso, an area of new growth had been opened in the Mesilla Valley. Farther west, part of southern Arizona had been reoccupied, after disastrous Indian raids in the late 1840s.[13]

In New Mexico, as a classic contemporary narrative by W. W. H. Davis makes clear, an old and very definite culture had made few gestures toward change during the "Anglo" occupation. By 1860 Santa Fe, the only big town, had a population of 4,635. It was a community of single-story adobe houses, each built around a patio, each with its dirt floor and its roof of dirt and mud, the whole town looking from a distance like "a colony of brick-kilns," Davis reported.[14]

New Mexico, like other parts of the Spanish-speaking southwest, was a land of social extremes. The rich minority (*ricos*) were a tiny layer at the top. Far below them was the great bulk of the population, the peons, some of them poor but free, some bonded for debt and rather worse off, Davis felt, than southern black slaves. All classes and both sexes loved gay clothes and jewelry, and the mounted caballero of the ruling class was a striking sight, with silver ornaments on his sombrero, his pantaloons, and his spurs, and more silver on his horse's saddle and bridle, but the peons had little save their serapes, which were a blanket with a hole cut in the middle for the wearer's head. Poverty, simplicity, and unchanging practices characterized the peons and the isolated little villages in which most of them dwelt. Commonly they were dependent on a rico or a *patrón* (local boss) for all relations with the unknown outside world, including protection when in trouble, credit when in need, and the few simple things that they might occasionally buy.

Communal irrigation the peons had developed to a high degree, but their crop-raising practices impressed Davis as being those of the Middle Ages if not of the Bible. The staple foods of the country were tortillas and beans (*frijoles*); the staple product of the territory was sheep, the small, scrawny New Mexican sheep. But if New Mexico ever adopted a coat of arms, Davis declared, the principal symbol on it should be the burro, the universal animal of the territory.

The level of education and literacy was deplorable. Davis was convinced that "there is a larger number of persons who cannot read and write than in any other Territory in the Union." They were, he pointed out, a people totally without previous experience in self-government, and yet the United States was trying to introduce universal male suffrage.[15]

All in all, Davis found them a contradictory people: ignorant, superstitious, and addicted to gambling—all classes—and yet courteous, gracious, and generous as hosts; the young women slender, lovely, and graceful; the older ones no longer slender or lovely, but kind. When a visitor came, the mistress of the house would roll and light a *cigarrito* and hand it to him. "The habit of [smoking cigarettes] is bad enough in men, but intolerable in women. . . . Some [ladies] even indulge the luxury while they lie in bed." One wonders how Davis knew.[16]

It is a pity, a very great pity, that the awkward and stiffly moralistic Horace Greeley did not get to Santa Fe. The mutual misunderstanding between the noted editor and his first hostess would have inspired the most expressive writing of the entire journey and would have created a local legend that would still be current in Santa Fe.

Taken together, Greeley's observations and these few additional comments suggest the nature and the relative size of settlement in the Far West and Great Plains in 1859. California was by far the largest and most varied in population and industry, its commercial center of San Francisco was the only real city in the farther west, and from San Francisco radiated lines of transportation and communication to most parts of the west and to New York and the Missouri River frontier. Reflecting its recent past as a mining region, California was still a man's world (276,337 men to 106,657 women in 1860). By contrast, the other three major western areas, being agricultural and pastoral in their base, were far more even in their division between the sexes. In Mormon Utah, despite polygamy, the census reported almost exactly equal numbers, 20,225 men and 20,018 women. New Mexico did nearly as well, with 49,091 men and 44,425 women, including an almost equal distribution of the 10,500 "civilized" Indians between the two sexes. Oregon, where so much of the immigration had been in family units from the valleys of the Missouri, Ohio, and Mississippi rivers, had 31,591 men and 20,874 women.

Again reflecting its past of the gold-rush and mining eras, and reflecting also the attractions of San Francisco for all kinds of people, California had a large number of foreign-born: 146,528 out of the total of roughly 380,000, and nearly 35,000 of these were Chinese, which means that to antagonisms toward Indians, blacks, and the Spanish-speaking, California had now added material for still another racist crusade. San Francisco was genuinely cosmopolitan, with its population almost equally balanced (28,454 foreign-born out of a total of 56,802). Utah, where determined overseas proselytizing by the Mormon church had brought in nearly 13,000 foreign-born among its 40,000 recorded residents, handled matters selectively, for more than 9,000 of its foreign-born were from England, Scotland, and Wales.

New Mexico, which included Arizona, was a special case. Its people were overwhelmingly native-born, but save for a very small minority of recent "Anglo" arrivals from the "States," most had been born into a Spanish-speaking culture that was a world removed from what might be found in New England or Indiana or Tennessee. Add to the New Mexicans the unknown number of people of Spanish-Mexican heritage who had persisted in California and western

Texas since Mexican days, despite the engulfing tide of Anglo settlement and despite ill-treatment, and it becomes clear that "culturally Spanish" American citizens were far more numerous than Anglo-written history has usually recognized.

Nor is that all. In 1860 New Mexico and Arizona had 4,815 foreign-born from Old Mexico, California had 9,150, and Texas listed 12,443, many of whom must have been in western and southwestern Texas. This means that the total of all "culturally Spanish" folk must have formed the third largest group in the farther west, ranking after the Anglo and Indian.[17]

The size of the total Indian population is mostly guesswork. In his report for 1858 the Commissioner of Indian Affairs estimated "the whole number of Indians within our limits . . . to be about 350,000," while the Eighth Census reported 44,020 "civilized Indians" (what a patronizing term!) and 295,400 others.[18]

Finally, the census gives a specific figure for Chinese (34,935 in California, 425 in Oregon, and one each in Washington and New Mexico). The information on blacks is less clear. There seem to have been over five thousand "free colored" in the Far West and Great Plains, together with nearly two thousand slaves, chiefly near San Antonio, Texas.

Here, then, was a bizarre mixture of native-born and foreign-born elements representing quite different cultures. Was there a chance that they could learn to cooperate with one another? Was there a chance that the sense of community so notable among Mormon, Hispano, and Indian groups might inspire a sense of common purpose among the population generally, or would the driving force be individual gain—private profit—as in most of Victorian America?

CHAPTER 2

The Mining Advance into the Interior

W ESTWARD from the Missouri the land rises gradually toward the base of the Rocky Mountains, traversing en route all those miles of rolling or level plains that Greeley found so monotonous and aridly useless. At the eastern edge of the Rockies begins what geographers call "the cordilleran portion of North America," by which formidable term is meant the vast elevated region that includes everything from the eastern Rockies to the western foothills of the Sierra Nevada and Cascade ranges. Between those two massive mountain systems lie the dry Columbia and Snake River plains in the north, the desert Great Basin of Utah and Nevada in the center, and in the south the high Colorado Plateau that straddles southern Utah and Colorado and northern Arizona and New Mexico. South of the Colorado Plateau, deserts and mountains extend endlessly into Old Mexico.

A more unpromising region for rapid settlement could hardly be conceived. Yet this is the region into which tens of thousands of would-be gold and silver miners thrust their way during the decade that began in 1859. By an extraordinary coincidence, almost simultaneously gold was discovered in Colorado, on the eastern edge of the cordilleran region, and silver was found on the Comstock Lode of Nevada, near the western edge. The one was the beginning of an abrupt advance of placer miners and gold-quartz operators into the Rocky Mountains, along a thousand-mile front that extended from southern British Columbia to southern Colorado; the other was the introduction to a new type of precious-metal mining—silver—that lured men into the Great Basin, the Rockies, and the southwest. Despite traditional notions of the frontier as a "westward movement," the mining advance was a series of thrusts from both east and west into the cordilleran middle. Men from California, Oregon, and Washington, calling themselves "Yon-siders" (yonder siders) crossed the Sierras or Cascades to meet "pilgrims" (greenhorns, tenderfeet) coming from the settled lands east of the Great Plains. Out of their joint efforts grew a succession of mining districts and supply centers that, however transitory some proved to be, forever altered the hitherto little-settled interior.[1]

The rush from the west was understandable. Greeley had been correct in recognizing the signs of decay in the California placer regions. Diggings that had been abandoned entirely or left to the Chinese were evidence that the average white placer miner, who possessed only limited capital and technical knowledge, no longer felt that he could earn enough to make mining worthwhile. The very fact that money and effort, and a growing technical understanding, were now being invested in quartz (lode) and hydraulic mining was proof that the day of simple placers—"the poor man's mines"—had passed. Few of the placer miners were burdened with families, businesses, or other encumbering responsibilities. Their occupation had accustomed them to change and to risk taking. For several years their jobs had been slipping away. By the end of the 1850s they were "industrially desperate," as a contemporary phrased it, and they were dragging down with them the storekeepers, boardinghouse keepers, saloon proprietors, mechanics, blacksmiths, lawyers, and other local service people whose incomes were dependent on the ability of their customers to continue paying. They were not the only restless ones. There were also the urban unemployed and the outright drifters who hung around the streets of San Francisco and some of the larger towns of the Pacific Coast.

A good insight into the degree of restlessness was disclosed in 1858 when exaggerated reports trumpeted the discovery of allegedly rich placers along the Fraser River in faraway British Columbia. The "Fraser fever" lasted only a few months, yet between twenty-five thousand and thirty thousand people from California, Washington, and Oregon hurried off to this unknown foreign wilderness.[2]

As it watched this alarming exodus, the widely read Sacramento *Daily Union* felt impelled to warn that

the fortunate strikes, and large piles made, are always published, whilst not a word is said about the thousands who are unfortunate. The good news from mining countries travels fast, while that which is bad scarcely travels at all.[3]

The placer men and their camp followers heard what they wanted to hear. What they were seeking was "regular '49 times," a new California as it had been in 1849.

Nor were they alone in their discontent. Among those who had gone into quartz mining, there were many who had learned the rudiments, had labored steadily, but had profited only moderately if at all. George Hearst, for example, founder of the Hearst fortune, had come to California from the Missouri lead mines in 1850, had tried both placer and quartz mining, and thereafter had spent five years near Nevada City, California, engaged in prospecting, "locating" (i.e., asserting title to), and selling lode "claims" while he tried to accumulate enough capital to develop even one of his discoveries. Hearst was a hard worker and never a spendthrift. When a friend told him, in "strictest confidence," of course, that silver had been discovered on the bleak desert slopes of Mount Davidson, on the far side of the Sierra Nevada, Hearst joined a veritable stampede of his neighbors (who must have got the word in similarly confidential fashion) across the mountains to the new Comstock Lode, where Hearst joined other Californians in buying what proved to be one of the richest of the early silver claims, the Ophir. Hearst had to dump his California holdings and borrow money besides to finance his share in this fortunate venture.[4]

Silver veins were new to Californians, and experience with gold veins was only partly relevant, but that did not deter anyone. Perhaps ten thousand people, mostly Californians, went storming across the Sierra passes as soon as the snow melted enough to make passage possible. Some must have returned as soon as they had seen the reality, for the census of 1860 recorded only 6,857 people as resident in Nevada Territory. Contemptuously the first real historian of the Comstock, writing in 1881–1882, remarked that only "a small part of the speculative troop" of 1859–1860 were working miners. "Probably half," he added, "were a swarm of drones, many of whom were penniless and worthless in any capacity."[5] Reflecting this, the silver-rush crowd left to a few able veterans of the California lode mines the unfamiliar problem of extracting silver, while the majority frenziedly bought and sold shares in undeveloped claims, most of which were of little value. This was their improvised substitute for the "poor man's placers"—something that could be entered upon with little capital or knowledge. Ultimately nearly seventeen thousand claims were located, but one half of the total production of the Comstock and four fifths of the dividends came from only two pairs of adjacent mines.[6] From an early date ownership of the best mines fell into the hands of Californians.

Since the Comstock Lode was distant by only a hundred miles from California mining camps, a Californian dominance was understandable, but a Californian role in the rush to Colorado and the northern Rockies was something else again. The Russell brothers were a good example of how indirectly the process sometimes worked. They had been raised on the former Cherokee lands of northern Georgia, which was one of the few parts of the United States to have significant gold mining prior to California. Mining had been practiced there since 1828–1829. Twice members of this family, under the leadership of their older brother, Green Russell, put to good account their Georgia-gained knowledge of gold. In 1848, when they heard of the original California discovery, they organized a party to go overland to the Sierras, and Green had hardly returned to Georgia from that successful venture before he turned around and took his two younger brothers back for two more years of apparently profitable work in California.[7]

A trip to Kansas in 1857 to investigate land claims unexpectedly caused the Russells to hear reports of possible gold in Colorado, and led to the formation of a party of Georgians and Cherokee Indians to prospect along the foot of the Rockies during the next year. While Green Russell's group found only the most limited placers in 1858, grossly exaggerated reports of their activities and those of another prospecting party were eagerly inflated by the newspapers and business-seeking merchants of the Missouri frontier towns in a successful attempt to precipitate what became known as the "Pikes Peak" gold rush of 1859.

Contemporaries spoke of the Green Russells, the George Hearsts, and other veterans of mining in California as "Old Californians." Old Californians were looked up to as wise old fellows who knew about such essentials as "indications" of mineral deposits, "locating" and registering claims, building and using the rockers, long toms, and sluices necessary for placer mining, and the stamp mills and arrastras that were basic to starting on vein mines. Perhaps equally important, Old Californians knew how to organize a self-constituted and self-governing "mining district" and draft a code of self-imposed rules, together with providing for a popularly chosen judge or court to adjudicate disputes over claims and to try men accused of crimes.[8]

The Old Californians, in short, were a new frontier type—a no-madic, resourceful, hardy, and experienced species that could be counted upon to do some of the first prospecting, mining, and organizing in any district. And if an Old Californian were not available, the chances were good that the pioneer work would be done by some former Georgian. As if to illustrate these twin origins, the Pikes Peak rush of 1859, started before there was justification for so much excitement, was saved from disaster by the discoveries of George A. Jackson, an Old Californian, and John H. Gregory, who had mined in Georgia. Both made their finds in the rugged mountain canyons drained by Clear Creek and its tributaries, due west of Denver and well above it in altitude. Somewhat later, the Russells added still another discovery when they opened diggings in what became known as Russell Gulch, not far from Jackson's and Gregory's diggings.

A similar role was played by "Captain" Elias Davidson Pierce in opening the northern Rockies. Pierce was a former California prospector and miner who had tried his luck in the British Columbia mines before going into partnership with a trader on the Nez Percé Indian reservation in northern Idaho, where he is said to have married a Nez Percé Indian. With a privileged position on a reservation that was supposedly closed to miners, Pierce was able to discover gold on the Clearwater River in 1860.[9] Despite the Indians' objections, a rush quickly invaded the Idaho Rockies along the Clearwater, moved south to the Salmon River late in 1861, and discovered the magnificent placers of the Boise Basin of southwestern Idaho in the spring and summer of 1862. Almost simultaneously in the summer of 1862 the John Day and Powder River placers were opened in eastern Oregon.

Hardships and dangers were not enough to deter gold seekers from entering the new regions. Survivors of the rushes to the Clearwater and Salmon rivers spoke of the extreme winters, when snow was many feet deep and temperatures went to thirty degrees below zero. One observer recalled watching a dozen snow-blinded men stumbling along a trail that had been beaten into the snow. Led by the only one who could still see, the others were strung out single file behind him, with each man clutching one end of a miner's shovel, while the next in line held the other, and so on down to the last man in this pitiable procession.[10] In the depths of winter new camps like Pierce City, Oro Fino, and Florence were cut off from supplies save for what men backpacked in. For want of fresh produce, scurvy became common. In speaking of Florence, which was for a time the most sought-after of the Salmon River camps, one pioneer, although he acknowledged the heavy snowfalls, high altitude, difficult mountain roads, and high cost of food, nevertheless concluded: "But nothing will stop an old miner when he hears of a rich strike, so they came from all parts of the Pacific coast."[11]

So volatile were these Idaho pioneers that each new discovery virtually depopulated diggings found only a few months earlier. Florence, for example, despite its temporary popularity, became almost a ghost town in the winter of 1863, and recovered so little that in 1864 Chinese miners were being allowed to buy Florence claims. "About 20,000" people were said to have been in Idaho's former wilderness of mountain and forest by the spring of 1863, but as the richness of the Boise Basin exerted its magnetic attraction during that summer, that basin alone was said to have acquired fifteen to twenty thousand people. A special census taken in late September 1863, which would be after the season had ended, claimed a population of just over twenty thousand for the territory as a whole, while the next regular Federal census (1870), taken after the boom had passed, recorded only 14,999.[12] A visitor claimed that at the peak of the boom twelve thousand claims were being operated in the Boise Basin, and he felt that individuals could profit if they really tried, for "a practical miner can always obtain from five to six dollars a day, boarding himself, which he can do very well for nine dollars per week—whisky and cards not included!"[13]

Montana started later but followed a similar pattern. Who first discovered gold is unclear, but some of the earliest prospecting and small-scale placer mining was done in 1858–1862 by James and Granville Stuart, who had been in the California placers from 1852–1857. Upon leaving California, they had intended to return to their parents' home in Iowa, but got no farther than frontier Montana, where they followed a mixed existence of raising stock, trading cattle with passing emigrant wagon trains, and prospecting. A letter from James and Granville to a third brother, Thomas, caused a prospecting party of sixteen to abandon Colorado and hurry north to unknown Montana in 1862.[14]

That year the first big gold rush in the Montana Rockies began in tentative fashion at Grasshopper Creek, where Bannack soon developed, but in 1863 was diverted to Alder Creek (Virginia City) where the richest diggings ever discovered in Montana were found along a creekbed less than twenty miles long. Not content with even that wealth, a party of Georgians opened Last Chance Gulch in 1864, where their camp, "Crab Town," was rechristened with the more dignified name of Helena. In October of 1864 prospectors found gold on Silver Bow Creek, site of the future Butte, and late that year discovered Confederate Gulch, which proved to be exceedingly rich. As in Idaho, each new discovery was likely to depopulate earlier diggings, at least temporarily; one observer remarked that Montana rushes tended to move in circles, with miners returning to a former camp after having become disgusted with a later one. Because the severe winters froze the streams and reduced the working season to eight months, many Montana placer men made an exodus each autumn to a warmer climate.[15] Something like that happened also in Idaho, where in the autumn of 1864 many miners went back to their homes in California, Washington, or Oregon, some intending to return in the spring, others to quit Idaho forever.[16] How many took part in the Montana "excitement" would be difficult to say. A modern historian has remarked that "the extent of the rush to Montana never equaled that to the California, Nevada, or Colorado mines,"[17] presumably because the Montana Rockies were so remote and climatically difficult. The assessors and tax collectors claimed that the population fluctuated between 21,000 and 24,000 between the autumn of 1864 and 1867, while the Federal census of 1870 recorded 20,595.[18]

The Colorado rush, although started largely by false reports, seems to have attracted more participants than any of the other rushes save the great original one to California in 1849. Although the Federal census credited Colorado with only 34,277 in 1860 and 39,864 in 1870, a well-informed contemporary estimated that more than 50,000 took part in the rush of 1859, and that 100,000 people were in Colorado for varying periods between 1858 and 1870, with no more than a third of that total present in the territory at any one time. In other words, as in Montana and Idaho, there was constant coming and going by the unstable gold-rush crowd, but the turnover seems to have been unusually large in the case of Colorado, probably because Colorado was closer to the "States" than were the camps of the northern Rockies. Dangerous though it might be to travel six hundred to seven hundred miles across the plains, nevertheless the journey between Colorado and the Missouri River towns was entirely possible. After all, as Greeley's trip demonstrated, stagecoach service between Denver and the Missouri frontier was available even in 1859.

Whatever local discouragements there might be, in Colorado as in Montana and Idaho prospectors soon moved deeper into the mountains. Although even the passes in the Colorado Rockies were at altitudes of eleven thousand feet or more, both prospectors and the miners who followed them crossed the Continental Divide in 1859 and opened diggings on both slopes. Especially notable was California Gulch, on the headwaters of the Arkansas River, where some of the best diggings in Colorado developed at an altitude of ten thousand feet, despite the fierce winter storms and short working season that that altitude implied. Although thousands tried their luck along the ten-mile length of California Gulch in 1860 and 1861, and some succeeded handsomely, thereafter the fickle crowd abandoned California Gulch as decisively as they left comparable diggings in Idaho and Montana.[19]

For the far southwest of Arizona, New Mexico, and Utah, the 1860s were anything but boom years, save for localized exceptions at Prescott and Wickenburg, in the northwestern interior of Arizona, and in diggings along the lower Colorado River. Numerous prospecting expeditions sent over from California to southern Arizona's Gadsden Purchase strip, below the Gila River, were driven back not only by the fierce desert climate and the remoteness from any supply base but also by the constant danger of Apache raids, to which were added, for a time, wartime attacks by Confederate troops and Sonoran bandits. In New Mexico the inevitable prospecting party of former Californians discovered gold at Pinos Altos in 1860, only to be forced out by Apaches in the next year. In much of the southwest, including Utah, mining received an unexpected encouragement when the Regular Army troops, called back to serve in the Civil War, were replaced by the California Volunteers, who could not forget that they had been miners before they donned a blue uniform. Wherever they marched, they found time to prospect, file claims, and plan for the future.[20]

If Old Californians and Georgians often served as leaders or first comers in these rushes to the cordilleran interior, the rank and file consisted of all sorts of people from both east and west. An early writer said of the Colorado Fifty-Niners: "Probably nineteen-twentieths of these gold-seekers were as ignorant and inexperienced as regards mining as they well could be, and had but a faint idea of the work to be done or the experience to be undergone in this wild rush for wealth."[21] Because of Colorado's greater accessibility to the "States," this is probably a much higher percentage of tenderfeet than would be encountered in other new mining regions. But on each mining frontier could be found farm boys or clerks, or a former apprentice steamboat pilot like Mark Twain (whose semi-autobiographical *Roughing It* is one of the best of all books on the mining west), or a journeyman printer like Henry George, the future author of *Progress and Poverty*, who took passage to British Columbia during the Fraser River rush.

The conversion of a tenderfoot into a miner was well illustrated by the career of Joseph H. Boyd, who in his old age dictated an account of his adventures.[22] Born in 1842 in the old British seaport of Plymouth, he followed local custom by going to sea while still a small boy. After years on ships trading to the African coast, Boyd landed at San Francisco in 1857,.only to be swept up in the Fraser River rush of 1858, when he was still but sixteen. After eight months of digging for gold on the bars of the Fraser, he quit and headed south for Puget Sound, where he worked on ranches and in logging camps until he heard the call of gold discoveries in Idaho. In 1861, after traveling south to Portland to pick up the Columbia River route to Idaho, he and four friends made their way to the Clearwater mines at Oro Fino, where Boyd found that "the first miners in the district were from Oregon and California and they introduced the California mining laws and regulations."

A summer's work near Oro Fino, starting with the crude-labor chore of shoveling mining tailings at four dollars a day, yielded enough money to see Boyd through the winter of 1861–1862, which he and seven partners spent in a cabin that they built and provisioned four miles from Oro Fino. As he remembered it,

a great many miners lost their lives in the mining country that winter. It was so cold that our thermometers froze and we never knew just how cold it was. I slept under four or five heavy blankets and by morning the blankets would be frozen together from my breath. Nights we men would gather together from the different cabins and have a social time. We had a fiddler in camp and often had stag dances. . . . Provisions began to be scarce. . . . Soon all we had left was some flour and a little bacon but by being frugal this lasted us through. Two Germans living a couple of hundred yards from us had two large sacks of beans but we couldn't persuade them to sell us any.

Made wise by experience, Boyd spent the following winter near Portland. The money so laboriously earned in the mines was lost through one friend's dishonesty and another's lack of ambition after Boyd had grubstaked him. By April, Boyd had to borrow enough money to get back to the mines to recoup.

Several years followed in which Boyd mined near Oro Fino and built ditches to bring in water for mining. He and his partners spent the winter of 1867–1868 having "a good time" in San Francisco. "Like most young men we only wanted money to spend. If I had taken my money and invested it I would have been a millionaire." Ultimately Boyd bought into a general store at Pierce City, invested in real estate, and served as deputy sheriff, but he never ceased to own mining claims. Successive moves to Portland and Spokane finally brought him moderate wealth and prominence, but his money seems to have been made in real estate, stores, and an ironworks rather than in mining. Yet to the amanuensis who was taking down his dictation he declared proudly:

For sixty years I have kept up my interest in the mining development of the Northwest and I have at different times invested in the development of most of the principal mining districts of the Northwest.

The instability shown in Idaho and Montana was characteristic. Much of the nature of the mining advance into the interior escapes understanding unless one allows for the peculiar psychology of the precious-metal regions. Bitterly the leading mining journal of San Francisco, the *Mining and Scientific Press*, denounced

the restlessness and wandering propensities continually displayed by the mining population of California. An unhealthy desire to amass a fortune in a year, has ruined many a man in this State. A marvelous story of fabulous riches hidden near the North Pole is caught up with avidity, just the same as we listened to early told tales of riches at Gold Lake, Gold Bluff, Kern River [in California], Fraser River [British Columbia], etc. Our desires run away with our reason and better judgment; we are bereft of common prudence and another disappointment awaits us.[23]

As a veteran of the Montana mines lightheartedly recalled it, in 1863 he was at Virginia City, Montana, when he heard that an expedition was assembling to prospect the Snake River:

I had always thought that there must be deposits of gold on the Upper Snake River, as I knew that the "color" had been found below; and as the country was unknown, distant, and dangerous, it possessed all the elements which combine, in the eye of a frontiersman, "to lend enchantment to the view." I therefore resolved to go.[24]

Neither the irritated criticism of the *Mining and Scientific Press* nor the cheerful cynicism of the Montanan should be allowed to hide two facts. The first was that real treasure in huge amounts did come out of some of the new mining regions. The Comstock Lode, to cite the most famous example, produced about $300 million from 1859–1882. Colorado had an unexpectedly small output of perhaps $25 million for the decade 1858–1867, whereas Idaho is said to have produced nearly twice that between 1862 and 1870, nearly all of it from placers.[25] An unconfirmed estimate alleges that Montana's placers also yielded $50 million (by 1880), and contemporaries even asserted, probably with decided exaggeration, that Alder Gulch gave up the extraordinary total of $30 million in three years, a figure that would indeed justify the Federal mining commissioner's calling Alder Gulch, "in yield, the first, perhaps, in the world." Last Chance Gulch, which contemporaries ranked next after Alder, has been credited with an impressive total variously estimated at $12 million to $16 million, chiefly before 1868. Confederate Gulch, too, was very rich, but stood third after Alder and Last Chance.[26]

The second fact was that while the individual often did badly, western society as a whole might actually profit. This the *Mining and Scientific Press* acknowledged on another occasion, when new wonders were being reported almost daily. "The restlessness of the California miner," the editor declared in 1863, "while, as a general thing it works only disaster to the individual, is exerting a most beneficial effect upon the community at large." The discovery and opening of the mineral wealth of the Rockies, the northwest, the Great Basin, and the eastern slope of the Sierra Nevada was "mainly" the work of "these hardy and determined explorers," and as a further result of their activities, "large cities and towns have grown up" to serve the new mines.[27] This reasoning sounds rather like Adam Smith's famous argument that even extravagance benefits society as a whole, because an "unseen hand" guides reckless spending so that it creates jobs and stimulates business.

In Idaho, Montana, eastern Oregon, and parts of Colorado, at least some of the gold-rush crowd found abundant placers, and with knowledge inherited from California and Georgia, they dug out shallow deposits with pick and shovel and washed them through rockers, long toms, or sluices, so as to start separating the gold—found as flakes, tiny fragments like grains of sand, or nuggets—from the worthless or low-paying debris in which it was hidden. The enormous waste of precious metal caused by reliance on this simple process was somewhat reduced by using quicksilver (mercury), which to the exclusion of other material would amalgamate with the gold, from which it could later be separated by heating in a retort. Deposits that were hidden beneath thick layers of debris could be reached by the slower and more expensive technique of sinking a shaft and then "drifting" along the "lead" of pay dirt. Far more costly, and requiring large capital investment before any return could be expected, was hydraulic mining, which necessitated building elaborate systems of flumes and ditches that could deliver water under high pressure, so that as it shot out of a cannon-like nozzle (a "monitor"), the water could disintegrate hillsides and send masses of material booming down long lines of sluices—a dramatic example of gold extraction on a mass production, laborsaving basis, at low cost per ton of dirt handled.[28]

Placer mining wasted a large part of the gold in any auriferous ground washed, and the waste was the higher because, working under conditions of maximum cost for all his supplies and any capital that he had borrowed, the placer man tended to skim the richest part of the gravel and impatiently move on. That is why Chinese, prepared to work for less, could so often make money out of abandoned diggings. J. Ross Browne, the first Federal commissioner of mining statistics, asserted in his report in March 1868 that "at a moderate calculation, there has been an unnecessary loss of precious metals since the discovery of our mines of more than $300,000,000, scarcely a fraction of which can ever be recovered."[29] This is quite aside from the damage done to the landscape by digging countless prospect holes and leaving piles and drifts of debris that the next heavy rains would wash down to choke the lands below. Nor does such a comment allow for the destruction of the forest cover to provide building lumber and firewood.

The tendency to go elsewhere as soon as the best was skimmed accentuated the instability inherent in superficial placer mining. Placer miners, other than those engaged in hydraulicking, were essentially small-scale independent entrepreneurs. In a given district there might be anywhere from several dozen to several thousand of them. It was the sum total of their individual decisions that decided the fate of the district—that is, whether it would continue until the inevitable day when its nonrenewable gold deposits would be exhausted, or whether it would suddenly, almost quixotically, be abandoned while recoverable gold still remained.

Operating usually in partnerships or loose associations, these entrepreneurs hired additional manpower when they could afford it, but they tended to be undercapitalized and constantly in debt to the local storekeeper, who had little choice but to extend credit to his only customers, thus becoming a kind of involuntary banker. Where natural conditions permitted hydraulicking, as notably in parts of Montana and Idaho, this bigger and potentially longer-lasting type of operation was tried, sometimes with real success, sometimes under such handicaps as inadequate water supply, or "the want of fall or descent" necessary to create high pressure,[30] or the lack of the massive thick beds of deep gravels that made hydraulicking so brilliantly possible in central and northern California.

The alternative to which not only miners but also local businessmen and distant investors kept turning was quartz, or lode, mining, also known as vein, or "hard-rock," mining. From the beginning it was recognized that this was potentially a more enduring type of activity but that it was also one that required patience, expertise, and capital. A determined miner or group or miners could open a vein by sinking a shaft to moderate depth and blasting out of the solid rock enough chunks of auriferous ore to test the potentialities. If funds were scarce, as they generally were, limited amounts of ore could be ground in a homemade arrastra. An arrastra, a device of Mexican derivation, was simply a shallow circular pit made level inside and lined with stone. From a rotating post in the middle projected a horizontal arm that dragged heavy grinding stones behind it as a mule or horse plodded in a perpetual circle. A quartz owner who wanted faster results could build or import a small stamp mill designed for steam power or waterpower. With this machine the ore was crushed in a sturdy mortar as heavy, iron-shod "stamps" rose and fell rhythmically.

In this distinctly limited fashion it was possible to open a claim, test its probable richness, and win a small income. The difficulty was that the further steps necessary to extract gold on a really significant scale demanded much more capital, required technical skills of several kinds, necessitated hiring both underground miners and surface operatives, and fundamentally envisaged operations that would have to be carried out over a considerable period of time to be profitable. For precisely those reasons local merchants eagerly welcomed the prospect of lode mines in their vicinity, for they saw this as bringing stability to a camp and attracting skilled workmen and men in service industries who would be good customers and might have families.

But where was the capital to be found to purchase larger stamp mills and build plants for treating the crushed ores? Where was the money to carry a mine through a long period of development before it could return much income? It took time and money to drive a shaft down to real depth and to identify and block out ore bodies. Underground chambers and passageways had to be timbered (braced with posts and beams) to prevent caving in, and pumps and hoists had to be installed, the one to get rid of underground water, and the other to lift out ore and lower and raise men as each shift went to work or returned to the surface.

Californians had faced these problems throughout the 1850s, and the dimensions of their difficulties are best indicated by the fact that after ten years of trial and error even their better-managed quartz mines were only just becoming financially and technologically viable by 1859–1860; the technological achievement was still only a qualified one, for the percentage of gold lost through imperfect treatment remained high. The effort and money that had gone into quartz since 1849 were out of all proportion to the returns. A modern statistician has asserted that 99 percent of the gold secured in California between 1848 and 1860 was derived from placer operations.[31]

Thus it was to an incompletely developed type of mining that men turned in the 1860s, when the thrust into the interior opened seemingly limitless new opportunities in lodes. The early tests came under two quite different kinds of circumstances. In point of time, the first was on the Comstock Lode, and here initial success was achieved between 1859 and the middle 1860s.

To be sure, early success was presently followed by the severely bad times that prevailed between 1864 and the opening of the 1870s, when a new and much bigger boom led into the Big Bonanza and the making of a new crop of millionaires. But that lay in the future. For the moment George Hearst and his associates were preoccupied with buying the Ophir mine in 1859 and investigating its value. They took out enough ore for a substantial test, and after grinding it in arrastras built on the scene, they selected thirty-eight tons to send to San Francisco for smelting. Packed across the Sierras on muleback, through the snows of that first winter, this "ore of Orphir" created a veritable hysteria in the queen city of the Far West when the first bars of smelted silver were shown to the public.

Hearst and his associates vigorously pushed the development of their mine, but they soon found themselves getting beyond their Californian experience. When they had gone down only to the fifty-foot level, underground water began flooding the Ophir, and the owners decided to install the first steam-powered pumping and hoisting equipment used on the Comstock. At a depth of 175 feet, their vein proved to be very broad by comparison with Californian precedent, and in rock that was soft and crumbling. Simple wooden pillars broke under the load, so that miners were in constant danger of cave-ins that would bury them alive. The Ophir's operators hastily sent back to California for Philip Deidesheimer, a resourceful young German engineer, then engaged in managing a gold-quartz mine in El Dorado County. After careful study, Deidesheimer solved the Ophir's problem by devising the so-called square-set system of underground timbering, which was eagerly seized upon for use not only at all other Comstock mines but throughout the west.

Simultaneously other former California gold-quartz men were trying to cope with the unfamiliar question of treating silver. The pioneer was a friend of Hearst's, Almarin B. Paul. Like Hearst, Paul was a true Old Californian. In addition to mining, he had tried merchandising, publishing, and real estate. He owned a quartz mine near Nevada City, California, but his mining experience had started long before that at Lake Superior, just as Hearst had begun in the Missouri lead mines. In 1859 Paul brought back sacks of ore from the Comstock, and after experimenting on them during the winter of 1859–1860, he returned to the Comstock ("Washoe," contemporaries called it) in the spring to build what for those simple days was a good-sized stamp mill (twenty-four stamps) and treatment plant. While he was able to cut his lumber locally, everything else had to come from San Francisco, by steamer to Sacramento and thence by mule power over the Sierras to the site of the impatient millman's prospective operations.

As Paul himself later remarked, "in 1860 and 1861 none of us knew anything about milling silver ores." He and his several rivals were fortunate in that the Comstock's ores, for reasons not yet adequately explained by geologists, were fundamentally simpler than most western silver ores. Most silver is found in association with base metals, usually lead, zinc, or copper, from which it can be separated only by the expensive, scientifically demanding process of smelting. The Comstock ores, by contrast, were in association principally with gold, and what's more, the percentage of gold was high. By intelligent experimenting with mechanical processes based on California gold-milling experience, and adding quicksilver, salt, copper sulphate, iron filings, and heat in the form of steam, by 1862

Paul developed what became known as the "Washoe pan process," soon to be copied in many parts of the world. For the particular ores available on the Comstock, and with the large percentage of gold that could be recovered along with the silver, this worked, and helped make possible that initial Comstock boom that lasted until 1864, a boom that is described in unforgettable terms in Mark Twain's *Roughing It.*

Washoe, in the early 1860s, became the great wonder, the great success story of western mining. Californians seized control of it and made western Nevada a colonial province, almost an industrial suburb of San Francisco. Washoe's day of reckoning was to come all too soon, but for the moment it seemed magnificent, and the public responded with undiscriminating enthusiasm when the owners of the new mines raised the capital they needed by incorporating the mines and offering shares to anyone who would buy, as the California and Nevada public all too unwisely did.

Elsewhere in Nevada and indeed throughout the west, most silver deposits occurred in more complex forms that required correspondingly complex treatment, usually smelting, and this circumstance does much to explain the slowness with which silver mining developed during the 1860s. Nor was it solely a question of silver. In Colorado experience showed that while some of the early "diggings" were true gold placers, others were really the heavily eroded, weathered, and broken outcroppings of gold veins. As Colorado's rather limited true placers waned after 1862, emphasis shifted to veins, which were worked through relatively short shafts and with resort to arrastras and simple stamp mills for grinding the ores. The trouble was that at depths that were often no more than one hundred feet, the Coloradans found that they were dealing with pyritic gold ores, popularly known as "sulphurets," which is another way of saying that the gold was in chemical combination with sulphides. This meant that their gold would not amalgamate with mercury and thus was lost in the tailings.

Californians had long known of this phenomenon, but with their gold ores the percentage of "sulphurets" had been small enough so that they could tolerate the loss. The Coloradans were less fortunate. In opening their mines, they made the usual mistakes of starting with too little capital, too little knowledge, too much untried equipment, and claims that were too small for efficient operation. To these relatively common errors was added the special problem of Colorado's pyritic ores. Soon the struggling mine owners found themselves going into debt to the bankers who handled their gold shipments, and presently the bankers were taking over ownership. Working through their eastern financial correspondents, the bankers succeeded in incorporating the mines and marketing them to eastern and middle western speculators. By 1863 and 1864 Colorado mines were being hawked in New York, Boston, Philadelphia, and other major cities, with the result that a flood of speculative money temporarily poured into Colorado, only to be dissipated by inexperienced, wasteful, or dishonest managers, some of whom proved distressingly gullible when pressured by salesmen for fake processes to capture the pyritic gold. The inevitable collapse of the boom came in 1864–1865, and only modest recovery was achieved prior to the late 1860s.

In other parts of the Rocky Mountain west the reliance upon vein mining proved equally uncertain during the 1860s. Quite aside from the usual difficulties of inexperience and insufficient capital, Montana, especially, and Idaho somewhat less so, were very distant from sources of supply, particularly for heavy equipment like boilers and stamp mills that had to be hauled in from California or the Middle West. As in Colorado, money was sought from investors in distant cities, and often was spent to poor purpose. As the yield of their placers declined, the vein mines were unable to sustain the former gold output in either Montana or Idaho, or even to make a reasonable return against their own costs. And yet, while the percentage of unprofitable operations in lode mining was extraordinarily high throughout the west during the 1860s, nevertheless those unhappy ventures played an extremely important role in the economy of underdeveloped regions. As historians of both Montana and Idaho have pointed out, quartz mining helped to carry the northwest through a long and painful transition from the boom days of placer mining to a quieter era in which varied industries, including agriculture, stock raising, lumber, and base metals, were ready to support the Rocky Mountain territories.[32]

By its very nature, quartz mining brought a change from the individualistic operations of the placer miner to corporate organization, which both attracted capital from within the region itself and gave local bankers and promoters a new role as middlemen in seeking outside capital. Outside and local capital together financed purchases of heavy equipment from San Francisco or Chicago and gave an immense amount of business to the freighters who hauled it in. The mines hired not only professional underground miners but also surface men, mechanics, ironworkers, bookkeepers, and lawyers. Proprietors of stores, boardinghouses, restaurants, saloons, and livery stables all found new customers. "Thus the entire base of operations was broadened with a constant effect on the entire community."[33]

To be sure, the flow of new money all too often proved to be only temporary, but "heavy" ventures like quartz tended to acquire a momentum that carried them beyond their allotted life span. The owners might become increasingly reluctant to put up more money, the miners might be left without wages for months at a time (and perhaps never thereafter receive what was due them), and the local storekeepers might be unable to collect the mounting debts owed them, but for the moment one more mining settlement was saved from becoming a ghost town. This peculiar tendency to prolong existence on credit and unpaid wages was quite unlike the rapid exodus from failing placers, where all were their own masters and only the unfortunate storekeeper stood to lose. In the end, of course, continued deficits for a quartz mine must lead to closure, unless—and here was the perennial western optimism—new investors, new technical improvements, lower operating costs, or cheaper transportation could make possible a fresh beginning.

That so happy a turn of events was actually possible was proven by the history of Virginia City, Nevada, which demonstrated that after falling from flush times into half a dozen years of *borrasca* (hard times), it could boom into the Big Bonanza at the opening of the 1870s. Virginia City became the classic mining town of the west, the biggest and gaudiest of them all. It was the classroom wherein men learned the essentials of large-scale underground mining and the use of massive, heavy equipment. There they learned about timbering, hoisting, blasting, pumping, and ventilation, just as they discovered how to incorporate and manipulate shares of stock in the interest of a favored few. Just as California had been the original "school" for western miners, so now the Comstock Lode became the center for advanced training in hard-rock mining, and presently its "graduates" wandered off to mines throughout the west, carrying with them their Comstock-acquired lore.[34]

To build Virginia City on the barren, sagebrush slopes of Mount Davidson required engineering skill of a high order and private enterprise of a most ambitious kind. Using gravity as the driving force, wood and water were shot down from high in the Sierras, through flumes and pipes, and conveyed across Washoe Valley to the consumers. Everything else—food, clothing, tools, heavy machinery, huge steam boilers, not to mention such necessities as whiskey, champagne, canned oysters, and cigars—had to come from California by mule teams across the high Sierra passes.

On the eve of the silver rush, the site of the Comstock Lode could count perhaps one to two hundred gold-seeking placer miners. By 1870 Virginia City and its immediately adjacent neighbor, Gold Hill, had a combined population of 11,359. By 1880 the total for the two was 15,448, but since the peak of the boom had come and gone during the 1870s, there must have been more than 20,000 in the middle of the decade, thus making it one of the largest cities in the west.

In the spring of 1860 Virginia City was a chaos of frame shanties, tents, brush huts, and mud-and-stone houses. Its prospective citizens, as they were observed en route to the new diggings, included Irishmen pushing wheelbarrows, Americans, Frenchmen, and Germans struggling under heavy packs, Mexicans leading burros, gamblers and confidence men on horseback, prostitutes dressed in men's clothing, Missourians trying to bring their families and household goods over the almost impassable roads, Jewish peddlers of clothing and miscellaneous goods, organ-grinders, and hog and cattle drovers whose "merchandise" was being made to walk to market.

As what Mark Twain called "the grand 'flush times' of Silverland" got under way, the city took on a much more ordered appearance, even though the sprawling mine and mill buildings and the heaps of waste rock and tailings were never far out of sight. Streets were surveyed on regular lines and the land subdivided into lots, which in preferred locations might sell for as much as ten thousand to twenty thousand dollars for a forty- or fifty-foot frontage. C Street emerged as the main business district and could claim handsome brick buildings and the elaborate International Hotel. Above C Street were the substantial, ornately furnished homes of merchants, lawyers, and mining company officials, whose elegant wives dressed in the height of fashion as they sat at ladies' luncheons, gossiping over "chicken, creams, ices, and Champagne."

Below C Street were the inferior quarters of the Chinese and the flimsy huts in which dwelt surviving members of the original inhabitants, Washoe and Piute Indians who lived a precarious existence by begging and raiding garbage heaps. To quote a recent writer, "The Mexicans and Chinese along with the Indians and the blacks formed the lowest rungs of the social ladder on the Comstock."[35] On D Street "the girls" of "the line" plied their trade in cribs whose fancy interiors contrasted with simple whitewashed exteriors.

The working miners, mechanics, and laborers found quarters where they could afford to live, the single men in rooming houses, cheap hotels, or their own shacks, the married men in simple cottages. One married man, James Galloway, paid $225 for a house lot and borrowed $800 to have carpenters build a home for his family. In 1870 men outnumbered women by more than two to one, while children were only about 10 percent of the population. By 1880 the increase in women and children had been greater than the increase in adult males, with the result that together they now formed about half the population. But regardless of numbers, the women of 1880 found themselves living in a community that still preserved many of the values established during the early years of the town. Those values were based on the speculative, free-spending, unstable attitudes of a predominantly masculine population whose key members, the miners, led a high-risk existence in which death or maiming might come during any day's work. In his contemporary history, Eliot Lord remarked that "merriment in a mining town amid barren mountains means to uneducated men drinking and gambling."[36] He might have added whoring and speculating in mining stocks.

This gaudy side of Virginia City has been well publicized. With a hundred saloons ready to offer a conviviality far more appealing than a boardinghouse room, the drinking and gambling became the more understandable. Nor was this simply a habit of Lord's "uneducated men." An upper-class lady complained that her husband seemed to find excuses for going downtown in the evening on business that she suspected was actually poker or billiards. She remarked acidly that the husbands of her set never seemed to have free time to squire their wives around, whereas unmarried men seemed eager to look after the ladies in the husbands' absence.[37]

Russell Elliott, a modern historian, has protested that "in back of the carnival city was another community of churches, schools, fraternal organizations, and homes," where family life was not too different from that in other parts of the nation.[38] The diary of James Galloway supports this assertion, for Galloway speaks of family picnics, Fourth of July fireworks, setting up the Christmas tree, a New Year's Day feast, attending church, watching a performance of *Hamlet,* and going on a rabbit hunt. He also speaks of speculating and losing on mining stocks.[39]

As at most towns devoted to underground mining, a high percentage of the miners were foreign-born. Particularly numerous were the Irish and the famous Cornishmen, those enduring experts who worked at their ancestral craft in deep mines all over the world. The 1880 census showed that of a total mining labor force of 2,770, only 770 were American-born. The Americans tended to become machine operators, maintenance men, or supervisors. Within the special category listed as "miners," 691 were Irish, 543 were "English" (which must mean Cornish), 394 were Americans, 132 were Canadians, and the remainder were of scattered origin. In the total population of Virginia City and Gold Hill, foreign-born slightly outnumbered native-born in 1870 but were in the minority in 1880. So cosmopolitan was the community that Germans, French, French Canadians, Cornish, Irish, Welsh, Scottish, Mexicans, and Chinese each had their own social organizations and national holidays, and sometimes also their own churches, orchestras, bands, or choral societies.[40]

CHAPTER 3

The Response to the Mining Boom: I. From the East

W HEN the mining rushes burst so suddenly into the cordilleran interior, they caused camps and towns to spring into existence where none had been before. Colorado and Nevada, for example, had no significant white population before 1859, yet even the censuses of 1860 and 1870, which caught only a fraction of this mobile and impermanent crowd, credited Colorado with more than 34,000 in 1860 and nearly 40,000 in 1870, while Nevada had nearly 7,000 at the former date and 42,500 at the latter. Idaho and Montana, with virtually no white populations in 1860, had 15,000 and 20,500, respectively, in 1870. In actuality, probably two or three times those numbers spent some time living in the new camps between 1860 and 1870 but moved restlessly on before any census taker recorded them.[1]

Such figures mean that a region that had been a wilderness inhabited by self-sustaining Indians suddenly became what nineteenth-century merchants regarded as a large consumer market, even though the customers were scattered through hundreds of separate mountain communities that could be reached only by hastily cut pack trails or rough, steep wagon roads. To supply the new localities required a massive operation, for the nearest major bases were far away, either in California to the west or on the Missouri River to the east. Californians could get supplies into western and central Nevada and Arizona, into Oregon, most of Idaho, and occasionally Montana, but Colorado, Montana, Wyoming, New Mexico, Utah,

46

and parts of Idaho and eastern Arizona and Nevada could best be reached from the Missouri.

To be sure, some of the food could be procured within the intermontane west. From the old Hispano settlements in the upper Rio Grande Valley of New Mexico, and from their recent extension into the southern valleys of Colorado, could come flour, melons, and vegetables for the markets of Denver. The Mormons, who by now were well established at Great Salt Lake and Utah Lake, could spare flour, vegetables, fruit, eggs, and butter, and could make delivery in their own wagons.

More important was the ability of Utah and Colorado to provide major regional distribution centers for goods coming from the east. Salt Lake City, despite its special status as the holy city of Zion, had begun during the California gold rush to develop into the only significant commercial entrepôt at the western foot of the Rockies. Presently Denver, the overnight creation of the misnamed Pikes Peak rush, would take on a comparable role at the eastern foot. The two cities, respectively twelve hundred and seven hundred miles from the Missouri, were destined to be places of transshipment, places to which merchandise and equipment from across the plains could be consigned and where they could be warehoused before being sent on their way to literally hundreds of destinations in the mining regions.

By now travel across the plains was by well-worn trails. There had been an enormous change since the beginning of the California gold rush in 1849. From 1849 to 1860 some two hundred thousand westward-bound individuals had taken the trail to California, fifty-three thousand to Oregon, and nearly forty-three thousand to Utah.[2] Trading posts or way stations had sprung up to serve them. Usually known as "ranches," these roadside places provided meals, liquor, supplies, wagon repairs, blacksmithing, fresh draft animals, and ferry or toll-bridge service across the rivers. "In 1859 and 1860 there were, literally, hundreds of supportive facilities en route," usually spaced twenty-five to thirty miles apart.[3]

Of course from Denver there was still a hard climb into the Rockies, and from Salt Lake City a four-hundred-mile haul north to Montana. New Mexico and Tucson drew their supplies by a different route, the famous old Santa Fe Trail.

All of these journeys required weeks of travel through a countryside dominated by Indians of a type new to many Americans. Unlike the earlier experience with eastern woodland Indians, the new westerners of the 1860s and 1870s found themselves in conflict with mounted nomadic opponents whose attacks made effective use of the harsh natural environment. The Spanish pioneers' unintended but decisive gift of the horse had revolutionized the lives of Commanche, Sioux, Cheyenne, Kiowa, Navajo, Apache, Nez Percé, and many others.

The warriors of these nomadic bands had developed into remarkably effective mounted guerrillas. Superb horsemen and tough, practiced individual fighters, their ability to live off that semiarid country was matched by their military tactics, which employed stealth and surprise, the quick strike and withdrawal, the ambush, and a frustratingly skillful retreat in which the warriors seemed to become an invisible part of the enveloping landscape. On the rare occasions when the usually determinedly independent bands could be persuaded to combine temporarily into a major force and accept overall leadership, the Indians could become an overwhelming opponent, as General George A. Custer so tragically demonstrated on the Little Bighorn in 1876, when he led more than 260 troopers to their death against several thousand Sioux and Cheyenne warriors; or as Captain William J. Fetterman proved in 1866 on the Bozeman Trail, when he was given a chance to test his boast that with eighty men he could ride through the whole Sioux Nation. What Fetterman proved was that an incautious commanding officer could be decoyed into a well-executed Sioux ambush in which the entire contingent of eighty-one men was killed.[4]

Fortunately for the safety of the white advance, the Indians usually operated in small bands, and they thought in terms of immediate and local objectives, not of some comprehensive crusade against the white invaders. They made devastating raids on way stations, isolated farms, and unwary travelers, and usually their murder and pillage were completed and the perpetrators gone before the nearest contingent of troops could be sent on a futile chase after them. Although a nation of nearly 31.5 million in 1860, the United States never committed more than a fraction of 1 percent of its population to the task of guarding the frontier, despite the enormous enlargement of military responsibility that had come with the acquisition of the farther west in the 1840s and the swelling tide of travel over the trails to Santa Fe, Oregon, California, Utah, and Texas.

On the eve of the mining booms that began in 1859, the secretary of war reported that out of the Army's total authorized strength of 18,165, other duties required so many troops that there were "left only thirteen regiments for actual service in the field. And upon this small force, numbering little over eleven thousand men, devolved the arduous duty of prosecuting all the Indian wars, which have extended this year from the British possessions on the Pacific to the border settlements of Texas."[5] A map of "the military west in 1860" shows sixty-five "major" Army posts, thinly scattered from Minnesota to Texas and from Fort Leavenworth to the blue Pacific— sixty-five posts in half a continent.[6]

After the interlude of the Civil War, during which volunteer troops held the frontier with notable vigor in the absence of the Regulars,[7] the professional Army returned, only to see Congress reduce the Army to a total of twenty-seven thousand officers and men available for all kinds of duty everywhere in the country, endangered western areas included.[8] From the west's point of view, the little garrisons and inadequate units of cavalry and infantry that these figures implied nevertheless served two purposes. First, they provided a minimal protection that was better than nothing—indeed, the west's constant cry for larger forces shows how much they valued the little that they had; second, the Army was the west's best customer for supplies and services.

The western Army was a major buyer of flour, beef, feed grains, and work stock. Even in peaceful years the Army's needs were large, but in time of crisis, the size of Army orders soared. Particularly important was the military role in encouraging overland transport. After an unsatisfactory experience with staffing and operating its own supply trains during the Mexican War, the Army turned during the 1850s to a primary reliance upon private—civilian—freighting contractors, and as a matter of convenience, after 1855 the quartermaster officers preferred to assign their business to a few large contractors, often to a single operator for one or more large military regions.[9] The quartermaster general reported that for the fiscal year ending June 30, 1865, the Army paid $6,187,525 for civilian freighting services from the Missouri frontier to the two big areas of Utah and New Mexico, including points along the routes thither.[10] If expenses for freighting to other parts of the west were comparable, then the Army's role in encouraging civilian freighters during the 1850s and 1860s was comparable to Federal subsidization of the aviation industry in modern times.

Nor was that all. Just as the Army's supply operations were justified by the need to control the Indians, so, as the Army gradually forced the Indians onto reservations, the Bureau of Indian Affairs (of the Department of the Interior) had to make large contracts with civilian suppliers each year for the "annuity" goods promised to the aborigines as a condition for their withdrawal to reservations. Contracts for hauling the goods to the reservations were sought as eagerly as the basic privilege of providing the treaty supplies themselves.[11] Because men with elastic consciences saw rich opportunities for profit by cheating, bidding each year was conducted in an atmosphere that steamed with politics and favoritism.

Government freighting, then, had become a big annual business by the time that genuine news of gold in Colorado was brought back to the Missouri River. If it seems miraculous that so many tons of supplies and so much heavy equipment could quickly be started across seven hundred miles of semiarid plains to Denver, the explanation is that by 1860 the eastern edge of this interior frontier was highly experienced, was already organized into large freighting companies that could command capital, and was resourceful enough to expand its existing operations so that it could service the new markets without abandoning the old.

The starting point from which both professional freighters and amateur wagon trains began their journeys was not concentrated at any one town but rather kept shifting up and down between new communities on the three-hundred-mile stretch of the river between Independence and Omaha. Council Bluffs, Nebraska City, St. Joseph, Atchison, Brownville, Leavenworth, Westport, Kansas City, and Independence each had its day of big operations, after which some faded into obscurity, while a few such as Omaha and Kansas City survived to grow into major urban centers.[12]

In some degree all the river towns were dependent on St. Louis, whose strategic position enabled it to tap not only traffic on the upper Missouri and Mississippi but also trade coming upstream from the latter's junction with the Ohio and from the seaport at New

Orleans. But St. Louis' influence as a major river port was already threatened by the oncoming railroads. Greeley's trip by railroad in 1859 from Hannibal on the Mississippi to St. Joseph on the Missouri showed that the lower section of the river could be bypassed, and the likelihood was great that additional rail lines would have their real origins in the bustling new city of Chicago.

The new border towns were raw places, hastily thrown together. Most of them were penned into the relatively narrow strip between the levee on the river's edge and the bluffs that rose up behind the town, at the point where the prairies and plains began. The warehouses, outfitting stores, and offices of the forwarding and commission merchants were built on that level strip, convenient to the all-important steamboat landing. A little farther back were the saloons, dance halls, brothels, and hotels that served the rough and boisterous crowd of rivermen and plainsmen, western veterans and eastern tenderfeet. On top of the bluffs were the few residences of what was usually called "the respectable element," and out beyond them stretched the corrals and wagon parks where the wagon trains were assembling their animals, equipment, and men for the long haul across the plains.[13]

Merchants at these river towns might buy their supplies from wholesalers as nearby as St. Louis, but a big mercantile house might get better prices by ordering directly from New York, Philadelphia, or Chicago.[14] The steamboats that brought their shipments were incomparably more efficient as carriers than the wagons that were to convey the cargo across the plains. In 1855 a local newspaper reported that a steamboat might carry as much as 150 tons of freight, but that it would require sixty wagons and over seven hundred oxen to move that same quantity across the plains.[15] The man who established the standard pattern for wagon trains was Alexander Majors, one of the most remarkable personalities on the frontier. Kentucky-born but raised in Missouri, he grew up in a rural district characterized by hard work and limited financial reward. Having married at twenty and fathered several daughters, Majors found that Missouri farming simply was not providing enough income to support his family in comfort. Therefore in 1848 he took the gamble of freighting between Independence and Santa Fe. His success was so notable that he came to be regarded as the preeminent frontier freighter.[16]

The freighting business was a tough, competitive field that rested ultimately on the underpaid labors of the rough, boisterous, profane, and unkempt "bullwackers" and "mule skinners" who actually handled the individual wagons. Yet Majors, a serenely devout Christian, maintained strict discipline over motley crews that might contain a mixture of Americans, Mexicans, Europeans, Indians, and half bloods. He required all employees to take an oath that they would neither swear, drink, gamble, nor mistreat animals while in his service. To each he issued a Bible to save their souls, and firearms to fight off Indians.

Majors settled upon oxen as being better suited to Great Plains travel than mules, even though the latter could go faster and farther in a day. The essential difference, he reasoned, was that mules could not subsist solely on the native grasses en route; oxen, if properly handled, could. Besides, oxen were more available and at lower cost, since work oxen could be broken in from either the local cattle raised in the Missouri Valley or from the abundant supply of longhorns available each year from Texas and from the Cherokee herds. But where speed was essential, and especially on winter trips where animal food had to be carried anyway, mules were the choice.

Majors, and the many who copied him, normally used six yoke of oxen (i.e., twelve oxen) per wagon, and one of his big wagons could hold five thousand to six thousand pounds of freight. At that time the practice of hauling one or even two trailers behind the main wagon had not yet been widely adopted. According to Majors' calculations, the best size for a train was twenty-five wagons to haul the freight, plus one additional wagon to serve as mess and supply vehicle.[17]

As it left the Missouri for Denver, Salt Lake, or Santa Fe, a "full train" was a splendidly impressive sight. With their white canvas, or Osnaburg, covers, blue bodies, and red wheels—the national colors in motion—the twenty-six wagons lumbered ponderously forward as the more than three hundred half-broken oxen responded to the shouts and long whips of the teamsters. A wagonmaster commanded the whole, with an authority comparable to that of a captain at sea. Under him served about thirty men, all of them armed. The hired hands were the cheapest part of the venture; Majors said that the average salary was a dollar a day plus expenses. For that the men were expected to plod beside their wagon fifteen miles a day for one to three months, through relentless dust and heat, and with periodic struggles to get the wagon safely down one bank of a wash and up the other, or to replace a broken axle, or tighten a wheel whose wooden spokes and felloe had shrunk away from the iron tire because of the extreme dryness of the air.[18]

The men who operated the freighting outfits were as varied as they were enterprising. Majors was not representative of them all. The famous Ben Holladay, later the stagecoach, steamship, and railroad king, was as well known a figure in freighting as Majors. On him Henry Villard, the distinguished journalist and railroad promoter, pronounced a harsh judgment, based on personal experience in 1874:

Holladay proved a genuine specimen of the successful Western pioneer of former days, illiterate, coarse, pretentious, boastful, false, and cunning.[19]

Another contemporary, who had known Holladay during the latter's early years on the Missouri River frontier, said more tolerantly:

He had faults of disposition and education, but he was brave, strong, aggressive, talented, and generous. The history of the man reads like a fable.[20]

A fable indeed. Holladay's career ranged from simple beginnings in rural Kentucky to great wealth acquired in transportation and lost in the same. At his peak he was the classic example of the new-rich westerner who ostentatiously built palaces in New York and Washington, filled them with tasteless art objects, and married his daughters to worthless European nobles whose only interest was in their father-in-law's lavishly spent money.

Yet Holladay was both a shrewd and aggressive promoter and an effective organizer. He got his start by freighting for the Army during the Mexican War, then bought oxen and wagons at bargain prices when the government dumped its surplus at the end of the conflict. With the foresight to realize that Salt Lake City would need merchandise for both the Mormons and the transient Forty-Niners, Holladay formed a partnership with a Missouri merchant and successfully took well-loaded wagon trains to Salt Lake City, where he opened a pioneer store to sell his goods. But so great was his restless energy that for several years he also conducted a cattle business in California and won new contracts for freighting supplies to Army posts from the military depot at Fort Leavenworth.[21]

The end of the so-called Mormon War of 1857–1859, when the Regular Army was sent to "invade" Utah, gave Holladay another chance to buy surplus Army animals, wagons, and harness at cheap prices during 1858 and 1859. By now he was associating himself with the leading freighting firm of Russell, Majors and Waddell. In this firm Majors was in charge of wagon operations, while finances were left to William B. Waddell, a cautious businessman resident in Lexington, Missouri; promotion was in the hands of a most incautious optimist, William H. Russell, then also of Lexington though a Vermonter by birth. Russell was a volatile, nervous man with the manner and dress of an aristocrat and a soaring imagination that inspired him to speculations greater than he could finance.

At a time when his freighting firm was already in financial trouble, Russell led his reluctant partners into first establishing the stagecoach service to Denver that Horace Greeley used in 1859, then taking over contracts to deliver the mail from the Missouri to Salt Lake City and from Salt Lake City to California, and finally embarking on a brilliantly imaginative folly. This was the costly notion of starting the famous Pony Express as a means of winning publicity and congressional financial support for an overland mail service. Ben Holladay, by now well-to-do, advanced money to the floundering firm, presently took out a formal mortgage on its physical assets, and in 1862 took over the concern at a foreclosure sale.[22]

While it is obvious that diversion from freighting to other activities had much to do with the collapse of the great firm of Russell, Majors and Waddell, nevertheless there was a saying on the frontier that anyone who stayed in the freighting business long enough would fail, because the risks were so great. Much of the capital employed in the trade seems to have been generated within the Missouri Valley itself. Frequently the core of a successful firm was a team of several brothers, sometimes supplemented by a brother-in-law. Probably the difficulty of finding partners one could trust had much to do with this reliance on relatives.[23]

Accurate figures that would show the size of the freighting business do not exist, but there are rough indications. During the Colorado boom of 1860, Alexander Majors seems to have dispatched 515 wagons from Nebraska City, while other firms and individuals seem to have sent off an additional 150 from that same river town. Omaha probably sent off 150 to 200 more, Leavenworth apparently more than six hundred, and Atchison claimed to have provided the massive total of 1,773 wagonloads, or 8,220,882 pounds, in 1860, as compared with over seven hundred wagons in 1859. About 70 percent of Atchison's total was directed to Colorado.[24]

With a veritable army of professional freighters plodding across the plains in the 1860s, with amateur trains of would-be settlers or miners marching beside them, and with road ranches and Army posts at intervals, the once empty expanses of the interior were well into a change of far-reaching importance, even though the Indians and the buffalo remained dominant throughout the immense open spaces that still existed between the narrow ribbons of travel. But in fact the invasion of what had been untenanted plain, mountain, and desert did not stop with the incursion of those associated with freight carrying or western migration. Americans are an active folk who like to travel fast themselves and to send their letters and packages even more quickly. Usually the two could be combined, for the obvious way for a contractor to get started in the business of transporting passengers was to have the Post Office subsidize him for carrying the mails in the same vehicles which he intended to operate for passenger service.

In 1857 Congress decided to have the postmaster general contract for an overland mail service between the Mississippi and San Francisco. This was to be in addition to the existing (and Federally subsidized) twice-a-month sea mail between New York and California via the Isthmus of Panama. On the alleged ground that a central route via the familiar California Trail or some variant of it would be too difficult in winter, the postmaster general, a Tennessean, restricted the proposed contract to an extreme southern route that would pass through El Paso, Tucson, Fort Yuma, and Los Angeles before turning north toward San Francisco—in other words, through a region noted for its deserts, its paucity of white settlements, and the ferocity of some of its Indian inhabitants. This circuitous approach was to use stagecoaches capable of carrying both mail and passengers and was to be ready to operate within a year.[25]

Twelve months would not have been enough for most promoters, but for John Butterfield, who became the driving force behind the new Overland Mail Company, it was sufficient, though barely so.

Butterfield was an example of how far ability and determination could carry an American in the nineteenth century. Born in 1801 near Albany, New York, of simple rural stock, Butterfield received a little formal education in a country school before turning to his real love—horses. After finding a job as a youthful stage driver at Utica, which remained his home for the rest of his life, he climbed to a controlling position in his employer's firm and then to a comparable domination over most of the mail and passenger stage lines in northern and western New York.

When he saw the new railroads beginning to cut off his business, this versatile genius shifted to packet-boats on the Erie Canal and steamboats on Lake Ontario, but found time to start Utica's first horse-drawn street railway and participate in a local steam railroad project. Presently he began to erect block-long commercial buildings in Utica, inevitably became a bank director there, and in 1856 was elected mayor.[26]

Butterfield was one of several upstate New Yorkers in the 1840s who sensed the possibilities for an "express" service that could give fast and safe shipment to letters, packages, items of merchandise, and things of especial value. After founding his own express company in 1849, in the next year he merged it with two leading concerns—Wells and Company, and Livingston and Fargo—to form the American Express Company, thus creating a great company that still does business today and thus bringing forward two names that were to become universal in western history, Henry Wells and William G. Fargo.

Both Wells and Fargo had grown up in upstate New York, and both had been expressmen since the 1840s. In the new consolidation Wells became president and Fargo secretary of the American Express Company. Just as Butterfield showed a never-failing concern for the welfare of Utica, so Wells became a devoted citizen of Aurora, New York, where he served as president of the bank, head of a local railroad, and founder of what is now Wells College, while Fargo displayed a comparable loyalty to Buffalo, where he was twice elected mayor and was very active in local economic enterprises.[27]

With the American Express prospering in the east and Middle West, Wells and Fargo wanted to expand in 1852 to the rich new opportunities that other express companies had already discovered in California. Since Butterfield and two other directors of American

Express were firmly opposed, the decision was to establish a separate but cooperating corporation, Wells, Fargo and Company, for the California trade. The outstanding success of Wells Fargo during the next half-dozen years amply justified what had seemed a speculative venture. When the chance came in 1857 to add the proposed overland mail contract to their other concerns, "men who had a substantial financial and managerial interest in one or more of the four major express companies—American, National, Adams, and Wells Fargo"—pooled their resources in a joint-stock association known as the Overland Mail Company.[28]

Butterfield took charge of organizing and equipping this massive undertaking, even though by the standards of that day he was at an age when many men thought of retirement. Something in him responded to this last and greatest challenge to the stagecoaching that had been his earliest enthusiasm. In the east and Middle West the new railroads had already eliminated the main stage routes; here, until that uncertain day when a railroad would be built across the plains, was a chance for staging on an almost continental scale. Nor was Butterfield alone in feeling so. When he made known his need for experienced hands, veterans of the old New York and Ohio stage lines were among the first and most numerous to apply.

They knew they would be working for a relentlessly driving, rigidly demanding perfectionist who did not know how to relax. To service his long route, he bought eighteen hundred head of horses and mules and over 250 coaches of the two famous makes, "Concord" and "Troy" (so called after the towns in New Hampshire and New York, respectively, where they were built), together with some rugged "celerity" or "mud wagons" designed for especially difficult country. Probably two thousand men staffed the route.[29] All this expenditure helps to explain why Butterfield, despite his immense accomplishment, was forced out by the other directors of the Overland Mail Company.

The Overland Mail Company continued under new managers, with Wells Fargo thereafter the "dominant" influence,[30] but upon the beginning of the Civil War, Congress, recognizing that operating through Texas was no longer possible, transferred the Overland Mail to the central route of the California Trail. The service was to be more frequent and there was to be a semiweekly Pony Express between the Missouri and California.

This action by Congress opened the way for consolidation of all overland services. The Overland Mail Company, under virtual Wells Fargo control, became the prime contractor.[31] Temporarily Russell, Majors and Waddell was allowed to subcontract for service east of Salt Lake City, but in 1862 Ben Holladay took over this operation along with the other assets of the bankrupt firm, while at the same time he developed an extensive network of branch and feeder lines in Colorado, Nebraska, Idaho, Montana, Oregon, and Washington. Holladay, in turn, came under financial pressure in 1865. When he sold out to Wells Fargo in the next year, the latter consolidated under its own name the major express and stagecoach lines operating west of the Missouri River.[32]

Thus emerged a single transportation giant from the financial reverses of Butterfield, Russell, and Holladay. As a part of the new pattern the gallant Pony Express, which had captured the popular imagination as no other means of communication could, was at last given the government subsidy that Russell had wanted, but in actuality, quite aside from its failure to earn enough to pay its very high costs, the Pony Express had only a limited future, for a new means of communication was a-building that even the foam-flecked ponies could not outrace. In New York State, whence came so much constructive investment in the west, Hiram Sibley of Rochester, in association with Ezra Cornell, had already formed the Western Union Telegraph Company and now, with a promise of forty thousand dollars' annual subsidy from Congress, incorporated the Pacific Telegraph Company to build a telegraph line that would run westward from Omaha and would connect eastward with the existing Western Union lines. Some masterly lobbying and reconciling of rival interests preceded the incorporation. His construction superintendent for the new Pacific Telegraph Company was Edward Creighton, who was already a veteran builder of telegraphs despite the newness of that industry. Born in Ohio of poor Irish parents and given very little schooling, Creighton had developed a practical intelligence and a determination that carried him through massive supply problems, while at the same time he had the diplomatic skill to persuade both Indians and Mormons to accept this newest form of intrusion. In late October 1861 Creighton's line from Omaha was connected at Salt Lake City to a new line coming east from California, thus reducing to a matter of seconds the west's distance from the east.[33]

While overland freighting and stagecoaching were the main avenues to the farther west, Montana had an alternative because it could be reached by water. With the Federal government seeking carriers for an increasing amount of cargo for the Army and Indians after 1855, the Chouteau family of St. Louis fur-trade fame were inspired to build a special steamboat, the *Chippewa,* designed for the shallow water of the upper Missouri. Drawing upon the experience of the builders on the Mississippi and Ohio rivers, who had already shown what could be done with lightweight, high-pressure, shallow-draft steamers, Pierre Chouteau, Jr., had the *Chippewa* built in 1859 and sent upriver in charge of his son Charles.

Low water forced the younger Chouteau to stop just short of Fort Benton, the usual head of navigation, in that first year, but Chouteau succeeded in 1860 and in all but one of the several years immediately following. By the time that news of the Montana gold discoveries filtered down to the lower Missouri, St. Louis steamboat captains were eager to accept freight and passengers for Fort Benton. The voyages proved the superiority of the river route over wagon freighting, despite the meandering river's length of three thousand miles and the limited annual period of deep water on the upper river, and in the middle 1860s St. Louis boomed into prosperity as its steamboats established "a virtual monopoly" over trade with the upper Missouri.[34] Cargoes were chiefly for the Montana mines, although government freight continued to be significant. Where only six steamboats had reached Fort Benton before 1864, a total of seventy arrived during the two years 1866 and 1867.[35]

Dominance by St. Louis could not last, for the very scope of the city's boom encouraged railroad promoters to construct new lines to tap the river well above St. Louis, just as the Hannibal and St. Joseph Railroad had done in 1859. Each new river port that had an eastern railroad connection drew off trade that might have passed through St. Louis. The Chicago and North Western Railroad reached Sioux City, just below the southernmost point of South Dakota, in 1868, to open a direct link to Chicago and New York. Use of Sioux City as the point of departure for steamers bound upriver shortened the river route by nearly a thousand miles. Sioux City, in turn, lost its temporary supremacy after 1872 when tracks were laid to two points still higher up the river, Yankton in South Dakota and Bismarck in North Dakota, both of which quickly attracted the upper Missouri steamers. Because the severe depression of 1873 checked further railroad construction, Yankton and Bismarck were left free of new challengers for seven years.[36]

As St. Louis' supremacy faded, much of the leadership on the river passed to men from the Ohio River valley, especially from the little town of Allegheny City, near Pittsburgh, Pennsylvania. From this small community, where steamboat builders were rivaled only by steamboat captains, came an extraordinary number of men who devoted the central years of their lives to operating, financing, and commanding boats on the upper Missouri. Some retained their homes in Allegheny City and returned to see their families in the off-seasons; others made a commitment to the Dakotas and Montana by building new homes there.[37]

Whatever their origins and degree of commitment to the west, river men shared with the freight wagon proprietors and the men who ran the express, stagecoach, and telegraph services in a readiness to invest in a variety of enterprises while still promoting their main interests. In the west the age of merchant capitalism, with its undifferentiated way of doing business, was yielding only slowly to the oncoming era of industrial and finance capitalism and business specialization. It was commonplace for freighting and steamboat firms to have wholesale and retail stores in connection with the warehouses they maintained at Missouri River landings. In both Denver and Salt Lake City, and in some of the mining towns, freighting firms opened stores. Merchants were often in partnership with steamboat captains or freighters and frequently served as bankers for the firm, its customers, and any qualified borrowers.

Edward Creighton, the telegraph builder, was also a grading contractor for the Union Pacific Railroad and proprietor of a freighting company operated in association with his brother and cousin. In November 1866 he became president of a wagon freighting company that was hastily formed to take advantage of a chance to profit temporarily from the extra short-haul business generated by the partial completion of the Union Pacific Railroad. His partners in the venture were two Omaha bankers (the Kountze brothers) originally from Ohio, an Omaha wholesaler grocer, the chief engineer of the

Union Pacific Railroad (General Grenville M. Dodge), and the latter's principal lieutenant for construction (General John S. Casement). No one seems to have worried about possible conflicts of interest.[38]

The New York–owned Wells Fargo concern followed the same course. It started as an express company and banker, but became stagecoach operator, mail contractor, wagon freighter, and shipper by steamship and railroad as well as by the stagecoaches and Pony Expresses, for which it is most remembered today.

To a man the new western entrepreneurs were ready to speculate in land, mines, urban real estate, and transportation in the areas that their operations were helping to open. Nor were they without public spirit. Almost all had come from someplace else, but when they finally settled upon a town or city as home, they gave to that community's welfare the same promotional zeal that they showed in their business ventures. Sometimes the new home was in one of the new western states where their business was centered; sometimes it was back in Aurora, Rochester, Buffalo, or Allegheny City. Biographical summaries of the merchant capitalists of the 1860s repeatedly list their election as mayor, state representative, state party committee member, or even occasionally as United States senator. Often they were appointed head of a committee to raise funds for a civic project. Henry Wells and Edward Creighton founded colleges or universities that still bear their names. Many successful businessmen endowed a hospital or orphanage or subscribed liberally to the building of a church.

Their great time was the 1860s and early 1870s, when the successive mining booms brought such a rapid increase in the volume of business, and when government freighting for the Army and Indians was continuing to mount because the very growth in traffic across the plains caused greater friction between aborigines and white intruders. The mining "excitements" as a stimulus to business fell off in the early 1870s but revived with the Black Hills gold rush to South Dakota in 1876 and the silver discoveries at Tombstone, Arizona, in 1877. But in the meantime the long-anticipated railroads were beginning to make an impact.

Until after the Civil War the influence of the railroads was indirect, in the sense that the tracks came up to the Missouri, where the trains turned their freight, mail, and passengers over to steam-

boats, wagons, and stagecoaches. This means that wagon freighting, stagecoaching, and steamboating did not come to an end the
day the first train appeared; rather they became supplements or
feeders. Each new "end-of-track" became a center for animal-
drawn or waterborne transportation. What the oncoming railroads
did was to shorten the distance that had to be covered by the
older, slower, and more costly means. Freighters continued operating throughout the 1870s and 1880s and into the 1890s, albeit
over constantly shrinking routes, and Concord coaches and mud
wagons continued to crisscross the west wherever the rails had not
yet been laid.

The beginning of a major change was foreshadowed in the later
1860s, when the Union Pacific Railroad at last began to build westward from Omaha up the familiar central route of the Platte Valley,
while the Central Pacific advanced eastward from Sacramento
through the formidable barrier of the Sierra Nevada. Although
Abraham Lincoln signed the original Pacific Railroad bill in 1862
and a revised, financially much more generous version in 1864, little
construction was completed until 1865 on the Central Pacific and
1866 on the Union Pacific. The primary reason was skepticism that
a railroad built through so challenging and thinly settled a stretch
of desert, mountain, and semiarid plain could pay a profit. In the
phrase of a modern economist, this was a case of "premature enterprise," where not only the cost of construction but the very high risk
deterred private investment.[39] In reporting out the Pacific Railroad
bill, the chairman of the congressional committee bluntly stated that
without government subsidy no one would undertake so unpromising a venture; yet it was a national necessity to link east and west
together.[40]

The congressman's argument meant that the justification lay in
the realm of national policy—of social good—rather than of economics. The leading railroad statistician of that day, Henry Varnum
Poor, who was secretary of the original incorporating group of the
Union Pacific, expressed the business community's attitude when he
asserted that

those who undertook the construction of the Pacific Railroad were leaders
of a forlorn hope. To be connected with it was enough not only to imperil
one's money, but to forfeit one's reputation for business sagacity.[41]

The Pacific Railroad bill, as revised, offered what seemed to be generous help.[42] The Federal government was to grant free right-of-way and was to issue thirty-year bonds that "were in the nature of a loan of credit by the United States." These bonds the railroads could sell to investors for cash, and since the government bonds would constitute only a second lien against the railroad's property, the roads could also market their own first-lien bonds, as a still further means of raising money to pay the contractors and suppliers. The amount of government loan per mile was to vary from sixteen thousand to forty-eight thousand dollars depending on the difficulty of the terrain. As a kind of delayed bonus that would reach real value only after the railroads were actually operating, the railroads were to receive twenty sections of unoccupied public land (12,800 acres) for each mile of track. Sales of the land to settlers or speculators would help to reimburse the railroads for their construction costs.

Modern critics have suggested that it might have been better to have waited until the distraction of the Civil War was over, and then assign responsibility for this huge project directly to the Federal government. Whether, in that unsavory period after the war that has come to be called the Grant era, this would have resulted in a less costly and more honestly handled enterprise is at least open to doubt. Be that as it may, the task of constructing the roads fell into two phases: a never-ending struggle to raise money by intricate negotiation and manipulation in New York and Washington, and the actual building of the roads out in the west.

As far as the Union Pacific is concerned, the financial story is painfully well known, because of the accusations and revelations of scandal that it produced. The Union Pacific, which was a corporation chartered by Congress and subject to very limited oversight by two governmental members of the board of directors, found that it could not possibly sell its stock at par and for cash as required by its congressional charter. In practice the controlling inside group handed over to a wholly owned subsidiary, the Credit Mobilier, a series of dubious contracts to build the railroad. The Credit Mobilier protected itself against loss by greatly exaggerating its costs, getting reimbursed by the Union Pacific (which had a desperate time maintaining cash flow), and then accepting Union Pacific stocks and bonds in payment, thus enabling the Union Pacific technically to meet the congressional requirement about selling its stocks and bonds.[43]

That circuitous scheme for payment helps to explain why the earliest objective history of the Union Pacific, written by an attorney, morosely concluded that "the capitalization of the completed road was nearly double the amount which was actually expended in the work."[44] Even genuine construction costs were run up to unnecessarily high levels by the directors' insistence on haste, and especially by the decision to keep building through the Wasatch Range of the Rockies throughout the winter of 1868, so as to get well into Utah ahead of the Central Pacific, even though this meant doubling and at times even trebling or quadrupling normal expenses.[45]

The operation of building the railroad out in the west arouses far more admiration than the labored and inexcusable financing of this undoubtedly "premature enterprise." The physical difficulties were awesome. No existing railroad reached the Missouri in the latitude of Omaha and its twin city on the east bank, Council Bluffs, and no bridge crossed that broad river between the two communities. The Chicago and North Western Railroad, under the driving direction of John I. Blair of Blairstown, New Jersey, had managed to keep building across Iowa during the Civil War, when many railroads found new work impossible, but his railroad did not reach Council Bluffs until 1867, and no bridge existed until 1872. As General Grenville M. Dodge, the engineer in charge of building the Union Pacific, remarked, until well into 1867 "the amount of road we built each year was limited to the material that we could bring up the Missouri River on steamboats during about three months' navigation."[46]

Similarly, from the end-of-track, supplies were hauled forward by "enormous" wagon operations. Dodge asserted that "at one time we were using at least 10,000 animals, and most of the time from 8,000 to 10,000 laborers."[47] This means that the prospective new means of transport initially relied upon the old: steamboats, wagons, and animals. Dodge illustrated the scope of the task by saying that as the rails advanced into the desolate Great Plains, where even water had to be hauled, the contents of forty railroad cars were required to supply each mile of track laid.[48]

The labor force, according to Dodge, had a high percentage of Irishmen, with veterans recently released from military service forming a most important element, because repeatedly they had to exchange their tools for rifles and go into skirmish lines to repel Indian attacks. As would be expected, the construction crews were a rough, brawling crowd whose off-duty wants were supplied by the famous "Hell on Wheels," a lawless aggregation of gamblers, saloon keepers, and prostitutes who moved into each new end-of-track as fast as the rails reached it.

From its slow progress in 1865 the Union Pacific accelerated rapidly in 1866 after Dodge, a highly experienced railroad engineer, took charge. Born in Massachusetts and educated as an engineer at Norwich University, Vermont, Dodge had been surveying railroad lines in the Middle West since 1852 and had been highly successful during the Civil War as Grant's and Sherman's specialist in rebuilding captured southern railroads. As understanding of politics and lobbying as of engineering, Dodge was able to work with the New York and Boston interests that were manipulating the railroad's finances, whereas his predecessor had resigned in disgust.[49]

Dodge's report for 1869 proudly chronicled the extraordinary achievement that he had directed:

40 miles of track having been laid in 1865, 260 in 1866, 240 in 1867, including the ascent to the summit of the Rocky Mountains, at an elevation of 8,235 feet above the ocean; and during 1868, and to May 10, 1869, 555 miles, all exclusive of side and temporary tracks, of which over 180 miles were built in addition.[50]

May 10, 1869, was the wonderfully dramatic moment when the Union Pacific tracks were joined at Promontory Point, Utah, to the rails built eastward by the Central Pacific. The railroad was not really finished at that date—Dodge continued with it for another eight months and bluntly told the directors that it would take an additional $6 million to put the railroad into the prescribed "first-class condition"[51]—but the central fact remained: the west was now linked to the east by bonds as strong as the steel rails that bore the new cars. The long distance and relatively slow journeys of stage-coach, wagon, and steamboat had given the west a sufficiently separate existence to encourage a distinctive character. Now that must change—not overnight, and in some areas not for years—but gradually a decisive change would come. The question was, what shape would the new pattern take?

CHAPTER 4

The Response to the Mining Boom: II. From the West

THE California to which came news of the mineral discoveries in the interior was a vastly different place from the tumultuous region of the gold-rush years. Even the cautious Equitable Life Assurance Society of New York tacitly conceded as much when it advertised, "No extra rate charged for residence in California!" Nowhere was the change more evident than in San Francisco.

By 1860 the crude little bayside village of 1848 had grown into an urban center of nearly fifty-seven thousand and was the fifteenth largest city in the United States. Its citizens boasted of their "elegant buildings of brick and stone," of their "elegant and handsomely-furnished houses," of the "beautiful gas-light" that illuminated their streets, and of the energetic merchants who had built the "huge hotels and stores, of the most beautiful and substantial character," that had made San Francisco queen of the Pacific Coast.[1]

As a seaport it ranked sixth in the nation in terms of incoming tonnage; its outgoing tonnage was a different matter. To balance their accounts the city and state were still too dependent on the export of what was termed "the prime source of prosperity and wealth to California," gold.[2] Gold production had reached its peak in 1851–1854, the richest year having been 1852, with $81.3 million. From that summit the output dropped sharply within four years down to an annual level of $42 million to $47 million that prevailed until 1862, when the final decline began down to a plateau of $17 million to $18 million per year that lasted from 1865 until well into the 1880s.

More immediately felt than this overall reduction was the exhaustion of the superficial placers, those shallow diggings that could be worked by men who possessed little capital save their own labor. "The Golden Era," as San Franciscans loved to call it, ended with the close of the mining season of 1853. Where once yields as high as ten to twenty dollars per day per man had been possible, by 1853 five dollars was common, and from 1856 onward three dollars was standard.[3] Thousands of miners quit in disgust and sold their claims to Chinese. Having miners idle was serious, for the miners were in debt to their local storekeepers, and the storekeepers were in debt ultimately to the San Francisco merchants, either directly or through intermediary regional wholesalers.

Economically and socially the San Francisco mercantile class was the ruling element in the city and state prior to the Comstock era. It was a proud class to whom financial credit was all-important. Many of the San Francisco offices were started by men trained originally in the countinghouses of New York, Boston, Philadelphia, or other northeastern cities, and began business with eastern backing. Some were sons or nephews of their eastern sponsors, others were promising young clerks from the home office. Soon a more cosmopolitan atmosphere developed as an unusually high percentage of foreign-born merchants, especially Germans and German Jews, joined the first comers. All were dependent on their financial standing with the eastern or European houses that normally honored their drafts and advanced credit.

Many were caught with excessive inventories when the decline in mining became evident. Mercantile hard times started in 1853–1854, but crashed down into sheer disaster in 1855. The major bank of Page, Bacon and Company failed, followed shortly by the collapse of Adams and Company, an express and banking company whose operations were the biggest in the state and reached into every part of it. The chain reaction set in motion by the Adams and Company closure ruined smaller banks and express companies and hurt hundreds of business and professional men. When the national economic panic of 1857 fell upon the local scene, it came as just one more disaster upon a suffering community.[4]

It was in this disturbed, insecure atmosphere that the merchant class rallied politically to strike against what it regarded as a corrupt and expensive city administration that was dependent on an Irish Catholic political machine which had been imported directly from that best of training grounds, New York City. The famous Vigilance Committee of 1856, a carefully organized, self-constituted, extra-legal, semisecret association led by merchants, temporarily usurped political, police, and judicial power over the city, arrested and tried men accused of crimes, hanged two, and drove many more into flight. Before returning power to legitimate authorities, the Vigilantes created a "People's Party" that for a full decade ruled the city by winning public elections for slates of candidates nominated by a businessmen's committee. The philosopher Josiah Royce perceptively termed this "that unique historical occurrence, a Business Man's Revolution," and a modern scholar has theorized that the merchants' readiness to take an action so uncharacteristic of their class can be explained by their discontent over the precarious state of their economic fortunes. Others have seen the 1856 revolt as a racist and nativist outburst against Irish Catholic politics. That prejudice was not lacking is shown by the consistency with which the merchants of the 1850s excluded Catholics and Jews from their chamber of commerce, volunteer fire companies, militia companies, and benevolent societies.[5]

The heritage of 1856 proved to be enduring. Having stood together through days of extreme tension, the several thousand Vigilantes never forgot their common experience, and the city as a whole came to accept their version of what had happened. Modern scholars have been critical of the episode, but throughout the 1860s and 1870s the memory of the "Great Committee" was a warm and living force that united those who had served.

Almost anything that gave unity and stability was an asset, for contemporary observers and modern scholars are in agreement as to the nature of the San Francisco business community. Writing in 1861, just as the boom in the interior mines was rescuing the city from its uncertain years, John S. Hittell, the best local economic commentator of his day, gave this description:

The business of California is conducted boldly. Men make money rapidly, spend it freely and hastily. Changes in occupation are frequent, and in wealth rapid. Hazardous speculation is the body of our commercial system. Most of our business men are young, and they still are under the influence of the feverish times of '49. Our business is unsteady. Hereditary wealth is unknown. . . . We are speculators by our very position. . . . We were dissatisfied with life in Europe and the Eastern states, because it was too slow. We came here to enjoy an exciting life and to make money rapidly. . . . It is no uncommon thing to see men who have been wealthy on three or four different occasions and then poor again.[6]

Instability such as this might be expected to drive men away from San Francisco to try their luck elsewhere. Modern research into urban mobility in San Francisco does indeed confirm this supposition, but it does so against a growing realization that everywhere in nineteenth-century America the turnover in urban populations was extraordinarily high. To cite two well-established cities, only 39 percent of Boston heads of households who were listed in 1850 were still there in 1860, and only 32 percent of Philadelphia's adult males persisted in their city throughout the decade that ended in 1860. What happened in San Francisco, while made extreme by the gold rush and the excessive unsteadiness of business thereafter, appears to have been more an exaggeration than a sharp deviation from behavior in other contemporary American cities.[7] In speaking of San Francisco between 1850 and 1880, a recent scholar has concluded:

Within the general employed population of the city, only one in ten had persisted within the city for three decades; three-quarters had departed within eight years after first arriving in San Francisco.

During the 1850 decade, the rate of failure was probably somewhere between half and two-thirds of all merchants. Only about two out of every ten merchants . . . remained in San Francisco through 1880.[8]

A similar doleful conclusion was reached by the compiler of the principal contemporary city directory, who discovered that in the "leading branches of trade" 1,570 firms or individuals failed in 1859, as compared with 2,056 "remaining in business," while "the yearly change among the small dealers will not fall short of fifty per cent, per annum."[9]

Evidence so unanimous makes clear that uncertainty was a part of the economic life of San Francisco, and that uncertainty was at a peak in the late 1850s. The city was waiting anxiously for a new opportunity, and suddenly it was rewarded by precisely what it had been yearning for: news of the Comstock Lode, news of Idaho and the northwest, rumors of Arizona. Here were new mines that could be served by the business facilities that had been created for the old. By 1860 an awesome amount of capital had been invested in the city and the services ancillary to it. San Francisco had made herself the center for warehousing, wholesaling, finance, communications, recreation, and travel for a huge region that included all of California and most of the Pacific Coast from Alaska down into Mexico. Across her docks and into her warehouses were trundled thousands of tons of merchandise brought round the Horn by the great clipper ships or up from Panama by the semimonthly steamers. As the vessels unloaded, importers, wholesalers, bankers, and insurance agents argued over the disposition of the cargoes, while clerks, accountants, teamsters, and longshoremen handled the details, and jobbers, retailers, and country merchants waited to place orders.

With her excellent harbor, San Francisco had become the transfer point where cargoes were shifted from oceangoing vessels, with their deep draft, to steamers and small sailing craft better suited to the shallow waters of the interior. Since few interior merchants ordered directly from New York, most of the business passed through the hands of the mercantile firms and warehousemen of San Francisco. From the latter city a chain of inland waterways led up the Sacramento River to the north or the San Joaquin to the south, while lesser routes ran to points around the Bay itself. "The ordinarily navigable portions of the streams and bays" open to regular steamer operations totaled about five hundred miles—a natural asset of the greatest significance in the pre-railroad era.[10]

The most important inland route by far was that between San Francisco and Sacramento. The departure of the Sacramento boat from San Francisco at four o'clock each afternoon was an event that inspired a burst of activity. Everyone who had an excuse, and many who did not, came down to the dock to watch passengers, mail, express packages, and freight being loaded onto the ornately handsome side-wheelers.[11] But that daily excitement was minor compared to the tumult caused twice a month by the impending sailing of the regularly scheduled steamer for Panama, there to connect with steamers for New York. As the authors of an early history amusedly remarked:

Once a fortnight, at the beginning and middle of every month, San Francisco, which is never without some feverish excitement, gets gradually worked up to a crisis.[12]

So important was the approach of each "Steamer Day" that businessmen throughout the city dropped all other concerns while they anxiously reckoned up their accounts and sternly dunned their debtors, so that there would be money to meet obligations due in New York. "A peculiar custom," as a contemporary termed it, was widespread in San Francisco "of loaning money from 'steamer-day' to 'steamer-day.' "[13] The custom was understandable, because each Panama steamer normally carried off a million dollars in gold for New York, but the practice automatically put financial and nervous pressure on bankers, importers, jobbers, retailers, and customers alike, twice each month. Simultaneously with settling debts, merchants wrote out orders for eastern or European goods, answered letters, and prepared drafts on their eastern or foreign financial "correspondents."

Even the beginning of overland mail service in 1858 did not destroy the significance of "Steamer Day," partly because the habit was so well established, and partly because with the aid of a railroad across the Isthmus of Panama, the sea mail could travel between San Francisco and New York in about the same time, or less, that it took the overland stage and its rail connections to get letters to the Atlantic Coast. The Pony Express in 1860–1861 and the telegraph after 1861 of course captured the field for fast communication of brief messages. In other categories than mail, for twenty years the greater comfort, safety, and carrying capacity of the ocean steamers enabled them to carry "most of the passengers, treasure, and fast freight between New York and San Francisco."[14]

While express shipments and high-value freight thus came to San Francisco by steamer, the big inbound cargoes of merchandise and heavy equipment arrived by the less expensive route around the Horn in sailing vessels. Coastal freight and passenger service, though less frequent and reliable than that to the interior, connected San Francisco with ports all the way from Mexico and San

Diego on the south to Portland, Puget Sound, and British Columbia on the north, while irregular offshore sailings linked San Francisco with islands scattered throughout the Pacific and with the big ports of the Far East, Australia, and Europe.

All told, San Francisco had become an intensely busy maritime center, but that was not all. By 1860 the need of the mines for machinery locally designed and custom-made, and the demands of the residents of their own city, who constituted by far the biggest single consumer market in the Far West, had caused San Franciscans to start iron and brass foundries, machine shops, a boiler works, a gasworks, flour mills, sawmills, meat-packing plants, whiskey distilleries, breweries, macaroni factories, and sugar factories. The foundries and machine shops were still dependent on imported iron and steel, and nails, screws, wire, copper goods, and cutlery continued to be imported.[15]

It took courage to venture upon manufacturing, for wages and interest on borrowed capital were high, although the former had fallen dramatically since the ending of the gold rush. A good carpenter who could earn sixteen dollars a day in 1849 was being paid only four dollars in 1861, and most craftsmen had suffered proportionately, even though there was a persistent shortage of blue-collar workers.[16]

It was not easy for blue-collar workers to finance the trip to California. The career of one who succeeded, Peter Donahue, illustrates what could happen.[17] Born of poor Irish parents, Donahue was brought to America as a child and at sixteen was apprenticed "to learn the millwright and engineering business" in Paterson, New Jersey. Later he held jobs with two ironworks, including the firm that built the Pacific Mail Steamship engines. He wandered off to a job in Peru before joining in the rush to California in 1849. There his few months in the mines were unsuccessful, and joined by his two brothers, who like himself had learned the trade by apprenticeship, he founded a blacksmith and boilermaking shop that grew into San Francisco's famous Union Iron Works. Reportedly the three brothers melted and molded the first cast iron in California, and soon were attracting orders for all kinds of ironwork, including those iron storefronts and doors that are today so valued a part of surviving historic buildings. Later the Donahues built steamboat engines, mining engines, and presently railroad locomotives.

It was Peter and James Donahue who conceived the immensely profitable idea of getting a franchise to supply San Francisco with its first illuminating gas. Later, Peter built San Francisco's first street railroad. Donahue and two associates took over the projected San Francisco and San Jose Railroad and carried it through to completion without government subsidy. Donahue repeated his success by building a railroad through Sonoma County up into Mendocino. Unlike the builders of the Central Pacific, Donahue insisted on constructing his railroad with white labor rather than Chinese, and thereby he partially answered the constant complaint of California newspapers that the cities and towns were filled with unemployed white men who refused to take hard jobs.[18]

Blue-collar work in California was apt to be unsteady. Even the leading manufacturers rarely kept a large number of hands employed for an extended period.[19] Both in the city and the country employers met each recurrence of "dull times" by laying off workmen and cutting wages.[20] The struggle of the young Henry George, then a typesetter, to find work in San Francisco and Sacramento between 1858 and 1866 illustrates the uncertainty of employment even for a skilled craftsman whose work bordered on white-collar status. When his second child was born and the doctor said that mother and child must have food even though the little family was destitute, Henry George went down into the street and demanded five dollars of the first stranger he met. George later claimed, doubtless with exaggeration, that he was so desperate that he would have killed the stranger had he refused.[21]

Unlike many new western communities, California was able to generate much of its own capital, as the Donahues' achievement demonstrates. But in the field of transportation this was only partly true. The all-essential Panama steamships, on both sides of the isthmus, together with the Panama Railroad that connected them, were owned and managed by a small group of eastern men who made their headquarters in New York City and were as ready to blackmail and trick an opponent as they were to extort all that the traffic would bear from travelers and shippers. After a period of ruthless competition and poor service during the 1850s, a truce was declared in 1860 that left the Pacific Mail Steamship Company supreme on the Pacific side and the notorious "Commodore" Cornelius Vanderbilt on the Atlantic. In 1865 the Pacific Mail finally bought out Vanderbilt and operated the whole run between New York and San Francisco.[22] San Franciscans resented New York control of a service that owed its profitability to California, but they acknowledged that "the agent of the company in San Francisco, by virtue of his position, was one of the leading business men of the city."[23]

Inland from San Francisco a pattern prevailed that was equally monopolistic but without absentee ownership. The fleet of schooners and sloops seems to have remained unorganized, despite an attempt at cooperative action in 1857,[24] but the steamboats created an unbeatable monopoly. After abortive attempts to form combinations in 1852 because there were too many steamboats for the available traffic,[25] the steamboat men tried again and on March 1, 1854, announced the formation of the California Steam Navigation Company. Steamboat ownership at that time was divided among many people, because individual boats often were owned on shares, with merchants, captains, boat builders, and what contemporaries called "capitalists" all holding shares, and sometimes shares in several boats at once. The California Steam Navigation Company was to be a joint-stock company capitalized at $2 million in shares of one thousand dollars each. Swept into it by the pressure of too much competition were all the important steamboats on all of the major runs from San Francisco to the interior. How contemporaries received the news was best indicated by the headline in the Sacramento Weekly Union: "Mammoth Company, and Monster Steamboat Monopoly."[26]

The California Steam Navigation Company proved to be remarkably durable and profitable. A contemporary asserted that "river steam navigation in California probably realized greater profits during the first fifteen years of our existence as a State than any other single line of enterprise" and made "fortunes" for the men who organized the monopoly and stayed with it.[27] This can hardly have been an exaggeration, for at its annual meeting in 1860 the company complacently announced that since its founding it had paid "102 percent in dividends upon the par value of the stock, which, upon the average market value, is over 200 percent, leaving at the present time, a handsome surplus of available assets on hand."[28] With the boom in traffic through Sacramento for the Comstock, the company was able to pay dividends of $162,500 in 1867, $375,000 in 1868, $250,000 in 1869, and $225,000 in 1870.[29]

This was possible despite the too frequent necessity of buying off would-be competitors by a process that the self-righteous company directors denounced as "paying blackmail." Demands that the legislature regulate the monopoly were skillfully blocked, and the public was placated by the good quality of the company's service, by its generosity in times of flood, and by its willingness to spend considerable sums to remove snags from the rivers and deepen their channels. As with similar steamboats on the Mississippi and Missouri, the public accepted with surprising equanimity the occasional disastrous explosions and fires. Control of the company centered in San Francisco, for city directories show that during the 1860s all of the corporate officers and most of the directors gave San Francisco as their address.

Passengers and freight delivered at Sacramento en route to the Comstock—"Washoe"—could begin the overland journey by taking the only railroad built in the Far West before 1860. The little Sacramento Valley Railroad was only twenty-two and a half miles long and stopped just as it reached the foothills of the Sierra Nevada at Negro Bar (which was renamed Folsom), but its construction between 1853 and 1856 was achieved by such a remarkable combination of determination, watered stock, large mortgage bonds, and extravagant expenditure as almost to arouse one's admiration.[30] The builders and lenders appear to have covered themselves by making ample allowance for the speculative nature of the enterprise.

On Washington's Birthday 1856 the little train chugged out of Sacramento with "a trainload of merrymakers" intent on enjoying every minute of the first trip by rail west of the Missouri. Despite its crushing burden of debt, the pioneer railroad continued in operation. Although capital for railroads continued to be very scarce in California, the boom in travel to Washoe was so encouraging that two more short lines were built, the one intended to advance traveler or freight an additional twenty-one miles toward passes north of Lake Tahoe, the other twenty-six miles toward passes south of the lake.

These were mere stubs of railroads, which means that until late in the 1860s the real work of ferrying freight and passengers across the Sierras fell upon those familiar instruments of western travel, freight wagons and stagecoaches. By the middle and late 1850s Sacramento and its sister cities of Stockton and Marysville had become important centers of land transportation. There the wagon freighters congregated and there their huge wagons, adapted from the Conestoga model, were built. The belief was universal that eastern-built wagons would not survive in California's dry atmosphere, but the California builders preferred to hire Pennsylvania craftsmen, and they further reflected the continuity of tradition by painting the wagon bodies blue. Stockton became especially notable for the immense size of its wagons, but Sacramento had the preferred position because it was on the most direct routes to Washoe.

The freighters were said to be predominantly "western men," coming especially from Missouri and Ohio, but with many also from Indiana, Michigan, Illinois, and Iowa, and an occasional individual from that original home of big wagons, Pennsylvania. Unlike their counterparts of the Great Plains, they relied entirely on mules. Since the distances were relatively short, wayside stations numerous, and Indian danger not a factor, there was no need for the large trains and large freighting concerns that characterized the Great Plains trade. Most teamsters owned their own "outfits" and were proud of the appearance and condition of their animals and wagons. They made their bases at veritable caravansaries, where hay and feed yards were available for the animals, and taverns for the drivers.[31] By no means unaware of the power of united action, the teamsters had formed rate-setting associations in California long before the Comstock boom, and they renewed the practice when there seemed to be too much competition in hauling to Nevada.[32]

At first the ability of the teamsters to pull large loads was limited by the poor condition of the early roads that crossed to Washoe, but very quickly individuals obtained franchises to build toll roads across the several major passes. The size of the teams increased proportionately, until it became commonplace to have from ten to sixteen mules pulling a single load. By the mid-1860s, when the business was at its peak, about fourteen hundred freighting teams were regularly employed in hauling across the Sierras, and the cargoes that they brought over the mountains from California totaled from forty-five thousand to seventy thousand tons per year.[33]

As they plodded their sweaty, dust-covered way over the steep slopes, the freighters had to make way for the clattering stagecoaches that hurried passengers, mail, and express packages between California and her new colonial area, Nevada. Stagecoaching had started in California in 1849, and despite a minimal expenditure for road building, had spread rapidly over the state.

By 1853 so many staging companies had entered the business that the leading proprietors decided to combine into what they hoped would be a statewide monopoly. The formation of the California Stage Company, with a capital stock of $1 million and headquarters at Sacramento, was announced on January 1, 1854. By the standards of that day this was a massive enterprise whose consolidated operations embraced nearly all the important routes.[34] For about two years the company "was particularly vigilant in 'crushing out all' opposition,"[35] but where the contemporaneous attempt at steamboat monopoly succeeded, the California Stage Company failed because it tired of constantly fighting off independent challengers. The California Stage Company withdrew to the northern part of the state, transferring its headquarters to Marysville and selling off its routes south of Sacramento. In 1860 the company accepted the mail contract for the long run from Sacramento to Portland, Oregon.[36]

The timing of this retreat was unfortunate, for when the rush to Washoe built up rapidly in 1859 and 1860, the big California Stage Company was only one of several firms that were strategically placed to exploit the sudden rush of business to Nevada. One of their strongest competitors was the Pioneer Stage Company, which was acquired by Louis McLane, Jr., of Wells Fargo, and run by his brother Charles. The famous Wells Fargo, immortalized in western story, was in its origins as much an absentee, New York–based company as the Pacific Mail Steamship Company, but it displayed greater shrewdness in permitting a larger degree of local operating autonomy. Organized and financed in New York in 1852, and with its headquarters and corporate officers in New York throughout the 1850s and 1860s, Wells Fargo grew rapidly as both an express company and a bank, even before the failure of its chief rival, Adams and Company, suddenly opened a unique opportunity. Cautiously the New York directors reorganized the company's affairs during 1855–1856 and appointed Louis McLane, Jr., as general agent for California, with a broad grant of authority.[37]

McLane was just the man to seize the opportunity created by the collapse of Adams and Company and the lesser firms. Blessed with what a contemporary termed "a fresh and unusually vigorous spirit of enterprise and improvement,"[38] he came of a well-known and influential Maryland and Delaware family. His father, a onetime naval officer, became Andrew Jackson's secretary of the treasury and, later, secretary of state, before retiring from politics to serve as president of the Baltimore and Ohio Railroad. Louis, Jr., and his brother Allan followed their father's precedent by serving in the Navy. Allan resigned to become a steamship commander for the Pacific Mail Steamship Company and rose to be president of that company from 1861–1871. Louis, Jr., resigned in 1850 to operate steamboats between San Francisco and the interior. His steamboat was one of the fortunate vessels that were taken into the California Steam Navigation Company in 1854.

When placed in charge of Wells Fargo's California operations, McLane pushed forward so energetically that after counting 55 offices in 1855, Wells Fargo could claim 147 in 1860. By the latter year the company had offices in every important California city and mining town, and had expanded northward to Oregon, Washington, and British Columbia, eastward to Nevada, Arizona, and Utah, and had offices in Honolulu and Guaymas, Mexico.[39]

So profitable were their operations that Wells Fargo, after establishing a 10 percent annual dividend in 1857, was able to increase that to 12 percent during all but one of the Civil War years, plus an additional cash dividend of 10 percent in 1865 and a 42 percent stock dividend paid out of surplus in 1863. In addition, the directors declared a stock dividend of 100 percent in the latter year, so as to increase the company's capital to $2 million.[40]

It would be superfluous to remark that Wells Fargo was in an unchallengeable position as it followed the mining frontier eastward from California. To further their express business, Wells Fargo had bought out a number of stagecoach companies, some of which continued under their existing firm names, apparently because it was expedient not to appear too monopolistic. Particularly interesting was the action of Louis and Charles McLane, who, as independent proprietors operating under Louis' name, operated the Pioneer Stage Line between Sacramento, Placerville, and Washoe. The McLanes expanded operations so rapidly that in 1863 Pioneer stages carried 10,500 passengers from California to Nevada, while at the same time hauling about two thousand pounds of bullion, mail, and express shipments each way every day. By 1864 they were sending off four stages daily in both directions, east and west.[41]

In the latter year, when their company was at its peak, the McLanes sold out to Louis' employer, Wells Fargo, for $175,000 in gold, but the purchase was not publicly announced lest it alienate rivals such as the California Stage Company, which was carrying Wells Fargo packages on its stages every day. In the west as a whole, Wells Fargo was emerging as the de facto controller of the Overland Mail and the famous Pony Express, and in 1866 it capped its development in transportation by buying out Ben Holladay in the "Grand Consolidation" that gave control over most of the stagecoach and express services west of the Missouri.[42]

In reward for his spectacular services, Louis McLane became president of the newly enlarged Wells Fargo and moved to its headquarters in New York, while his brother Charles became general agent at San Francisco. Soon orders were being placed for new Concord coaches. But the future of stagecoaching was much less certain than the costly purchase of the Holladay interests and the McLanes' orders for new equipment would suggest. The Central Pacific and Union Pacific Railroads were now building toward their prospective meeting in Utah. Once the rails were joined, Wells Fargo would lose its transcontinental mail contract and its through passengers, and would be dependent on the railroad's goodwill for transportation of express shipments. In their enthusiasm for the familiar, the McLanes were probably relying too much on the correct assumption that for many years stagecoaches would function as feeders to carry mail, passengers, and express to and from the relatively few rail points.

Recent experience seemed to justify optimistic expectations. When the new Central Pacific Railroad, starting out from Sacramento, decided to cross the Sierras by a pass north of Lake Tahoe instead of going through Placerville and south of the lake, the Pioneer Stage Company responded by buying out the California Stage Company's operations over the routes north of the lake, so that the

Pioneer could run services from the successive railheads of the Central Pacific. Travel between end-of-track and Virginia City increased so sharply during 1866 and 1867 that Wells Fargo kept putting on additional stagecoaches and building new offices.[43] But in 1868 the tracks were complete from Sacramento to Reno, and only the short feeder run to Virginia City was left to the stagecoaches. What now?

The denouement might have been less disastrous if Louis McLane's faith in continued stagecoaching had not caused him to forget how ruthlessly cutthroat San Francisco business could be. As Wells Fargo's first general agent for California, before being succeeded by his brother Charles, McLane had for more than a decade occupied a position of importance in San Francisco comparable to that of the resident agent of his brother Allan's Pacific Mail Steamship Company. His significance was suggested by the companies of which he was a director, incorporator, or large shareholder: the Bank of California, Pacific Insurance Company, California Dry Dock Company, Pacific Rolling Mills, San Francisco Gas Company, Sacramento Gas Company, and the California State Telegraph Company. If he ever stopped to think about it, McLane must have considered himself to be beyond challenge.

But the essence of success in San Francisco's constantly changing business world was to recognize opportunities before anyone else did. Lloyd Tevis and his partner James Ben Ali Haggin[44] (the middle name commemorated a Turkish grandfather) had lived by their wits ever since they formed a law partnership in Sacramento in 1850. Both were from Kentucky and were the sons of lawyers. Their already close relations were further strengthened when Tevis married the sister of Haggin's wife. Both were adept at analyzing carefully and judging with shrewd, informed insight. Haggin was the "silent, phlegmatic, cold, imperturbable" partner; Tevis, the "vivacious, talkative, active, ubiquitous" one. Yet of the two, Tevis was even more cautious than Haggin. "He feels his way as though he were blind," someone said.[45] Tevis was a master of detail and a master at self-control, supposedly capable of suppressing all personal or emotional considerations.

Tevis had tried mining for a few months in 1849 before deciding that the placers were too uncertain a way to wealth. The historian Hubert Howe Bancroft was not often guilty of humor, but there was barbed wit in his comment that years later when Tevis was talking with another erstwhile '49 miner (the by-then highly successful Sacramento and San Francisco banker D. O. Mills), the two agreed on "how much more satisfactory the gold-fleecing of men in town was to the argonaut business in the mountains."[46]

Haggin and Tevis quickly discovered that they could make more by managing money than by practicing law, and in 1853 moved their office to San Francisco, where they became a strong force in business and finance. Tevis' forte was in what might be termed the diplomacy of business—that is, in conducting intricate negotiations that ended in business mergers and handsome fees or profits for the chief negotiator.

As he studied the changes foreshadowed by the Central Pacific and Union Pacific Railroads, Tevis noted that the Union Pacific was creating an express company of its own to have a monopoly on service over its tracks, to the exclusion of Wells Fargo, American Express, or any other company. Tevis now proposed to form a comparable new express company to seek a monopoly over the Central Pacific tracks, again to the exclusion of Wells Fargo. The banker D. O. Mills and one of the Central Pacific's major promoters, Charles Crocker, agreed to join in the venture. When their scheme materialized in the Pacific Express, Wells Fargo's future became precarious, and the price of Wells Fargo stock fell to a low point at which Tevis, Mills, and Crocker gathered in enough shares to gain control. In 1869 they forced Wells Fargo to buy out their new Pacific Express at a high figure and merge it into Wells Fargo, which then received shipping privileges over the railroads. McLane was out as President, Wells Fargo began selling off its stagecoaches, and after a brief interval Tevis himself took over the presidency of Wells Fargo and moved its headquarters to San Francisco. Tevis remained president for twenty very remunerative years.[47]

In similar fashion he stepped into the telegraph business at a critical moment and again arranged a very profitable merger. Telegraphy had started in California at a surprisingly early date, only nine years after Samuel F. B. Morse had sent his epochal message from Washington to Baltimore. In October 1853 the California State Telegraph Company opened a line that ran from San Francisco through San Jose to Stockton, Sacramento, and Marysville, thus connecting the major communities in the state.[48] The company had hired a veteran telegrapher, James Gamble, to build and superintend their lines. Profits began to appear so quickly that by 1855 the company was paying dividends of 1 percent a month, and the firm's only serious trouble was that its success had inspired a chaotic assortment of rivals. By the time Congress passed the Pacific Telegraph Act in 1860, two California companies had already started building eastward in the hope of a Federal subsidy.

Western Union's Hiram Sibley of Rochester, New York, had taken the lead in lobbying the Pacific Telegraph bill through Congress and in reconciling some of his eastern rivals while evading others, so that he would have a clear field for Western Union's subsidiary, the Pacific Telegraph Company, to build from Omaha to Salt Lake City. There the Californians were supposed to take over. Realizing that nothing could be accomplished until the warring California companies were rationalized, Sibley sent a skillful negotiator, Jeptha H. Wade, a future president of Western Union, to California. Wade succeeded in merging the major California lines into the California State Telegraph Company in 1860, and this enlarged concern created the Overland Telegraph Company to build toward Salt Lake City.

The reliable James Gamble was put in charge and worked in harmony with the equally reliable Edward Creighton, who was building west from Omaha. Despite distances, aridity, rough country, and anxieties about Indians, the two men pushed their crews so determinedly that their lines connected at Salt Lake in October 1861 and a message was flashed from California to President Lincoln in Washington. A project that was expected to take two years had been completed in something over four months. What's more, by charging rates so high that only the rich could afford to use it, the transcontinental service "proved immediately and highly profitable."[49]

Lloyd Tevis was not listed as a director of the newly consolidated California State Telegraph Company when it was formed in 1860, but by 1862 he was.[50] He handled the negotiations by which Western Union bought a controlling interest in the California State Telegraph Company, and then used the latter as the vehicle for absorbing all the important lines west of Salt Lake City, including new lines to the Pacific Northwest. These lines were leased to Western Union and became the Pacific division of that huge national company, with

James Gamble as general superintendent. Contemporaries reported that Tevis was handsomely rewarded for his part in this transaction.

Quite aside from the significance of linking the farther west to the rest of the nation by quick communication, Tevis' role in the telegraph merger and in a series of other mergers he arranged involving San Francisco gas, water, ice, and railroad companies illustrates an important characteristic of the flourishing new San Francisco that was rebuilding itself out of the profits of the incoming flood of Comstock silver. Business operations were getting bigger, a greater diversity in types of business was lessening the significance of the merchants (especially the import traders), the corporate form was replacing partnerships, and the "inside" few were finding rich opportunities for profit.

A new group of Comstock millionaires was becoming prominent in San Francisco business and society, and soon even they were overshadowed by the supermillionaires of the Comstock's "Big Bonanza" era of the 1870s. The "railroad crowd," associated at first with the Central Pacific and later with railroads, land, and politics everywhere in California, was signaling its rise to opulence and power by moving to San Francisco, there to build their ostentatious mansions on Nob Hill.

A comparison of the boards of directors of important corporations based at San Francisco shows the same names recurring many times, which suggests that a small coterie of newly rich men, of newly influential men, had taken command, supplanting the old mercantile class. In its long front-page obituary review at the time of Tevis' death in 1899, the San Francisco *Chronicle* stressed that in addition to his constant partner Haggin, Tevis had a score of western business leaders as his frequent associates, and that he exercised great influence over those around him.[51] In addition to mining investments, Tevis served as director, officer, or large stockholder in a wide range of businesses: the California Steam Navigation Company, California Dry Dock Company, Risdon Iron Works, Pacific Ice Company, Pacific Coast Oil Company, the California Street Market and California Railway, and the Spring Valley Water Company.

This broad spectrum of interests reflected the rapid growth of San Francisco during the Comstock years and its impressive response to the demand for a local industry, especially in the iron and machine trades, that could meet the needs of the mines, railroads, and shipping companies and such civic services as street railways. From less than 57,000 in 1860, San Francisco grew to nearly 150,000 in 1870 and 234,000 in 1880. She ranked tenth in the nation in 1870, ninth in 1880. As early as 1870 the number of hands employed in iron, machine, boiler, and engine works in San Francisco came to the very respectable total of 1,369, and the products they were turning out were valued at almost $3 million per year.

A decade later a special census survey revealed that San Francisco's industry towered above that of other communities west of Omaha and Kansas City, and probably far exceeded the sum total of all of them combined. In 1880 San Francisco's total industry, covering the manufacture of everything from beer to locomotives, represented capital of $35,368,139, paid out $14,928,534 in wages that year, turned out products valued at $77,824,299, and employed 28,442 hands, several thousand of whom were women or children. For illustrative contrast, Denver's establishments represented capital of $2,301,850 in that year, and Salt Lake City's $860,415. Because of the continuing demands of the mines of Nevada, Idaho, California, and places as distant as Montana and Arizona, San Francisco had become a national leader in mining machinery, which meant that foundry and machine shop work continued to be the city's most important industry.[52]

The rich opportunities latent in this expanding economy caught the imagination of one of the most extraordinary figures in California's history. William Chapman Ralston was an attractive and self-confident promoter with a talent for friendships. He was one of those able young men from the Middle West who played such a large part in the opening of the region beyond the Missouri.[53] Born in 1826, he had grown up on the Ohio and had begun his business training as clerk on a steamboat. Service on the Ohio and Mississippi introduced him to a group of river men who were later to be his close associates on the Pacific Coast. In 1849 Ralston got as far toward California as Panama before joining in a business that ultimately involved dealing with trans-isthmian traffic as merchant, banker, and shipping agent. In the almost lawless atmosphere of that tropical land, where the Pacific Mail Steamship Company and Commodore Vanderbilt were mighty warring powers, Ralston received a harsh training that more than prepared him for San Francisco, to which he came in 1854 to join friends of his river days in establishing a bank.

Ten years later, when he founded the Bank of California, Ralston had moved upward through a succession of bank partnerships (there were as yet no incorporated banks), had become active in the chamber of commerce, and was a director of the Sacramento Valley Railroad and of the two new short lines. He became a director of the steamboat monopoly, just as he did of the California State Telegraph Company after its consolidation into a monopoly. Meantime he was treasurer of two leading mines on the Comstock Lode and a director of the Pacific Insurance Company.

Despite the California constitution's prohibition against banks, Ralston incorporated the Bank of California under the state's general incorporation laws and persuaded the prominent banker D. O. Mills to serve nominally as president, while Ralston as cashier did the real work. The other incorporators and early stockholders included some of the most influential men in California, such as Louis McLane, A. J. Pope of the big Pope and Talbot lumber firm, and two of San Francisco's most successful mining investors.

The bank became the base from which Ralston, through his friendships, alliances, and aggressive opportunism, took over the chief mines and mills of the Comstock when they were in the trough of depression after 1864, consolidated and refinanced them into a profitable monopoly, and then launched into a general campaign to back enterprises that would promote the growth of California and the regions tributary to it. His ambitions for his adopted state seem to have been limitless. His largess extended to San Francisco's only woolen mill, a sugar refinery, a vineyard and winery, and a tobacco plantation. He advanced money to complete the San Francisco and San Jose Railroad, invested in agricultural lands and urban real estate, put money into a carriage factory, a railroad car factory, a watch factory, a silk company, and a dry dock. He helped finance a steamboat monopoly in the Pacific Northwest and brought Ben Holladay's coastal steamships to that area. He was co-founder of the big Pacific Insurance Company, and political wire-puller on its behalf when it needed special legislation. He began construction of the Palace Hotel, the most luxurious of San Francisco hostelries.

Behind these overly ambitious projects was the income from the Comstock silver mines. Ralston's nonmining enterprises were what

economists would call "premature." With high-cost labor and capital, and a relatively small regional market, they were marginal at
best, and once the railroad began to bring in merchandise from the
east and Middle West, they could not meet the competition. Failure
was widespread and unemployment became acute. The value of
Ralston's investments shrank as drastically as did the collateral behind the loans he had granted. Temporarily new bonanzas on the
Comstock enabled him to manipulate and conceal what was happening to his own and the bank's resources.

When the crash came in 1875, panic broke out in San Francisco,
and so widespread was the bank's influence that mines and businesses closed throughout the west. At a dramatic meeting with the
bank's directors, Ralston was stripped of his position (he had become president in name as well as in fact) and was forced to sign
over his great personal holdings in partial satisfaction of the huge
sums that he had borrowed from the bank. Ralston evaded the
curious, and went down alone to North Beach for his daily swim.
Whether he committed suicide or in his agitation swam out too far
and was caught by currents has never been determined definitely;
probably he took his own life. His death symbolized the collapse of
a remarkable attempt to transform California quickly into a land of
varied industries. Industrialization and diversification were increasing, but for decades more, California and the west generally would
have to rely primarily on extracting wealth from natural resources,
be it mines, forests, agricultural land, or pastures.

When Louis McLane failed to foresee the implications for Wells
Fargo of the prospective spanning of the continent by a "Pacific
railroad," his thinking was in harmony with that of San Francisco's
business leaders as a whole. In 1859 and 1860 Theodore D. Judah,
an optimistic, dedicated young railway engineer and promoter who
had been in California since the early days of the Sacramento Valley
Railroad, tried to stir up financial support in San Francisco for the
long-discussed notion of a railroad between the Pacific and the
Missouri. He received little response. His San Francisco audiences
were finding ample uses for their funds in Comstock and other
mines, in California real estate, and in California-based enterprises.

Receiving no help there, Judah perforce turned to Sacramento,
which had been his home base for several years. This must have
seemed a weak second choice. Sacramento had but 13,000 inhabi-

tants in 1860, compared to San Francisco's nearly 57,000. By 1870 Sacramento would grow to a little over 16,000, and by 1880 would be less than 21,500. Sacramento was, then, a large town or very small city, more important as a transportation crossroads than as a center of wealth or industry.

The Sacramento men who finally responded to Judah's persuasive estimates and predictions were prosperous rather than wealthy, preponderantly storekeepers and politicians.[54] Collis P. Huntington, the ablest of the group and the one destined to be the real leader, was in partnership with the quiet, conservative "Uncle Mark" Hopkins in a successful hardware store. Charles Crocker, the huge (250 pounds) and loudly energetic proprietor of a dry-goods establishment, was to become head of construction; his brother, E. B., a practicing attorney, was to become chief legal counsel. Leland Stanford, the best-educated but not the brightest of the associates, was a lawyer with strong political ambitions who in California had become a storekeeper in charge of a Sacramento grocery firm established by his brothers. When two miners failed, owing large bills to the Stanford store, he took over their quartz mine just in time to profit handsomely from his involuntary investment.

The whole group was politically minded and was to display a notable talent for using the rising new Republican party as a vehicle to assist their railroad project by any convenient means, ethical or unethical. Stanford had already run unsuccessfully for state treasurer and governor and now was running again, to win a single term as governor just as the railroad got started. Usually he was the one to handle the railroad's relations with successive pliant legislatures. Hopkins and Charles Crocker had been aldermen in Sacramento and Crocker had run for state assembly. E. B. Crocker served a term on the state bench.

Since none of this group had large wealth, nor experience with large projects, nor with physical construction, and none had a record as an important promoter, one is left to wonder why they decided to make this drastic break with the relatively simple pattern of their lives. Probably a part of the answer is that the initial cash investment required of each, a 10 percent down payment, was trivial, about fifteen hundred dollars apiece. That was enough to have Judah make surveys and have him lobby in Washington for a Pacific Railroad bill, and even the down payment was retrievable, for Judah

stressed that in his preliminary reconnaissance he had already discovered a pass over the Sierras by way of Dutch Flat and Donner
Lake, where a profitable wagon road could be constructed while
waiting for the railroad. With the Nevada trade booming, a wagon
road and a short railroad connecting with it would give a handsome
return even if most of Judah's Pacific railroad proved visionary.
Perhaps, too, the observant Sacramentans had already noted that in
railway projects the profits went to the inside group who controlled
construction, rather than to the ultimate operators of the functioning road. It was over ethical questions connected with construction
that the Sacramento group parted company with Judah, who resigned in sharp disagreement.

When ground was broken for the railroad in January 1863, Stanford was the president of the Central Pacific and the governor of the
state. Huntington instinctively preferred to manipulate events from
behind the scenes, while Stanford posed and orated ponderously as
the "front man." Huntington was a shrewd, determined, and ruthless individual whom a witty contemporary described as being
"scrupulously dishonest."[55] He must also have been exceedingly
able, for no second-rater could have made the transition from running a local hardware business to negotiating and planning on a
national scale to obtain the money and supplies that the Central
Pacific needed. Finance, in particular, was a continuing nightmare
for Huntington, who established himself in an unostentatious, inex-
pensive little office in New York City and from there learned the
intricate, carefully hidden manipulations by which he kept funds
flowing to Crocker, the construction head. Huntington's biographer says that in 1864 there was one particularly desperate period
when for seventeen days there was not a dollar in the company
treasury.[56]

Crocker, although he had had no previous experience to qualify
him for his job, functioned at first as Charles Crocker and Company,
later as the Contract and Finance Company, which was the Central
Pacific's version of the Credit Mobilier. The results were the same
as with the Union Pacific: excessive costs and transfer of stocks and
bonds to the construction company, leaving the builders rich and
the railroad overcapitalized and poor. The details of construction
financing will never be known, for Huntington and his partners

thoughtfully burned fifteen volumes of records to avoid a repetition of the Credit Mobilier disclosures.[57]

Several factors helped to increase the Central Pacific's income during the critical phase. The demands of the Comstock mines provided traffic revenues as soon as enough track had been laid to make it worthwhile to operate over a portion of their route. The state of California and the counties of Sacramento, Placer, and San Francisco all voted financial help in one form or another to supplement the much bigger Federal assistance. By the legerdemain of persuading Abraham Lincoln that the Sierra Nevada mountains began on the flat plains seven miles outside Sacramento, the railroad won the maximum Federal subsidy intended for mountains, instead of having to build for at least twenty miles further before it could honestly claim compensation for mountain terrain.[58]

But there could be no question as to the difficulty of the project. The railroad had to reach a summit more than seven thousand feet high by the time that it had built a hundred miles. It had to drill and blast tunnel after tunnel through the granite of the Sierra and to invent and construct snow sheds to prevent the numerous deep cuts from being clogged by impassable drifts in winter. It was only after the road had made its way down the eastern slopes of the Sierra that more level terrain was encountered in the Nevada and Utah deserts.

Just as Dodge hired crews of Irish, so Crocker hired Chinese, though Crocker also employed Irish. In 1865 he had seven thousand Chinese and twenty-five hundred Irish working for him.[59] Crocker claimed that when he tried American labor, they quit to go to the mines as soon as they had accumulated a little cash.

Long before they were ready for the ceremonies at Promontory Point, the associates who were building the Central Pacific sensed that in their as yet incomplete road they had a weapon through which they could establish a monopoly over transportation in California and between California and the outer world. Despite their always precarious corporate finances, the Central Pacific managed to absorb virtually all of the new railroad projects that were struggling into existence in California, while also acquiring the California Steam Navigation Company by indirection (they took over a smaller railroad that had just "saved" the steamboat company by buying it before the Central Pacific could), and they still found the money and political adroitness to win a monopoly over the Oakland waterfront on San Francisco Bay, together with a site accessible to the San Francisco waterfront (public outcry had stopped their plot for a much richer deal at San Francisco). Over and above the huge land grant that they received from the Federal government, they squeezed potentially valuable real estate out of every county and city that feared economic strangulation if it were left off the new railroad routes.

On their way to monopoly the "railroad crowd," as contemporaries angrily termed them, came virtually to control the state legislature and some of the local governments. A few individual Californians were shrewd enough and rich enough to win favorable terms from them. Peter Donahue sold a succession of his railroad investments to them. Lloyd Tevis probably actually bested them, though his maneuvers were hidden by such an impenetrable screen that it is hard to judge Tevis' role in the Oakland waterfront deal, or his sale of an unbuilt railroad, the Southern Pacific, to the Central Pacific (which would presently exchange its original name for that of its purchase), or his ploy in having the Southern Pacific buy out the San Francisco and San Jose Railroad, in which Tevis had come to share an interest with Donahue. The San Francisco and San Jose happened to be essential if the Central Pacific were to enter San Francisco by land.

These were murky affairs, arcane in nature and clear only in their demonstration of Lord Acton's aphorism that "power tends to corrupt and absolute power corrupts absolutely." Legislative inquiries into the behavior of the railroad usually ended in whitewash. How the discerning public felt can best be indicated by two quotations, the first from a notoriously independent private citizen, Caspar T. Hopkins:

It is enterprise—often of the most deserving kind—to build railroads. It is business—thoroughly legitimate business—to operate them. But when enormous fortunes are created out of their construction by means of Credit Mobiliers, Contract and Finance Companies, by corrupting public officers, by over-issues of stock or bonds, or by any other of the thousand tricks resorted to by sharpers for obtaining money without consideration, and yet under cover of the law, the tidal-wave of speculation sweeps the business almost out of sight.[60]

The second is from the leading California newspaper of its day, the Sacramento *Daily Union*. Having been an earnest advocate of a Pacific railroad in the beginning, and a supporter of subsidies as the way to get construction started, the *Union* felt compelled to explain in 1871 why it had reversed its stand:

And we may add that if the *Union* has changed from any view it entertained on the subject ten years ago, so have the people, Congress, and even the Courts. Experience with private subsidized corporations has caused the changes. They have dealt in a spirit of fraud with those whose generosity has aided them in the acquisition of property, and bitterly disappointed every reasonable expectation. Instead of serving the public interest, they oppress the public, corrupt its servants, and employ the gifts secured in the furtherance of schemes for cheating the nation and bankrupting the counties. Ten years ago railways were properly regarded as the great desideratum. Now, since this bitter experience with the plundering scamps who managed most of them has intervened, the desideratum is how to prohibit the further progress of the game of plunder.[61]

CHAPTER 5

Build Thee More Stately Mansions: Leadership in Three Western Cities

A THOUGHTFUL western historian has argued that even
though most westerners did not live in cities, nevertheless "society was remarkably urbanized." Newcomers were apt to go first to
"Salt Lake City, San Francisco, Portland, or one of their later rivals," and even if they decided not to settle there, they returned for
frequent visits, while in the meantime virtually the whole population
was "economically and culturally" tributary to one or the other
of these regional centers.[1] Two specialists in urban history have
suggested how this fits into the broader pattern of national development. Between 1860 and 1890, they point out, "the rapid
development of new regions . . . created great opportunities in
building new cities." The period saw "the emergence of a national
urban network—a complex interrelated system of national and regional metropolises, specialized manufacturing cities, and hundreds
of smaller subordinate cities."[2]

The farther west's contribution to this emerging "network" was
the founding of regional metropolises that came into being as centers of commerce, transportation, finance, newspaper publication,
and recreation (places to escape to periodically). "Specialized
manufacturing cities" were hardly a western feature; instead the
regional metropolises attracted to themselves most of the very limited amount of manufacturing that grew up in what was basically a
land of high-cost labor and capital, limited markets, and vulnerability to eastern competition once the railroads were built. Up to 1880

San Francisco alone developed an extensive industry. Between 1880 and 1900 Denver began to be significant industrially, and modest industrial advances were made at other regional metropolises.

Of "smaller subordinate cities" there were quite a few, but given the volatility of the west, it is not surprising that many failed to survive. Those that were better situated and had varied sources of income became permanent, as in the case of Boise, which started as a small military post and mining supply center hard by the Oregon Trail, presently was surrounded by a cluster of irrigated farms, and became a governmental center by capturing the territorial capital and county seat. Its stores serviced a wide reach of miners, farmers, and ranchers, and its *Idaho Daily Statesman* circulated extensively. Far too often the smaller cities were overgrown mining towns, such as Virginia City, whose future was cut off when its only industry declined. Even the better-endowed Leadville, Colorado, which produced lead, copper, and zinc as well as silver and developed extensive smelting facilities, barely lasted into the twentieth century.

When the census of 1880 set out to list the one hundred principal American cities, it found six cities west of the Missouri that qualified. San Francisco, with nearly 234,000, ranked ninth in the nation and dwarfed every other western community, for the next in size were Denver and Oakland (respectively fiftieth and fifty-first and each with about 35,000), then Sacramento (ninetieth, with 21,420), Salt Lake City (ninety-third, with 20,768), and San Antonio (ninety-sixth, with 20,550).[3]

It was gospel among promoters of western communities that to grow, a city must have access to railroads. San Francisco and Portland were the obvious exceptions, made possible by their fortunate location at the point where oceanic shipping met inland water transport. To most westerners the approach of the first railroad was the most exciting prospect since the opening of the mining booms. In oversimple terms merchants, land speculators, and other boosters saw it as a matter of their community's life or death to be on the route of the Union Pacific or Central Pacific, only to have reality prove much more complex than their expectations. The Pacific railroad gave a greater stimulus to Omaha, the eastern terminus, than it did to Sacramento because Sacramento was not so much the real Pacific terminus as the unloading point for freight and passengers bound for San Francisco, whose position by 1869 was beyond challenge despite the city's awkward location at the end of a peninsula. Oakland, on the eastern shore of San Francisco Bay, was closely linked to San Francisco by ferries that carried railroad cars as well as passengers and assorted freight. It received much of the rush of new business from the railroad toward the queen city, while at the same time it was developing as a residential and industrial suburb of San Francisco.

In between Sacramento and Omaha the new railroad created, almost overnight, communities like North Platte, Nebraska; Cheyenne, Wyoming; and Reno, Nevada; yet who would describe any of these as ranking among the nation's more promising cities? The Pacific railroad managed to miss entirely the only two prospectively important commercial cities that were close to its route, Denver and Salt Lake City, just as it bypassed by a few miles the most important mining center along its path, Virginia City.

Unlike the railroad, the historian cannot afford to neglect the rise of cities nor to overlook the importance in western development of the little groups of politically minded merchants, bankers, and land speculators that thrust their way forward in each city to volunteer a leadership that was crucial not only to the struggling new community itself but also to the much bigger region that was tributary to it. To illustrate the process, sketches will be given here of two inland regional metropolises, Denver and Salt Lake City, and one seaport equivalent, Portland, adding to what has been said already about the earliest and greatest western metropolis, San Francisco.

Of the three to be considered here, Denver's experience is especially intriguing because with immense problems to overcome in the early years, "Denver leaders consistently demonstrated promotional zeal and skill" that carried them and their city to an ultimate triumph.[4] Theirs is a classic case of what could be accomplished under the leadership of a local elite.

Among the early arrivals none was more important than the first newspaper editor, William N. Byers, who had tried Ohio, Iowa, Oregon, California, and Omaha before he hauled a printing press across the plains to Denver in the spring of 1859. He barely got his first *Rocky Mountain News* off the press ahead of a would-be rival journal, whose proprietor promptly sold out to the victor. Something in the straggling little mining depot appealed so strongly to this wanderer that he went back to Omaha for his wife and children and settled into a lifelong career of boosting Denver to the outside world, providing local leadership as editor and very vigorous citizen, and promoting his own money-making schemes. His wife, who seems to have been quite conscious of her prestige as a First Settler, launched into typically Victorian good works for the Methodist church, the poor, and orphaned boys.[5]

The early years were a trying time for Denver. Congress had a well-deserved reputation for procrastination in providing territorial status and government for new areas, and in those dying days of the Buchanan administration, with the crisis over the South dominating Congress, unusual speed was impossible. Congress finally "organized" Colorado Territory by a bill passed early in 1861, and Abraham Lincoln's nominee for governor, Colonel William Gilpin, arrived in Denver by stagecoach at the end of May of that same year to govern a region that had needed a government since 1859.

During the two years of no legal government, Denver experienced both the constructive and the negative happenings so characteristic of a frontier hamlet that was trying to leapfrog into urban status. With enthusiasm it celebrated a succession of "firsts" that revealed not only the physical needs but also the psychological wants of the little outpost: the first issue of the *Rocky Mountain News* on April 23, 1859, signifying that the town had found a spokesman; the arrival of the first stagecoach from Leavenworth two weeks later, which implied that Denver was now in regular communication with the "States" (with "home"); the birth of the first white child in July, symbolic of family life in a town filled with male transients; the opening in August of the first brick kiln, with its promise of building material that would be more fireproof and more impressive in appearance; the arrival from the Missouri of large wagon trains of merchandise and supplies; and the first theatrical performance, late in October, as a recreational alternative to the omnipresent saloons and gambling houses.[6]

Negatively Denver suffered from absence of governmental authority and from the footloose nature of its people. In a period in which most American cities, east or west, were subject to a high turnover of population, Denver went to extremes. Its population was essentially transient, and the few who stayed put and tried to improve their new home sometimes found their efforts nullified by violence-prone drifters from other frontiers. With doctored whiskey plentiful at twenty-five cents per drink, everyone armed, and many harboring antagonisms based on sectional allegiance to south or north, it's a wonder that homicides, robberies, and fights weren't more prevalent than they were. In 1859 and 1860 Byers took time out from his promotional activities to help organize vigilance committees and people's courts that carried out their "swift, terrible and . . . irrevocable decrees"—and these were not the last vigilance committees and lynchings in Denver's history. At one point a self-constituted militia patrolled the streets to cow a defiant gang of desperadoes called the "Bummers," while land occupiers formed a "claim club" to render mutual assistance against claim jumpers.[7]

Pioneers with long experience in creating their own government on frontiers held one election under the laws of Kansas Territory (whose governor, James Denver, contributed his name to the new town), then drafted a constitution for the "State of Jefferson," and when that was rejected by the voters drafted a stillborn organic act for the "Territory of Jefferson." Governor Gilpin got legitimate territorial government under way during the summer of 1861, and Denver was incorporated in that year, but Gilpin remained governor only during 1861–1862 and was preoccupied with the outbreak of the Civil War. A military veteran with service in two wars, and a convert to the west whose soaring imagination and unbearably long speeches were unrestrained by common sense, Gilpin made enemies of influential local men like Byers, while at the same time he had the audacity to raise a volunteer military force without authorization from Washington and without money to pay or equip it. The fact that Gilpin's "army" had helped turn back a very real Confederate invading force that had marched from Texas up through New Mexico became known too late to save Gilpin from dismissal by the Lincoln administration.[8]

His successor, John Evans, made a deeper mark. A Quaker by birth and education, Evans became in mature life a leading Methodist, a well-known doctor, medical teacher, and founder of hospitals, and a founder of Garrett Biblical Institute and Northwestern University, which last is located in the Chicago suburb that bears Evans' name. Later he was to found the institution that is the ancestor of the present University of Denver. Evans made a considerable fortune out of Chicago real estate and devoted years to railroad promotion and a Nebraska land scheme, even while finding time for

Chicago civic affairs and the new Republican party. When angry Methodists accused President Lincoln of not making enough political appointments from the ranks of their denomination, a weary Lincoln used the Colorado governorship to reward this prominent individual from his own state.[9]

Like Byers, Evans had the optimism and physical and nervous energy that the territorial challenge demanded, and as a veteran promoter, he stepped easily into the simultaneous advancement of Colorado and of his own fortunes. His appointment, like that of the notably effective Chief Justice Moses Hallett, who joined the Colorado bench in 1866, suggests that the old notion that only hacks were sent to govern the territories is too undiscriminating a generalization. Modern evaluations have shown that the little group of Federal appointees played an important transitional role in creating a political structure within which settlers' impatient efforts at self-government could be directed into orderly democratic processes, and within which statutes and court decisions could work out a reasonable compromise between traditional common law precedents and the innovative practices demanded by the peculiarities of western circumstances, such as the necessary diversion of water for mining and irrigation.[10]

Precisely because Washington sent so few, it was important that the territorial officials be able and diligent and avoid the frequent absenteeism and overenthusiastic dedication to whiskey that lessened the usefulness of quite a few of them. The standard crew was a governor, a territorial secretary, and three or more judges, together with lesser officials appointed by the various departments to serve as United States attorneys, collectors of internal revenue, surveyors, land office officials, and postmasters.[11] Economically the disbursements supervised by this scattering of officials, like the contracts issued by the Army and Indian Office, were of great importance in a new land that had few sources of income. The financial incentives offered to those at the top were not great: Evans was to be paid fifteen hundred dollars per year as governor and commander in chief of the militia, and an additional thousand dollars per year for serving as superintendent of Indian affairs. His friend and future son-in-law, Samuel H. Elbert, late of Plattsmouth, Nebraska, was to receive eighteen hundred dollars a year as territorial secretary.[12]

The Denver to which Evans came in 1862 was "treeless, grassless, bushless" because no water for irrigation was available as yet. "Its motley, irregular, ugly structures of brick, frame, or log" were soon to be replaced, because in the spring of 1863 a terrible fire destroyed most of the flimsy structures, and when the town courageously rebuilt, Cherry Creek flooded disastrously one year later, with severe loss of life and property.[13]

Replacements for items lost were particularly costly because this was a period when embittered Indians were cutting the lifeline that connected Denver to the Missouri River bases. By the winter of 1864–1865, virtually all communication between Denver and the east had ceased, and the wayside ranches and stagecoach stations had been burned. Already alienated by white intrusion, the Arapaho and Cheyenne had been aroused to fury by the Colorado militia's sadistic massacre of sleeping men, women, and children whose camp at Sand Creek was supposedly under the protection of the nearest American military post.[14]

To complete the list of disasters, the winter of 1864–1865 was unusually cold, and 1865 brought the first grasshopper invasion to devastate the new little farms that had sprung up along the river bottoms near the city. Prices of all commodities soared and wages rose with them, although mechanics at the then-high rate of seven to eight dollars a day and common laborers at four to five dollars had little to show for their work after they had paid for their basic necessities.[15]

These nearly fatal setbacks must be viewed against the fundamental circumstance that Denver was still largely a crossroads for transients—of men going to or coming from the mines, or arriving from the east or returning to it. The census credited Denver with no growth between 1860 and 1870 (4,749 in 1860 versus 4,759 in 1870). The fortunes of the place and the size of its population vibrated in response to the collective performance of the mines, but the middle and late 1860s—roughly from 1864 to 1868—were the nadir for the Colorado mines.[16]

Nor could Denver be entirely sure of its regional supremacy. Other Colorado towns had ambitions to displace it, and one, Golden, west of Denver, was a dangerous rival that for a time stole from Denver the distinction of being the official territorial capital. A "Golden crowd" emerged in Colorado politics under the able leadership of Henry Moore Teller, the future United States senator, who was then a leading attorney and an influential, Republican-oriented political figure in the mining counties of Gilpin and Clear Creek, which were the center of Colorado's principal surviving mining efforts. Teller, of western New York origins and a former schoolteacher, had practiced law in a little town in Illinois before a lawyer friend persuaded him to come to Colorado.[17]

Despite his stern Calvinism and membership in the Good Templars temperance society, Teller fitted into the life of the mining town of Central City and prospered well enough so that he was able to return to New York State to marry his fiancée, Harriet Bruce, and bring her back to Colorado on a wedding journey that his wife later described as "by stage over barren and uninhabited plains." The new Mrs. Teller was a determined Methodist who made the Teller home a headquarters for Methodist activity, just as her husband became a leading Mason and grand master of Colorado.[18]

Opposed to Teller's "Golden crowd" was a "Denver crowd" that was at least as able, more numerous, and better placed geographically for controlling trade. A modern scholar has remarked that

in each western territory the early years of organization were characterized by a type of disruptive, confused, intensely combative, and highly personal form of politics that can best be described as chaotic factionalism.[19]

This was decisively true of Colorado in the 1860s, where the rivalries of local communities and the related ambitions of individual personalities built factions and territorial parties that cut across Colorado's allegiance to the Republican party. Colorado might have achieved statehood in the 1860s, especially in 1864 when Nevada did, if its divergent political groups could have united instead of blocking each other.[20]

Governor Evans was a part of a Denver faction that included his close associates Byers and Elbert and drew together a notable group of politically minded businessmen who considered it normal to speculate in land and mining and to be none too ethical in their speculations. All had been restless movers before finding in Denver and Colorado a field into which they could channel their creative energies and imaginations. Jerome B. Chaffee, born in New York State of a comfortably situated family, had taught school in Michigan before moving to St. Joseph to enter banking. After an unsuccessful try at town promoting in Kansas, he came to Denver, where he linked his fortunes with David H. Moffat, Jr., another New York State man and a poor boy by origin. Moffat worked in banks in New York City, Des Moines, and Omaha before coming to Denver as a partner in a book and stationery store. Moffat joined Chaffee in mining and real estate speculation, and when Chaffee opened the First National Bank of Denver in 1865, Moffat was his partner and soon became cashier. Both men became very wealthy; very active in promoting mines, railroads, and land ventures; and very political.

Bela M. Hughes, formerly of Kentucky and Missouri, was a well-educated lawyer who came to Denver as local head of Ben Holladay's stagecoach operations, and turned back to the law after Holladay sold out. Luther Kountze—one of a team of four brothers from Osnaburg, Ohio, that opened banks in Omaha, Denver, and elsewhere—was sent to Denver in 1862 to inaugurate what became the Colorado National Bank. Amos Steck, born of well-to-do Ohio parents, read law in Philadelphia, went to California in 1849, returned to Pennsylvania, and tried Wisconsin before migrating to Denver in 1859, where he succeeded in real estate speculation, served as mayor, organized a hospital and a fund for the poor, and in association with Luther Kountze obtained from the legislature a charter for Denver's first horse-drawn street railway.[21]

This richly experienced group met their big test in 1867 when they had to face the reality that instead of drilling tunnels through the formidable Rockies west of Denver, the Union Pacific was going to lay its tracks along the gradual ascent through southern Wyoming, where Cheyenne, a hundred miles north of Denver, would be the nearest rail stop to the disappointed city. The only alternative to the Union Pacific was a weak one: a railroad with an erratic history and uncertain finances, soon to be rechristened Kansas Pacific and recently authorized by Congress to build from Kansas City to Colorado. But Colonel James Archer of the Kansas Pacific proved no more encouraging than General Dodge of the Union Pacific about building through Denver.

It was a critical moment that might determine Denver's fate for years to come. There had been signs of improvement lately. Planting and gardening had brightened the city, and nearby farms were feeding it. Rebuilding after the fire and flood of 1863 and 1864 had been in more substantial style. The worst of the lawlessness and violence seemed past. Golden's pretensions to being the territorial capital had been crushed.[22]

Despite these gains, "it was evident that the city could not and would not enter upon a career of active growth and prosperity until the coming of railroads."[23] The need was the greater because since 1865 Teller, in association with the determined promoter-politician William A. H. Loveland and other members of the "Golden crowd," had been planning a Colorado Central Railroad that would connect the mines of Gilpin and Clear Creek counties to the Union Pacific in such a way as to promote Golden at the expense of Denver.[24]

Evans—by then out of the governorship because of criticism of the Sand Creek massacre—and the other Denver businessmen-politicians were congenitally unable to sit idle while their city was bypassed and their own futures were jeopardized. To focus the strength of the business community on the crisis, they organized a board of trade, in imitation of similar bodies that they had known in Chicago, St. Louis, and other cities. To arouse the public, they held a series of open meetings. To have a possible vehicle available, Evans, Moffat, and Hughes incorporated the Denver Pacific Railway and Telegraph Company, in which Byers undertook to build the telegraph line. They persuaded Arapahoe County to vote five hundred thousand dollars in bonds for the proposed Denver Pacific, and drummed up individual promises to subscribe perhaps three hundred thousand dollars more. Then public enthusiasm sagged; no more money was forthcoming, and a minimum of $2 million was believed to be needed (the actual cost proved to be far higher).[25]

Evans assumed the presidency of the railroad and turned for help to the Union Pacific, which first agreed, but then reneged. Evans himself then contracted to build and equip the Denver Pacific and pay its outstanding debts, in return for all of the road's remaining stocks, bonds, and other assets. He decided to seek the help of the Kansas Pacific, which had resumed building toward Denver, and after three weeks of negotiation with President Robert E. Carr of the railroad, a half interest in the Denver Pacific was ceded to Carr, in trust for the Kansas Pacific, while Evans, Moffat, and a third Denver man, Walter S. Chessman, retained the other half. After five years, control of the Denver Pacific was to be surrendered to the Kansas Pacific, and as a further restraint, the Denver Pacific was to agree that the two roads would share equally in their respective gross receipts for a distance of 106 miles on either side of Denver (the equivalent of the distance from Denver to Cheyenne).[26]

These were hard terms that reflected the weak bargaining position of a depressed western trading town that was threatened by isolation. The terms were sweetened by the assurance that both the Kansas Pacific and Denver Pacific would be completed into Denver and together would build a branch to Boulder, where there were important coal fields on land granted to the Denver Pacific by Congress.

For Evans personally, there was the prospect of good profits from an agreement that construction would be by a joint construction company modeled after the Credit Mobilier and directed by Evans and General William Jackson Palmer of the Kansas Pacific. There would be further profits from land sales out of the congressional land grant and from coal revenues, not to mention gaining control over much of the coal business of northern Colorado. A scholar of a later day concluded that probably the Denver Pacific "was built for approximately one-third of the claimed cost,"[27] which must mean that as with the Union Pacific and Central Pacific, the men controlling construction were the ones who made money, while the railroad was left to operate under a heavy burden of debt. Evans' biographer has concluded that "Evans and his Denver associates seem to have invested very little cash in the road."[28] The future was to demonstrate that the Denver Pacific would have trouble operating profitably under the restrictions imposed by the Kansas Pacific and with the burden of interest on its debt. Besides, the alliance with the Kansas Pacific drew down upon the Denver Pacific the hostility of the Union Pacific, which continued uncooperative until Jay Gould in 1880 forced the three roads to merge.

But in the eyes of contemporaries, the important consideration was that the job got done. With his Kansas Pacific backing and a congressional land grant for collateral, Evans was able to market Denver Pacific bonds in New York, London, and Frankfurt, and to persuade Dutch purchasers to absorb a considerable chunk. The Denver Pacific was completed in June 1870, amidst ceremonies that saw Indians and fur trappers mixing with bankers and politicians, so recent was the passing of the frontier. When the Kansas Pacific arrived in August, Denver had its outlets to both east and west. These two successes, in turn, started a wave of railroad construction that won back for Denver its old primacy as a transportation center. An aroused Union Pacific advanced money to Loveland to extend his Colorado Central approximately to Denver in September 1870, and finally to Cheyenne in 1877. The short Boulder Valley Railroad reached the coalfields at Erie by 1871. When the "Golden crowd" continued hostile, Evans built the Denver, South Park and Pacific up the South Platte River to the mines, amidst a burst of criticism of his management. General Palmer of the Kansas Pacific, a cultivated and imaginative Philadelphian who had served with the Pennsylvania Railroad, was so taken by Colorado that he bought large tracts of land and planned the narrow-gauge Denver and Rio Grande Railroad, incorporated in 1870 and first built south from Denver to Pueblo parallel to the line of the Rockies. Palmer was the leading force in founding the resort town of Colorado Springs in 1871 and its Colorado College in 1874.[29]

For Denver signs of progress became numerous during the early 1870s, and contemporaries gave the new railroads full credit for them. With travel so much easier and quicker, strangers were crowding Denver's hotels. Not only businessmen, mining men, and settlers were appearing, but also two new breeds, tourists and health seekers. Along with them came types that suggested that Denver had indeed become a part of the general American scene: Susan B. Anthony, who arrived in 1871 to lecture on women's voting rights; the Kit Carson baseball team, bearing a great frontier name, to play the Denver club. City real estate values were advancing, new buildings were going up, commerce and bank deposits were increasing, and long overdue civic improvements were being started.[30]

An English lady who passed through Denver on a cold, snowy day in late October 1873 found it "a busy place, the *entrepôt* and distributing-point for an immense district," where the "sportsman, hunter, miner, teamster, emigrant," and asthmatic could find a complete outfit at any one of "fifty different stores." On the streets she saw Indians and trappers mixing with kid-gloved Broadway dandies and rich English tourists. Indian women accompanied their men, but only five white women were visible.[31]

The ubiquitous Byers, hired to promote land sales for the Denver Pacific and Kansas Pacific, helped place a series of agricultural colonies: Horace Greeley's Union Colony at the new town of Greeley, well north of Denver, in 1870; the Chicago-Colorado Colony at Longmont in 1871; and the St. Louis–Western Colony at Evans, also in 1871. Up in the mountains, whose mines were all-important to Denver's continued growth, the first technologically successful smelter began working the intractable gold ores in 1868 and improved its performance in the early 1870s. By 1878 the smelter's owners had decided to move their plant down to Denver, now that the new railroads could bring in Colorado coal and coke for fuel and now that Denver was becoming a central point to which ores for smelting could be hauled from numerous mining districts. Similar recognition of Denver's improved accessibility attracted ten modest-sized foundries and machine shops that by 1880 were turning out products valued at over $770,000 and were employing over 250 hands, as they responded to demands from the mines.[32] Between 1880 and 1900 Denver's industries developed markedly, although they remained far behind San Francisco.

Meanwhile progress was evident up in the mountains themselves. Silver in Clear Creek County, discovered as far back as 1864, began to produce modestly in 1870 and 1871 and much more rapidly thereafter. As railroads penetrated the mountain canyons, lower transportation rates supplied one of the essentials for a mining revival. The one big element still lacking was the discovery of a true bonanza. This good fortune finally blessed Colorado in the middle 1870s when the identification of rich silver–lead carbonate ores at Leadville (altitude ten thousand feet) triggered a major rush that started in 1877. By that time Denver was as well prepared to profit from Leadville as San Francisco had been to exploit the Comstock Lode. From a population of less than 5,000 in 1870, the city shot up to 35,629 by 1880, thus becoming the second largest city in the Far West. Fittingly, Congress had granted the long-desired statehood in the centennial year of 1876.

* * * * *

The full bulk of the Rockies loomed between Denver and Salt Lake City. If the Mormons had had their way, a social and psychological wall of equal proportions would have separated the two. The Mormons, whose story will be told in a later chapter, had founded Salt Lake City with the intent of having it serve several quite specific functions: to be the holy city wherein would be built the most sacred temple of the Kingdom; to be "the new gathering place and head-quarters city of the Mormons";[33] and to be the hometown of thousands of rural Mormons. In short, Salt Lake City was to be at one and the same time the place of the temple, the administrative center from which the Mormons would be ruled by their own leaders, the reception center and temporary stopover for the refugees and converts brought in by the annual church wagon trains, and a major permanent settlement of self-sustaining farmers. It was not to be a commercial center.

Reflecting these purposes, Brigham Young's advance guard in 1847 started by choosing a site for a temple and setting aside space near it for the homes and working quarters of church officers, then from the Temple Block as a center laid out the prospective city as a series of rectangles. Each rectangle was divided into house lots of ample proportions (one and a quarter acres each), so as to permit kitchen gardens, fruit trees, chickens, a milk cow, and other means of family self-support. Since lumber was scarce, houses were usually of sun-dried adobe brick and of a plain, unadorned design that suggested the simple, primarily rural origins of the early population.[34]

Visitors always commented on the pleasant contrast between the desert that had to be crossed to reach Salt Lake City and the sudden impression of well-planted yards and tree-lined streets as the traveler entered the city. The noted British explorer and scholar Sir Richard Francis Burton remarked on the rows of cottonwood, locust, acacia, and poplar, and spoke of the fruit trees and vines. He was critical of the one-story, dull-colored adobe homes because they seemed too much all of a single pattern, and, besides, the poorer houses were "hut-like."[35]

The Right Reverend Daniel Sylvester Tuttle, a thirty-year-old Episcopal missionary bishop, wrote back to his wife that

Salt Lake City is beautiful. . . . streets straight and wide, rills of irrigating water running along the sides to refresh the growing shade trees, . . . yards and gardens filled full of peach, apple and apricot trees, of grapes and all vegetables. . . . Almost every family here has a cow.[36]

As the bishop's description suggests, even after twenty years of growth the atmosphere of Salt Lake City was more rural than urban. In every aspect of life the directing hand of the church could be sensed: in maintaining decorum, in allocating land to prospective occupants, in building the all-essential water system, in encouraging local manufacture of articles that would otherwise have to be imported from across the plains, and in governing. The Federal government's decision to appoint Brigham Young as the first territorial governor was no more than a recognition of the reality that Brigham Young was in fact the ruler, and subsequent insistence by the distant Washington administration that non-Mormon ("Gentile") governors, judges, and other Federal officials must be thrust upon a resistant Mormon population produced endless friction that distorted the pattern of politics characteristic of most western regions during their territorial eras. One result of appointing non-Mormons was the creation at Salt Lake City, the capital, of a little group of Federal officeholders who felt isolated from the predominant society and were only too eager to serve as the nucleus around which anti-Mormon sentiment could collect.

In the first years of most western cities the merchant and banker class was a major if not the dominant force, as exemplified by the San Francisco merchants and bankers of the 1850s and 1860s and the Denver leaders of the 1860s and 1870s, but in Salt Lake City the merchants had an uneasy position despite the profitableness of their occupation. Brigham Young denounced trade, especially through non-Mormon merchants, because it created a dependence on an outside and presumably hostile world and enabled merchants to send out of Utah profits squeezed out of Mormon consumers. At a time when the church was boldly exercising domination over other aspects of economic life, the governing hierarchy "left to Gentile freighters and merchants the opportunity of supplying the Salt Lake market,"[37] with the result that in 1849 and the decade of the 1850s non-Mormon (i.e., "Gentile") merchants, notably including Ben Holladay, made fortunes by hauling goods to Salt Lake City. They opened retail stores and provided financial services. Their early successes encouraged additional firms to enter the field in the 1860s, including several teams of Jewish brothers. In effect, the Mormon leaders left commerce to the forces of private capitalism, with only occasional attempts to regulate prices of essential foodstuffs that were proposed for shipment out of Salt Lake Valley.

The merchants' profitable operations proved that even as determinedly self-contained a group as the Mormons could not exist without trade with the outer world. But in fact this same point was demonstrated repeatedly by unplanned intrusions throughout the 1850s and 1860s. The California gold rush, for example, occurred at a time when the success of the settlement at Salt Lake was threatened by severe shortages of hardware, iron, clothing, processed foods, coffee, tea, and cash. The gold rush brought to Salt Lake City a disorderly crowd of California-bound gold seekers, who abandoned or dumped for whatever they could get the excess equipment and supplies with which they had unwisely burdened themselves before leaving the Missouri River. In return the Mormons made the travelers pay high rates for fresh draft animals, for the services of blacksmiths, wagonsmiths, and laundresses, for board and lodging, and for whatever flour, potatoes, animal feed, and other foodstuffs the hard-pressed Mormons could spare. When a reverse flow of returning gold seekers set in, the Mormons acquired still another greatly needed item, gold dust that could be melted into a circulating medium for use in an economy that was otherwise reduced to barter.[38]

The gold and silver booms of the 1860s had a similar beneficial effect. By that time the Mormons' predominantly agrarian economy was producing food surpluses that Mormon teamsters could haul to mining camps throughout the Rockies, thus bringing cash into what was still primarily an economy of barter. Salt Lake City merchants stepped vigorously into this trade by assuming responsibility for assembling and shipping large quantities of flour, dried peaches, and other farm produce to Idaho, Montana, Colorado, and Utah's own new mining districts.

When President James Buchanan ordered a major force of Regular Army troops to occupy Utah during the so-called Mormon War of 1857–1859 (so as to compel the Mormons to accept Federal authority and officials), he unintentionally did the Mormons an economic service, for with four thousand troops and nearly as many civilians to be fed, the Army permitted its dependents to barter with Mormon villagers, who traded vegetables, eggs, butter, potatoes, dried fish, buttermilk, and "Valley Tan" whiskey for cash, clothing, tea, coffee, pieces of iron, or stoves. When the troops were withdrawn at the start of the Civil War, the Army dumped as surplus a huge accumulation of property that ranged from wagons and draft animals to tools, food, and iron. At an auction in 1861 the Army was said to have received about one hundred thousand dollars for property that had cost $4 million. Among those who snapped up bargains were the Mormon church, the ever-alert Ben Holladay, and several men who presently became prominent as merchants in Salt Lake City.[39]

Throughout the 1860s successive intrusions from the outer world helped to strengthen the Mormon economy, bring in much-needed cash, and build up Salt Lake City as a place of many uses not anticipated by Mormon planners. When the Lincoln administration decided to station the California Volunteers at a camp overlooking Salt Lake City, to serve as a wartime garrison in place of the departed Regulars, a profitable local market for Mormon goods and services was again created. The operation of the Overland Mail and Pony Express brought an influx of cash to Salt Lake City in return for Mormon supplies, labor, and skilled services. So did the stringing of lines for the overland telegraph in 1861. Both Edward Creighton and James Gamble had the political shrewdness to make Brigham Young the prime contractor, and therefore their ally, for supplying poles, subsistence, and transportation for a section of the line. When the Pacific railroad was approaching from east and west, the Union Pacific repeated this wise maneuver by granting a construction contract to Young, who was acting on behalf of his church, and the Central Pacific quickly followed suit.

Inexorably, then, the Mormon world was drawn into closer contact with the "Gentile" nation from which it had fled, and Salt Lake City was the point at which contact was most frequent and significant. However much the Mormons might have preferred to keep Salt Lake City to themselves, the tide of economic forces was against them. The journalist Albert Richardson, who visited the city in 1865, declared: "Salt Lake City is the city of the future—the natural metropolis of all Utah and portions of Nevada, Idaho, Montana, and Colorado." A distinguished Mormon historian has concluded that despite Brigham Young and the Mormons, "Salt Lake City did become the entrepôt of the Mountain West."[40]

The city grew from 8,236 inhabitants in 1860 to 12,854 in 1870 and 20,768 in 1880. By the last-named date Denver had far surpassed it, but prior to the late 1870s Salt Lake City was the largest population center in the Rocky Mountain region. As merchants, freighters, Overland Mail personnel, telegraphers, travelers, soldiers, and Federal officeholders crowded into the expanding city, the paradox emerged that Salt Lake City, the holy place of the Mormons, was acquiring the most cosmopolitan and least exclusively Mormon population in Utah, even while the cleavage along religious lines diminished not at all. Burton, a sophisticated observer of alien societies, was convinced that no matter how long or apparently intimately a Gentile lived in Salt Lake City, he would never penetrate beneath the surface of Mormon life. On the other hand, Burton described the anti-Mormons and apostates as "venomous" in their attitude toward Young and his church.[41]

Mercantile activities centered in Main Street, which attracted both Mormon and non-Mormon merchants and won the revealing nickname Whiskey Street. While non-Mormon merchants and freighters predominated, the field was not exclusively theirs. William Nixon, an English convert to Mormonism and formerly a merchant in St. Louis, became known as the "father of Utah merchants" because he trained so many young Mormons. Nixon was one of those who opened a store on Main Street.

It took courage to enter upon such a career. Edward Tullidge, a Mormon who was excommunicated by his church, plaintively remarked that "there grew up a conflict between the merchants and the Church. To become a merchant was to antagonize the Church and her policies."[42] Horace S. Eldredge, who unlike Tullidge had impeccable credentials as a Mormon trusted by Brigham Young, observed that there was "a degree of prejudice against merchants, particularly Mormon merchants."[43]

Tullidge, who became an articulate critic of his church's attitude toward commerce, argued that Utah would have long remained an isolated rural community on a barter economy but for the chance coming of the Forty-Niners, the soldiers, and the Overland Mail, and "the extraordinary activities of her merchants," whose operations converted Utah's simple agricultural produce into cash through trade with the mining regions and through contracts with government or Overland Mail. And if the Mormons' hunger for finished goods was to be satisfied, only a merchant class had the knowledge and the financial credit to obtain merchandise from eastern suppliers.[44]

From Brigham Young's point of view, the danger was that in a Utah economy that was still "relatively self-sufficient, relatively

equalitarian, and relatively homogeneous,"[45] commercial success
was steering "all the money to a few hands"[46] and was creating a
class of merchant princes who were mostly Gentiles (in the Mormon
sense), Jews, or nonconformist Mormons, and whose incongruously
large wealth and power might ultimately challenge the church itself.
Since the arrival of the California Volunteers, under their flamboyant colonel, Patrick Connor, the whole debate over the church's
economic role had become exacerbated, for Connor and his California and Nevada soldiers were filing claims to mineral discoveries
and were seeking to precipitate a mining boom. At the same time,
the prospective completion of the Pacific railroad would obviously
lessen greatly the Mormons' protective economic isolation.

Feeling that the time had come for a change in church policy, in
1869 Tullidge, William S. Godbe, an English-born mercantile
leader, and other prominent Mormon merchants and intellectuals
in Salt Lake City launched what became known as the New Movement or Godbeite heresy. Their thesis was that the Mormons should
abandon their self-imposed economic isolation, and should encourage exploitation of Utah's mineral resources as the quickest way to
prosperity. Brigham Young was too decisive a personality and too
accustomed to command to accept threats to his authority. The
Godbeites were tried and excommunicated, even as the Mormon
hierarchy brought to fruition a series of measures that they had been
developing in planning conferences in which several thousand
members of the priesthood had taken part.[47]

The most important had to do with merchandising. The church
leaders had already begun a boycott of "hostile" merchants, and in
1868 had enlarged this to a general boycott of Gentile stores and
businesses. Now a Mormon-owned wholesale house, known as
Zion's Co-operative Mercantile Institution, or "ZCMI," was to be
founded at Salt Lake City, with affiliated retail stores in Salt Lake
City and throughout the territory. The faithful must buy only at
these stores. Uniform retail prices were to be set. ZCMI was to get
started by taking over the inventories of the principal Mormon
merchants in exchange for capital stock in the new concern, while
the inventories of some other merchants were to be purchased
outright. Only one Mormon merchant, Henry W. Lawrence, a Cana-
dian-born member, had the temerity to protest publicly, but other

leading Mormon merchants had to be coerced into acquiescence by Young's threat to isolate them if they did not join.

In actuality, the reluctant merchants were well taken care of, for they became the principal stockholders and officers in the new cooperative, while their Salt Lake City store buildings were leased by the cooperative at profitable rates. The so-called Parent Store of ZCMI "was an immediate and outstanding financial success" that "captured virtually all the wholesale trade of the territory and much of the retail trade in Salt Lake City," thanks to the compulsory patronage of the faithful.[48]

This unblushing attempt at Mormon monopoly did not drive out all competition. The weaker merchants did indeed sell out and leave, but the stronger firms, such as Walker Brothers and the Jewish houses of Kahn Brothers and the Auerbachs, survived and after a period of uncertainty resumed their growth.[49] The Walkers were perhaps the most notable of the families that established themselves in business in Salt Lake City. Born in Yorkshire, England, they were the sons of a once comfortably situated man who had lost his money and had converted to Mormonism "during his days of adversity." Upon coming to America, the elder Walker had gone into business in St. Louis, where he came to know William Nixon, who undertook to train one of the Walker sons in his store. When cholera carried off Walker and his two daughters, his widow and four sons decided to go to Salt Lake City in 1852. There Nixon joined them and gave two of the sons mercantile training. The young Walkers were among the merchants who profited from the presence of Buchanan's Army troops and from the surplus sale when the Army withdrew. Working as a team, the brothers became wealthy and powerful as merchants, established a major bank that is still in business in Salt Lake City, and after a difficult beginning in 1870, made a success of mining when that industry finally got under way in the Great Basin. But in the process of becoming successful the Walkers ceased to pay their tithes and became symbols of resistance to economic domination by the church. An admiring apostate claimed in 1872 that the Walkers "own more real estate, and more wealth in Zion" than any one man or firm in Utah save Young himself.[50]

Quite obviously, the non-Mormon merchant-bankers of Salt Lake

City could not hope to gain a political influence commensurate with their economic authority or comparable to the political power exercised by members of their class in San Francisco or Denver. But they were too ambitious not to try. In 1869 a group began to coalesce around the most prominent Godbeites and in February of 1870 founded the Liberal party. Connor, the wartime commander of the California Volunteers and now an enthusiastic promoter of mining in Utah, assumed responsibility for summoning the new party to its first annual convention, which nominated its first (and of course unsuccessful) candidates for public office. Corinne, a disorderly new freighting center on the Pacific railroad line, became for a few years the focus of the Liberals' hope that a major non-Mormon community could be developed in Utah, but Brigham Young's skillful offer of superior attractions at Ogden, a few miles to the east, drew the business of both the Union Pacific and Central Pacific to that Mormon-settled junction point.[51]

By promoting a church-sponsored merchandising system, Young and his associates strengthened not only the hold of the church on its members but also the position of Salt Lake City as the Mormons' commercial center. Parallel schemes in the fields of communications and transportation further ensured dominance of both church and city. The completion of the overland telegraph in 1861 had so impressed Brigham Young that he began at once to plan for a local system that would link settlements along a north-south line that was to run the length of Utah, from the border with Idaho to that with Arizona. Wartime shortages of copper wire and equipment delayed the project until 1865–1866. When resumed at that time, the effort illustrated dramatically how the Mormons could make a major capital investment without incurring a large bonded debt.

Money to pay for the wire and technical equipment was raised by the local church units under the leadership of their bishops. To haul the eighty-four tons of copper wire, batteries, insulators, and instruments across the plains, wagon teams and teamsters were contributed by the same local sources. Each settlement was made responsible for cutting and erecting poles in its particular area, for learning how to string the wire, and for sending young men and women to Salt Lake City to be trained in telegraphy.

By mid-February 1867, a five-hundred-mile line was in operation; by 1880 the line was twice that long. Although legally operated as an incorporated concern—the Deseret Telegraph Company—the system was actually a cooperative, justified by social, religious, and theocratic considerations rather than as a money-maker, which last it seems never to have been. Church business, including long Mormon sermons, went free of charge. Personal and community social messages passed at nominal rates, because the church felt that as settlement spread geographically, it was becoming increasingly important to "bring us into more speedy and close communication with one another." News reports from around the world were forwarded from Salt Lake City to the outlying settlements at low fees, thus greatly extending the church's effort to control news, an effort which dated back at least to 1850 when the *Deseret News* was founded at Salt Lake City to be the voice of the church. Finally, with Salt Lake City as the central point in the system, the telegraph immensely increased the church hierarchy's ability to direct the daily mix of spiritual and temporal business that was so characteristic of the Mormons. As the church's instructions concerning the telegraph explained, "the center should be in position to communicate at any moment with the extremities."[52]

Building railroads proved far more difficult, because the initial investment had to be so much bigger and because it was inherently inefficient to operate small railroads that were largely feeder lines for the Union Pacific. As with the telegraph, social objectives seem to have been greater than expectations of making money. The purpose was to provide passenger and freight service between dispersed settlements and Salt Lake City.

The determination to have railroads was born when Brigham Young learned that the main line of the Union Pacific and Central Pacific would bypass Salt Lake City in favor of the more level terrain through the Mormon town of Ogden, about thirty-seven miles north of Salt Lake City. Before the Pacific railroad was even finished, church leaders began planning a feeder railroad, the Utah Central, to save Salt Lake City from being cut off. Like the businessmen of Denver, they would not tolerate this threat to their city's future. At that time Mormon subcontractors were completing the construction work on the Union Pacific for which Young had contracted. When the Union Pacific defaulted on its obligations to the Mormons, leaving the better part of a million dollars unpaid, Young accepted surplus Union Pacific rails and rolling stock in part payment of what was owing. This material was to be used for the Utah Central, whose bonds were then to be sold to reimburse Young and the subcontractors for the losses suffered on the Union Pacific. The other costs for the thirty-seven-mile railroad, such as grading, laying ties, and building bridges, were to be borne by Mormon labor recruited by the bishops and remunerated at minimum rates.

The Utah Central began operating early in 1870 and inspired the building of a series of additional feeder railroads during the 1870s. Soon there was a Utah Southern to tap the country south of Salt Lake and a Utah Northern that headed toward Idaho from the Utah Central terminus at Ogden. Later there was a Utah Southern Extension and a stillborn Utah Eastern.

Financing these railroads proved an uncertain business, despite encouragement by church leaders and despite the sacrifices of the common folk who contributed much of the labor. Like any of the big railroads, these local roads issued their impressive-looking stocks and bonds—and found that they sold badly. Again like the big roads, they incurred debts that necessitated seeking help from outside interests, which most commonly meant the Union Pacific. By 1879 the Mormons had ceased to boast of their "peoples' railroads" and had allowed most of their completed projects to slip into the control of the Union Pacific. Despite the denouement, the social objective had been achieved, and by bringing the local lines to it, Salt Lake City preserved its importance even though Ogden was the point at which the Utah lines made junction with a national railroad.[53]

* * * * *

Up in the prairies and forests of the lovely Willamette Valley, the little village of Portland was struggling to make itself the San Francisco of the Pacific Northwest. It had a reasonably good location, situated a dozen miles above the Willamette's confluence with the Columbia and an equal distance below its falls at Oregon City. Although the water route to Portland from the ocean was 110 miles long, and impeded by a dangerous bar across the mouth of the Columbia, nevertheless oceangoing vessels could navigate as far up as Portland and could find good deep-water moorings at docks along the river front. At Portland cargoes could be transferred to steamboats for the long journey up the Columbia to the vast and as yet largely unoccupied interior. This was a difficult route because it was interrupted by unnavigable rapids and falls at the Cascades and The Dalles, but once portages were built around those obstructions, river commerce could move from Portland for 240 miles to the frontier landing at Wallula, where pack mules and wagon trains were based; or, when the water level was favorable, river craft could turn from the Columbia into the Snake and go as far as Lewiston, Idaho, to complete a voyage of 401 miles.

Portland was well placed to attract produce from Oregon's pioneer farms. The rich Tualatin Plains, whose 460,000 acres were Oregon's first important wheat area, were linked to Portland in the 1850s by a difficult but passable canyon road cut through the hills west of Portland, while the river made it possible to bring shipments down from upper Willamette Valley farms by steamboats, although with a portage around the falls at Oregon City.

Yet Portland grew slowly. By 1860 it had only 2,874 people and by 1870 only 8,293. Even by 1880 its population rose only to 17,577. The reason for slow growth, of course, was isolation. The city was far indeed from the world's markets.[54]

In the 1840s and 1850s the farms accessible to Portland had been settled primarily by rural families that had come overland in wagon trains from the interior of America, roughly the region of the Mississippi, Ohio, and Missouri valleys. These simple folk of southern, nonslaveholding background found little outlet for their small rural surpluses until the California gold rush suddenly created a market for all the foodstuffs and lumber that the Oregon colony could supply and thereby stimulated investment not only in farming and lumbering but also in transportation and town building.

The town dwellers of Portland, who served as middlemen for the export of Oregon produce to San Francisco and the import of finished goods from that same city, were quite unlike their rural clients and customers. Like the early San Francisco merchants, many had come by sea from New England or the Middle Atlantic states. Again like the San Franciscans, when they first came most were single young men in search of careers. Their early years were lonely, but after the California gold rush had brought prosperity to the little frontier outpost, the more successful went "home" for wives or found eligible women of their own kind among the incoming population.[55]

Portland's lively prosperity of the early 1850s withered as news came of the hard times that were descending on San Francisco after 1853. Local gold rushes in Oregon and the northwest, and contracts to supply militia recruited to fight Indian wars, provided temporary new customers in the middle and later 1850s, but by the end of the decade it was all too clear that with little foreign commerce and few domestic alternatives Portland was narrowly limited, and even with the trade it did have was inescapably dependent on San Francisco.

These gloomy prospects vanished suddenly with the beginning of the northwestern mining excitements. Initial discoveries in the Clearwater country of Idaho in 1860 led to disorderly stampedes southward to the Salmon River and Boise Basin in Idaho and to the John Day and Powder rivers of eastern Oregon. By 1862 gold seekers were going clear to western Montana. The crowds were the bigger because Idaho, Montana, and eastern Oregon had placers that were far better suited to the modest skills and resources of the ordinary man than were the industrialized operations of the Comstock.

To the editor of the Portland *Oregonian* this abrupt change was "absolutely bewildering," but he quieted his doubts with the comforting thought that now there would be "tremendous stampedes from California,—a flood of overland emigration,—a vastly increased business on the Columbia river, the rapid advance of Portland in business, population, and wealth,—and the profitable employment of the farmers of this valley."[56]

This was precisely what happened, and for the leaders of Portland's young business community the rewards were high. As in California, river transportation prospered especially and was of crucial importance in promoting Portland. After an ineffectual attempt to combine in 1859, the pioneer owners of steamboats and portages on the Columbia had been induced to pool their investments in 1860 in order to form the Oregon Steam Navigation Company, a combination that was obviously inspired by the example of the California Steam Navigation Company. Never was a corporate merger timed more fortunately. With the mining rush to the interior starting almost immediately, in 1861 the Oregon Steam Navigation Company carried 10,500 passengers up the Columbia; in 1862, some 24,500; and by 1864, about 36,000. So great was the pressure for freight that in Portland an unbroken line of drays stretched back from the steamboat docks as the teamsters waited their turn to deliver their loads.

The company followed a policy of charging all that the traffic would bear. Over the nineteen years of its existence the monopoly spent $3 million on steamboats and other capital improvements, as against paying its stockholders $4 million in dividends, and still was regarded as being worth $5 million. The attitude of the leading members of the company was crucial to Portland's future. One faction wanted to take out quick profits, the other to think in less immediate terms, which meant plowing back some of their bulging profits into improvements.

When the latter faction won, they gave Portland a big boost. Large sums were spent directly by the steamboat company for wharves, warehouses, and payrolls, and less directly by travelers and shippers for the services of the hotels, saloons, express companies, outfitters, and teamsters required by the heavy flow of people and goods en route to the mines. Less directly still, the successful proprietors of the steamboat monopoly invested some of their personal profits in city real estate, public-service companies, and a wide range of other local ventures.[57]

In handling this booming trade of the 1860s, Portland served in large part as regional distributor for merchandise that came to it by way of San Francisco. Flour and other foodstuffs could be supplied from Oregon's own productions, but equipment and other finished goods were either purchased from San Francisco merchants and manufacturers or were ordered from New York but delivered at San Francisco for reshipment northward. Either way San Francisco took its percentage, and Portland's newspapers complained constantly of the "tyranny" of San Francisco. They complained even more when Californians, under the leadership of the California Steam Navigation Company, sought to open an "inside" route to southern Idaho via Sacramento River steamboats to Chico and thence overland, thus bypassing the Columbia route.[58]

As warehousing, wholesaling, finance, and transportation matured at Portland, that city became as much the dominant center within the northwest as San Francisco was within the Far West as a whole. Portland was slower than San Francisco to diversify its economy by investing in industry, presumably because its opportunities were limited, although with the discovery of iron-ore deposits six miles from the city, the leading businessmen incorporated a company and began exporting pig iron—to San Francisco.

The unusual aspect of the city's growth was the continuing predominance throughout all changes, and until very late in the century, of a small group of local businessmen who had been among those early comers from the Middle Atlantic states and New England. Their family names became omnipresent in the growing city's life: Corbett, Ladd, Failing, and Lewis, starting in 1851; Reed, in 1852. In business, civic, social, and cultural affairs alike they were always prominent, frequently dominant, and some of their descendants have continued to be so almost until today. Such stability was in decided contrast to the rapid turnover among San Francisco's merchants and their eventual displacement by the newly rich and powerful men of the Comstock and Central Pacific eras. Doubtless Portland's much smaller size and its continuing relative isolation—it did not win a transcontinental railroad connection until 1883—do much to explain this.

The members of this increasingly wealthy and powerful elite were closely linked by marriage and business partnerships. For example, Henry Failing married Henry W. Corbett's sister Emily. Corbett gave Failing's younger brother his training as a clerk (the traditional first step in a business career in that era). Later Corbett and Failing merged their mercantile firms and took in two younger Failing brothers as partners, while together the two families bought control of Portland's second bank. William S. Ladd, Portland's first banker and an important figure in the Oregon Steam Navigation Company, had as his constant business associate Simeon G. Reed, who became vice-president and manager of the steamboat monopoly in 1864–1865.[59]

The Portland people liked to think of themselves as culturally superior to their rustic neighbors of the Willamette Valley farms and as more stable and churchgoing than the chance-taking and probably godless San Franciscans. They were immensely flattered when the famous Samuel Bowles of the Springfield (Massachusetts) *Republican* said of them that "they keep Sunday as we do in New England, and as no other population this side of the Missouri now does." To Bowles Portland had "the air and the fact of a prosperous, energetic town, with a good deal of eastern leadership and tone to business and society and morals."[60]

The census statistics for 1870 give evidence of a much more varied community than Bowles reported. In Multnomah County, which consisted chiefly of Portland, the census found that over 20 percent had been born in what would today be called the Middle West, that the Irish constituted nearly 10 percent, and the Germans 7.5 percent, which included the German Jews who had been taking a vigorous part in the mercantile life of the city since 1851. Over 400 immigrants from England, Wales, and Scotland, 500 Chinese, less than 150 blacks, and a tiny remnant of American Indians completed the listing.[61]

Judge Matthew P. Deady, one of Portland's leaders who was in no sense a New Englander or New Yorker but rather a product of the Ohio Valley, summed up the occupational distribution with the bluntness for which he was famous. His fellow ruling citizens, he said, were mostly engaged as merchants or in the building industry, while unskilled labor was left to the Irish, and laundry, woodcutting, and domestic service to the Chinese. A few Irishmen had risen to be tradesmen or mechanics. "The merchants and businessmen are principally Jews, and Americans from New England and New York—particularly New England." He added that "church-going" was "comparatively common," whereas "theatrical amusements" barely existed.[62]

Deady, the Federal judge who had been president of Oregon's constitutional convention and had written the new state's first general incorporation act and its code of civil procedure and code of criminal procedure, was the outstanding case of a powerful figure who stood outside the New England–New York elite but often worked with it.[63] A massive recent study of the latter shows how, by the late nineteenth century, their directorships, trusteeships, and investments had come to penetrate every major activity in Portland, and had led inevitably to a considerable manipulation of urban and state politics.[64]

* * * * *

A recent scholar has maintained that "little was unique or new about the young cities of the West," and that "westerners sought to build cities that looked as much as possible like those in the older sections."[65] That was true of their architecture, which was largely imitative; of their grid pattern of streets; of the chambers of commerce, Masonic lodges, and volunteer fire companies that they founded; of their support for a few churches and schools, an occasional college or library; and of the mobility of their inhabitants.

But was there no new flavor to urban life in so new a land? The young Episcopal Bishop Tuttle, newly arrived in Denver in 1867, wrote back to his wife that he found the conversation there "unusually sensible and intelligent," characterized by "a freedom from 'airs,' and a directness of manner. . . . And they are very little impressed by dignitaries. . . . There was a self-respect which allowed none of them to attempt any flattery or fulsome eulogy."[66] A dozen years later a tourist guidebook claimed for Denver that "there is a dash and animation to the place, along with a finish and elegance that suggests prosperity, wealth, and Eastern stability, as well as the progressive and aggressive frontier. It is the healthy vigor of the thriving trade centre, the prodigality of the mining metropolis."[67]

Generalizations about western cities should be phrased with care. Beneath undoubted similarities of function and practice, there were basic differences. Portland was not simply a smaller San Francisco, nor was Denver merely a secular Salt Lake City. Each had its own character.

CHAPTER 6

Many Peoples:
I: White Immigrants, Black Americans,
and Red Indians

DESPITE the predominance of native-born Americans in "western" movies and paper novels, the native stock was in fact only one element among many. The west was a land of many races, many ethnic backgrounds, many national origins. The Indians had been there ever since their ancestors had crossed the land bridge from Asia, and in the thousands of years since then had developed so many different cultures that there were more mutually unintelligible languages and dialects than were to be found on the whole continent of Europe. The Hispano-Americans had been in the southwest since Oñate led his pioneer settlers up the Rio Grande to northern New Mexico in 1598, and they had been on the Pacific Coast since a little band settled at San Diego in 1769. A few French Canadians had trapped fur-bearing animals and left French names on mountains, rivers, and lakes before making permanent homes, especially in the Oregon country.

Subsequently a series of major events drew in an extraordinary variety of peoples. The California gold rush attracted fortune hunters from all over the world, including the first big waves of Chinese immigrants to come to America. While some of the gold-rush crowd soon went home or died prematurely in California, many thousands remained, to give California important groups of Germans, French, German and Polish Jews, British, Mexicans, a few Chileans, Peruvians, and Italians. When the mining frontier turned eastward to the cordilleran interior, it carried with it members of all of these groups.

The building of the Pacific railroad led to the recruiting of thousands of Irish and Chinese to do the hard, dangerous physical labor. Owners of the new deep vein mines hired all the veteran Cornish miners they could find and employed an even larger number of Irish who were willing to learn. Experienced Welshmen appeared as soon as the mines found that they needed smelters. Germans served as mining technicians, engineers, and assayers.

In California the boom in agriculture that got under way as the gold rush faded gave French horticulturists a chance to show their notable skills with orchards, vineyards, and nurseries. Hispano-Californian landowners, Germans, Italians, and Americans joined them. Their labor needs, together with the huge seasonal needs of the new wheat ranches, and the demands of smaller crops such as hops, led to the employment of Mexican, native Californian, Chinese, and California Indian workers. The early irrigation systems of southern California drew manual laborers from these same sources, while contracts for the services of hundreds of Chinese were made for the laborious, unhealthy work of reclaiming the potentially rich but swampy lands of the Sacramento–San Joaquin delta.

In the intermontane west the Mormons were so determined to bring in more fellow believers and useful workers that they founded the cooperative Perpetual Emigrating Fund Company. By the time the Federal government intervened in 1887 to stop the work of the Fund, the latter had aided over one hundred thousand immigrants, of whom eighty-seven thousand were from Britain and northern Europe, many coming from Scandinavia.

As additional railroads penetrated the west late in the century, Mexicans by the thousands were imported to do the construction and maintenance work. Italians and Yugoslavs were recruited both by the new railroads and by the mines. In South Texas, when agriculture replaced livestock, thousands of Mexicans crossed the border to join native-born Spanish-speaking Tejanos in doing the field work. Other Mexicans flocked into Arizona as it began to offer jobs in mines, on ranches, and in irrigated agriculture. At the end of the century Japanese were appearing in the Pacific Coast and northern Rocky Mountain states.

The Great Plains were never the exclusive domain of cowboys and American-born farmers. Foreign-born farmers were particularly numerous on the western fringe of settlement, where land was cheaper than in the older, better-watered eastern plains. North of Nebraska immigrants bulked especially large in proportion to total population, although in Nebraska itself and in neighboring Kansas immigrants were very numerous. Germans were by far the largest immigrant stock to settle in the Great Plains, and their occupation extended clear down into West Texas. By 1900 it was estimated that one third of Texas' white population was of German ancestry. Under the term *German* contemporaries included German-speaking Swiss, Alsatians, and Austrians, together with the Germans who had lived for generations under Russian rule on the Volga and in Bessarabia. English, Scottish, Welsh, Irish, and English Canadians formed still another large element. Scandinavians flowed into the Dakotas to farm, just as after 1890 they moved into the Pacific Northwest to lumber. Czechs were an important factor in Nebraska.

While no one would accuse the decennial census figures of being precisely accurate, nevertheless they are the best indication of the relative proportions of native-born and immigrants, and of the shifting balance between the sexes as the west matured. The Federal census shows that in most of the western states and territories from 1860 to 1900 there was a preponderance of native-born stock, ranging between 60 and 90 percent. But in 1870 both Idaho and Arizona recorded less than half native-born, while Nevada in 1870 and 1880 and North Dakota in 1890 all listed a native-born stock that fell short of 60 percent. By way of contrast, over the United States as a whole in these years native-born people constituted 85 to 86 percent of the total. In California, by far the largest and most developed of the western states, the foreign-born formed about a third from 1860 to 1890 and about a quarter in 1900.

If allowance be made for immigrants' American-born children, and for the children of native-born Spanish-speaking citizens—two groups that were apt to be raised in a family environment dominated by the language, religion, and customs of the old country—then the influence of foreign cultures must have been distinctly more pervasive than the figures suggest. On the other hand, many an immigrant, especially among the ubiquitous Irish and Germans, went through an "Americanizing" transitional experience in the east or Middle West before venturing farther west.

The distribution of the sexes varied with the stage of the west's development. In 1860, when mining was just beginning in the inte-

rior, Nevada and Colorado recorded an overwhelming preponderance of males—90 to 95 percent—and by 1870 the mining and
pioneer ranching territories of Montana, Idaho, and Wyoming still
had about 80 percent males, while six others in that year were not
far below that figure. By 1880, however, the proportion of females
was increasing throughout the west, so that most states and territories could claim a third and some over 40 percent. In California
females were less than 30 percent in 1860, about 37 percent in 1870,
and 40 percent in 1880. By 1900 nearly all states and territories
were well above 40 percent, and the laggards—Wyoming, Montana,
and Nevada—were close to 40 percent. This means that while the
west was heavy on the masculine side in the early years, when mining, ranching, and freighting were the chief occupations and transi-
ency was very high, thereafter the west gradually ceased to be a land
of lonely men. The corollary, of course, was that children became
less of a rarity.[1]

Foremost among the uncertainties raised by the mixing of races
and nationalities were the twin questions of how native-born Americans would treat European immigrants, and how the white majority
as a whole would treat nonwhite minorities, including under that
term the mestizos, who formed by far the largest part of the Spanish-speaking population. This would be one of the great tests of the
west's claim to be the land of opportunity, equality, and democracy.
It would be a test also of the Turnerian theory that the west, as the
land of new beginnings, was capable of assimilating people of many
backgrounds.

The first massive peopling of the west in the 1850s, during and
after the California gold rush, came at an inopportune time. In the
east, after an erratic growth in the 1830s and 1840s, a venomous,
often riotous opposition to Catholics and immigrants, directed especially against the Irish, had boiled up into the nativist Know-
Nothing party of the 1850s.[2] In the southwest and west the Texan
Revolution and the Mexican War had left a mutual antagonism
between "Anglos" and the darker-skinned "Hispanos." The former
acted too often with contemptuous arrogance, the latter with quick
anger, or sullen bitterness, or despairing acceptance.

It would have been illogical not to expect this established attitude
toward foreigners to reappear in the disorderly atmosphere of the
mining camps and San Francisco. But the targets of abuse were

different. Mobs set upon Mexicans, Chileans, Peruvians, Frenchmen, Kanakas, and Chinese. Indiscriminately they drove out of the mines the native-born Californians, who under the Treaty of Guadalupe Hidalgo had as much right as their persecutors to be there. Yet, strangely, the California nativists "completely neglected to heckle the Irish, a favorite ploy of eastern xenophobes."[3]

Perhaps the Irish owed their escape partly to the irrelevance of the issue of Catholicism in a state where Catholicism had been established long before Americans arrived and where Catholicism was probably the largest single denomination. Perhaps it was simply that religion was not that important in that turbulent society. But whatever the explanation, the antiforeign agitation of the 1850s set a pattern that was to prevail throughout much of the west during the next several decades: relatively moderate attitudes toward most Europeans and English-speaking people; harsh prejudice toward nonwhite minorities.

The Germans, for example, in regions as varied as California, Texas, and Nebraska, seem to have made their way successfully into American society, even while supporting churches, clubs, and newspapers that enabled them to maintain their cultural identity. The Irish, although scattered throughout the west as unskilled or semiskilled labor, tended to concentrate in cities, most notably in San Francisco, where by 1880 they were said to constitute one third of the population of the community. Economically they ranged all the way from millionaires, such as the Donahues, to paupers. Socially the Anglo-Americans tended to exclude the Irish from their clubs and activities, but as a whole the Irish must have been relatively satisfied, despite periodic hard times such as those of the 1870s, for they were less prone than most to move out of the city. A modern scholar has concluded: "The central core of Irish experience in the city [San Francisco] was whole and satisfactory."[4] Western Irishmen did not, however, escape scot-free, for there were always employers whose "want ads" warned, "No Irish Need Apply," and the 1880s and 1890s saw a revival of anti-Catholic nativism.

The Jews, similarly, often had to tolerate a bullying and domineering attitude upon the part of their customers in the early years when many young Jews were getting their start as peddlers or small dealers in mining and rural areas. And the Anglo-Americans who controlled credit ratings were all too apt to view them suspiciously, as poor risks for loans. But through the close-knit families from which these upwardly mobile young German and Polish Jews had come, they were able to borrow funds and rise to merchant status and prosperity, at a time when many an American was losing money because of unwise speculations.

As merchants whose stores grew into department stores, as manufacturers whose products circulated everywhere, and as financiers, the early Jews, who were mostly German in origin, though sometimes Polish, left names that have become household words: "Levi's," the creation of Levi Strauss, once of Bavaria, who came to San Francisco in 1850; Zellerbach paper, named for a family who came down from the mining town of Nevada City to San Francisco in 1868; Goldwater's, the Arizona success that finally rewarded Michael Goldwater after he had failed in previous ventures in Sonora and Los Angeles; Meier and Frank's in Portland, founded in 1857 by Aaron Meier, formerly of the California mining town of Downieville; the Auerbach brothers, who opened their store in Salt Lake City in 1864, after previous starts in Rabbit Creek and La Porte, California, and Austin, Nevada; and I. W. Hellman's Farmers and Merchants Bank, in Los Angeles.

Just as these pioneer Central European Jews had become successful economically and had partly assimilated socially, they found themselves faced by a wave of Yiddish-speaking Jews from eastern Europe, who were poor, orthodox in religion, and given to building synagogues and clustering around them in dense little pockets of settlement. Subsequently, still a third element, the Sephardim, came from the Mediterranean with another language, Ladino (Spanish-influenced), and a different pattern of worship and customs. As the successful German Jews morosely predicted, the new groups stimulated a new wave of anti-Semitism more severe than anything encountered in the earlier years. The creation by Jews of their own communal and fraternal organizations in the larger cities suggests a sense of only limited acceptance and hence a need for mutual support.[5]

For all that, the record of the leading pioneer immigrant groups from Europe showed that economic success was possible and that social integration would come ultimately, if not in their own generation, then in their children's.[6] The experience of smaller groups such as the Italians and Norwegians appears to have been similar.[7]

This is not to say that adaptation to the dominant culture was easy. On the contrary, as a sympathetic historian of the Nebraska Germans has explained:

There was nothing in the typical immigrant's experience to prepare him for the myriad frustrations, disillusionments, and negative encounters with American people and American customs, the sum total of which we call cultural shock.[8]

The newly arrived foreigner was all too apt to discover that "his clothes, his mannerisms, and his speech often became objects of derision and contempt."[9] He was also likely to find that it was far easier to adjust his behavior to the practices of his American neighbors or business associates than to win acceptance into the ruling social structure, a circumstance which suggests the wisdom of Moses Rischin's warning that too much emphasis upon the greater ease of European immigrants' adjustment to life in the west "has obscured the vigorous nativism that flourished in the region from its inception and the equally vigorous continuity of group diversities."[10]

And yet the discriminations against white European immigrants seem moderate when compared with attitudes and actions against nonwhite minorities. Racism has been defined as "the belief that one or more races have innate superiority over other races,"[11] more specifically, whites over nonwhites. Since the nineteenth century was the great era of white technological and commercial dominance and expanding empires, and in America a time of black slavery until 1865, it was all too easy to assume that nonwhite peoples suffered from inherent deficiencies that condemned them to an inferior existence unless some missionary instinct caused whites to uplift them.

To illustrate what this meant in practice, it is worth starting with a case that is relatively simple because it involved so very small a percentage of the western population and because the people in question, the blacks, had lived closely with whites for generations.[12] By 1860 the west had copied the east in refusing to permit free blacks to vote, give evidence in court cases involving whites, have their children attend public schools with white children, marry whites, or serve in the militia. California, Oregon, Kansas, and Nebraska proposed to exclude free blacks from their boundaries, and after the Civil War Oregon and California rejected the Fifteenth

Amendment, which promised that the right to vote would not be denied because of "race, color, or previous condition of servitude." These actions of the 1860s were equivalent to saying that western whites did not shed their old attitudes when they crossed into a new country.[13]

Faced by prejudice, most western blacks found work in the new urban communities and mining towns, usually in menial jobs or in service positions that traditionally had been open to them, such as barbers, porters, cooks, or janitors.[14] A very few did notably well and rose to be merchants, hotel keepers, and property owners. The San Francisco blacks, while small in number, included some unusual individuals—better educated than most of their group and more experienced in race relations—who made San Francisco a place of leadership for blacks throughout the Pacific Coast. They led an ultimately successful twenty-year fight to open the schools to their children, and they organized state conventions to fight for their rights.[15] But real equality of economic opportunity and treatment as social equals lay very, very far in the future.

In the Indian wars blacks provided the enlisted personnel for the famous Ninth and Tenth Cavalry and the Twenty-fourth and Twenty-fifth Infantry.[16] Blacks frequently served with cattle outfits, most often as cooks, sometimes as remuda men, and perhaps a few thousand as cowboys.[17]

Most colorful of all was the "Exoduster" hysteria that aroused southern blacks to migrate to Kansas in 1879–1880 to escape the hopelessness of their lives in the South. A few succeeded, one or two permanent black towns were founded, but most of the participants were pathetically lacking in everything necessary: knowledge of farming in a strange land, money, tools, winter clothing, seed, food. They became indigent cases dependent on such charity as could be hastily organized.[18]

*   *   *   *   *

Among racial minorities the Native Americans, historically known as Indians, were unique. Two centuries of terrifying folktales about the scalping knife and tomahawk, the raping of white women and bashing in the heads of little children, had bequeathed to westward movers an attitude of distrust and fear that, in coarse-grained individuals, led to actions as ruthless and sadistic as any committed

by those termed "savages." Two centuries had also seen the expro-
priation by whites of most of the "ample domain," as Chief Justice
John Marshall termed it, that the Indians had been accustomed to
use. Unlike any other racial group, Indians were, in Marshall's
words, wards of the United States government, members of "domestic dependent nations," and as such dealt with by treaties prior
to 1871 and subject to a bureaucracy that had its head in Washington, its agents out in the field.[19]

There were enormous cultural differences not only between red
man and white, but also between one Indian group and another.
John C. Ewers, an ethnologist of long experience, has commented:

> They had no common language, no political or cultural unity. They were
> divided into a host of independent tribes or villages, which distrusted one
> another as much or more than they distrusted the first white invaders.[20]

Modern anthropologists have concluded that in all probability
whites killed fewer Indians than were killed by other Indians in
intertribal wars.[21] The introduction of firearms, sold by white traders, increased the Indians' ability to kill each other, and white pressure on one band for land or trade often caused that group to
intrude upon its neighbors, at the cost of still another intertribal
war. To the losses by wars was added the much bigger factor of
almost unbelievably high death rates when American aborigines
were exposed to diseases of European origin for which, in their
continental isolation, Native Americans had no inherited immu-
nity.[22] Smallpox was by far the worst, but cholera, scarlet fever,
measles, influenza, and tuberculosis all were deadly to people with
no previous exposure. Venereal disease is a less clear case; it is
uncertain which of the two races gave it to the other.[23] Liquor, which
proved to be disastrously appealing to Indians, was an important
trade item, and modern scholars are unsure whether a genetic factor
caused Indians to be so explosively susceptible to liquor's worst
effects, or whether Indians learned their drinking behavior from
watching frontiersmen's debaucheries.[24]

Beyond these specific ills was the more elusive factor of cultural
disintegration. In bewilderment Indians witnessed the shattering of
the intricately achieved religious, social, and governmental patterns
that they had developed over many generations. Individual bands
found the delicate traditional balance between aboriginal man and

his accustomed food sources being upset as rival Indian groups, finding the wild game increasingly scarce, invaded adjacent hunting grounds and raided crop-growing Indians' carefully accumulated stores. Competition from white game hunters, a growing dependence on trade goods, and the increasing intrusion of white land seekers, Indian agents, missionaries, and the Army all accelerated what to the Indians was devastating decay.[25]

The sum total of all these assaults on the Indians' lives, health, and basic patterns of existence must have been awesome, for if it is really true that when white men first came to North America there were perhaps 2.5 million Indians in what is now the United States,[26] consider the implications of the massive special report of the census of 1890, which concluded that there were only 250,000 Indians in the nation, exclusive of Alaska.[27] This seems to have been the nadir; a figure for 1860 would probably have been higher by about one hundred thousand, and a slow recovery seems to have begun about 1900.

It was thus with a dwindling remnant of a once powerful and numerous race that whites dealt in the latter part of the nineteenth century, and of this remnant a goodly part had become so demoralized and defeated that it better deserved pity than fear from whites. The "intruded" Indians of the "permanent" frontier had been overrun by white land seekers and repeatedly condensed into ever smaller tracts, while the three hundred thousand overland emigrants who had marched through the Indians' lands by 1860 had killed off the wild game and stripped the scant timber. The Civil War was a major disaster regardless of which side individual intruded tribes favored, for it brought hunger, sickness, homelessness, and guerrilla fighting during the war and loss of land at the end of it.[28]

In California, where the Spanish and Mexicans had reduced many Indians to laborers and servants, some Americans after the gold rush followed the Hispanic precedent by using Indians as underpaid farm workers or cheap domestics, while in the mines a limited employment of Indians by whites in the early days was replaced by a ruthless disregard for them thereafter, until, as the commissioner of Indian affairs reported, "from a position of independence they were at once reduced to the most abject dependence. . . . They are almost compelled to become vagabonds—*to steal or to starve.*"[29] In Oregon and Washington the outcome was the same: Indians "began to

pilfer and steal to prevent actual starvation," and won white retalia-
tion in a series of small wars.[30] When mining began in Nevada, the
story was repeated with the Great Basin Indians. In Texas the situation was perhaps the worst of all, for the Texas Rangers attacked the
guilty and the innocent with undiscriminating ferocity, and the militia and private citizens abetted them and cheered them on, while the
Plains Indians retaliated by regarding Texans as a special people
distinct from Americans.[31]

With decay on the eastern and western flanks, most of the fighting
of the 1860s and 1870s was left to the still-virile mounted Indians
of the Great Plains, the Rockies, and the southwest. Great warrior
names such as Sioux, Cheyenne, Arapaho, Nez Percé, Commanche,
Kiowa, Ute, Apache, and Navajo dominated these wars. Some committed the ultimate in cruelty and torture when they fell upon their
white victims. Bitterly Harvey W. Scott, the pioneer editor of the
Portland *Oregonian,* declared in 1867 that "the people of the Western border, the plains and the Pacific Coast . . . have learned something of the inborn perfidy and fiendish barbarism of the Indians."
As he surveyed recent carnage in eastern Oregon and Idaho, Scott
explained his anger:

There has not been a day when it was entirely safe to travel or reside
beyond the limits of the larger settlements. The frequent murders, burn-
ings and robberies . . . sufficiently attest this statement. A season of quiet
has been only the precursor of a tragedy, or some villainy perpetrated by
redskins incapable of good faith and knowing no law but that of fear or
savage hate.[32]

To this strong language two famous westerners, William Bent (of
Bent's Fort) and Kit Carson, gave a surprising retort when ques-
tioned by an investigating commission sent out by Congress in the
wake of the Sand Creek Massacre of 1864. Speaking of his thirty-six
years in southern Colorado, Bent testified:

Since I have been there nearly every instance of difficulties between the
Indians and the whites arose from aggressions on the Indians by the
whites. . . . [His friend Carson agreed: Bent's observations] coincide per-
fectly with my own. . . . I think, as a general thing, the difficulties arise
from aggressions on the part of whites. From what I have heard, the
whites are always cursing the Indians, and are not willing to do them
justice.[33]

Another witness before the investigating commission was a Colorado militia major who in civil life was a lawyer and who was a westerner only by adoption (he was a native of Albany, New York). Bluntly he told the commission:

I think and earnestly believe the Indians to be an obstacle to civilization, and should be exterminated.[34]

In short, a Hitlerian "final solution." Others shared the major's views, for the Reverend Charles A. Huntington, who served in the Indian Service in Washington Territory in the 1860s and 1870s, sadly concluded that efforts to civilize the Indians failed

not by reason of impossibilities inherent in the race itself, but by reason of the damnable heresy on the part of the civilized race, that Indians are not men. . . . With the old saw in their mouths! *"the survival of the fittest,"* they say "God never intended the survival of the Indian race. The Indian is in the way; and the sooner he is put out of his misery and out of the way, the better."[35]

By the mercy of the Indians' dwindling power to resist, wars became infrequent after the fierce campaigns of the 1860s and 1870s, as most tribal groups were forced to agree to withdraw to reservations. The Apache raids in the 1880s, culminating in Geronimo's capture in 1886, and the bungled fight that became a slaughter of Sioux men, women, and children at Wounded Knee in 1890 were exceptions. The Plains Indians had lost their food supply through the whites' extravagant slaughter of the buffalo that had been the basis of the Indians' existence. Technology had come to the whites' assistance with the completion of the railroads and telegraphs that made possible rapid movement and control of troops and supplies. The Missouri River steamboats served a like function. Despite frustrating bureaucratic delays, better artillery and repeating rifles finally reached the troops in the 1860s and the Gatling gun, one of the first rapid-fire weapons, in the late 1870s. Meantime the Army had learned to attack in the dead of winter, when Indians were holed up in winter quarters, not expecting war. The Army had also discovered that Indians could be enlisted to fight Indians who were their traditional enemies, such as Pawnee and Arikara against Sioux and Cheyenne, or one band of Apache against another.

Indian defeats usually meant compulsory withdrawal into a desig-

MANY PEOPLES: I

nated reservation, to which the Federal government promised to
supply food, clothing, tools, instructors to teach the children, and
a farmer and blacksmith to teach the adult males agriculture, so that
presently they could become self-supporting. Usually a Christian
missionary was included. For years the Federal government had
been sliding uncertainly into a resort to reservations, and by the late
1850s and early 1860s officials of the Bureau of Indian Affairs were
repeatedly urging this as the only alternative to continued wars or
an ultimate extermination of the Indians.[36] By the 1870s the need
was even more apparent. Francis A. Walker, the economist and
future president of the Massachusetts Institute of Technology, had
gained an unusual insight from serving as both director of the 1870
census and commissioner of Indian affairs. At the opening of the
1870s he explained:

Instead of exposing to Indian contact, as heretofore, a clearly defined
frontier line, upon two or three faces, our settlements have penetrated the
Western country in every direction and from every direction.

Indian treaty lands had been violated "at a hundred points," and
no place was too remote to have attracted "some solitary ranchman
or miner." The Indians were losing both their homes and the game
upon which they normally subsisted. This meant, Walker concluded, that "the freedom of territorial and industrial expansion,
which is bringing imperial greatness to the nation, to the Indian
brings wretchedness, destitution, beggary."[37]

A great anthropologist, Clark Wissler, who began his field work
on reservations at the turn of the century, when native life was near
its lowest ebb, remarked that each band, when forced onto a reservation, "in almost total economic and social collapse, entered upon
a period of sullen passive resistance, attempting, as far as possible,
to rehabilitate in isolation their old aboriginal life."[38]

Their efforts were made the more difficult by the poor quality of
so many of the whites sent to guide the Indians in their new confined
existence. Cynics asked why so many were eager to be appointed
Indian agent in charge of a reservation, when the post paid only
fifteen hundred dollars a year and the isolation, hardship, and danger were considerable. The answer seemed to be that a few years
as Indian agent, in profitable collusion with contractors and politicians, could be made to assure a competence for life. All too often

the politics-ridden system sent to the reservations shoddy goods (clothing, tools, blankets) and food that was too poor in quality and too inadequate in quantity to support the Indians. "Starvation and near-starvation" were present annually on some reservations, and increased death rates and sickness rates were commonplace during the first few years of confinement.

Epidemic diseases, venereal disease, and illegal whiskey were bad enough, but to them was added the cultural shock of exchanging freedom for boredom, while seeing their tribal pattern of leadership and decision making undermined by the agent, who evolved into de facto ruler. Nor did the Federal government ever provide adequately for schools, least of all schools that would respect Indian culture, despite the obvious opportunity to move toward a better mutual understanding by a discriminating teaching of the oncoming generation. Much of the burden of operating schools on insufficient budgets was contracted out to missionary-minded church denominations.[39]

Quite aside from specific shortcomings, it was hard for even those sympathetic to Indians to visualize their salvation in any terms save conversion to the whites' way of life. With anthropology still a discipline practiced only by a few, ethnocentric thinking was so nearly universal in the nineteenth century that it was almost impossible to appreciate the values that a "primitive" race might find in its accustomed way of life.[40] Firmly the agent of the Sioux agency at Yellow Medicine declared: "The prejudices and habits of the Indian must be eradicated." His superior, the head of the northern superintendency at St. Paul, agreed:

There is something more necessary to be done to educate the Indian than to teach him the arts and sciences or religion. His whole nature must be changed. He must have a white man's ambition, to be like him. He must have the objects and aims of a white man.

To accomplish this, the superintendent continued, the Indian must be taught to be more "mercenary and ambitious to obtain riches." Then he would come to understand the laws concerning private property, and "tribal relations would be broken down."[41]

So extreme a point of view cannot be dismissed as the unreflective thinking of bureaucrats, for when the Civil War was over and slavery ended, reformers whose energies had been absorbed in the antislavery movement channeled them now into the battle for Indian rights. Such reformers were apt to be well educated. They have been categorized as "middle class idealists" and "social-gospel Christian humanists" who were members of mainline Protestant churches.[42] From modest beginnings shortly after the Civil War, their numbers grew rapidly from 1879 onward until they had founded a whole cluster of organizations dedicated to this one issue. Their headquarters tended to be in Philadelphia or Boston, although some notable individuals, such as the exceedingly active Episcopal Bishop Henry B. Whipple of Minnesota and the determined John Beeson of Oregon, were former easterners who had firmly established themselves in the west.

Where many a westerner hated and feared Indians and was contemptuous of the Indian way of life as seen in the not too impressive daily reality, the reformers saw Indians as children of God and therefore the white man's brothers. To them the objective was to assimilate the Indian into American life by teaching some of the arts of white civilization. Their thinking had the same central thesis as that expressed by the officials just quoted. The Indian must be "saved" *as an individual,* just as Protestant evangelists sought to "save" individual white backsliders, and this meant "freeing" the Indian from his familiar, psychologically supportive communal life. Essential elements leading toward salvation were conversion to Christianity, education, manual arts, and individual ownership of land that was to be worked by the Indian as a farmer, regardless of how unfamiliar with agriculture the Indian might be. How the transformed Indian was to slip into a society as race-conscious as that of white America was not explained; assimilation did not include intermarriage.[43] One is reminded of the warning of two modern anthropologists that "ethnocentrism means acting in accordance with one's own values in a situation to which they are not relevant."[44]

In the unlikely atmosphere of the Grant administration, Quaker and Episcopal leaders teamed up first to persuade Grant to let religious denominations nominate Indian agents, so as to get honest men, and then to convince both Grant and Congress to create a board of Indian commissioners, which would be composed of ten unpaid philanthropists drawn from the religious denominations, and charged with scrutinizing operations and recommending reforms. To complete the new arrangements, in 1873 the Episcopalians lobbied through Congress a statute to appoint five inspectors who would visit the agencies and examine the financial accounts of each.

This unusual involvement of church and state, in a nation dedicated to keeping the two separate, worked unevenly at best. The Indian agents sent out by the denominations brought greater honesty than common sense and leadership qualities, and gradually they were replaced by political appointees. Missionary and educational work by the churches continued, despite unseemly rivalries and a very inadequate attempt to get along with the Catholics, who had a long record of missionary accomplishment. The board of Indian commissioners had an erratic record because its effectiveness was largely dependent on the fluctuating goodwill of the successive secretaries of the interior, who were responsible for both policy and administration, although day-to-day operations were of course carried out through the Bureau of Indian Affairs and its commissioner.[45]

The reformers were convinced that the reservations were retarding and corrupting influences that must be broken up in favor of individual farms, if the Indians were ever to be assimilated into American life. In the 1870s and 1880s enthusiasm was high for "severalty" legislation—i.e., statutes that would divide tribal holdings into individual ownerships. Had they been more realistic in their thinking, the reformers might have wondered why this proposal that they were pushing so energetically was winning support from the land-hungry westerners and speculators who were usually their opponents. The fact was that severalty legislation had been tried with a few Indian groups, and the results had been disastrous. For example, when the Chippewa received land allotments about 1871, they were so unenthusiastic about farming and so inexperienced in land transactions that by 1878 five sixths had lost their lands to whites.[46]

At least one influential senator, Henry M. Teller of Colorado, realized that most Indian tribal bands were not ready for independence, and the Five Civilized Tribes in Oklahoma presented an effective argument against the whole mistaken idea, but the enthusiasm of the crusade swept all before it, including Henry L. Dawes of Massachusetts, who held the key position as chairman of the Senate Indian Affairs Committee. The Dawes Severalty Act was passed in

1887, with the safeguard that the individual Indian would not be permitted to sell his land for twenty-five years. Unscrupulous whites circumvented this in numerous ways, for example, by persuading Indians to lease their lands for unreasonably low rents, or by getting themselves appointed guardians for Indian minors. After the individual allotments were made, surplus lands went on sale to eager whites. Thus did a measure intended for reform result in stripping the Indian race of most of its remaining land base.[47]

Meantime, earnest people were trying to prepare Indians to cope with white civilization. Starting in 1870, Congress at last began to appropriate money specifically designated for schools, and by 1899 over $2.5 million was being spent annually to support 148 boarding schools and 225 day schools that together served almost twenty thousand children.[48] The widespread conviction that a complete break away from the tribe was necessary caused off-reservation boarding schools to be very popular with reformers in the late nineteenth century. The best-known was that established by Captain Richard H. Pratt at the old Carlisle barracks in Pennsylvania, in 1879, and made famous in part by its athletes, especially Jim Thorpe. Pratt was simultaneously a firm believer in the worthwhileness and educability of Indians, and an equally firm enemy of the reservation system because it segregated Indians from American society, and yet he opposed severalty legislation as coming too soon.[49]

Boarding schools had the central weakness that they separated the boy or girl from home long enough to graduate a person who was ready neither to earn a living in white society and win acceptance there, nor to return to the reservation with assurance of either finding a job appropriate to his or her newly acquired skills or being welcomed back by relatives and friends—who resented the young person's break with traditional ways. Congress and the Bureau of Indian Affairs were dishearteningly slow to develop and finance schemes that would encourage adult Indians to play an adult role in providing for themselves. Instead of being so single-minded about teaching agriculture to reluctant grown-up pupils, much could have been done with livestock, as the successful examples of the Navajo with sheep and the Choctaw and Cherokee with cattle would suggest. Or again, where the government had been paying large fees to white firms to haul agency freight, Agent John D. Miles of the Cheyenne and Arapaho reservation tried having Indians take over the job. This they did willingly, at a considerable saving that still enabled them to make money for themselves.[50] Most significant of all was the successful though grossly underfinanced experiment of enrolling Indians as policemen on their own reservations, and later as judges. They proved an invaluable and reliable link between rulers and ruled.[51]

As the century ended, the confusing business of finding a place for the widely varied Indian groups in the ever-engulfing, ever-growing white society was far from complete.[52] Perhaps the most knowledgeable summary was that given by the anthropologist Clark Wissler, who had seen it all firsthand:

There was no other place for the Indian to go [save the reservation]. . . . The reservation gave the Indian a haven. He was, in a sense, a prisoner in a concentration camp, but his scalp was safe. He enjoyed free medical service, and free schooling. At times he was hungry, his food poorly chosen, but few starved to death after 1890. Naturally, the Indian was far from happy . . . because the foot of the conqueror pressed down upon the neck of the Indian.[53]

CHAPTER 7

Many Peoples:
II. The Spanish-Speaking
and the Chinese

FROM the time when Oñate led his pioneer band up the Rio
Grande to build homes in the land of the Pueblo Indians, the
Native Americans of the southwest had had to share their thinly
occupied domain with a scattering of Hispanic villages, farms, ranches, and mines, most of which were in New Mexico and not far
from Oñate's original area of settlement. After Mexico's revolt from
Spain, and the consequent withdrawal of the Spanish garrisons from
the presidios, nomadic Indians such as Apaches, Navajos, and Com-
manches swept down on the isolated Hispanic communities with
devastating effectiveness. At many points the advance of the Hispanic frontier was checked, and at some it receded.[1]

For a time Arizona, which had been settled only in the southern
strip below the Gila River, was abandoned save for the garrisoned
town of Tucson, while losses of lives and livestock were heavy all the
way from Texas to California. When the United States acquired the
southwest, it promised more military protection than it actually
provided, but New Mexicans continued to thrust their way outward
from the upper Rio Grande Valley. In the 1840s they were pushing
north and east from Santa Fe and Taos, and under the new American rule they advanced northward into the San Luis Valley of
Colorado and eastward into the upper valleys of the Pecos and
Canadian rivers. In the latter area their herds of sheep and cattle
grazed well out beyond the little fortified villages (*plazas*) that the
pioneers built. By the 1870s New Mexicans were as far east as

Tascosa, in the Texas Panhandle. Far to the south, on the lower Rio Grande, other New Mexicans opened the Mesilla Valley, while still others invaded southeastern New Mexico, especially along the lower course of the Pecos River and its tributaries.[2]

Taking advantage of the Army's operations against the Navajo and Apache in the Civil War era, New Mexicans moved westward in the late 1860s as far as the pastures of eastern Arizona. In the 1840s a remarkable group of New Mexicans migrated all the way to the San Bernardino Valley of southern California, where they had been promised land if they would defend the area from Indian attacks.[3]

The burden of these pioneering thrusts was carried by the sturdy *mestizos*—the mixed bloods—who constituted most of the Hispano population. Living with them were detribalized, Hispanicized Indians, known to the New Mexicans as *genízaros,* who founded villages of their own or were incorporated into mestizo settlements. Without the fighting abilities of genízaros, the San Bernardino colony could not have succeeded.

In New Mexico most of the mestizos lived in the small villages that nature permitted them to crowd onto the patches of irrigable land that were all that arid region provided. Their livestock, mostly sheep, grazed on less-valuable land that the village held in common as pasture. Some New Mexicans were retainers on the great ranches (*haciendas*) of the *ricos* (rich men). In either case the illiterate mestizo was dependent on his *patrón* (local boss), who alone knew something about the economics, laws, and politics of the world that lay beyond the parochial limits of the village. The patrón might be a resident village leader or he might be a big landholder. The New Mexicans carried these arrangements with them when they moved northward into Colorado, where new settlements tended to be pioneered by groups from a single family.[4] In Texas, where patróns exercised a comparable authority, the mestizos again formed the bottom of the social pyramid, but in California the widespread use of Indians as cheap labor created a class below the mestizos, who were thus able to serve as *vaqueros* (cowboys) or to move up to positions comparable to foremen on the ranches, or become independent small farmers or craftsmen or small shopkeepers in the few towns.

In each province the upper class formed a thin layer, distinctive in that they tended to be whiter in skin color and prone to boast,

with varying degrees of justification, of their "pure Spanish blood."
An Anglo visitor to Texas spoke of the Tejano aristocracy as being
"a fine-looking and elevated race" who looked down upon "the dark
Mexicans with contempt."[5]

When it became evident that, willy-nilly, their future lay with the
United States, many of the New Mexican ricos sent their sons to St.
Louis, New York, or other American cities to be educated, or apprenticed them to one of the mercantile houses that handled supplies and freighting across the plains, so that they could learn English and American business methods. Ambitious Anglos who had
come to New Mexico intermarried with them, and business partnerships between Anglos and New Mexican aristocrats were frequent.[6]
The early Anglo arrivals were few in number, mostly territorial
officials, Army, or merchants, together with a clutch of men who
mixed law, politics, and land speculation to their own profit.

Of the merchants, in New Mexico as in other parts of the farther
west, a goodly percentage were German Jews who started in a small
way, learned Spanish, and rose to prominence in both business and
finance. As in the case of the notable Spiegelberg and Seligman
families, or Charles Ilfeld, they tended to rely on relatives when
their expanding firms required additional personnel.[7]

For New Mexico, with its preindustrial economy, it was essential
to have big freighting and merchandising firms to haul wool across
the plains to the "States," and to return with the supplies and
merchandise demanded by the Army, Indian reservations, Santa Fe,
and lesser distributing points in New Mexico and Arizona. Frequently Hispanos and Anglos were partners in these firms, which in
that undifferentiated economy simultaneously handled transportation, exports and imports, and credit and loans. As railroads approached, the wagon journey became progressively shorter, but the
Atchison, Topeka and Santa Fe Railroad did not enter New Mexico
until 1879. By that time mining and cattle raising had become significant alternatives to sheep, and with the beginning of through rail
connections, the pace of this sleepy colony's activities began to
quicken.

Many of the ricos shared in the prosperity both before and after
the railroads, but the same could not be said for the masses of New
Mexicans. Economically they failed to advance, and in the key field
of education and learning English, so important if mestizos were to

protect themselves from exploitation and win rewarding jobs in the evolving economy, little was accomplished, for Hispano politicians fell into a fierce and continuing debate with determined Anglo Protestants over whether priests, especially Jesuits, should be allowed to teach in public schools and whether English should be required. The issue became a symbol of an underlying rivalry between the traditional New Mexican leaders and the recently arrived Anglos. Not until 1891 was a statute passed that required common schools and specified that they were to be nonsectarian and were to teach English. But progress under this law was discouragingly slow.[8] As late as 1911, a linguist reported that while use of at least a mixture of English and Spanish was common in the cities and towns, comprehension of more than a few English words was rare in the rural districts.[9]

Why did not the ricos make more effort to help their poorer fellow countrymen? Perhaps it was not even to their advantage to do so. When the strange American custom of popular elections was introduced to a largely illiterate and uninformed electorate, it was obvious that the patróns and ricos would control the vote and that most local elected officials and members of the territorial legislature would be Hispanos. The ambitious new American politician-lawyers were quick to recognize this and to form alliances accordingly. The most successful of them were Stephen Benton Elkins and his partner Thomas Benton Catron, who made it their first concern to learn Spanish fluently.

These opportunistic politician-lawyers saw their chance in the failure of Congress to create any special agency to deal with the tangled land titles until 1891. For more than forty years land titles were determined by special acts of Congress and by surveys, investigations, and decisions made by appointive officials in Santa Fe and Washington. This was just the type of opening that wire-pullers could exploit, and in doing so they formed what came to be known as the "Santa Fe Ring," an informal, frequently changing group dedicated to fattening their own pocketbooks through speculation in land and through handling land title cases for Hispano clients, who frequently had no other means of paying their attorneys than to cede to them part of the land in dispute.[10]

Catron and Elkins became so successful in politics and law as to be almost beyond challenge, so long as they tended carefully their alliances with Hispano leaders and with the frequently changing territorial officials. Catron was particularly good at stretching the boundaries of confirmed claims beyond anything reasonable, and he was equally adept at quietly acquiring title to undocumented common pasturelands that, by unwritten custom, had been used by the peasantry since time immemorial.[11] At best, New Mexican rural life offered the peon no margin for safety against droughts, erosion, or more children than the land could feed. It took only the manipulations of an Anglo sharper and his Hispano accomplices to win control of carelessly held lands and force the peons to go wandering off in search of seasonal employment elsewhere, while their wives held the family together.

There were limits to how far chicanery could go. Violence and feuds were already a part of eastern New Mexico's life, partly because of an aggressive thrust by Texas cattlemen into ranges where New Mexicans were already grazing sheep, partly because of a bitter antagonism between Texans and New Mexicans. Now outright racial warfare was added, although it was warfare that sometimes found members of the Hispano elite on the side of the Anglos.

The Las Vegas Community Grant, of five hundred thousand acres, had been occupied by a substantial number of Hispano families since at least 1841. When Anglo cattle ranchers forced their way into it and erected barbed wire fences, the angry New Mexican rural folk—*los pobres* (the poor ones)—found a leader in Juan José Herrera, a native New Mexican who had lived outside the territory for years and during that time had learned English and a considerable amount of Anglo law, and had become an organizer for the Knights of Labor.[12]

With some aid from the Knights, but more importantly by organizing themselves as a masked night-riding outfit known from their costume as Las Gorras Blancas (the White Caps), the New Mexicans set out to make life impossible for the Anglos. With perhaps seven hundred men joining them, in 1889 and 1890 they raided throughout the three counties of San Miguel, Santa Fe, and Mora, cutting fences and burning the fence posts, and sometimes burning haystacks, barns, and houses. Under Juan José's leadership, other New Mexicans, operating as the Knights of Labor, rose in revolt against the price paid them for railroad ties for the Atchison, Topeka and Santa Fe, and burned thousands of ties owned by the railroad.

Out of this violent activity came a brief political victory, for the dissidents united momentarily to form the People's party, ultimately affiliated with the Populists, and swept local elections in 1890, 1892, and 1894. Catron, who was running for Congress, was one of their victims in 1892. But the representatives they sent to the territorial legislature proved singularly ineffective as reformers, save in their success in getting the Las Vegas Grant incorporated. (Later it was fully confirmed to the community that had occupied it for so many years.) More than any other single episode, the activities of Las Gorras Blancas refuted the notion that simple Hispanos could always be beaten into submission, no matter how outrageous the circumstances.

In Texas the treatment of the Spanish-speaking Americans was worse than in New Mexico, where the sheer bulk of the Hispano population, relative to the small number of Anglos, set limits. Frederick Law Olmsted, later to become the famous landscape architect, made a long horseback journey across Texas to San Antonio in the 1850s. An experienced observer, he warned that there was "between our Southern American [i.e., Anglos from the Deep South] and the Mexican, an unconquerable antagonism of character, which will prevent any condition of order where the two come together." Continued Olmsted:

The mingled Puritanism and brigandism, which distinguishes the vulgar mind of the South, peculiarly unfits it to harmoniously associate with the bigoted, childish, and passionate Mexicans. They are considered to be heathen; not acknowledged as "white folks." Inevitably they are dealt with insolently and unjustly. They fear and hate the ascendant race.[13]

At an early date the better lands of eastern Texas had been taken over by southern Anglos and their slaves. In central Texas German immigrants, followed by smaller groups of Czechs, Poles, and other Europeans, had joined the slave-owning southerners in occupying the land. Farther west, to quote a distinguished geographer, "by 1860 the Anglos had gotten control, by fair means or foul, of nearly every ranch worth having north of the Nueces." Where Hispanos continued to live in the towns, "Anglo and Hispano lived physically adjacent, but socially separate."[14]

Beyond the Nueces, which runs through southernmost Texas to the Gulf at Corpus Christi, the Rio Grande border country was for decades a lawless region repeatedly invaded by hostile Indians, Anglo and Mexican brigands, cattle thieves, filibusterers, guerrillas, punitive expeditions of the United States and Mexican armies, and the all too race-conscious Texas Rangers. In that tense atmosphere, and with Anglo strength visibly growing, it was not difficult for shrewd men, familiar with legal and political processes and willing to take a chance in a dangerous region, to pressure landholding Tejanos into sales at bargain prices. Great estates such as those acquired by Richard King and Mifflin Kenedy had their start in this era.[15]

With this widespread transference of ownership "Anglo-American immigrants to south Texas rapidly appropriated not just lands but the foundations of the region's economy." They became rulers of a region "where persons rooted in the older Spanish-Mexican heritage composed at least 73 per cent of the total population through the last half of the nineteenth century."[16]

Some of the Tejano ranchers held on to their land, while others formed alliances by marrying their daughters to Anglos, but by the pattern of their lives the Tejano aristocrats passed on to the incoming Anglos "a legacy of feudalistic rule" based on the dependence of *peónes* upon patróns.[17] To be sure, there was a limited mutuality about the relationship, for the patrón, in Texas as in New Mexico and southern Colorado, advised and protected "his" peons, advanced them credit or started them as sheepherders on a shares basis, sold them goods, and won goodwill by contributing the cost of weddings, funerals, and fiestas. When Anglos bought out Hispano rancheros, they became patróns who assumed the obligations as well as the opportunities of the former owners.[18]

Incoming Anglo politicians, who were often lawyers, recognized the political potentialities of the relationship, just as they did in New Mexico, and men such as James B. Wells, Jr., who was Texas-born of New England seafaring stock, became undisputed political bosses over South Texas counties. Wells was in close alliance with the dominant rancher class, both Anglo and Tejano, because they could deliver the illiterate peons' vote. Wells did not hesitate to work with a notoriously corrupt Anglo boss such as "Archie" Parr of Duval County, or with an authoritarian Tejano boss such as Manuel Guerra of Starr County.[19] The bosses were sufficiently aware of the expectations of their constituents to see to it that some lower-level patronage jobs always went to Spanish-surnamed people, but only well-to-do Hispano ranchers and merchants had significant influence, and all too often the Tejano lords found it more important to curry favor with the Anglo leaders than to worry about the education and welfare of the peons who served them.

At first the impact of the shift to Anglo control was cushioned for the bulk of the population by the continuance of life in its familiar pastoral and agricultural pattern. Tejano ranch hands were hereditary experts at handling cattle and sheep, and as ranching revived and expanded, their services were needed on both Anglo and Tejano ranches. Other mestizos went about an equally familiar work as teamsters or mule packers. Hauling to and from the Texan ports was a major activity, while in all parts of the west, but especially on the mountainous trails to the mines, could be found mule packers whose long trains of pack animals picturesquely followed the tinkling leadership of the bell mare.

But late in the century railroads penetrated the southwest to put hitherto isolated places within reach of markets. All along the American-Mexican border, from South Texas to southern California, the 1880s and 1890s were a period of decisive change, as cotton and vegetables replaced ranching in South Texas, a smelter was built at El Paso, copper mines opened in Arizona, and irrigated agriculture boomed in southern California. Each of these new industries, together with the construction and maintenance of the railroads themselves, required large numbers of cheap unskilled laborers. So, too, did the growing cities along the railroad lines, such as El Paso, Albuquerque, Tucson, Phoenix, and Los Angeles. While Hispano-Americans filled some of these unfamiliar and low-paid jobs, often the need for manpower was supplied by immigrants from Mexico, who began in the 1880s and 1890s to cross the border in numbers that would grow to massive proportions after 1900. The jobs so filled were ones in which pay was low, hours long, and conditions often unhealthy, dangerous, or uninviting. Modern historians with Spanish surnames have termed this critical change in the late nineteenth century the "proletarianizing" of their race, or the reduction to "second-class status."[20] Interestingly, the native-born Hispano-Americans tended to look down upon the struggling newcomers and to maintain their distance from them, even though the Hispano-Americans themselves were becoming hard pressed as the older types of jobs in which they were skilled disappeared in this changing economy.

Many of this increasing number of natives and immigrants drifted into the southwest's growing cities and towns. There they were segregated in *barrios*—Spanish towns—and that at least had the advantage of preserving areas where comfortably familiar customs could be continued in the face of daily pressure to the contrary, where the traditional extended family could remain together, albeit in an atmosphere of poverty, poor health standards, and limited education. Small merchants and professional men came forward to serve the barrios, thus enlarging the middle class in a society where that class traditionally had been weak. In cities such as San Antonio and El Paso, where the total Spanish-speaking population was large, the Anglo-run political machines and "rings" conceded some local political offices, and under pressure from Hispano leaders learned to pay some attention to the needs of the barrios.[21]

Conditions in California differed from those of either New Mexico or Texas. Because it was settled late, and because Mexicans were unenthusiastic about migrating to so remote a place—a veritable Siberia to them—the civilian population grew very slowly and never became large. The garrisons at the presidios were correspondingly tiny, and a mere handful of padres taught Christianity and useful arts to the Indians (neophytes) whom they brought to the missions.

Bancroft's researchers estimated that by 1845, on the eve of the war between Mexico and the United States, the Hispano-Californian population numbered only about seven thousand, while foreigners (mostly Americans, often married to Hispanos) were about seven hundred, and "domesticated" Indians were a few thousand.[22]

The Hispano-Californians might have been fewer still if a revolution in landholding had not taken place during the preceding dozen years. Spain had been very slow to grant land to private petitioners and the first Mexican governors were equally slow. But in 1833 land-hungry Californians linked with revolutionary Mexico's anti-clericalism to obtain a Mexican statute that called for the breaking up of the missions' huge landholdings, and the liberation of the neophytes.

This late secularization meant that, with relatively few exceptions, the most desirable land in the province was distributed to private ranchers only within the thirteen years before the American military invasion. In that brief period California governors granted over five hundred concessions to private petitioners,[23] and indeed, of the 813 land claims ultimately presented for adjudication by the United States, 341 had real or alleged granting dates within three and a half years before July 1846.[24] The much-romanticized era of the ranchos was thus a brief one, and local society did not have time to congeal into as rigid a structure as New Mexico's. It is true that a few great landholding *rancheros,* mostly self-made men, became the new dominant force, exercising supreme authority on their ranches and a patrón-like influence in the towns, and occupying local public offices; but the class structure they created did not include a feudalistic relationship of patrón to mestizo-peon comparable to New Mexico's. That was partly because Indians formed a bottom class, economically and socially lower than anyone else. Freed from the missions, some Indians returned to traditional ways of life, while others took ranch jobs (for little more than their subsistence), and still others drifted into the towns, where most found only a precarious and irregular existence. Like Indians under Anglo jurisdictions, the former mission Indians and the survivors of deteriorating bands fared badly when left to their own resources in white society.[25]

In part the absence of mestizo peonage reflected the availability of land. This permitted a class of small mestizo farmers and ranchers to develop, while also encouraging mestizo town dwellers, who carried on subsistence farming on the side and pastured a few head of livestock on the common land of the pueblo, meantime working as artisans, skilled laborers, and at seasonal jobs.

Of all the ills this small Californian population suffered after they passed under the American flag, the most drastic was their submergence beneath the unprecedented flood of immigrants that started with the gold rush and continued throughout the rest of the century. Those 7,000 Californians of 1845 were overwhelmed by a population that rose well above 100,000 by 1850, reached 380,000 in 1860, and stood at nearly 1.5 million by 1900. In northern California the rancheros, mestizos, and Indian workers were swept aside by this torrent of newcomers who came from a different cultural background and quickly changed pastoral California into a commercial, city-centered, speculative, and money-minded capitalistic economy. Unsophisticated *Californios* found themselves struggling with such unfamiliar institutions as property taxes, mortgages and professional moneylenders, American-style politics, and the Protestant work ethic. Change came more slowly in remote, backward southern California, but even there it was only a question of time.

Nor were the Californios' own numbers strengthened materially by permanent immigration from other Spanish-speaking countries, prior to the Mexican immigration of the 1880s and 1890s. Most of the gold-rush crowd of Sonorans and other Mexicans went home after facing the wrath of the nativist-minded miners. The censuses for 1860, 1870, and 1880 all credited California with a Mexican-born population of about nine thousand. Even if the census counts under-enumerated Spanish-speaking persons, still the error could not have been big enough to lessen materially the growing imbalance between English-speaking and Spanish-speaking elements.[26]

The size and cohesiveness of the Spanish-speaking population was of crucial importance politically, if the Hispanic element was to maintain any degree of self-government. By the 1870s, when the new railroads were bringing crowds of would-be settlers even to southern California, the game had been lost everywhere, and Spanish-speaking people had become a permanent minority. In Los Angeles, for example, the Spanish-surnamed part of the city's population fell from more than three fourths in 1850 to 19 percent in 1880.[27] Reflecting this, Spanish-named people, who had held a wide variety of local offices in southern California throughout the 1850s, had to be content with less in the 1860s and early 1870s, and with very little thereafter. And at state level they never did play an important role.[28]

Santa Barbara's experience illustrated the process. For years the most important center of Spanish and Mexican culture in California, it had a class of vigorous and well-to-do ranchero families who were accustomed to ruling themselves. The younger generation was well symbolized by the able De la Guerra brothers, who learned English, learned American politics, served in the state legislature, and in concert with other leading families, such as the Carrillos, and with their own innumerable relatives and dependents, kept a firm control over Santa Barbara city and county officeholding until late in the 1860s. The De la Guerras and other aristocrats built a machine that worked through mestizo managers to organize an ethnic vote that was highly effective because the Anglo vote was split between the two national parties.

As late as 1867 Spanish-surnamed voters were nearly 63 percent of the electorate in the city and nearly as much in the county. But with a continuing influx of Anglo voters, by 1871 the electorate was close to being equally divided, and elections were contested with a fierceness that bode ill for permanent race relations. By 1873 Spanish-surnamed voters had dropped to about 34 percent in the city and county. This was still enough to give them the balance of power until the Anglos dropped their normal party allegiances to form a "People's Convention" that put forward a unified ticket that was anti-Californio, anti-Catholic, and antiforeign. In the elections of 1873 the Californio candidates lost almost all the city and county offices. With control now in their hands, in 1874 the Anglos hastened to reincorporate the city on a basis that gerrymandered the Spanish-speaking vote into futility. By 1880 the Anglos had been equally successful in winning control of the county.[29]

Contemporaneously the ranchero class was losing the land grants that were the basis of their wealth and power and the source of jobs for mestizos and the dwindling number of Indians. The gold rush, with its sudden demand for vastly greater amounts of food, had brought the ranches what Robert Glass Cleland vividly termed "seven fat years of inflated prices and treacherous prosperity."[30] Had the rancheros put their profits into improving their livestock, pasture, and water supply, they might have had some chance when competition for the glutted northern beef market became severe, but 1855 and 1856 brought to an end what Cleland called "the golden age of the cattle industry."[31] The rancheros, having become accustomed to luxuries for themselves and their families, and loving ostentatious clothing and parties, had built up no reserves. Now they found themselves forced to borrow at exorbitant rates of interest. A contemporary remarked that the rancheros "knew not the value of money or the crushing power of compound interest."[32] At the same time, many had failed to pay their taxes and had to borrow again on costly and risky terms that ultimately proved disastrous.[33]

Worst of all, they were already struggling to pay for a slow-moving, expensive process by which the validity of their land grants was being tested—a process that kept their ownership in a state of uncertainty, made sale of land difficult, and encouraged challenges by squatters and alert speculators. To quote the leading student of this subject, "a rough estimate" of the total amount of land involved

in the 813 claims would be 14 million acres, which included much
of the best agricultural and pastoral land in the state, and the sites
of most of the future cities.[34] By American standards, California
land titles were incompletely documented and boundaries were
only vaguely described. Some grants were forgeries or last-minute
bestowals made under dubious circumstances by the defeated outgoing government. Oral evidence, as a substitute for missing or
questionable documents, was often contradictory. The Mexican requirement that a grantee occupy and use his land had not always
been lived up to, nor had the very generous Mexican limitation as
to size always been obeyed.

Obviously some screening process was needed, and in northern
California the need was immediate, because the gold rush had
started a rapid escalation in land values and had encouraged an
army of speculators, squatters, and lawyers. Yet not until 1851
could Congress agree upon a commission to examine and adjudicate claims; not until 1853 was the commission seriously at work.
Little if any effort was made to staff the commission with men who
could read and speak Spanish and were familiar with Spanish and
Mexican land laws. Nor were the commission's decisions necessarily
final, for appeal could be taken to the Federal courts in California
and to the United States Supreme Court, with all the delay that
implied. And after titles had been determined, there still remained
the uncertainties of boundary surveys. In southern California, distant by several hundred miles of poor transportation from the new
world of San Francisco, Sacramento, and the mines, the settlement
of land titles proceeded more smoothly than in the north because
land values continued low and rival claimants and squatters were
fewer. But throughout California, the Californios' lack of cash
meant that when they hired lawyers to defend their claims, they
often had to surrender part of their estate in lieu of fees. What is
more, while some lawyers were honest, competent, and compassionate, others were frauds and thieves.[35]

A distinguished Los Angeles attorney once declared that of all the
Mexican and Spanish grants in the huge area that then constituted
Los Angeles County, he knew of only one, that to the Dominguez
family, that remained in the ownership of descendants of the original grantees, and even that grant was fought over in internecine
legal battles between members of the Dominguez family.[36]

While the lawyers struggled to salvage grants for their clients, the latter were in serious trouble because of the continued low price of beef. Then nature, too, turned against them. As Mark Twain observed, California never does things by halves: throughout the state the winter of 1861–1862 brought the most damaging floods in memory, while immediately following in 1862–1864 came two years of unprecedented drought. Somberly a Monterey correspondent wrote as the second rainless winter ended:

The cattle, sheep and horses (in which the wealth of this county consists) will nearly all die this year, if they are not "killed" to prevent them from dying. . . . There is, then, no prospect ahead for the stock raiser in this part of the State, except destitution and poverty.[37]

By September of 1865 the Monterey County Assessor reported that instead of the seventy thousand head of cattle in his county a few years earlier, only thirteen thousand now remained.[38] Southern California was at least as hard hit. The once proud rancheros were either ruined or drastically reduced in circumstances, while what was left of their estates passed into new hands, usually American or European. This accelerated a movement to break up the great ranches into smaller tracts intended for sale, especially where irrigation was possible. Only a few of the rancheros made the difficult transition to American-style careers.[39]

Indirectly the passing of the ranchero class hurt the mestizos and what was left of the Indian workers. For the Indians the future held little hope save a continued struggle against poverty, sickness, and abuse, until they ceased to be significant even in the cheap-labor market. The mestizos were more enduring. Their central problem was that they had been trained primarily in the skills and crafts required by a rural and simple pastoral economy. Most were illiterate and ill-equipped to learn new ways. In the new California that was now emerging even in the south, there was a big demand for unskilled and semiskilled labor, and a quite separate need for highly developed skills. The mestizos were caught between the extremes, not qualified for the latter and hating to enter the former.

What were they to do? Some experienced vaqueros could still find work on Anglo-owned ranches in California, while others found similar jobs as far away as southeastern Oregon and southern Arizona. A limited amount of seasonal work was available for sheep-shearing and periodic farm tasks. Some families retreated into the isolation of mountainous country, where the new age would leave them alone. Many simply drifted into the cities, where white prejudice, poverty, and their own sense of identity caused them to congregate in barrios. Increasingly the mestizos found themselves with no alternative save to accept jobs at the bottom of the new capitalistic economy. Even in Santa Barbara, "by 1870 the Spanish-surname work force was steadily becoming a downwardly mobile, unskilled, displaced working class." As Mexican immigrants entered the southern California labor market from the 1880s onward, the two elements fused into "a proletarianized, ethnic working class in the lowest stratum of the economic order."[40]

Arizona proved to be the Johnny-come-lately of the Hispanic southwest. By 1856, when the United States took formal possession of the Gadsden Purchase strip south of the Gila, most of the survivors of the Apache raids were still huddled in Tucson—if they had not abandoned Arizona entirely. But the California gold rush had transformed Tucson and the Gila Valley into one of the routes to the new Golconda. Through it in the 1850s came gold seekers, Texan and New Mexican ranchers driving cattle and sheep to the California market, the Butterfield Overland Mail, and the United States Army, which became the region's biggest customer for supplies and freighting.[41]

This evidence of Tucson's importance for trade and transportation encouraged a heterogeneous assortment of Anglo-Americans, European immigrants, and Mexicans from Sonora and Chihuahua to seek Tucson and there to set themselves up as merchants, freighters, storekeepers, butchers, blacksmiths, and liquor dealers. Ranchers began raising livestock once more and a little farming was resumed on irrigated lands. A few old mines were reopened and new ones claimed. Unskilled and semiskilled labor flowed up from Sonora and Chihuahua in response to rumors of jobs.

By 1860 Tucson and the reviving area tributary to it were developing into an unusual bicultural community. The great majority were Spanish-speaking, but among the leaders a disproportionately large number were either Americans or European immigrants. This predominance by outsiders developed despite the presence of upper-class natives of Tucson and immigrants of comparable status from Sonora and Chihuahua, who had the background to take lead-

ing roles, as in fact some did. Relations between the American and
European leaders and their Spanish-speaking compeers seem to
have been good from an early date. Anglos and Hispanos joined in
business partnerships, and Anglo men, in this region where there
were but a tiny number of American women, courted and won wives
or mistresses from among the Spanish-speaking, with all that that
implied about influence exerted via the bedroom, nursery, and
kitchen.

At lower social levels and especially outside Tucson, relations
were often marred by racism and misunderstanding. One student
has concluded that in this early era "there was a decided race feeling
between the Mexicans and the American inhabitants," and epithets
like "greaser" and "gringo" were common.[42] At a mine whose
managers were Americans and Europeans, the laborers were Mexicans or New Mexicans and seemed to their bosses to be irregular
in habits, slow, and less orderly and careful than was needed. But
the Mexicans and New Mexicans were paid less than others and
were irritated by a visible "Anglo-American racism, a sense of cultural superiority and ethnic hostility."[43]

This duality of relatively good relations in Tucson, where the
Spanish-speaking were numerous and influential, and frequent ill-
feeling or prejudice elsewhere, was to characterize Arizona for
decades. For the moment the issue was thrust into the background
by the outbreak of the Civil War, which caused the recall of the
Regular Army garrisons. Once more the Apache swept down upon
the exposed settlements, and what they missed was pounced upon
by Sonoran bandits up from Mexico. A small force of Texan
Confederates completed the area's misery by invading Arizona to
"annex" it to the Confederacy.

Out of these disasters unexpectedly came the beginning of Arizona's permanent growth. California volunteer troops under General James H. Carleton drove out the Confederates, and launched
a series of campaigns against the Indians. Carleton's men had little
success against the Apache, but Carleton had the good sense to
entrust operations against the Navajo to Colonel "Kit" Carson and
his New Mexican militia. Carson's decisive victory in 1864 brought
permanent peace with that hitherto dangerously effective foe. Some
of Carleton's men decided to remain in Arizona and became leading

citizens. Congress, with Lincoln's approval, made Arizona a territory in 1863.

Despite the continuing dangers of these turbulent years, the middle and late 1860s saw changes that were greatly accelerated in the 1870s and 1880s. Mining booms drew in crowds of newcomers. Despite the glitter of Tombstone's silver, the really important development was the opening of great copper mines and their attendant smelters and company towns, which meant that full-scale industrialization had come to Arizona. Irrigated agriculture transformed the Salt River valley and brought into being Phoenix, destined to become the territory's largest city. Railroads and telegraphs joined Arizona to the hitherto distant outer world. Population soared from less than 10,000 in 1870 to over 40,000 in 1880 and nearly 123,000 in 1900.

What did these extensive changes mean for racial relations? In Tucson Anglo and Hispano continued to get along relatively well. As James Officer has pointed out, the intermarriages between leading Anglos and daughters of Hispano families long prominent in Tucson or in nearby Sonora brought the former into "the complex kinship network which bound together the Tucson Mexican colony," and thus helped bridge the gap between the two cultures.[44]

Similarly, a major business firm such as that of Pickney Randolph Tully and Estévan Ochoa, freighters and merchants, united the talents of an American frontier entrepreneur—who had lived successively in Mississippi, Arkansas, Missouri, and Santa Fe before settling in Tucson—with those of a Chihuahua-born aristocrat who had gone to Independence, Missouri, to learn English and American business. Tully served twice as mayor of Tucson, four years as territorial treasurer, and was a strong supporter of public education. Ochoa also served as mayor of Tucson, and while a member of the territorial legislature introduced Arizona's first public-education bill—and then donated land for Tucson's school and served as president of the board of education. On the debit side, Tully and Ochoa were accused of being part of a "Tucson Ring" that won lucrative government contracts.

Or there was Mark Aldrich, proprietor of the first permanent store in Tucson, and the first American to serve in the old Mexican office of alcalde. He was a member of the territorial legislature and president of the territorial council. Formerly from Illinois, he was not in a position to marry in Tucson, for he had left a wife and children behind him when he departed for the southwest, but that did not prevent him from living with a Hispano girl, having a child by her, and being accepted in Tucson society.[45]

After 1880 this harmonious association lessened. The railroad had come, bringing with it many more Anglos and easy access to supplies from the main part of the United States. Trade via Sonora and through Spanish-speaking merchants dwindled, while simultaneously Tucson lost its small-town feeling of being an isolated outpost that was united by an omnipresent fear of Apache attack. Prominent Spanish-surnamed citizens found that they were no longer invited to be guests at parties given by well-to-do Anglos who had Anglo wives. To check this slippage, the upper-class Hispanos formed, in 1894, the Alianza Hispano-Americana, which proved to be the inspiration for many similar self-help groups formed by Hispano business and professional men in southwestern cities to lobby for recognition.[46]

Meantime the poorer class, the mestizos of Tucson birth and the comparable immigrants from Sonora, were faring better in Tucson than they would have in, say, Los Angeles, even though wages were lower in Tucson. Spanish-speaking people were in the majority in Tucson until the early 1880s, which was well after they had lost the battle of numbers in Los Angeles. In Tucson a smaller percentage were laborers and there was a better chance to be self-employed. Job opportunities were better and land was cheaper. The percentage of Spanish-speaking men in white-collar jobs was higher.[47]

Over the territory as a whole, the status of the Spanish-speaking was not that good. A directory published in 1881 lists numerous Spanish-surnamed people as running small stores and shops, but the larger businesses and professional offices outside Tucson were dominated by Anglo-Europeans.[48] A large part of Arizona's population was composed of Mexican immigrants and the children of immigrants, few of whom had highly developed skills or much education. Employment as laborers was their principal opportunity. In the new copper and silver mines they might get low-paying surface jobs, but it was common for the "white" miners and their unions to refuse to permit either Mexican or Chinese underground.[49]

In the rural parts of the territory similar prejudice was likely to appear. Texan cowboys, who moved into Arizona late in the century, were scornful and arrogant toward vaqueros of Mexican descent.[50] In the Anglo-founded farm town and supply center of Phoenix, when "Mexicans" became numerous, animosities increased. In 1877 a burst of violence involving two Anglos and a very drunken Mexican led not only to vigilante hangings of the two Anglos and the killing of the Mexican but also caused crowds representing the two ethnic groups to assemble in tense confrontation until dispersed by armed Anglo vigilantes. By happy contrast, the new little farm town of Florence attracted a population that was about evenly divided between Anglos and Hispanos, and there a degree of real harmony seems to have prevailed.[51]

*   *   *   *   *

No ethnic or national minority has had a history that is so intractable—so ill-suited to generalization—as the Chinese; yet few have occupied so conspicuous a place in western history. The Chinese were by no means the largest minority in the west. Even at their peak in the 1870s and 1880s, they can't have numbered much over 120,000,[52] which was several times less than the total of native-born and immigrant Spanish-speaking people at that time. Unlike the Hispano, the story of the Chinese does not involve a state-by-state, territory-by-territory displacing of established cultures and imposing of new economic and political orders.

Instead, at a time when they constituted a remarkably versatile and effective work force in a west that was crying for manpower, and at a time when they were famous for being unobtrusive and withdrawn from white society, the Chinese were hit by the most violent assaults ever launched against an immigrant stock. As a distinguished historian of immigration has remarked:

No variety of anti-European sentiment has ever approached the violent extremes to which anti-Chinese agitation went in the 1870s and 1880s. Lynchings, boycotts, and mass expulsions still harassed the Chinese after the federal government yielded to the clamor for their exclusion in 1882.[53]

Why so extreme a reaction? Was it unfair economic competition, as so frequently alleged;[54] or nativism—antiforeignism—carried to the ultimate against a people who were peculiarly unable to defend themselves, since they were not permitted to testify against white people;[55] or was it racism, aroused by a contemptuous conviction that the Chinese were a strange and backward race? Was the antagonism caused by the belief that the Chinese were essentially slaves— that is, "coolies"? Was it, as one major study has concluded, caused by the belief that the Chinese were transient fortune seekers who sought only to make money and return home, and in the meantime lived in self-contained enclaves without seeking assimilation into American culture?[56] Or, as another major study has claimed, was there already an established American distrust and dislike of China and the Chinese, based upon our limited contacts through merchants, missionaries, and diplomats?[57] Was the anti-Chinese agitation largely a device for uniting the embryonic western labor movements?[58] Or for diverting hostility from other immigrants, particularly that favorite eastern target, the Irish? How did Chinese immigration grow from a Californian issue to one that aroused the whole west, and finally to a national concern that caused Congress and the President to bludgeon their way past imperial China's diplomats and enact our first restrictive immigration statutes? And, finally, why did the most murderous attacks on the Chinese occur *after* Congress had passed the Exclusion Act of 1882?[59]

The trouble started soon after the Chinese first appeared in California during the gold rush. At that time some went no farther than San Francisco, where job opportunities were abundant. The leaders in San Francisco were what a British observer termed "the swell Chinamen," meaning the merchant class, who went about magnificently clad in "sky-blue or purple figured silk jackets, and tight yellow satin continuations, black satin shoes . . . and a fan in the hand, and a beautifully plaited glossy pigtail."[60]

The merchants and lesser Chinese created a distinct Chinese quarter, easily identified by its unintelligible signs, its restaurants, its stores that sold Chinese goods and foods, its laundries, theater, ill-lit gambling saloons and brothels, and "a peculiarly nasty smell" popularly attributed to the use of rats for food.[61] Sarcastically another observer alleged that Chinatown was "entirely occupied by these singular people, who industriously pursue the professions of clothes washing, restaurant keeping and swindling. Here a man may ask for and receive a fricasse of dog, cat, or rat, cooked in the best culinary style of Canton or Hong Kong."[62] Apparently, even at that early date Chinatown was to outsiders a place that was bizarre, mysterious, and not to be trusted. But to Chinese it was the head-quarters of Chinese America, and would remain so throughout the century.

Most of the early Chinese moved right on through San Francisco to the mines. As they passed through Sacramento the local newspaper said of the newcomers that "their orderly and industrious habits make them a very desirable class of immigrants."[63] Yet everything about them was strikingly distinctive. Not only did they have slant eyes, pigtails, and yellow skin, but they also wore big basket hats and flopping blue clothes, and carried a jumble of curious equipment and supplies on bamboo poles, while all the while they kept up a "gabbling and chattering" in "their horrid jargon," which produced "a noise like that of a flock of geese."[64] There was no chance that a nativist-minded or racist-minded American would fail to notice them.

Up in the mines they faced the hostility of Americans, who felt no compunctions about "driving off the poor Chinese, the Mexicans and the chilenos from their coveted claims," on the theory that "none but Americans have a right to work the gold mines."[65] But so long as they were content unprotestingly to work the less profitable diggings, or to buy supposedly worked-out claims from discouraged whites, the Chinese were often left alone. They must have done well, for as early as February 1852 a San Francisco newspaper was reporting a reverse flow of successful Chinese back through the city, en route home to China. "By their industry, frugality, and strict attention to business" they had "all made money."[66] Thereafter, for the next two decades, several thousand Chinese departed from the port of San Francisco every year, and in the 1870s and 1880s the annual exodus doubled.[67] But their very success and return to China seemed to justify the protest that they came to America only to make money, and while here lived a self-contained existence that included patronizing only Chinese merchants, thus contributing nothing to the American economy.

Perhaps the localized hostility to this most unique group of gold seekers was fated to grow anyway, for in 1852 the number of Chinese in California surpassed twenty thousand and perhaps reached twenty-five thousand, which would be about 10 percent of the state's whole population; but the growth of antagonism toward them was accelerated immensely by an enterprising state senator

who, impressed by the usefulness of Chinese workers, introduced
a bill to legalize and make possible the enforcement of contracts by
which Chinese laborers could sell their services for a period of
years, on the pattern of the nefarious "coolie trade" that had supplied semi-slave Chinese labor to Southeast Asia, Cuba, and Peru.
Out of this obscure political misjudgment by a senator who has long
been forgotten burst an uproar that produced not only widespread
and enduring opposition to the Chinese, but also most of the stock
arguments that were to be used against them for the rest of the
century.[68]

Newspapers were suddenly aroused, protesting miners held
meetings in the Sierra camps, and rival politicians thundered their
views. The politically sensitive governor declared that he was
"deeply impressed" by the need "to check this tide of Asiatic immigration."[69] The state legislature's committee on mines *"Resolved,*
that the importation by foreign capitalists of immense numbers of
Asiatic serfs, and Mexican and South American peons, is daily
becoming more alarming."[70]

Were the Chinese "serfs" or "coolies"? Were they like debt-
bonded peons in Old or New Mexico? Poverty forced most of them
to borrow their passage money. Usually this meant that a merchant
or broker advanced the necessary funds, the loan to serve as a kind
of indenture until repaid out of the emigrant's earnings in America.
But in default of adequate policing of the system, there probably
were times when illiterate and inexperienced emigrants were shang-
haied into true "coolie" or contract status.[71] A recent writer with
unusual access to Chinese sources argues that if they came on the
usual credit-ticket basis, the Chinese were essentially free agents.[72]

Once in this bewildering land, the newly arrived fell under the
control of the San Francisco Chinese merchants, to whom the loan
had been assigned and who would act as labor contractors in sending out gangs to work. The merchants were organized as the powerful Six Companies, originally only four, that collectively dominated
Chinatown and most of the Chinese. Formed on a basis that reflected village, clan, and family ties back in South China, the Six
Companies and their Chinatown were the continuing link between
the ancient civilization these peasants and laborers had left and the
confusion, opportunities, and dangers of life in western America.
To Chinatown the tired worker would return periodically, to find

congeniality among his own kind, safe from white harassment, and to indulge in escapism in the gambling halls, opium dens, and brothels. More benevolently, the Six Companies served as the agency that would look after individuals when they were sick, in trouble, or needed legal help, and would ship their remains back to China if they died. To protect their own interests, the Six Companies, in collusion with the shipping companies, saw to it that no Chinese was allowed to buy a return passage to China until he had paid his debts. The Six Companies, rather than the American authorities and courts, really set the rules by which Chinese immigrants lived.[73]

The combination of the credit-ticket indenture and the control exercised by the Six Companies caused many Americans to assume that the Chinese were in fact true "coolies," and the term "coolie" passed into political oratory as a synonym for Chinese. That impression was strengthened by what white miners saw. Writing his recollections of mining in 1857 in the backwoods county of Siskiyou, California, Herman Francis Reinhart said of a company of Chinese near him, "They were sort of bound out to superiors, who had charge of them" and who "collected all their earnings until they had reimbursed themselfs [sic]," after which the individuals "were at liberty to work for themselfs."[74]

The practice of organizing the Chinese into gangs, under a designated headman who handled all business details, including relations with white employers, was transferred to many other fields when California and the west diversified their economy. The most famous example was the building of the Central Pacific Railroad. Where the Union Pacific, advancing from the east, turned to Irishmen for a large part of their grading, tracklaying and bridge-building crews, the Central Pacific, starting from Sacramento, used Chinese, after a futile attempt to recruit white laborers who would stay on the job instead of quitting to try the mines as soon as they had earned a little money. Charles Crocker of that railroad testified before a congressional committee that he never dealt directly with the Six Companies, but rather commissioned white labor brokers in San Francisco to find workers. Apparently the Central Pacific's agents at first were able to hire Chinese from the placer mines and Chinatown, but later recruited directly in China, advancing the passage money. The labor brokers then organized the Chinese into gangs, with one

worker in each gang serving as bookkeeper and comparing his record every night with the tallies kept by the construction company's
white foremen. In theory, by having Chinese do the pick-and-shovel
work, whites were promoted to supervisory and skilled jobs.[75]

Other Californians, when seeking Chinese to reclaim swamplands
(an unhealthy, unattractive job) or do farm work, said they contracted with Chinese headmen, or with local Chinese storekeepers,
or through the good offices of Chinese who were already in their
employ.[76] In either case, it was both more convenient and more
economical for the employer to get his entire work force by hiring
a single disciplined gang that would complete its contract, without
labor turnover and usually at lower cost than where whites were
employed. Often the saving was the readiness of the Chinese to
provide their own meals and tolerate primitive lodgings.

While the majority continued to huddle together in California
and especially in San Francisco—according to the census of 1880,
of 105,000 Chinese in the United States, 75,000 were in California
and 21,000 of those in San Francisco—thousands followed the
whites to the new mining frontiers of the Rockies and Great Basin,
where they not only engaged in placer mining when the whites
would permit but also served as cooks at "hard-rock" mines and ran
their own restaurants and laundries. Because of strong white opposition and because Chinese miners had a reputation for quitting
immediately if there was any delay in their being paid, very few
mines hired Chinese for work underground, but "throughout the
West, Chinese labor is employed for certain inferior purposes, such
as dumping cars, surface excavations, etc."[77]

They were especially numerous in Idaho, Nevada, Oregon, and
Montana in 1870. Indeed, they formed more than a quarter of
Idaho's population and nearly 10 percent of Montana's. With the
decline of the placers, by 1880 their numbers had decreased somewhat in Idaho and Montana but had increased in Washington, Oregon, Wyoming, and Colorado, and by 1890 they were to be found
at least in small numbers all over the west.

Within California, agriculture proved to be the chief channel for
upward mobility. Chinese operated at every level: as farm laborers
and harvest gangs, as farm cooks, as common laborers on construction projects required by agriculture, as tenant farmers or sharecroppers, as market gardeners, fruit and vegetable peddlers, com-

mission merchants, and ultimately as owner-operators who hired their own crews of Chinese. For most, despite the success of some entrepreneurs, agriculture meant a permanent turning to wage labor and dependence on the white economy for jobs.[78]

To the white agriculturist, on the other hand, "Chinese labor was indispensable,"[79] for the white rural labor supply was scant and irregular, and filled with transients who did not like either the poor living conditions on farms or the highly seasonal work cycle which left long periods of unemployment. The newspapers often preached that the urban unemployed should seek jobs in the country, but this simply aroused the bitter reply that white men would not take farm jobs at "Chinamen's wages" and under "Chinamen's living conditions."[80]

After being occupied during the 1850s, 1860s, and early 1870s in the placers and on major construction projects, many Chinese turned toward the cities and new industries. San Francisco was the mecca for most, for it was both the industrial capital of the Pacific Coast and the headquarters for the Chinese. The timing was unfortunate, for it brought the Chinese into conflict with the struggling labor movement that had been trying to organize itself in San Francisco during the preceding two decades, and it did so at a time when unemployment and threats to the traditionally high level of western wages made white workers angrily sensitive to the dangers of Chinese competition. A very high percentage of those workers were themselves immigrants, especially Irish and Germans—but they were white immigrants.

Californians had expected that completion of the Central Pacific Railroad in 1869 would lift the state to new heights of prosperity; instead, the railroad brought middle western and eastern finished goods that easily undercut the prices asked for the products of California's high-cost, high-wage manufactories, while at the same time cheaper and easier transportation brought in thousands of workers and small farmers who, having neither the capital nor knowledge to set themselves up in business or agriculture, had no choice save to enter the already overcrowded San Francisco wage-labor pool.[81] The railroad itself intensified the crisis by laying off thousands of Chinese and whites formerly employed on construction.[82] From being a land of labor scarcity and high pay, California now became a discouraging place for workmen. These were the years that inspired Henry George's pessimistic reflections that culminated in his classic book *Progress and Poverty*.

Labor had long viewed the Chinese with distrust, and the city's experience with vulnerable industries suggested that the distrust was justified. In the San Francisco cigar-making trade, a "protective union," or guild, had been formed as far back as 1859 to protest the increasing hiring of Chinese in that field and to boycott Chinese-made goods. Save for stirring up more enmity toward the Chinese, little was accomplished, for throughout the 1860s both the absolute number and the percentage of Chinese employed kept increasing, until by 1870 the industry was staffed primarily by them; twenty-eight hundred in number, the Chinese were setting themselves up as proprietors of their own firms. In similar fashion the boot and shoe workers of San Francisco organized themselves as a lodge of the national order of the Knights of St. Crispin. In 1867 they had lost a violent strike against wage reductions attributed to Chinese competition. Now, in 1869 and under the leadership of the Knights, they struck once more and were defeated again.[83]

Finding themselves weak in labor organizations, workers took to founding "Anti-Coolie Clubs" and establishing boycotts. They soon discovered that while differences between trades and differences in philosophy and political party allegiances made it difficult to secure comprehensive action through unions, there was one cause upon which all could unite: "anti-coolieism." Further, they found that they could win allies from the employer class. In industries that did not require a large initial investment, the small proprietors discovered that Chinese who had learned the trade through working for whites were now copying the example of the Chinese cigar makers by setting up small manufactories to compete with whites.[84]

By 1870 urban labor was bitter toward the Chinese, and each crusade, such as that for the eight-hour day, included an accompanying denunciation of Chinese competition. As San Francisco was already the industrial leader, so it now became the center of labor activity for the whole Pacific Coast and some of the inland regions. What was said and done in San Francisco had reverberations elsewhere. Thus the propaganda value was considerable when even in 1870, when the trade unions were losing power because of the widespread unemployment and the employers' fight to get rid of the eight-hour day, the Knights of St. Crispin were able to organize an anti-Chinese meeting to which seventeen unions sent representatives, and to follow this with a mass meeting of ten thousand people.[85]

Agitation continued through the 1870s. If state or local action could have solved the problem, it would have been settled long before, for beginning in the 1850s California had passed every kind of state and municipal law or ordinance to harass the Chinese and impede further immigration, but the courts had rejected nearly all on constitutional grounds.

Ultimately what had been primarily a Californian issue moved onto the national political stage in 1876. In that year both the Republican and Democratic parties put an anti-Chinese plank into their platforms, and Congress appointed a commission to come to California to investigate the problem. The sudden readiness to recognize the anti-Chinese movement nationally reflected the close balance between the two parties. To seem to favor continued Chinese immigration would be to lose at least California's electoral vote and probably that of other western states.

A year later agitation broke out at meetings held on the famous "sand-lots" (vacant lots) of San Francisco, and the anti-Chinese faction found a leader in a self-educated, demagogic Irish drayman, Denis Kearney, who for the next two years kept the city in nervous anxiety as he became more and more radical in speeches that attacked both capital and the Chinese that capital employed. San Francisco had a potentially dangerous combination of working men who felt alienated from their employers, unemployed men, and drifters and hoodlums. The discontented elements were well aware of the suffering that was being caused contemporaneously in the east by the severe depression that had started in 1873, and they had been stirred by news of the spontaneous nationwide popular uprising inspired by the great railroad strike of 1877 and the labor warfare at Pittsburgh.

At a meeting intended to express sympathy for the eastern workers, an uninvited anti-coolie club and a fringe of hoodlums turned the assemblage into a riot that assaulted Chinese laundries and the Chinese Methodist Mission. When the police had extreme difficulty restoring order, the nervous merchants and propertied men organized a Committee of Safety under the leadership of the old Vigilance Committee hero of 1856, William T. Coleman. Four thousand men were enrolled and equipped with pickhandles as weapons. The Federal government was asked for help and made available weapons, soldiers, marines, and sailors, and sent warships to positions off the waterfront.

When a mob burned more Chinese laundries and tried to burn the docks of the Pacific Mail Steamship Company, which was blamed for having brought so many of the Chinese to America, the police and "pick-handle brigade" beat them into retreat, but at the cost of creating the impression that the propertied classes were united against the poor, the unemployed, and the working men. Class struggle was thus united with Kearney's slogan, "The Chinese must go!"[86]

Kearney's agitation carried over into the California Constitutional Convention of 1879, which wrote a new state constitution filled with such extreme anti-Chinese provisions that most were thrown out when cases involving them reached the courts. Meantime by 1879 Congress had reached the point where it was ready to act. When its first bill was vetoed by President Hayes, outraged Californians held a statewide referendum on the issue and recorded an overwhelming vote of 154,683 in favor of totally excluding Chinese, as opposed to 883 against. At stake was the awkward diplomatic consideration that in 1868 the United States had granted most-favored-nation status to China in the Burlingame Treaty. A new diplomatic mission managed to extract a new treaty from China in 1880. Using this as justification, Congress passed the nation's first piece of restrictive immigration legislation, the Exclusion Act of 1882, which was renewed in 1892 and extended indefinitely in 1902.

That should have settled the matter, for all save the Chinese had got what they wanted, but in fact some of the worst violence of the whole crusade broke out after the statute of 1882 had been passed, and it broke out in new places, notably in the big northwest corner of America, where the feeling was so intense that even the judges of the highest courts began to hand down decisions that did less than justice to the Chinese.[87] Perhaps the last-minute crowding in of fifty thousand Chinese in 1881 and 1882, in an attempt to beat the deadline, had something to do with the new violence, but in most cases there were special local circumstances that precipitated and thereafter helped shape events. Further, across the nation the middle 1880s, like the 1870s, were a time of anarchic relations between capital and labor, with Chicago's tragic Haymarket riot of 1886 perhaps the most famous symbol. Talk of class warfare and the evils of "capital" and "monopoly" were common in both east and west.

At Rock Springs, Wyoming Territory, in 1885 white coal miners, who seem "to have been almost all aliens," attacked Chinese coal miners and the local Chinatown with Winchester rifles and murdered twenty-eight of the Chinese. The Union Pacific Railroad, owners of the coal mines, had brought in Chinese a decade earlier as strikebreakers. White miners had then sought the help and leadership of a national union, the Knights of Labor, which was expanding rapidly in the 1880s. In the fight that followed, race hatred seems to have been joined to hatred of the Union Pacific, the local symbol of monopoly and capital.[88]

In Tacoma and Seattle an economic depression existed in 1885–1886, with resulting unemployment that was the worse because the completion of the Northern Pacific Railroad in 1883 and the Canadian Pacific in 1885 had cost thousands of Chinese their jobs. In Tacoma anti-Chinese feeling was strong, and the help of the Knights of Labor was sought. Repeated popular protest meetings had made it clear that the Chinese must indeed go, and the propertied element and the ministers from the local churches tried merely to arrange for their expulsion without violence; an anti-Chinese group, however, forced the Chinese out of their homes and business places, marched them off in a cold rain, and burned their quarters behind them.[89]

In Seattle "class cleavages" were as apparent as anti-Chinese feeling. "Monopolies" were blamed for bringing the Chinese to the Pacific Northwest. As in Tacoma, the propertied elements met to arrange an expulsion that would be without violence, and a newly formed labor organization promptly denounced them as "capitalists." A sheriff's "home guard," militia, and intervention of Federal troops were all arranged for; ultimately the Knights of Labor tried to exercise a restraining influence, but the anti-Chinese leaders forced as many Chinese to flee as the only available coastal steamer could carry, leaving behind two hundred more who crouched helplessly within a hollow square of militiamen while the latter opened fire on the rioters.[90]

At Eureka, far up on California's northern lumber coast, all Chinese were ordered out of Humboldt County in 1885 on a day's notice, and at the Sierra Nevada lumber town of Truckee, employers were pressured into firing their Chinese workers. With Tacoma, Seattle, Eureka, and Truckee as precedents, a wave of violence, pressure, and hostile legislation swept the Pacific Coast from Puget Sound to southern California, and extended even up into Alaska, where the Chinese lasted only through 1885–1886 before being expelled. Colorado had already passed through its anti-Chinese hysteria, with outbursts against hiring Chinese miners in 1874, Leadville (the leading mining town) boasting in 1879 that no Chinese were allowed in town, and Denver suffering a disastrous riot in 1880 in which the local Chinatown was burned to the ground and one Chinese killed. In Idaho, vigilantes hanged five Chinese in 1885, and in 1886 an anti-Chinese meeting in Boise drew representatives from mining camps throughout the territory as they prepared to force all Chinese to leave.[91]

Many of the Chinese so displaced sailed home to China; others sought safety in San Francisco's Chinatown. The durability of the latter was remarkable. The Chinese merchants had built political and economic alliances with influential whites, they had hired their own "special" police force of white men, the residents had apparently stockpiled weapons, and the sheer number of human beings jammed into that badly overcrowded and unsanitary firetrap made it unlikely that a mob would have the courage to rush, pillage, or burn Chinatown.[92]

So the story ends, in greater violence and prejudice than when it began in the mining camps of the 1850s. Caught between the rival white forces of labor and capital, rich and poor, in a time of anarchic industrial relations, the Chinese were easy victims—because of their differentness, because after the early mining days they let themselves be used as strikebreakers and wage cutters, because they were helpless to fight back, and because racism so easily appeals to man's worst instincts.

CHAPTER 8

Self-Proclaimed "Peculiar People"

I F THE treatment of nonwhite minorities seems profoundly disturbing, what was the fate of minorities that were white but eccentric? The story of the Mormons is illustrative. Basically they were an old-fashioned, unsophisticated American rural people, who were joined by British and European immigrants of working-class and shopkeeper status, but they stood apart from the majority of Americans, partly by their own decision, partly by their attitude of self-conscious rectitude, partly because the majority disliked and persecuted them. While they are of course best remembered for their practice of polygamy—which struck at that most central of American institutions, the family—polygamy would not have been possible if the Mormons had not been creating a very special, very distinctive society. Social scientists have long classified the Mormons as a separate "cultural group." Some scholars have concluded that at their peak in distinctiveness in the nineteenth century the Mormons came to constitute "almost a separate nationality," or a "near-nation."[1]

What made possible so extensive a deviation from the American norm? Of the major influences, the most important was the creation during Joseph Smith's lifetime of a strong sense of group identity, purpose, and uniqueness, based upon sharing a dramatically new faith. Mormonism, as Smith introduced it from 1830 onward, was more than just another Protestant splinter belief. It was founded upon two types of modern revelation: upon an angel's disclosure to Smith of the existence of a hitherto unknown sacred book comparable to the Bible, and upon direct communications from God to his modern "prophets, seers, and revelators," who were Smith and his successors as heads of the Mormon church. To accept the faith, one had to believe literally, unquestioningly in the authenticity of the Book of Mormon and the word of God as revealed to Joseph Smith. The God whom Smith presented to his followers was unlike the traditional deity of Christian religions. He was an almost human figure, a self-improved Being whose progress toward perfectness mortals could hope to imitate. A Mormon maxim runs, "As man is, God once was; as God is, man may become."[2]

By taking the enormous intellectual and emotional step of committing oneself to this body of belief, the nineteenth-century convert to Mormonism cut himself or herself off from the great majority and withdrew into a small world of like believers. In their own eyes the Mormons became a "chosen people," the elect of God, the only true believers, or, as they termed themselves proudly, a "peculiar people." When their rough, jeering rural neighbors harassed them, the persecution hardened the Mormons in their religious belief and in their loyalty to one another. Nothing so unites a group as the sense of standing together against a hostile world. And the non-Mormon world was exceedingly hostile. By threats, riots, and killings the Mormons were driven from their successive homes in New York, Ohio, Missouri, and Illinois before they set forth for the Great Basin in the hope that in that remote and arid land they would be left in peace. Their prophet, Joseph Smith, was murdered by Illinois militiamen and thus became a sainted martyr in his people's eyes.

Second only in importance was the creation by Joseph Smith of an elaborate theocracy that Brigham Young inherited, matured, and used as an omnipresent, omniscient instrument for ruling every aspect of his people's lives, religious and secular. Young was one of the remarkable men of his generation. Like Smith the son of an unsuccessful small farmer of New England stock, Young had been a painter, glazier, and carpenter until the leaders of the new church recognized his unusual combination of common sense, fervency in defense of the faith, and capacity for command. A pragmatist with an extraordinary mastery of details, Young could also think in comprehensive terms and could make and enforce decisions.

A kindly father to his numerous wives, children, and foster children, Young was a "father figure" and benevolent despot to thousands of Mormons who revered, feared, and obeyed him. Although he was a harsh disciplinarian, his "people were yet unbelievably loyal to him."[3] His very large surviving correspondence shows that his followers felt free to solicit the great man's advice on even the smallest details of household life. On his frequent journeys of inspection in Utah he showed an astonishing knowledge about what was happening in each little town. To a hard-working rural Mormon it meant everything that so great a person knew that Sister Eliza had had an unusually hard time after the birth of her sixth child, or that Brother Isaiah had been the principal carpenter in rebuilding the local church after it had suffered storm damage.

"Brother Brigham's" visits to local communities were rustic versions of a royal progress. The villagers put on their best clothes, buildings were cleaned and decorated, the streets were strewn with flowers, the brass band played, and the schoolchildren sang:

> Come join the army, the army of our Lord,
> Brigham is our leader, we'll rally at his word.
> Sharp will be the conflict with the powers of sin,
> But with such a leader we are sure to win.[4]

Young's was a contradictory personality. While he could be compassionate, he could also be ruthless, demanding, and crude. His public utterances, particularly his sermons, could be coarse and marked by the provincialisms of his Vermont boyhood and New York young manhood. But of his ability to head and mold the elaborate theocratic organization that he inherited from Smith, there could be no question. He proved that by the almost military skill with which he organized and transported thousands of Saints across the plains from the Missouri frontier to Utah in 1847 and subsequent years. He proved it again by his uncompromising insistence that as head of the church he must not be "trammeled" as "the principal spokesman for God on earth."[5]

In Utah, for the thirty years from 1847 until his death in 1877, Young was the undisputed leader, but he made constant use of a corps of experienced lieutenants. Young was assisted by two counselors, who with Young constituted the very influential "First Presidency of the Church." Nominally at least, Young was elected to his high office by the Council or Quorum of the Twelve Apostles, who were leading Mormons.

Below the central officials were the "stakes," which were essentially regional administrative units responsible for seeing that all went well in the basic unit of the church, which was the "ward," roughly equivalent to a parish or congregation. In charge of each ward was a "bishop," who was an influential layman engaged in a normal lay occupation—most commonly farming—while somehow finding time to lead his flock in prayer, in building public works, in allocating land and water, in dealing with local Indians, and in settling disputes that developed between the faithful.

There was no professional priesthood in Mormonism; every adult male of good character could qualify as a priest, and any adult male whose talents called him to the attention of the hierarchy might be appointed to any office, religious or secular. As a gesture toward democracy, all appointments were subject to a "sustaining vote," which meant popular concurrence by voice vote in open meeting. In a society as closely disciplined as the Mormons, failure to win concurrence was very unusual. Women and blacks were not permitted to enter the priesthood, but women were expected to bear numerous children, keep house, labor on the farm, do such chores as the washing, making soap and candles, and putting up preserved fruits, and still find strength to serve in the church's philanthropic efforts. Blacks were exceedingly few in number.

United by their faith, leadership, and theocracy, the Mormons found it easy to function with a degree of cooperation rare in the American west. They were true communitarians, by instinct and necessity. Since almost all were poor in the beginning, and lacking in such luxuries as heavy equipment and trained engineers, they built their Great Basin towns, irrigation systems, roads, and bridges by pooling their labor, work animals, wagons, plows, and tools under the direction of their bishops and in accordance with Young's commands and the church's traditions.

This means that in an age in which most of the west was being developed on an extravagantly uncontrolled basis—true laissez-faire economics—the Mormons expected their church to "play the central role in erecting and maintaining an improved economic system for its members."[6]

From Joseph Smith's day onward they had believed in planned communities, as the pattern for Salt Lake City showed, and the New England background of their earliest members had given them an appreciation of the values of compact settlements in which neighbors could live close to one another and to the church, school, and meeting hall. Accordingly, when towns were laid out in the Great Basin, the residences were within the town and on house lots big enough to permit kitchen gardens, fruit trees, and a milk cow. Out beyond the residential district were the farming lands, and still farther out a common pasture. In terms of intangible values, few western communities save for the Spanish-American villages in New Mexico and southern Colorado could rival the Mormons in neighborliness.[7]

Since farming, of necessity, was irrigated and little more than subsistence, individual landholdings were small enough to permit this pattern. Had Congress been less dilatory or less angered by the Mormons and polygamy, the Federal land laws might have been a serious obstacle to carrying out the standard Mormon scheme of settlement, but in fact until 1869 titles under the Federal laws could not be obtained. Brigham Young was thus left free to announce to his people, soon after the founding of Salt Lake City, that lands would not be sold but rather would be apportioned in relatively small units, and that water (and also timber and mineral resources) would be regarded as belonging to "all the people"—the community—rather than to private owners. The old common-law, humid-land doctrine of riparian rights, which stipulated that an owner of land along a stream was entitled to have the water continue to flow past him undiminished in quantity and quality by upstream neighbors, was simply abrogated in practice. Thus the Mormons magnificently dismissed centuries of Anglo-Saxon legal precedent and decades of Federal land legislation.

The earliest Mormon settlements were in the slender longitudinal valleys that lie along the base of the Wasatch Mountains, where the rainfall was rarely more than twelve to fifteen inches per year. In the mountains above, precipitation might be as much as forty inches, much of it in the form of snow, and many small streams brought the water down through steep canyons as the snow melted.

For the task of damming the streams and building lines of irrigating canals and ditches, the Mormons had no precedents. Among English-speaking people irrigation had not been a necessity. The Mormons met the challenge in their accustomed way. Under the leadership of their bishop they chose a committee to construct an irrigating system, the prospective users contributed their labor, teams, and tools, and when all was completed, the construction committee was released from its responsibility and a water-master was elected to control the distribution of water. Annual maintenance was done by contributed community labor. The similarity to the practice in Spanish-American villages is striking.[8]

As a pioneer student of irrigation has remarked, in this informal fashion thousands of miles of canals were built without incurring any debts or floating any bonds, although at times the church contributed money to help completion.[9] This does not mean the system was error free. Through lack of better materials the early dams were built of brush, logs, mud, and stones, which washed out almost annually, and through lack of experience in an arid land, the Mormons increased the alkalinity in the soil by watering too much. Modern engineers point out that by creating many small, inefficient irrigation systems, the Mormons preempted the whole of a water supply that could have been handled better by a few big systems—which the Mormons of the 1850s and 1860s could neither have financed nor engineered.

In litigation over water, a field that was a costly disaster in most of the west, the Mormons again were satisfied with simplicity. For decades most disputes over the use of water were settled quickly, quietly, and inexpensively through the mediation of church authorities, and when appeal was taken to the civil courts, it was "often for the purpose of giving the force of a court decree to an agreement reached through the influence of the church."[10]

A similar reliance upon cohesiveness under church leadership carried the Mormons safely through what could have been a very bad land-title crisis. When the completion of the Pacific railroad caused Congress finally to extend the Federal land laws to Utah in 1869, most of the better land had long been occupied by the Mormons' characteristic villages and small farms, where boundaries did not coincide at all with Federal specifications. The church met the challenge partly by explaining to its followers how to file claims under the Preemption and Homestead laws (and then redistribute the land in accordance with existing occupancy) and partly by having Hosea Stout, a leading Mormon lawyer, steer occupants through legal procedures, especially when serious danger appeared, such as the threat of having railroad grants extended over Mormon lands.[11]

If this quiet, clannish handling of land and water problems seems sharply unlike the often violent litigiousness over "squatters' rights" in most western communities, then it may also suggest that one of the characteristics that distinguished Mormon villages from other western towns was their sedate and law-abiding atmosphere. As one contemporary observer remarked, "the gin mill and the gambling hall" simply were not present.[12]

The Mormon village, as thus developed in Utah, was the agency for settling not only the lands first occupied but also every bit of the scant irrigable soil that could be discovered. Wherever settlement was possible, loyal Mormons must preempt the land and water to cut off the danger of ungodly neighbors intruding later and to shut out permanently from Zion the evil influence of the increasingly urban and industrial world, which to the rural-minded Mormons was Babylon incarnate. The Mormons regarded themselves as people of destiny who must prepare the way for the return of Christ by building up His world. To the new Zion that they were creating in the southwest must come American and all the British and European converts that the Perpetual Emigrating Fund could transport. A historian of Mormon colonization has remarked: "The gathering to Zion, with its emphasis upon withdrawal from a corrupt world, was in practice antiurban and agrarian."[13]

To make this ambitious program possible Brigham Young would "call" a trusted lieutenant to head a colonizing project. It was a rare individual that had the courage to decline to serve, even if his family were sick and his home lacked a roof, as was the case when John D. Lee was "called."[14] With the prospective leader were "called" a nucleus of men with frontier experience and a representation of the essential vocations, such as a teacher, blacksmith, mason, carpenter, veteran farmer and livestock raiser. The bulk of the party might well consist of greenhorns, such as newly arrived Welsh or Danish immigrants. If, in accordance with Brigham Young's determination to make Utah self-sufficient, the settlement was to have a special purpose, such as starting a woolen mill or raising cotton or making iron, then men whose background was most nearly appropriate would be added.

It has been estimated that in Utah less than 5 percent of the land is suited to tillage. Yet most of the one hundred towns and villages established during the first decade were in Utah. During the second decade, when about 135 were founded, settlement in Utah continued but was accompanied by pioneering in southern Idaho, southern Nevada, and northern Arizona. In the third decade, with about 127 new villages, an especial effort was made in southwestern Utah and northern Arizona, because Brigham Young had a misplaced fixation about the possibilities of that difficult region. Young may also have underestimated the potentialities of southeastern Idaho, but before his death there were thirty-one Mormon settlements there.[15]

Genuine heroism and self-sacrifice were demanded by this expansion. The attempt broke some men and killed their wives, especially if they were immigrants unfamiliar with the tasks at hand.[16] A sociologist concluded: "The pioneers indubitably accomplished goals which seemed to lie beyond their power largely because of their willingness to pool their efforts in the common interest."[17]

In the late 1870s and the 1880s Mormon settlement in the Snake River valley of Idaho increased greatly, while new thrusts were made into the valleys of eastern and southern Arizona, southern Colorado, New Mexico, and Wyoming. In these new areas the Mormons found themselves no longer entering virgin territory but rather colliding with earlier comers, including non-Mormon ranchers and miners, Spanish-American villages, agricultural Indian villages, and Indian reservations. Even though Mormons could sometimes buy out their predecessors' land and water rights, nevertheless they found themselves returning to the situation they had hoped to leave forever when they departed from the Middle West in 1847: Mormon enclaves in the midst of non-Mormons.[18] Ultimately the Mormons also occupied farms in eastern Oregon and founded outposts in Canada and Mexico to which they could take polygamous families. No other single group, religious or secular, played so important a role in colonizing the intermontane west.

But the very success of the "gathering to Zion" and the rapid engrossing of the land and water raised a major problem. As a historian of Scandinavian immigration once remarked, each arriving immigrant was "both an asset and a liability in Zion's hazardous economy—a liability as one more mouth to feed from resources always marginal, an asset as another squatter to secure Mormon title to the domain."[19] Even before Young's death it had become apparent that population pressure and land scarcity were putting a heavy strain on the hitherto so carefully organized pattern of settlement. Families were drifting off in less planned, more scattered fashion. Cooperation sometimes lessened as competition crept in. In a difficult region such as the Little Colorado River of eastern Arizona, where floods washed out the primitive dams and droughts seared the crops, some villages were abandoned entirely and others were kept alive only by repeated infusions of church-directed charity and reconstruction funds.[20] In some villages, such as Ephraim and Escalante, Utah, the physical environment caused livestock raising to displace agriculture as the main occupation.[21]

If the Mormons accomplished so much in a forbidding land, why were they targets for relentless attacks, from 1847 until well after 1890? Modern Mormon historians feel that four aspects of their culture aroused the recurrent wrath of the national majority. These were: the highly publicized, often luridly painted institution of polygamy ("plural marriage"); the domination of every aspect of life by a theocracy, which means a government by priests, headed in this instance by a priest who was president, prophet, and receiver of communications from God; the Mormons' practice of voting as a bloc in political elections and obeying their church leaders' guidance, to the exclusion of jealous non-Mormon politicans; and the Mormon drive for self-sufficiency and its concomitant, the exclusion of non-Mormon businessmen from as many economic transactions as possible.[22]

Antagonism aroused by these basic causes was increased by unnecessarily provocative rhetoric by Brigham Young and his fiery associates Heber Kimball and Jedediah Grant during the 1850s, and by angry intolerance felt by Protestant ministers who faced the Mormons' unshakable conviction that they had been set aside by God as keepers of the only true faith, which faith included polygamy.

Polygamy was justified to Mormons because when Joseph Smith asked the Lord why Old Testament leaders sometimes had numerous wives and concubines, the Lord answered with a revelation that sanctioned modern man's taking more than one wife. When Smith gradually disclosed "The Principle" of polygamy to his ruling coterie in the later 1830s and the 1840s, they were shocked, but recovered and began to practice "The Principle" in secrecy while denying it in public. No public announcement was made until 1852, when the Mormons were far off in Utah.[23]

While only a minority of Mormon households became polygamous, that minority was a very influential one. It included "all the central church leaders" and most of the bishops and stake presidents and their immediate counselors. A readiness to take more than one wife became almost a requirement for high office, for it was the ultimate test of a man's loyalty to the church's teachings; once caught in the net of plural wifedom, a believer was attached to the church by bonds not easily broken. Polygamy had the further very important significance of leading to extensive intermarriage between the well-established Mormon families that ruled the nineteenth-century church, thus creating a pattern of interlocking family dynasties that monopolized the closely intermingled religious, economic, and social concerns of Utah.[24]

Just how numerous polygamous families were is not yet definitely known. Modern research has shown that the church was incorrect in saying that at no time were more than 3 percent of the families polygamous; rather, at times the percentage was 15 to 20, within Utah, and still more recent case studies of a few individual towns and counties have disclosed some local percentages of 30.[25]

Polygamy was thus an institution that united the leadership of the church. It became the prerogative of the economically well situated, because a poor man was apt to find himself hard pressed to support even a single family. As the decades passed, a wide disparity developed between the top and bottom of what had been originally a relatively egalitarian society. Joseph Smith had dreams of a genuinely communitarian society, and in Utah Brigham Young vigorously sought to make a reality of his predecessor's hopes by successive efforts to build cooperative institutions, such as the ZCMI stores and whole towns that would be based on principles of sharing equally and using common facilities.[26]

There were limits to how much even Brigham Young could cajole his people. Perhaps his greatest success was the tithing system. Mormons were expected to pay a tenth of their income to a "tithing house" run by the bishop. Since cash was always in short supply, payment was commonly in produce, farm animals, building supplies, or labor. Despite constant exhortations to pay up in full, there was always some delinquency. In an economy that for years was based on barter, the tithing offices served the functions of church support, bank, investment capital, tax office, poor relief, emergency aid, and general redistributor of the Mormons' forced savings. By a system of credits, the local tithing offices were linked to the central office in Salt Lake City so that supplies could be made available where needed.[27]

To attack the monolithic power of the church in Utah was inherently troubling, for doing so meant that, despite our being a constitutional democracy, the nation would be negating the will of a large territorial majority and would be brushing aside the First Amendment's assurance that "Congress shall make no law respecting an establishment of religion, or prohibiting the free exercise thereof." Further, the ineffectiveness of the non-Mormon and apostate minority in Utah had made it evident that the Federal government alone lacked power sufficient for the task. As an anti-Mormon exposé remarked, if the Mormons were scattered over the nation, they would be too weak to be a challenge, but "collected into one Territory, and ruling there with almost absolute power, they present a painfully interesting problem."[28]

By contrast, during the 1880s Idaho, where about a quarter of the population was Mormon, and Arizona, where the percentage was perhaps 11, were able to cut down Mormon power by manipulating local politics so as to disfranchise Mormons and deprive them of constitutional rights in court. Idaho contrived a "test oath" that required a voter to swear that he neither practiced bigamy or polygamy nor belonged to an organization that advocated such practices. Arizona followed suit, and the United States Supreme Court upheld the Idaho statute. In Wyoming and Colorado a shrewd retreat from bloc voting and a readiness to maintain a low profile averted a comparable disaster.[29]

But Utah, predominantly Mormon, was a different story. There President Buchanan had inadvisedly sent in Regular Army troops to occupy Utah from 1857–1861, supposedly to install territorial officials appointed from Washington in place of the administration headed by Brigham Young, who was Federal governor of Utah from 1851–1857.[30] During the Civil War, Connor's Californians replaced the Regular Army. Mormons continued to monopolize the territorial legislature, the county and local governments, and juries, and gave original jurisdiction in civil and criminal cases to the probate courts, which they controlled.

Congress now took over with a succession of acts aimed nominally at polygamy, because that was the attention-catching issue upon which a horrified nation could unite, but aimed also at breaking the political and economic power of the church. In 1862 Congress passed the Morrill Act to ban polygamy in the territories, disincorporate the Mormon church, and prohibit churches in the territories from owning real estate worth more than fifty thousand dollars. When this act produced no results, Congress added the Poland Act of 1874, which gave exclusive criminal and civil jurisdiction to the United States district courts and abolished the Mormons' territorial marshal and attorney general in favor of the usual Federal marshal and district attorney.

With these new powers the Morrill Act went to the courts for testing and was upheld by the United States Supreme Court in 1879, on the ground that prohibiting the "practice" of polygamy was not an infringement upon "mere religious belief and opinions." But prosecution of polygamy cases lagged, and in 1882 a leading Republican, Senator George F. Edmunds of Vermont, persuaded Congress to amend the Morrill Act so as to punish polygamy or unlawful cohabitation with prison sentences and fines and with loss of the right to vote or hold office. Drastically, the act put a presidential commission (the "Utah Commission") in charge of territorial elections, in obvious imitation of Reconstruction in the South. In its first year the commission disfranchised more than twelve thousand Mormons by requiring a test oath of anyone seeking to vote. To the infinite relief of the Mormons, the Supreme Court disallowed the oath.[31]

But prosecution of polygamists, or "cohabs," as they were nicknamed, now went forward vigorously. Swarms of Federal marshals were recruited to arrest "cohabs," who "went underground," in ceaseless flight from one house or hiding place to another, when "spotters" warned of a marshal's approach. Mormons called this grim period "The Raid."

Still the Mormons refused to renounce polygamy and conform to American norms. Senator Edmunds tried again, this time aiming straight at the church's material and political power. The Edmunds-

Tucker Act of 1887 dissolved the church as a legal corporation, declared all but fifty thousand dollars of its perhaps $3 million worth of property escheated to the United States, and dissolved the Perpetual Emigrating Fund. A new test oath, requiring a pledge of obedience to the antipolygamy laws, was required of prospective voters, jurors, or officeholders. Most curious of all, the one area in which the Mormons had pioneered in regard to women's rights had been to grant them the franchise in 1870, in the well-founded belief that their wives, singular or plural, would vote with the rest of the Mormon community; this was now abolished.[32]

By 1890, perhaps twelve thousand had lost the right to vote, the leaders of the church, being polygamists, were in flight and unable to carry on the church's business effectively, much church property was in Federal hands, and the Supreme Court had upheld the confiscation; the Court had also indicated that it would be constitutional to disfranchise all Mormons, not just polygamists. As they watched their world crumbling about them, the leaders agonizingly debated what to do. All eyes turned toward their president, white-haired Wilford Woodruff, then in his eighties, a convert in 1833, a co-worker with Joseph Smith and Brigham Young, a man whose career had spanned the whole history of the church.

Earnestly and repeatedly the old man prayed to the Lord for guidance. In late September 1890, "in broken and contrite spirit," he announced, in a statement referred to ever since as "The Manifesto," that since "the court of last resort" had upheld the antipolygamy laws, he personally would "submit to those laws" and would use his "influence" to persuade others to "do likewise."[33]

While polygamy did not disappear, and many doubts remained to be resolved, the Manifesto nevertheless broke the Mormons loose from an unbearable pressure. The courts suddenly became lenient with polygamists, Presidents Harrison and Cleveland granted amnesties in 1893 and 1894, and Utah was admitted to statehood in 1896. The experience had taught the Mormons the unwisdom of too much bloc voting. The leaders now urged their followers to distribute themselves between the two national parties, so as to have friends in both big camps. As wealthy men, the leaders' natural allegiance was to the Republican party, as the guardian of property and business, but hitherto that party's harshness toward their faith had driven them away. With surprising quickness Mormons and Republicans now became political associates in Utah, Idaho, and Arizona.

With the church heavily in debt after the confiscations, and with their own conservative tendencies, the church leaders began to liquidate church property and to turn away from the "common ownership of property and classlessness" that had characterized Mormonism in its heroic age. In their desire to rejoin the nation, they emulated the economic elite of turn-of-the-century America. It was a strange outcome for a once radically experimental society.[34]

CHAPTER 9

Into the Pasturelands:
I. Cattlemen Occupy the Ranges

IN THE hopeful months after Appomattox, many a writer sat down at his desk to appraise the future that would open for his favorite economic interest, now that peace had come. Lewis F. Allen, of Black Rock, New York, was an example. A noted breeder of high-quality livestock and a prolific writer for agricultural journals, he was famous for his advocacy of Shorthorn cattle, although his enthusiasm extended also to Devon cattle, Southdown sheep, and Guernsey dairy stock.[1]

As he surveyed the prospect for beef cattle, he was excited by the potentialities of the distant lands west of the Missouri. "It is true," he acknowledged, "that hostile Indians and the buffalo may retard the settlement of those vast plains, but those obstacles will rapidly disappear before the grand march of civilized industry. The telegraph poles are already planted there; emigrant, passenger, and traffic [i.e., freight wagon] trains have taken permanent possession of the route over the plains; the great Pacific railway, tapping it on both sides, is making rapid progress in construction," and soon will be "reaching the innumerable mines, and the hundreds of towns and cities scattered among them."

Starting from a north-south line five hundred miles west of the Mississippi, he predicted, "the great plain thence to the Rocky Mountains will mostly be devoted to stock growing, as will also the great basin west to the Sierra Nevada. California will be devoted to mixed farming. . . . In time," he reasoned, "will these plains grow their herds, to be transported to the richer grain regions east and west for feeding [i.e., fattening] and consumption." The local population, he believed, will be "composed chiefly of herdsmen," while the miners will be the consumers.[2]

This was a remarkably perceptive prediction, complete even to such details as a future reliance on the grain belt. Allen added some comments on the cattle available for the forthcoming boom. There were, he said, two basic types of "unimproved" cattle in America: the so-called native cattle, which were the result of many generations of uncontrolled breeding between the stocks brought by English-speaking and North European settlers, and the "Spanish" or "Mexican" cattle that were descended from stock that the Spanish had gradually disseminated throughout the Caribbean, Mexico, Florida, New Mexico, Texas, and California.

Associated with the two distinctive strains of common cattle were two quite different cultural heritages. For generations most English-speaking settlers had regarded livestock as an adjunct to agriculture, although there had always been a minority who became specialists in grazing herds upon large tracts of unused land and driving them considerable distances to market. Among Spanish-speaking peoples, raising livestock on unfenced pastures and herding them on long seasonal drives had long been a major occupation. Along with the mission and presidio, the ranch, like the mine, had moved through northern Mexico into what is now the southwestern United States, and after the decline of the missions had become the prevailing institution, controlled by the upper class.

That was how Americans found it when they came drifting into Texas, New Mexico, Arizona, and California during the 1840s, 1850s, and 1860s. Presumably for the pragmatic reason that the system worked, the newcomers tended to accept most of what they found. The journalist John S. Hittell wrote an illuminating description that suggests the extent of Anglo-American acceptance of Hispanic ways. The time was 1860, a dozen years after the engulfing tide of the gold rush had swept over the small Spanish-speaking population; the place was unlikely, across the bay from the urban, modern, cosmopolitan bustle of San Francisco. Here was being held the annual cooperative spring *rodeo* (which at that time still meant a roundup, not an exhibition of cowboy skills), so that every ranchero for miles around could reclaim such of his cattle as had strayed onto someone else's grazing grounds. The basic rule was that since a calf would follow its mother, therefore an unbranded calf belonged to the owner of the mother's brand. Prominent ranchers with the title *juez del campo* (judge of the plain) presided and settled disputes.

Hittell guessed that between 200 and 250 rancheros and attendant vaqueros were present. It was a colorfully mixed group that included "picturesque [native] Californian figures, swarthy faced Mexicans, [and] thick-bearded Americans, [who were] mostly rough looking fellows, some from the San Joaquin, fifty miles off." He noted that "all were mounted on Californian saddles, with the accompaniments of Spanish bits, long spurs, leggings [i.e., chaps] *sudaderas* [bandana or scarf], *tapaderas* [stirrup cover], *reatas*, &c." With a remark that in cattle raising the old California persisted, Hittell concluded:

The native Californians have sold most of their land to the Americans, but the latter have adopted the pursuits of their predecessors, and prefer swinging the lasso to following the plow.[3]

If Hispanic livestock practices and personnel could survive that long in northern California, where replacement of the original population had been so massive and changes so comprehensive, then it becomes understandable why in thinly settled, less developed parts of the west, Hispanic influence could persist for decades. But the Hispanic was not the sole influence. It has already been suggested that mountain men and wayside ranchers inaugurated cattle raising on the plains and in the Rockies by building up herds based on tired-out stock acquired cheaply from westward-moving wagon trains bound for Oregon and California. Mormon settlers enlarged their herds and flocks in the same fashion. In the Pacific Northwest the earliest stock raising was started with cattle and sheep from California, although with an admixture of stock from across the plains and perhaps a few imported by sea. Subsequently so many settlers entered the Willamette Valley that by 1860 the thousands of immigrants coming overland had brought with them "perhaps tens of thousands of livestock."[4]

The livestock industry, then, had Anglo-American origins as well as Hispanic, but if the irritatingly incomplete census for 1860 is any indication, then the parts of the farther west that led in cattle and sheep by that date were all areas of original Hispanic settlement. In cattle, Texas had experienced during the 1850s such a "remarkable increase"[5] that by 1860 it was easily the leader not only of the western states and territories but also of the entire nation, with a huge total that probably exceeded 4.4 million head, of which nearly 800,000 were "milch or dairy cows" or "working oxen." California apparently had at least 1,234,000, including well over 200,000 "milch or dairy cows" and "working oxen," although when the stock growers of that state met in a convention, they generously estimated their horned cattle at 3 million.[6]

In New Mexico cattle had always been regarded as secondary to sheep and in 1860 were reported as being only one tenth as numerous. Josiah Gregg, in his classic *Commerce of the Prairies* (1844), declared, "Sheep may be reckoned the staple production of New Mexico, and the principle article of exportation."[7] Although by far the most important sheep country in the farther west in 1850, by 1860 New Mexico had yielded primacy to California, despite more than doubling its total. With more than 1,111,000 sheep, California ranked fifth in the nation in 1860, followed by Texas, whose true total must have been just over 1 million, and New Mexico, whose figure was probably just under that round sum. Reflecting the poor quality of western sheep and the tendency to raise a considerable percentage for mutton, the west did less well if measured in terms of wool produced. In 1860 California ranked sixth in the nation in pounds of wool, Texas was thirteenth, and New Mexico was well below that. The only other parts of the farther west where the census takers recorded significant numbers of cattle and sheep in 1860—Oregon, Utah, and Washington—reported totals that by comparison were small.[8]

Common to all these regions was the problem of markets for a perishable commodity like meat. That was why hide and tallow factories flourished on the Texas coast between the Mexican War and 1875.[9] New Mexico's great sheep owners had managed to get rich by driving tens of thousands of their small, scrawny *churro* sheep down into Mexico each year for sale as mutton in the mining camps and cities of the mother country.[10] When the California gold rush gave the west a market for meat, far-off Texas started thousands of cattle on the long, arid, dusty journey via southern New Mexico and Arizona, despite the grave Indian danger.[11] The grandees of the

New Mexican sheep ranches responded in similar fashion—and some famous Anglos like Kit Carson and Dick Wootton joined them. Probably six hundred thousand sheep were driven from the Rio Grande valley to California between 1849 and 1860, chiefly to be slaughtered for mutton, but partly to stock California ranches.[12] Oregon sent south as many cattle and sheep as it could spare.[13] From east of the Missouri drovers brought thousands of cattle and sheep to California, to sell for fattening and slaughter, or to stock new ranches that Anglo-American growers were establishing on the hitherto sparsely occupied lands of the central and northern interior valleys, where Hispanic settlement had been minimal. Here, despite the well-advertised uncertainty over land titles (caused by delay in adjudicating Spanish and Mexican grants), the more progressive Americans began using good breeding stock from the east or Britain to upgrade the "native" American and "Spanish" cattle, and the New Mexican churro sheep.[14]

Within California the native Californian rancheros and the Englishmen and Americans who had intermarried with them jubilantly responded to the high beef prices of 1849 and the early 1850s by sending off trail herds of seven hundred to one thousand, or occasionally two thousand, to the new markets without holding back enough cows for future breeding, without importing high-quality bulls for upgrading the stock, and without setting aside financial reserves for future needs. They did not appreciate that with cattle and sheep coming in from all parts of the west, the principal meat market at San Francisco and the lesser ones at Sacramento, Stockton, and the mining towns were becoming oversupplied. By 1860 the *California Farmer* was asserting that "beef and cattle are selling at rates that *cannot* pay," while in that same year a convention of cattle growers declared that "there being no market open to us beyond the limits of the State, this branch of industry has become profitless and ruinous."[15]

What economics began, nature completed. A severe drought in 1855–1856, another dry year in 1858, and excessive rain in 1859–1860 killed thousands of cattle and compelled ranchers to market stock at distress prices. Then in the winter of 1861–1862 came abnormal rains and disastrous floods, followed by a prolonged drought that started in the winter of 1862–1863 and did not break until late in 1864.[16] A local newspaper reported the result:

Any quantity of cattle may still be seen dead and dying between this place and Monterey. They stagger over the uninviting hills and plains, and should a blade of grass be discovered, death overtakes the skeleton animal that attempts to pluck it, for the force of the blade breaking capsizes the poor beast, and he is unable to rise again.[17]

For the ranchers, the mortgages and personal debts so confidently incurred in the 1850s, like the taxes left outstanding, became impossible to pay in the 1860s. Everywhere ranches were lost through foreclosure or tax sale. Often they were broken into smaller tracts and offered to prospective farmers. As agriculture began to compete for the better lands, the future for cattle became correspondingly limited.[18]

That success was possible was shown by the rise of the great firm of Miller and Lux. Henry Miller, of German birth, and Charles Lux, from Alsace, were working as rival butchers in San Francisco before they became partners in the later 1850s. To keep a large and steady supply of beef moving into the big San Francisco market, they started buying good ranch land, fencing it, stocking it with "improved" cattle, and ensuring supplies of water and feed. In the troubled 1860s and 1870s, when other cattlemen were selling land, Miller and Lux were buying, whenever the price was right. By 1880 they were said to own eight hundred thousand acres, purchased at an average cost of six dollars per acre, and with perhaps five hundred thousand acres under fence. They bought large ranches in Oregon and Nevada to supplement California holdings so vast that Miller liked to boast that he could ride from one end of the state to the other and sleep on his own land each night. At peak, the firm must have been one of the greatest in the American cattle industry. Everything was systematized and departmentalized; nothing was too small to escape Miller's personal scrutiny.[19] His subordinates were carefully chosen. "He had an army of them and they were splendidly drilled, loyal and intense workers."[20] To John Clay, a Scottish-born expert on ranches, Miller seemed "a nervous little German" who was at once selfish, grasping, and scheming, yet resourceful, indomitable, thrifty, and a man of his word.[21]

But Miller and Lux were not representative of California ranching as a whole. The 1870 census credited California with only half as many beef cattle as in 1860. A leading San Francisco newspaper dismissed the beef-cattle business as an unprogressive industry.[22] While the census of 1880 reported a partial recovery, it was not until 1890 that California's total reached (and surpassed) the high figure recorded in 1860. But 1890 was too late. By then farming, because it could bring a bigger return per acre worked, was elbowing aside the improving cattle business. California ceased to produce enough beef to supply its own market, and became instead a customer for cattle driven in from Nevada, Oregon, Idaho, and Utah, or shipped by the Central Pacific Railroad. By 1880 a special report for the census, prepared by Clarence W. Gordon, declared,

Except in the southern part of California, stock-raising is usually associated with agriculture, and not many persons keep sheep or cattle exclusively.[23]

The future belonged to Texas and to the Great Plains ranges that Texas was soon to stock. In Texas, Anglo-Americans had thrust their way into the (to them) new business of raising almost wild cattle on the limitless unfenced ranges, some of which were privately owned, while many were public land where the grazer could claim only the "range right" of being first user and the one who controlled the water.

A key area of exceptional natural richness was the big triangle south of the old city of San Antonio, where Texas thrusts its boundaries out to the Rio Grande on the west and the Gulf on the east. During the turbulent twenty years that began with the Texan Revolution and continued into the 1850s, much of the land here slipped from an original Hispano-Texan ownership into the grasp of Anglo-Americans. The new proprietors were a varied lot, sometimes of quite unexpected origins for future cattle kings.

Richard King, for example, was a rugged, determined steamboat captain of the type usually described as "two-fisted." Born in New York City of poor Irish immigrant parents, he was a self-made, self-taught man. In 1853 he bought for three hundred dollars the first 15,500 acres of what was to become the Santa Gertrudis Ranch, located on the Gulf Coast south of Corpus Christi. His partner in the steamboat business and, for years, in the Santa Gertrudis and other ranches, was Mifflin Kenedy, an erect, almost prim Pennsylvania Quaker who had been a teacher before he turned to steamboating, which he followed first on the Ohio and Mississippi rivers, later in Florida, where he met King.

King had started a cattle camp on the Santa Gertrudis even before the sale had been completed, and in 1854 purchased fifty-three thousand additional acres for eighteen hundred dollars. At the time, the Santa Gertrudis properties had been virtually abandoned by the Hispano-Texan ranchers to whom title had been granted, because in that lawless region the physical danger had seemed too great and the chance of success in the new American era too small. For working hands, by contrast, King had no difficulty in hiring Hispano vaqueros, and indeed a whole village of simple Hispanos picked up their belongings and moved to the ranch in return for the promise of regular wages. They became, in effect, hereditary retainers.[24] A Federal report in 1870 said that King kept "300 Mexican herdsmen and 1,000 saddle-horses . . . in constant requisition" to handle his 65,000 cattle, 10,000 horses, 7,000 sheep, and 8,000 goats.[25]

Another newcomer to the South Texas coast was a lanky New Englander, Abel Head Pierce, better known as "Shanghai." Originally from Little Compton, Rhode Island, he served an unhappy apprenticeship in his uncle's store in Virginia before he stowed away on a schooner bound for Texas in 1853. In Texas he sought employment from a fellow New Englander, Richard Grimes, formerly a sea captain from Rocky Hill, Connecticut, but had to settle for a chance to learn the ranch business by working for Grimes' son Brad, who proved to be a skinflint. On the Grimes ranch the working hands were a mixture of Anglos, Hispano vaqueros, and black slaves. When Pierce was ready to start his own operations, he centered his land and cattle in the region where the Colorado drains out toward the Gulf at Matagorda Bay, north of Corpus Christi.[26]

King, Kenedy, Grimes, and Pierce went into business on relatively lush coastal plains and prairies where cattle multiplied with such enthusiasm that their owners' chief problem was how to market them. Charles Goodnight began his long career in a very different geographic setting and with an equally different personal history. His German grandfather had immigrated to Virginia; his father had been born in Kentucky; Charles began life in Illinois. As a boy he rode his white-faced mare behind his family's wagon as they made the long journey from Illinois via St. Louis, Little Rock, and Dallas, to settle near the new town of Waco. There the prairies meet the narrow forest belts known as the Cross Timbers, and beyond the

Cross Timbers the land rises gradually through rolling plains, plateaus, and broken country.

By tracing the winding Brazos River upstream through the Cross Timbers, the young man could reach the Palo Pinto country, where he and a partner established their cattle camp in 1857. Herding cattle on these partly timbered upland ranges was quite a different experience from working on the coastal plains, and even the cattle of central Texas were not precisely the same as those of the coast. In this new region, which was then regarded as being the northwest fringe of settlement and dangerously subject to Indian raids, Goodnight met Oliver Loving, who was later to be Goodnight's partner and close associate. Loving was of Kentucky birth and the owner of slaves. In Texas he tried a variety of livelihoods: farming, storekeeping, dealing in cattle, and owning cattle. Like Goodnight, Loving supplemented an uncertain income by operating freight wagons. Years older than his future partner, Loving had the reputation of being an unusually resourceful and experienced frontiersman.[27]

In the last years before the Civil War these men were groping for a market that could absorb their enlarging herds. A careful manager like King, who gave close attention to the quality of his livestock, was able to sell his better cattle for breeding stock on ranches in Texas and Mexico while making a limited use of the hide-and-tallow expedient to dispose of the culls. Shanghai Pierce was dispatched to New Orleans with a trail herd of his employer's best beef cattle. Oliver Loving drove herds directly to New Orleans and took others to the river ports of Shreveport and Alexandria, from which they could be sent by boat down to New Orleans.[28]

Many ranchers in South Texas sent their stock from coastal ports to New Orleans and Mobile by the Morgan Line of steamers, only to find that the unaccommodating steamship company regarded cattle as low-paying freight that was worth carrying only to fill the holds of returning ships that had brought more profitable cargoes from New Orleans.[29] Exports to the West Indies and Cuba encountered comparable difficulties with shipping. Drives to California continued, as did the practice of trailing stock to outfitting points on the Missouri, where cattle were bought for many purposes: for beef, for work animals, for stocking farms and ranches, and for filling Army or Indian contracts.[30]

But the real potential was in markets to the north. In 1858 Loving drove a herd up through Illinois, in what seems to have been the first instance of Texas cattle reaching the Chicago market directly (others had gone to farms in Illinois). When the Civil War broke out, Loving was in Denver, selling cattle that he had driven up through New Mexico in order to tap the markets offered by the new Rocky Mountain mining region.

Then came the intervention of the war, with Texas cut off from external markets by the Union forces and with few men at home to tend the cattle. Left by themselves on the ample ranges, the long-horns multiplied so freely that the returning veterans after the war found their ranges crowded with stock far in excess of the demands of familiar markets. Yet in the meantime the continued industrial and commercial development in the Middle West was constantly enlarging the urban market for food. A cow that would sell for three or four dollars in Texas was worth ten times that amount in the north.[31] What is more, with railroad transportation now well established west of the Mississippi and increasingly available west of the Missouri, there was no need to repeat Loving's exploit of trailing cattle all the way through Illinois; at any one of several railheads stock could be loaded for Chicago or St. Louis.

The chief problem was the resistance of farmers in Arkansas, Missouri, and eastern Kansas. The Texans' experimental drives in the 1850s had shown that the trail herds would get into the farmer's growing crops, and that the South Texas cattle would infect local dairy and beef cattle with the "Texas fever." Not understood in its own day, the Texas, or splenic, fever is now known to have been a disease to which South Texas cattle were virtually immune because of long exposure. It was transmitted by ticks, and when the latter transferred themselves from Texas stock to local cows that had never before been exposed, death came quickly. As early as 1855 Missouri passed a law against the admission of Texas cattle. A stiffer statute followed in 1861, and Kansas copied Missouri in 1859 and 1861. Armed gangs of farmer-vigilantes undertook to enforce the prohibitions by turning back trail herds at gunpoint.[32]

In the lawless atmosphere of the Kansas-Missouri-Arkansas border, vigilante activity blended easily into cattle thievery, violence, and intimidation, and yet the drover who had the good sense to stay west of Arkansas and Missouri had to make his way through the uncertain reactions of the tribes that occupied Indian Territory (i.e., Oklahoma), not to mention the turbulence of Texas' own northern frontier.

No one ever accused Charles Goodnight of lacking courage, but in 1865 and 1866, as he debated how to market the stock that he found when he returned from wartime service, he decided that rather than strike directly north to Kansas, he would risk the hazards of fierce Indians and extreme aridity in order to sweep southwest through Texas to the Pecos River, and up that stream and through the length of New Mexico to Colorado. In Colorado, he reasoned, there must be money because of the mines, and there would be ample free pasture in case he had to hold his cattle for a rise in prices. The result was the Goodnight or Goodnight-Loving Trail that Goodnight blazed in 1866 in partnership with Oliver Loving when the two men, with a Texas crew that included Bose Ikard, a notable black trail hand who had been born a slave, forced their herd of two thousand head through to Fort Sumner, New Mexico, where they sold some of their stock to the contractor charged with feeding the starving Navajo and Mescalero Apache imprisoned there.

At Fort Sumner, Goodnight started back on the seven-hundred-mile journey to Texas for another herd, while Loving went on to Colorado to sell the remainder of their existing stock to John W. Iliff, who was soon to become known as the "cattle king of the plains." Originally from Ohio and the son of a prosperous stock raiser who was able to send him to college, Iliff had been a part of the 1859 Pikes Peak rush, but soon turned to buying work cattle from incoming travelers at Denver and built up a grazing empire that ultimately spread over northern Colorado and southern Wyoming. Goodnight admired Iliff's talents as a stockman, and in 1868 extended the Goodnight Trail as far as Cheyenne, to deliver to Iliff what was believed to have been the first Texas herd taken directly to Wyoming. The Goodnight Trail became a heavily used route to the western part of the Great Plains.[33]

Most Texans wanted a more direct route, straight north to Kansas and a railroad, and the northern men who came down from Illinois and Iowa to buy cattle and drive them home had the same desire. The attempt to push a very large number of cattle—allegedly 260,000—north from Texas in 1866 was reputed to have gone badly because the anticipated difficulties in fact materialized and most of the drovers lacked the experience and resourcefulness that Goodnight and Loving were showing on the Pecos in that same year. The drive in 1867 was correspondingly small, and since the Texas fever broke out in virulent form in Illinois in 1867 and 1868, the whole future of the effort was in doubt.[34]

Up to that time no pattern had emerged: no one northern destination, no certainty that a railhead could be reached, only informal agreements between Texas stock raisers and the professional drovers who took most of the herds north, and equally informal contracts governing sales to the ultimate buyers. Goodnight, as a drover, repeatedly assumed responsibility for a herd on the basis of an oral contract.[35]

As part of a stillborn scheme to promote a town as a center for the cattle trade, influential politicians in Kansas lobbied through the legislature of 1867 a statute that would permit cattle drives to points west of a quarantine line that would be beyond the principal farm areas. Joseph G. McCoy, then age twenty-nine and the youngest of three brothers in a prosperous Illinois cattle-shipping business, seized upon the statute to establish a meeting place for drovers and buyers on the route of the advancing railroad that was about to assume the name Kansas Pacific.[36] He chose Abilene, which he described as "a very small, dead place, consisting of about one dozen log huts, low, small, rude affairs."[37] A possible trail toward it had been laid out by a trader named Chisholm, who could never have guessed the immortality he had thus won for himself.

McCoy's choice was daring, for Abilene was actually a little east of the quarantine line, and public officials would have to be persuaded to overlook the illegality. Not one to be stopped by technicalities, McCoy bought 250 acres for a stockyard, started plans for a hotel, livestock scales, livery stable, offices, and a bank, and sent out a rider to attract Texas herds with promises of friendly and profitable treatment.

While McCoy's scheme matured too late for full results in 1867, nevertheless he made a well-advertised good beginning, and for the 1868 season he had ready a hotel, the Drovers Cottage, that quickly became a favorite, while stores, saloons, and brothels seem to have come to the raw new site without urging. McCoy's advertising had made Abilene widely known, and he had had the Chisholm Trail resurveyed and shortened as a step toward making it what it soon became: a route that ran straight north from San Antonio to Abilene.[38] The results were impressive. In 1870 the Federal government labeled Abilene "the great primary depot of the Texas cattle trade," and the general superintendent of the Kansas Pacific reported that his railroad shipped 30,000 head in 1867; 57,000 in 1868; only 47,000 in 1869 (because Illinois had just passed a statute aimed at the Texas fever); and 125,000 in 1870.[39]

Abilene's reign was brief, frenetic, and gaudy. During the few months each year that constituted its busy season, the place became as well known for the flamboyant misbehavior of transient Texans as for the large business deals that were negotiated there. Abilene's fall was symbolized by the decision in 1872 to load the popular Drovers Cottage onto railroad flatcars and carry it sixty miles farther west to the upstart town of Ellsworth. All the cattle towns suffered from the key weakness that they were dependent on the free use of large quantities of vacant public domain, where cattle could be held at very small expense while awaiting sale. As soon as farmers were attracted to the neighborhood, fights developed—over fences that cut off pasture or interfered with the trails, over crops eaten or trampled by cattle, over outbreaks of Texas fever, and over the transient cowboys' reputed immorality and violence. The Federal land laws were designed to encourage the farmer and made no provision for the stock raiser. The tendency was for the cattle trails to get pushed farther west, away from encroaching farmers, until finally Dodge City, in western Kansas and on the Santa Fe Railroad, and Ogallala, in western Nebraska and on the Union Pacific, came to constitute a kind of last stand.[40]

The significance of the Long Drive was enormous. A well-informed Federal official estimated that from 1866 through 1884, less than twenty years, more than 5.2 million cattle were driven north from Texas.[41] That meant that in a normal year a cattle army of 150,000 to 400,000 went plodding north, divided into herds of about 2,500, each shepherded by a dozen hands and advancing ten or fifteen miles a day, on a journey that might last two to three months—or might take longer, if the drive started at the Rio Grande and finished in Montana, as did the convincingly detailed narrative told by Andy Adams in his famous story of the trail, *The Log of a Cowboy* (1903).

That many "cows" could never have been absorbed solely by the slaughterhouses. At Abilene or some other northern destination the fat, mature animals might indeed be sold for immediate shipment by rail to Chicago, Kansas City, or St. Louis, while the less fat were taken over by men who had beef contracts for Indian reservations. But dealers from the corn states of Illinois, Iowa, and Missouri were eager to buy young steers for fattening, and the statutes directed against the Texas fever could be circumvented by a notarized certificate that the cattle had been "wintered" in Kansas and were safe. A very important link with the states east of the Missouri was thereby forged, and as land values rose in the corn belt, a reverse exchange developed, for it proved profitable to ship young middle western cattle out to the low-cost ranges of the west for a part of their maturing before returning them for "finishing" on corn-belt farms.[42] Few paused to reflect that cattle from the Middle West, accustomed to more care and less severe climatic conditions, might prove more vulnerable than the Texas longhorns if nature should provide unexpectedly harsh weather.

These uses for trail stock could perhaps have been predicted. What few save Lewis Allen foresaw was the revolution the Texas cattle brought to the Great Plains. Their arrival was the most recent in a sequence of related changes. The Army and the Indian Office were forcing the Plains Indians onto reservations, and their task was being made the easier by the extravagant slaughter of the buffalo that had been the Indians' food. As Indian and buffalo withdrew, ambitious men swarmed out to the virgin pastures to become ranchers. Most did not at first seek legal title to the bulk of the land that they used. It was enough to take possession of the few sources of water and to occupy the natural pastures—the "range"—that the water controlled in that semiarid land. Housing could start with a dugout or a log cabin or palisaded hut. The cattle, initially, could be some of those Texan longhorns just arriving from the south; very soon more cattle reaching Kansas were being sold for stocking the northern ranges than for the slaughterhouse.

With incredible rapidity pioneer ranches spread throughout the Great Plains and spilled over into the Great Basin, the southwest, and the part of the Pacific states that lies east of the Sierras and Cascades, until by 1885 Joseph Nimmo, Jr., the government specialist in such matters, felt justified in asserting that "the range and ranch cattle area . . . very nearly corresponds with the great dry area of the interior" and with the lands above fifteen hundred feet altitude.[43] The lesser part of this notable expansion was the occupation of the dry ranges of eastern Oregon and Washington and adjacent Idaho, in the rain shadow of the Cascades. Here cattle and sheep appeared in the 1860s as part of a thrust toward the markets offered by the new mines of Idaho, eastern British Columbia, and western Montana. Cattle escaping from the drought in California joined stock coming from western Oregon and Washington. During the 1870s and 1880s this big region east of the Cascades and west of the Rockies developed into a cattle kingdom of its own. It sent some of its cattle eastward to help stock the new ranches in the northern Great Plains and received some Texas cattle in return.[44]

But as Nimmo pointed out, the really distinctive part of this expansion of the 1870s and 1880s was that into the Great Plains, which Nimmo measured as extending for a thousand miles from Texas to Montana and for two hundred miles in width. Here, east of the Rockies and north of New Mexico and Texas, suddenly there were 7.5 million head of cattle valued at $187.5 million.

Theodore Roosevelt, then an aristocratic young New York politician and scholar, but for the moment in flight from tragedy in his immediate family, became in the early 1880s a part of this invasion of the northern plains. He acquired two ranches in western North Dakota, "where the Little Missouri flows through the heart of the Bad Lands." He marveled at the suddenness of what he was witnessing. "It is but little over half a dozen years since these lands were won from the Indians," he mused. "Cattle-raising on the plains, as now carried on, started in Texas, where the Americans had learned it from the Mexicans whom they dispossessed. It has only become a prominent feature of Western life during the last score of years."[45]

It could now become "prominent" among well-to-do easterners like Roosevelt because it promised not only financial profits but also the excitement, the sheer romance, of cowboy life in "a land of vast silent spaces, of lonely rivers, and of plains where the wild game stared at the passing horseman." Roosevelt's ranches were typical of moderate-sized outfits: "no neighbor for ten or fifteen miles on either side of me . . . no fences . . . the cattle wandered free . . .

[restrained only by] what we called line riding," which meant that cowboys rode along the boundaries to turn back cattle that were straying.[46]

The cowboys form a class by themselves. . . . They are mostly of native birth, and although there are among them wild spirits from every land, yet the latter soon become undistinguishable from their American companions. . . . Sinewy, hardy, self-reliant. . . . They are far from being as lawless as they are described; though they sometimes cut queer antics when, after many months of lonely life, they come into a frontier town in which drinking and gambling are the only recognized forms of amusement, and where pleasure and vice are considered synonymous terms.[47]

In Roosevelt's opinion, although many from Kansas and other northern states had entered the business, "the Texans are perhaps the best at the actual cowboy work." With his big hat, silk kerchief, high-heeled boots, and chaps, the cowboy was a colorful figure whose dress, "like many of the terms of his pursuit, is partly of Hispano-Mexican origin."[48] It was this cowboy that another eastern aristocrat, Owen Wister of Philadelphia and Harvard, established as one of the personae of American fiction when he depicted him in *The Virginian* (1902).

The possibility of making big profits while enjoying this wild life seemed real. Clarence Gordon's report of 1880 claimed that a rancher could begin in Texas on thirty thousand acres of free range, with one thousand three-year-old cows and forty bulls, for an initial capital investment of only $12,350 and annual operating expenses of $1,562.50. In these totals the least costly items were for buildings and corrals (seven hundred dollars) and wages (cowboys at twenty-five dollars each per month plus ten dollars board). Others listed cowboy pay at somewhat higher rates, thirty or forty dollars, but labor costs were minimal, especially when compared with the hardships and dangers of the job.[49]

British investors were as intrigued as eastern Americans by the opportunity. The thrust into the Great Plains happened to coincide with a period of high meat prices in Britain, where an epidemic of the anthrax disease during the 1860s had cut heavily into the stock of cattle available in Britain and on the Continent. By now, just as it was possible to ship cattle live to the Atlantic Coast cities by railroad, so was it possible to export them live to ports of the United

Kingdom, or, alternatively, to use the newly invented refrigerator car and refrigerator ship to send dressed (or fresh) beef almost anywhere. Less attractively, canned beef was available from American packing centers.[50]

American alternatives to high-priced British sources made the newly publicized cattle industry of Texas and the Great Plains so important to the United Kingdom that elaborate investigations were made into the opportunities for investment. This was, of course, the day when Britain's economic power was at its zenith and overseas investments were commonplace. A royal commission reached the electrifying conclusion that "the average profit of the [western American] stockgrower has been for years fully 33 percent," while the titled head of a Scottish investment group concluded that it had been "not uncommon for a cattle breeder to clear 80 or even 100 percent on his capital," although because of rising competition new investors should not count on more than 25 to 30 percent per year![51]

With endorsements such as these, it is no wonder that western cattlemen found moneyed British and urban Americans eager to invest or loan funds. Charles Goodnight, for example, after nine years as a drover, wanted the more settled existence of a rancher. He made one start in Colorado, then in 1875 began to shift his base to Palo Duro cañon in the Texas Panhandle, where no ranches existed as yet because of Indian danger and because it was 250 miles to the nearest railroad or supply base.

Goodnight found his capital by going into partnership with a well-to-do, upper-class British individual, John George Adair, of Ireland, once of the Foreign Service, later a stockbroker in New York and Denver, and married to one of the notable Wadsworth clan of New York State. Although Adair proved to be a caricature of the arrogant British visitor, nevertheless Goodnight went ahead with an agreement by which Adair put up the money at 10 percent interest plus assurance of capital gains, while Goodnight supplied the cattle, operated the ranch, fought off Indians, cattle thieves, and intruding sheep men, and acquired more land as fast as Adair supplied funds.[52]

On a much bigger scale, incorporated English and Scottish companies bought up large ranches, added greatly to the latter's working capital, and sought to manage them from a remote distance, at first usually through the American who had negotiated the original sale. When the Swan Land and Cattle Company was offered to Edinburgh investors in the spring of 1883, its promoter, Alexander Hamilton Swan, claimed to control a block of land in southeastern Wyoming that was 130 miles long by a width of 42 miles at its east and 100 at the west, and allegedly supplied with one hundred thousand head of cattle. Swan, born on a Pennsylvania farm and experienced in handling livestock in Ohio and Iowa before he and his brothers began in Wyoming in 1874, was retained by the Scots as manager.[53]

Often younger members of the families of the new British owners came out to try this romantic ranching business. Roosevelt's neighbors in the Bad Lands, the Langs, were Scots from Ireland. Having been sent out from the United Kingdom to look after the investment of Sir John Pender, "a rich London capitalist," they found themselves entertaining at various times the younger son of an Irish baronet, Pender's oldest son, and a variety of "scions of English nobility." The son of the Irish baronet proved "to be the right sort," but young Pender was upset by the refusal of the hired hands to address him as "Mister."[54]

With foreign and urban American money hurrying out to supplement local capital, and with Texans coming north to teach newcomers the art of raising cattle on unfenced ranges, the Great Plains launched into an unrestrained boom. Where early comers had enjoyed ample elbowroom only a few years before, now they found that they were acquiring new neighbors—neighbors whose stock got mixed up with theirs and whose operations interfered with their own. The Federal land laws, traditionally shaped by the ideal of the family-sized farm, made no provision for the stock raiser who needed thousands of acres in that dry region where "it takes thirty acres to graze a cow." Even when land was for sale, as in the railroad grants, few individual ranchers could afford the capital necessary to purchase big tracts. Instead, they tried to control the public domain, partly by exercising locally acknowledged "range rights," partly by filing homestead or preemption claims that blanketed the few water sources. Some of the claims were, inevitably, based on false affidavits that cowboys were hired to swear to. When outside capital was brought in, usually one of the first new expenditures was to acquire land by purchase or lease.

If left to his own wishes, the pioneer rancher would have preferred isolation, "unsocial" isolation that made it unnecessary to cooperate with anyone.[55] But as neighbors intruded just over the ridge or up the valley, cooperation was forced upon the rancher. Neither the limited new local government nor the remote Federal government that was the actual—though silent, unpaid, and unseeing—landlord could meet the need. Therefore, like pioneers on many other American frontiers, the cattlemen formed their own organizations to establish rules governing marks and brands, to arrange schedules for the spring and fall roundups, to determine the ownership of mavericks, to hire detectives to catch cattle thieves, to control bulls on the range, and, most difficult of all, to regulate grazing on the public domain.

Local associations sprang up everywhere in the 1870s and soon united their efforts in bigger organizations that could exercise jurisdiction over whole states or territories, and often over adjacent out-of-state lands as well. Wyoming was the most striking example of how strong an association could become. With no rival industry to challenge its rule, the Wyoming Stock Growers' Association was, in the words of a scholar, "for at least a decade . . . the unchallenged sovereign of the Territory of Wyoming,"[56] or, as a famous cattleman expressed it, the Wyoming Association "grew up to be a mighty power."[57] Although Alec Swan was the president from 1876–1881, the key person was Thomas Sturgis, the secretary, who came to know everyone's business through his work with the Association and through his ties with the influential Stockgrowers National Bank of Cheyenne. Sturgis was a well-educated, well-informed easterner who became by 1883 "the leading man in Wyoming." The Association's great power drew it deeply into politics, "and politics in Wyoming then, as now, is of a very sordid kind."[58]

In Montana, by contrast, mining and an agriculture developing in the river valleys constituted rival interests, and there was also a divergence between the big livestock growers and the small ranchers who had neither the time nor desire to participate in the large roundups needed by the big outfits. The result was that while local stock-growers' associations became strong in parts of Montana primarily devoted to range cattle, over the territory as a whole the Montana Association never achieved a power comparable to that wielded in Wyoming.[59]

The associations were least effective when dealing with excessive grazing on the public domain. Cattlemen were slow to acknowledge that continued exclusive reliance on the natural grasses was no longer safe, that they must provide supplementary hay and feed or risk killing their stock. Because they did not own the range, they disregarded warnings that the dry, overgrazed range was visibly deteriorating as the undernourished cattle attacked every growing thing. Noxious weeds were replacing the grasses, springs were being reduced to "filthy trampled mudholes," and as the cattle wandered farther and farther in their daily hunt for dwindling food and water, their hooves cut pathways down through the parched soil, thus starting "the thin end of the wedge of erosion."[60] A thoughtful newcomer like Theodore Roosevelt found little support when he brought the problem before the Montana Stockgrowers' Association.

Beef prices were too high for anyone to welcome Cassandras. In the summer of 1882 prices for the better grades reached the highest point registered at Chicago since 1870, while prices for poorer grades rose to their own peak in 1883. From that prosperous level the direction was erratically downward, until by late 1886 western newspapers were speaking in panicky terms of the pronounced decline.[61]

As in California in the 1860s, so now in the Great Plains in the 1880s nature finished what man had begun. On the southern ranges a severe winter in 1885–1886 caused very heavy losses which were somewhat increased by President Grover Cleveland's determination to have the Army evict cattlemen who were illegally grazing their stock on the big Cheyenne-Arapaho reservation in Indian Territory. This forced over two hundred thousand head onto the already overcrowded ranges of adjacent states, just at the start of this bad winter. Cleveland further upset the prevailing pattern by ordering the removal of the extensive fences that cattlemen had strung illegally across public lands. The northern ranges did not suffer heavily in the winter of 1885–1886, and some northern cattlemen took last-minute precautions to head off trouble.

Then nature struck. To this day, a century later, Great Plains folklore preserves the memory of the terrible winter of 1886–1887. A fiercely hot, dry summer preceded a winter that began unusually early and "caught us unprepared," as Roosevelt's neighbor, Lincoln

Lang, confessed. A soft initial snowfall turned into the first of successive blizzards whose deep snows and very low temperatures paralyzed life on the ranges. Each storm roared in on the heels of its predecessor, until the cattle, their strength as low as their will to live, drifted in bunches into fence corners and there quietly froze to death. Cattle that fought their way down to the limited shelter of banks, cuts, and coulees along the river were still there when warm, dry chinook winds abruptly melted the accumulated snow and ice into floods that swept away the weakened survivors.[62]

Lincoln Lang said that his ranch's loss of about 80 percent of their stock was less than that of most ranchers near him. John Clay, speaking generally of the plains north of Texas, said that losses varied from total among cattle recently arrived from Texas, down to 30 to 60 percent among cattle that had had the acclimating adjustment of a previous winter in the north. It was, he concluded, "a catastrophe," caused by "recklessness, want of foresight and the weather." By the spring of 1887

[t]he cowmen of the West and Northwest were flat broke. Many of them never recovered. . . . They disappeared from the scene. Most of the eastern men and the Britishers said "enough" and went away.[63]

The great Scottish-owned Swan Land and Cattle Company was able to stay in business only because they voted to reduce their capital by wiping out "80 percent of the investment of the ordinary shareholder."[64] They hired their fellow Scot, John Clay, to be their new manager. He reduced labor and management costs by one half, and yet still the company paid no dividends until 1897. Thereafter the company paid about 2 percent per year.

Another very large Scottish company, the Matador Land and Cattle Company, owned by Dundee businessmen and located in northwest Texas, recognized as early as 1884 the danger of overstocking their home-ranch ranges and initiated a policy of using their original Texas holdings as a breeding ground only. From there yearling steers and spayed heifers were sent to leased or owned lands in the Texas Panhandle, and from there were sent as two-year-olds up to leased or owned lands in the Dakotas, or occasionally Montana or Canada, from which they went later to the corn belt or market. In 1890 the Matador Company entrusted its destiny to an exceptionally able Scotsman, Murdo Mackenzie, who became one of the most influential cattlemen in America, welcomed to the White House by Theodore Roosevelt as an ally against the railroads and the "Beef Trust."

Mackenzie's first action was to make a careful count of the company's herd. By so doing he demonstrated that the actual number of cattle was so much less than the alleged figure that the company had to write off one third of its paid-up capital. Under Mackenzie's leadership the company sank wells and installed windmills and threw up shallow dirt walls to retain water in what westerners call "tanks"; it bought purebred bulls; and upon Mackenzie's decision it settled upon the Hereford as the standard breed. And still the Scottish directors kept pressing Mackenzie for more economies.[65] The steps taken by the Matador Company were characteristic of the measures necessary to survive in the new era. There was, as a distinguished scholar has remarked, "a real recession of the cattle frontier,"[66] as rangelands were abandoned and herds were reduced still further by growers forcing onto a weak market whatever stock had survived because they had to pay something on what now seemed mountainous debts incurred in boom times.

As open-range grazing declined, a gradual shift to ranching took place, with cattlemen concentrating on smaller herds that were of higher quality and capable of yielding more pounds of meat per animal. A changing public taste toward younger beef helped, because it lessened the number of years of feeding and care required per animal. Harvesting hay and using a crude, minimum-cost type of irrigation to raise forage crops such as alfalfa and sorghum became commonplace. The new barbed wire that became available in the later 1870s made it possible to control the use of pasture and water and to persuade high-grade bulls to confine their activities to the rancher's own cows. The mowing machine and the hay rake became as important as the lariat and branding iron—to the intense disgust of the cowboys.

The cowboys' bosses had little sympathy for them. They were struggling to raise capital to finance the new improvements, to acquire legal title or leases to a higher percentage of the lands they used, and to carry the stock through to the most favorable moment for sale. A limited recovery that began at the end of the 1880s was stifled by the nationwide depression of 1893, which kept money tight until 1898.[67] Essential to a new readiness to lend to the cattle industry was the increasingly close relationship between the cattle ranches and the corn-belt feeding farms. Lenders were more ready to advance money when a regular and reasonably predictable cycle could be discerned. A frequent though not invariable pattern was for cattle to be bred in Texas or the adjacent southern grazing areas, matured on northern lands, and fattened in the corn belt. Whether they were moved from south to north by trail or railroad depended at first on the rates charged by the railroads, but presently the trail drives disappeared. At the same time, shipment by rail directly from Texas to corn belt or slaughterhouse became important.

Between 1890 and the close of the century several channels for funds developed. "Stockyard banks" were founded for the chief purpose of lending to cattle raisers and feeders. The commission merchants who handled sales and purchases began to make loans as a part of their business, and special cattle loan companies were formed, often at the instigation of the stockyard banks or the packers. John Clay remarked that it was a big step forward when the cattlemen succeeded in getting short-term cattle loans classed as commercial paper that lending agencies could rediscount at regular banks.[68]

To cope with problems as varied as these required more talent than just the ability to raise animals. In his fine study *The Cattle Kings,* Lewis Atherton has correctly stressed the importance of flexibility in the leading cattlemen's approach to their operations. They had to be alert to change and to ways of meeting change. The fact that so many had tried other jobs and had known other regions before they turned to raising cattle in the farther west helped to make them versatile.

Leading figures such as King, Kenedy, and Goodnight of Texas, Iliff of Colorado and Wyoming, and Miller of California had had substantial experience in merchandising, transportation, land speculation, or trading—above all, in trading—before they began to center their attention on cattle, and after launching into the livestock business, they were constantly engaged in buying, selling, or bartering for cattle, horses, sheep, land, water and pasture rights, supplies, partly finished raw materials such as lumber and salt, and services such as droving and wagon freighting, not to mention speculating on the side in town sites, mines, and moneylending. After they began to win recognition, most of them either served on the boards of directors of banks or founded their own banks. They became, in short, skilled in the art of entrepreneurship, which means assuming the risk and management of business.[69]

What attitudes went with these talents? Speaking generally of Texas and southwestern ranchers and drovers, Joseph McCoy said in a famous phrase:

They are, as a class, not public spirited in matters pertaining to the general good, but may justly be called selfish, or at least indifferent to the public welfare.

McCoy added:

Each man seems to feel himself an independent sovereign, and as such capable of conducting his affairs in his own way.[70]

CHAPTER 10

Into the Pasturelands:
II. Sheep Men Also Enter the Ranges

B ECAUSE of the sheer drama of the cattle kingdom, far too little
attention has been paid to its principal rival, the sheep industry.
The neglect is a pity, for as a report to the United States Department
of Agriculture once remarked, "sheep raising has always been one
of the world's leading pioneer enterprises." That comment was as
true of the American west as of any other new region, despite a
tendency for westerners to look disparagingly at sheep men.[1]

Sheep, tended on foot by a lonely, unkempt herder and his
dogs, were inherently less colorful than half-wild cattle driven by
booted and spurred cowboys; yet sheep were in many respects
more resourceful than cattle in living off difficult country.[2] Of
course they preferred lush valley pasture, but in summer they
were willing to browse high up on the slopes of mountains and
into the forests, while in winter and spring they found food in the
lower hills, plains, and deserts. They would eat weeds and scrubby
forage that cattle normally scorned; they clipped any growing
thing right down to the ground; and they could go without water
for two or three days if necessary, provided they had access to
some kind of succulent feed. Their pronounced herd instinct,
reinforced by their herder-guardian's daily discipline, made them
much more manageable than cattle.[3]

That last was an important consideration, for in the semiarid west,
where edible vegetation was thinly scattered and most of the land
was unoccupied public domain, the logical way to handle sheep was

to imitate the practice of the Spanish-speaking settlers of the south-west. Instead of raising sheep in small flocks as an adjunct to agriculture and keeping them in fenced pastures, the New Mexicans, to quote Josiah Gregg, sent out "immense flocks" of "itinerant" sheep to graze their way across the open countryside under care of a herder and dogs, sometimes being "taken to water [only] once in two or three days."[4]

Gregg did not explain how big was "immense." Sheep men of a later day commonly operated with flocks or "bands" of two thousand to twenty-five hundred head, although some felt that three to five thousand made for a unit that was more efficient and yet still manageable. Under the Spanish system practiced in New Mexico and Texas, and copied elsewhere, the herders (pastores) were ruled by hierarchy composed of the owner, his foreman (mayordomo), a caporal, and a subordinate vaquero (the same term as for "cowboy"). Often a single owner would hold title to numerous flocks but lease them out to herders on shares under the partido system. Throughout the west many an ambitious poor man climbed the first rung toward independent ownership by contracting to handle sheep on this basis, where months of isolation and vigilant care of his charges might lead to success, or might end in a costly run of extreme weather or sheep disease, or a dispute with cattlemen who resented intrusion on an unfenced range.[5]

As the former annual drives down into Mexico had demonstrated, and as the drives to California in the 1850s confirmed, sheep were as capable as cattle of covering a thousand to two thousand miles if properly handled and if abnormal weather did not intervene. Such a drive could be a slow business—men sometimes spent two years on the trail between the Mississippi Valley and California—and in the 1850s the losses could be severe, almost half of the stock.[6] But as knowledge of the business grew and the country became less wild, sheep men accomplished extraordinary marches. One big California "outfit" drove thirty thousand sheep from California to Montana in 1878, decided that it did not like Montana, and with its stock increased to thirty-two thousand head, presumably through births outnumbering deaths, turned around in 1880 and pushed south through Utah to Arizona.[7]

Sheep differed from cattle in offering a choice between two major products. In the era of the mining booms the demand was for mutton. As that market became satiated, sheep raisers turned to breeding for wool. Late in the century the trend turned back toward an emphasis on meat, partly because refrigerated shipments became possible, but partly because eastern consumers were showing an increasing fondness for lamb. By the turn of the century more than half of the receipts from sheep came from the sale of meat.[8]

But during most of the years after 1860 wool was the important product. It was a good frontier crop because it could be transported long distances at manageable cost, with little danger of spoilage, and it brought a relatively high value per pound. To illustrate how flexible wool transport could be, New Mexico, which before the 1880s received its supplies by wagon train, used those same trains to haul wool to the Missouri River as part of their eastbound cargo, while California, which exported wool by sea prior to 1869, found that after that date it was more profitable to ship via railroad because the saving in time and insurance compensated for the extra cost of carriage.[9]

Much less favorable was the obvious circumstance that wool was a national and international commodity that was subject to great fluctuations in supply and price. Because of the Civil War, prices were high in the early 1860s when the sheep industry began to spread over the farther west. After Appomattox, prices broke sharply downward when the military demand ceased and the government began dumping its surplus. Congress responded in 1867 with a protective tariff whose essential features remained in all wool tariffs passed down to 1913, save for a brief and (to the wool grower) disastrous experiment with free trade in 1894–1897. Even with protection against foreign wools, prices still showed a disconcertingly wide fluctuation. The Franco-Prussian War, for example, helped to push prices up to a high level in 1871–1872, just before the national panic of 1873 brought them down abruptly and kept them down until 1879. A brief period of high prices from 1879 to 1881 proved but the prelude to a new decline when competition from the Southern Hemisphere—Australia, Argentina, South Africa, and India— was felt. By 1891 prices had already dropped even before sheepmen felt the impact of the national panic of 1893. At the turn of the century a moderate improvement was under way and continued into the early 1900s.[10]

Wool, then, was a volatile commodity whose periodic downward swings were discouraging and puzzling to the western sheep man. The biggest American market was in distant Boston, with additional trading in Philadelphia, New York, and Chicago. Successive middlemen handled the annual wool "clip" as it moved from range toward textile manufacturer.[11]

What made wool-growing financially appealing was the same combination of favoring elements that produced the cattle boom: abundant land that was cheap or free, large stocks of low-priced, hardy animals that were acclimated to semiarid ranges, and labor for hire at minimal cost. The initial capital required was much less than for cattle. Clarence Gordon's report, which had estimated at $12,350 the initial capital to start raising one thousand head of cattle on free land in Texas, quoted a Texas sheep man as estimating that for $3,565.25 a prospective grower could start with one thousand sheep and twenty rams. This same source claimed that wages for a Texas herder, who was usually a Spanish-speaking person, were only twelve dollars a month plus six dollars for board. That was less than half the California rate of twenty-five dollars plus board.[12]

The inspiration for all the rosy dreams was the unimpressive-looking churro sheep, sometimes unflatteringly called the "common sheep" of Spain and Mexico. Its wool was coarse and light in weight, its body small and bare-bellied, but its meat was as good as Josiah Gregg claimed it to be, and generations of hardscrabble existence had made it a sturdy, resourceful animal. The churro was expert at foraging under adverse conditions, was capable of traveling long distances, had become strongly imbued with a herd instinct, and ewes were unusually faithful about looking after their young. The churro was to the pioneer sheep industry what the longhorn was to the early cattle business: the initial breeding stock. Just as the longhorn was gradually bred out in favor of animals that would yield more pounds and better quality, so the churro was "improved" by being bred to rams of a famous Spanish type, the merino. An infusion of merino blood produced a sharp improvement in the quality and weight of the wool (though not of the meat), and since the merino was itself a hardy species long accustomed to Spain's annual migrations between winter lowlands and summer mountain pastures, the crossbred offspring was suited to the demanding conditions of the American west. Later, when a better grade of meat became important, breeders started using other types of merino rams, either the French Rambouillet or the Delaine, or turned to rams of the several British stocks that had always stressed mutton.[13]

The Californians were the first to make extensive efforts to upgrade their stock by breeding churro ewes to high-quality rams, although in Texas, German settlers brought in Saxon rams at an early date, and an inspired newspaperman, George Wilkins Kendall, spent the 1850s and 1860s promoting improved sheep breeding in the Hill Country of West Texas. In California, at a time when tens of thousands of churros were still being driven in annually from New Mexico, Texas, and Sonora and Chihuahua, Mexico,[14] observant men began warning that the local market for mutton was becoming oversupplied and that the future lay in wool. "Wool growing," a trade journal argued, "cannot be overdone in California, for we have the world for a market,"[15] thanks to oceanic transportation.

Regular exports on a modest scale commenced in 1854 and by 1860 had increased tenfold. The earliest wool clips were of the coarse churro type and were still further lessened in value by being carelessly prepared, with a high ratio of dirt and grease, a fault characteristic of early western wools. As good breeding stock was brought in from well-established sheep regions such as Vermont, New York State, Ohio, Missouri, Australia, Vancouver Island, and Britain,[16] most of the flocks in the state received some infusion of new blood, and the quality of the wool became correspondingly better. By 1863 or 1864 a flock of unmixed churro blood was rarer than an improved flock had been in 1856. Careless handling of the clip, however, continued to be a serious problem that gave California a poor reputation abroad.[17] A small local outlet for wool opened at the end of 1859 when a group of San Francisco merchants financed California's first woolen mill.[18]

What stands out from these early years in California was the ability of the sheep industry to rise above a succession of troubles. When the cattlemen suffered disastrous losses in the heavy floods of 1861–1862 and the extreme drought of 1863–1864, they were unable to recover; during the same calamitous years the sheep raisers lost hundreds of thousands of animals and drove many others out of the state in search of pasture, yet according to the census of 1870 they achieved a huge gain in numbers of sheep as compared to 1860, even though the census takers of 1870 made no effort to include the multitudinous "range sheep" that in fact were grazing in California but were not a part of a recognized farm or ranch.[19] California's total in 1870 made it the second-largest sheep-raising state in the nation, exceeded only by Ohio, which had been the nation's leader for twenty years.

In southern California a new drought struck in 1871, reportedly causing a loss of 20 percent of the stock, and again in 1876–1877, when 2.5 million sheep were said to have died, while many were driven out of the state. In northern California severe winters in 1874–1875 and 1879–1880 killed many sheep.[20] Yet the census of 1880 recorded such a massive increase that California had by then easily surpassed Ohio to become the leading sheep-raising state. Thereafter, as agricultural demands absorbed more and more of the pasturelands, California declined both in number of sheep and relative position among sheep-raising states.

In wool the record was almost similar. California was credited by the census with being the second-largest wool producer in the nation in 1870 and 1880, ranking after Ohio, and the first in 1890, before the decline began. The account books of the commercial companies that handled sales and shipment of wool seemed to show that California produced nearly twice as much in 1870 and nearly three times as much in 1880 as the census recorded.[21] The San Francisco *Daily Alta California* editorialized that "during the last seventeen years sheep have been more profitable and have increased more rapidly than any other domestic animals in California," and the San Francisco *Daily Evening Bulletin* agreed, commenting that "no branch of agriculture had proved so well or been so safe and unvarying in its yield as sheep raising."[22]

Quite obviously, sheep were replacing the depleted herds of cattle. In this, California's experience was a foreshadowing of what was soon to be a common sequence in the west. As Clarence Gordon expressed it:

The common order in the progress of agricultural civilization is often first the exclusive occupation of a region by cattle, next sheep, and last agriculture.[23]

In California, as in the west generally a few years later, real sheep men, as distinct from absentee speculators, proved both resourceful and aggressive about fitting their flocks into the rapidly changing economic patterns. They learned to drive their sheep into the Sierra Nevada and Tehachapi Mountains in summer and run them on the lower hills in winter, and to put them into the grain fields after harvest to glean the stubble, eat the weeds, and fertilize the fields. Particular success was often achieved by family teams, such as the Bixbys (originally from Maine), their cousins the Flints, their friends the Hollisters, or the Dibblees, the McConnells, the Pattersons, and the Whitneys. The great firm of Miller and Lux, not content to dominate the cattle business, became a major sheep raiser, on a typically well-organized, well-staffed basis. Frenchmen from the old province of Béarn (in the Pyrenees), French Basques, and Spanish Basques became important in the region that centered in Bakersfield, the chief town in the Tulare Basin.[24]

In the 1860s and early 1870s, these pioneers were operating under conditions that made for maximum profits. The land was free or cheap to rent, the flocks received no food or shelter save what nature provided. Urban newspapers condemned this "most careless and inhumane system of feeding and treatment"[25] because it led to many deaths in years of abnormal weather, but growers were too impressed by the extraordinary fecundity of sheep in California to pay much attention to the death rate. A rapid increase in the number of sheep came as a long-term capital gain in addition to the basic yearly income from wool, which more than paid for the annual expenses of keeping, herding, and shearing the flocks. When farmers began to compete with livestock men for use of the land, the sheep men had to increase their capital investment materially, and yet this led them into a still bigger long-term gain. Forced to buy land when it was still cheap, sheep raisers acquired an asset that rose sharply in value as population increased and agriculture sought more and more cropland. By the late 1870s much had been accomplished in "breeding up" to a level of crossbred sheep that had a high percentage of merino blood. Other western states and territories that were not so far along in the sheep business were eager to buy such stock, and when the droughts of the 1870s lessened the pasture in California, Californians began to send their flocks elsewhere. In 1877 and 1878 about 50,000 sheep per year were driven out of California, twice that number in 1879, and three times that in 1880. The destinations of the 1880 drives showed where the future lay: 72,000 to Montana, 30,000 to Wyoming, 15,000 to Utah, 10,000 to Colorado, the same to Nevada, half that to Oregon, and 7,500 to Washington Territory.[26]

As the figures suggest, outside California, sheep raising had not advanced rapidly until the 1870s. Texas had been held back by neglect of sheep during the Civil War years and by the generally poor level of understanding of sheep shown by most Texans. Until well into the 1870s most Texas sheep were of the "unimproved" or "common Mexican" type and the wool was described as "nondescript." While German settlers in the Hill Country pioneered in developing ranches that combined sheep and cattle raising, a much greater sheep region was emerging in southwestern Texas, between the Colorado and the Rio Grande, centering in the Rio Grande Plain but embracing also the vast, semiarid Edwards Plateau. Here big holdings predominated and here some of the most notable leadership came from men of German ancestry. Charles Schreiner, an Alsatian who made his headquarters at Kerrville, northwest of San Antonio, not only raised sheep by the tens of thousands, but pioneered in building warehouses for storing wool until market conditions were favorable. He became storekeeper and banker to lesser sheep men, and took the lead in bringing in railroad transportation. His ranch was said to have reached a total of six hundred thousand acres. His brother-in-law Caspar Real, of German birth, had a big sheep ranch six miles from Kerrville. Herman Steiler, also German-born, was trained in sheep raising by Schreiner and married Real's daughter, who was, of course, Schreiner's niece. To the west of them, and out in the center of the Edwards Plateau, was Karl Albert Anton von Schauer, son of an Austrian field marshal, who stocked his pioneer ranch in that bleak region by driving three thousand sheep overland from California.[27]

In New Mexico the sheep industry was still in the control of the rico class of great sheep owners and the *partidarios* (sharecroppers). Both tended to be complacent, uninformed, and slow to recognize the need to shift from meat to wool and to improve the quality of the sheep and the care given them. As late as 1892 a Federal report remarked that "the chief drawbacks to the industry are the poor quality of the sheep and the primitive methods of conducting the industry." Much of the blame was placed on the *partido* system, which gave neither owners nor lessees enough incentive to improve the flocks.[28]

As American sheep men came into the territory, bringing with them merino rams for breeding, and as Americans and German-Jewish immigrants who had started as storekeeper-bankers ended by owning their customers' flocks, the territory gradually changed. By 1880 New Mexico had received 40,800 part-merino sheep from California and in sheer numbers was once more in a leading position among sheep-raising states. Finding their own rangelands crowded, New Mexicans were taking their flocks far out into the Texas Panhandle, where they found good grazing in the Canadian and Red River drainage systems, but met strong opposition from Texas cattlemen and Texas legislation. Sheep from New Mexico were constantly being drawn off to newer regions because the cheapness and hardiness of New Mexico sheep made them a favorite with men throughout the Rockies and Great Basin who wanted a low-priced stock that they could "breed up."

Utah was still too small in its operations to have much influence. Its rapid growth did not begin until the later 1870s and was much more pronounced during the 1880s and 1890s. Prior to that most of the meat and wool were used locally by farm families. Sheep were handled either in small flocks near predominantly agricultural towns, or were put together into large, cooperatively owned flocks that were sent out, in care of herders, to graze the non-arable lands.[29]

In Oregon the dominant fact was that land west of the Cascades was primarily agricultural. Sheep were raised in small flocks as an adjunct to farming, or were regarded as a temporary means of putting to use the less valuable land. As early as 1861 Oregonians tried sending sheep eastward across the Cascades into the Yakima country of Washington Territory, where open-range grazing in large flocks would be possible, and while this first experiment proved disastrous, other flocks soon followed and succeeded. The range east of the mountains was extensive, untenanted, and open to whoever came first. Friction with cattlemen was endemic in eastern Oregon and Washington, and led to real shooting wars of the type later dramatized in fiction. Both sheep men and cattlemen tended to upset the delicate ecological balance of this dry-land region by overgrazing it. The total of Oregon sheep increased sharply between 1870 and 1880, and Washington made a beginning in those same years. By the latter date cattlemen and farmers were pushing sheep men out of the treeless plains and up into the Blue Mountains of northwestern Oregon, and presently back to the forests and slopes of the Cascades. As in California, a seasonal rotation developed between the mountain pastures and lower lands better suited to winter use.[30]

By 1880 western sheep raising was ready to expand out of its original home in California, Texas, and New Mexico, and out of the newer centers of Oregon, Washington, and Utah, into the big interior grazing regions that had been opened by the cattlemen. The census of 1880 showed that from the Great Plains westward all of the states and territories save the Dakotas had the beginnings of a sheep industry. Indeed, in the late 1870s and early 1880s large drives from California, Oregon, New Mexico, and Texas were already reaching these new feeding grounds. The collapse and retrenchment of Great Plains cattle raising soon gave sheep raisers their chance. As cattle ranchers withdrew the remnants of their herds from the overgrazed ranges, sheep moved in, with their customary advantage of being able to feed high up in mountains, down in "bad lands" canyons, or wherever else forage had escaped the desperate cattle.

Wyoming's conversion was especially dramatic. Here had been the unchallenged empire of the cattle kings, and the lordly rulers had been arrogant in their dismissal of rival economic activities. Sheep had been the least industry, and now they bid fair to become the most. Sheep men from outside trailed in new flocks, while stockmen who had suffered disasters in cattle turned now to sheep, convinced that that was where the profits lay. Their newfound enthusiasm reflected the fortunate circumstance that the capital necessary for a venture in sheep was only a third of that required for cattle. By 1892 there were more sheep than cattle in Wyoming.[31]

An all-engulfing craze swept the state. A participant who entered the business at the turn of the century amusedly reported what he found in the little town of Douglas:

I found myself in a community of sheep-men. Not only were there sheep-men, pure and simple, who were nothing else; but all the saloon-keepers were interested in sheep, so also were the hotel proprietor and the leading lawyer and doctor, and all the officials of the First National Bank, and the newspaperman, . . . and the men in the Land Office, and the taxidermist, and all the merchants but one; even two of the preachers had retired as pastors and became shepherds. It was a sheep town, sure enough. They worshipped not the golden calf, but the golden fleece.[32]

Montana had a similar experience. Abandoning their cattle, Montanans turned to sheep and horses and plunged so heavily with the former that by 1900 Montana led the nation in number of sheep, with New Mexico second, Wyoming a very close third, Ohio fourth, and Utah a close fifth. Regions of slow development such as Idaho and Arizona joined the trend, while Nevada promptly overdid it— accepted more sheep and cattle than its scant desert ranges could support.

Idaho received its sheep from Oregon and California; Arizona's came from Utah, California, New Mexico, and Colorado. Colorado had been a late entrant into the field. Until 1870 most of its sheep raising was concentrated in the southern part of the state, which was culturally an extension of New Mexico. Not surprisingly, initially its livestock and stock-raising practices were those of New Mexico and remained so until Anglos drifted into the region and part-merino breeding stock were driven in from California and the Middle West.[33]

Even Kansas, Nebraska, and the Dakotas, whose western counties had recently been cattle grounds that were infiltrated by agrarian "nesters," went into sheep raising in a small way because, having found that reliance on grain alone was unsafe in so dry a land; the farmers began to buy small flocks which they fed for market on what grain could be grown.[34]

Federal investigators who surveyed these new sheep regions near the end of the century were surprised at how little provision was being made for shelter from winter storms and shelter during lambing, and at the reluctance of sheep owners to spend money on feed crops that could carry the flocks through winters and drought cycles. When they encountered this attitude even in so northerly a latitude as Montana, they were told, in effect, that in most winters the deaths weren't numerous enough to justify the expenditure.[35]

That attitude persisted into the first decade of the new century. At a time when they were already losing grassland to misguided farmers who had been attracted by a few years of abnormally high precipitation, sheep men allowed their flocks to keep on increasing beyond the capacity of the thin natural forage. In Wyoming "men with a few hundred dollars and a knowledge of the business" could find someone to "stake" them to a band of sheep on shares.[36] Discriminating observers noted two warning signs. As winter approached each year, some stockmen shipped cattle and sheep eastward to be wintered on hay, while others imported hay and corn, at considerable expense, to supplement the local range feed.

Here was the tacit evidence that some at least recognized that "the demand for free grass exceeded the supply, and the range was overstocked."[37] Had the Rocky Mountain sheep industry paid more attention to such portents, there would have been no necessity for their flocks to suffer widespread deaths when the years of good rainfall and moderate winters gave way to drought and blizzards. But the sheep men of the early twentieth century were no more eager than had been the cattlemen of the 1880s to acknowledge that now they must spend money if their animals were to survive.

If that suggests callousness toward the sheep, the attitude toward the guardians of the flocks was not much better. Wages were low everywhere. They were highest in remote Montana, where it was necessary to pay the abnormal rate of thirty-five to fifty dollars per month, plus board, to get anyone.[38] Some of the owners had come up by the hard road of tending sheep themselves, but many, including some of the greatest, had bought into the business and were quite content to hire men to live with the sheep. An eccentric visitor to California, who had seen much of sheep raising while covering thirteen hundred miles on foot, bitterly remarked that the old-fashioned word "shepherd" had been discarded in favor of "sheep herder," and the latter had become a term of scorn.[39] In New Mexico and Texas the herders and their caporal and mayordomo supervisors were Spanish-speaking and presumably native to the country, though Mexicans, too, took employment after slipping across the unguarded border. In Texas the only non-Hispanic employee was usually the ranch superintendent or administrator, the man who handled the money and had final responsibility.[40] In California, Basques, today so universally associated with western sheep, appeared as early as 1858[41] and by the 1890s had achieved a dominant position in the industry in the huge area from Fresno southward. English-speaking sheep raisers came to have as much antipathy for them as white laborers had for Chinese. Like the Chinese, they were accused of being skilled at their work, industrious, frugal, illiterate or only slightly educated, secretive, and clannish.[42]

As sheep raising expanded over the interior of the west, the Mexican, Hispano, and Basque herders went along with their charges, and an ever-increasing number of Basques rose through the ranks to become independent owners. Theirs was a highly nomadic existence, based on a determined search for free pasture and not always respectful of locally established customs concerning grazing.

As pressure upon the land increased, itinerant or purely nomadic sheep grazing became impossible. Sheep raisers found themselves forced to imitate cattlemen by gaining title to a permanent base camp, usually acquired under the Federal laws and strategically placed so as to command sources of water. From this base their sheep roved outward on seasonal migrations that were increasingly to leased or purchased ranges, often obtained from railroads. Ultimately permanent summer leases became possible in the new national forests that were created at the end of the century. But as late as 1892 a government survey reported that in the newer sheep regions such as Wyoming, "very little land is owned or leased by the sheepmen. They use for the greater part Government land."[43]

At shearing time the owners brought their animals to central points from which wool shipping would be possible. There they usually turned the job of shearing over to migratory crews that were "generally Mexicans, . . . or expert California shearers, who command higher wages, as they are more rapid and skillful."[44] Colorful shearing crews of Mexicans, handsomely dressed and handsomely mounted on horses with silver-ornamented bridles, were annual visitors to sheep ranches and sheep centers throughout much of the west, thus serving as picturesque reminders that theirs was the race that had pioneered this vast industry.[45]

CHAPTER 11

Farming in a Land of Limited Rain

A S PART of his report for 1910, the director of the census bureau had his geographers prepare a series of maps that would show "the density of the rural population" in each recent decade. In American thinking, "rural" comes close to meaning "agricultural,"* and in the *Statistical Atlas* of the 1910 census the degree of ruralness was linked to the prevalence of agriculture. The map for 1870 was the first to include the west, and in so doing it revealed patterns that were to persist in each census until the turn of the century.[1]

Starting approximately from San Antonio, close to the ninety-eighth meridian, the eastern frontier extended northward in fairly solid fashion until Sioux Falls, South Dakota, near the ninety-seventh meridian. West of that the situation was quite different. "Settlements in the West, beyond the frontier line, had arranged themselves mainly in three belts." The easternmost of the three followed the Rio Grande through New Mexico and went on through central Colorado to a point north of Cheyenne. To the west of it was a second belt, essentially of Mormon settlement, which extended from the few occupied spots in Arizona north through the center of Utah to southeastern Idaho. The final belt was the Pacific Coast, including western Nevada. As interpreted by the census director:

*Webster's New International Dictionary, 3d. ed., defines *rural* as "living in country areas: engaged in agricultural pursuits."

220

These three great western groups comprised nine-tenths of the population west of the frontier line. The remainder was scattered about in the valleys and the mountains of Montana, Idaho, and Arizona, at military posts, isolated mining camps, and on cattle ranches.

Later maps in the atlas depicted the eastern frontier as growing denser with population after 1870 and advancing westward along a north-south front, while the three belts to the west continued to be the distinct, separate entities that they had been in 1870—essentially elongated islands in a vast sea that the census classified as "unsettled," used chiefly by hunters, prospectors, and stock raisers. The belts thickened as settlement within their own limits increased, and as growth spread into lands immediately adjacent, but their isolation from each other and from the eastern frontier was only lessened, not eliminated, by the occasional fingers of settlement that thrust out tentatively in an east-west direction.

This failure of the rural population to fill in the west's huge open spaces illustrated a harsh reality: to advance beyond cattle and sheep grazing into an agriculture more extensive than the essentially subsistence level of the New Mexicans and the Mormons required water, transportation, and understanding. Over most of the western half of the country a precipitation of only eight to twenty inches a year was painfully common, and an abundance of sunshine and a low relative humidity made for a high rate of evaporation. The New Mexican and Mormon farmers had been able to satisfy their water requirements by a relatively primitive, cooperative type of small-scale irrigation, although Mormon agriculture in the 1850s had been disappointing.[2]

Thereafter, as new markets offered new opportunities, the New Mexican villages found it difficult to respond on a large scale because of the antiquated nature of their farming practices and the poverty and illiteracy of the villagers. By what must have been a great effort, accompanied by self-denial, the Mormons squeezed out of their small farms a surplus of food for man and beast when the 1860s and 1870s brought new customers: the mines, the Army, and the personnel and work animals of the successive transportation companies. By using their own wagons, they were able to begin delivering flour, potatoes, eggs, butter, dried peaches, and early vegetables to towns and mining camps throughout the Rockies and

Great Basin even before the newly completed railroads could provide a more efficient and extensive distribution.[3]

The need for western-grown food was immediate, and beyond that was the allure of raising big crops for export. Colorado, with its many new consumers, was making a manful effort, but even in the early 1870s meat and flour were the only staples produced in quantities large enough to satisfy the local market. With a rainfall of only fourteen inches at Denver, there was much to learn. Enthusiasts such as Byers, the newspaper editor, and Evans, the governor, had proved that farming was possible, for both operated general farms on land that is today within Denver's city limits, while in the valleys of the South Platte, Arkansas, Cache la Poudre, Saint Vrain Creek, Huerfano, and Fontaine-qui-Bouille good crops were coming from small farms that used the rich bottomlands, where short ditches and brush-and-stone diversion dams turned the water out of the river to irrigate the crops.[4]

There were two areas where a bigger effort was possible, on the Pacific Coast and on the eastern frontier. Both possessed transportation, the one by river steamer and oceangoing vessel, the other by the increasingly numerous railroads. The Pacific Coast north of San Francisco and west of the Cascades and Sierras had sufficient rainfall; elsewhere the Pacific Coast shared with the Great Plains a precipitation that was sufficient for crops in some years and disastrously inadequate in others. Neither area had enough farmers who understood dry-land agriculture.

In the 1860s and 1870s, as the atlas showed, most settlers on the eastern frontier were still east of the Great Plains, east of the ninety-eighth meridian, which is to say, still on the safer side of that line of semiaridity that marks the point where special crops or special practices are needed. By the late 1870s settlers were starting what in the 1880s would become a rush into the heart of the Great Plains, in such areas as the Dakotas, western Kansas and Nebraska, and presently eastern Colorado. A swarm of land promoters, journalists, and railroad agents persuasively assured both American and immigrant farmers that there was no longer a drought problem west of the ninety-eighth nor even the hundredth meridian. Pamphlets were printed in most of the North European languages, and agents were sent abroad to find more recruits. Railroads offered attractive rates to transport farm families and their goods, and made railroad land available on time payments.[5]

Long before that the Pacific Coast had gone into grain raising on an immense scale, as the Great Plains farmers would do in the 1880s. Although the Californians raised very large amounts of barley for animal feed, and the southern plainsmen at first tried corn, the predominant crop on both the Pacific Coast and the Great Plains was wheat. As J. R. Dodge, the veteran statistician of the United States Department of Agriculture, explained, "The pioneers of agricultural settlement have been wheat growers, and exclusive wheat growing has been the advance guard of agricultural forces in this country."[6]

Both Oregon and California plunged quickly into wheat, even though early experience showed that more intensive crops were possible. Because it was situated at the point where Pacific storms dumped their load as they crossed the Coast Range and collided with the Cascades, the Willamette Valley had a rainfall that was extraordinary for a western region, perhaps forty inches a year. A pleasing mixture of prairie, hill-slope, and timbered land gave the valley further potentialities.

Among leaders in the early Willamette were the Luelling, or Lewelling, family (the spelling varied even between brothers). They were Quaker abolitionists from North Carolina who moved to Indiana to get into free territory, then shifted to Iowa before forming a wagon train in 1847 to haul to Oregon several hundred boxes of grafted fruit and nut trees, vines, and berry bushes. In the Willamette Valley they joined a former Iowa neighbor, William Meek, who soon married one of the Luelling daughters. Meek had hauled twenty grafted trees across the plains.[7]

Together the Luellings and Meek put in orchards and established the first nursery on the Pacific Coast. Apples from their young trees established an Oregon specialty when successfully marketed in San Francisco in 1853 and 1854. Annually thereafter Oregon exported large quantities of apples to California, but by the 1870s production had gone so far ahead of demand that farmers were feeding apples to pigs—and were looking for something more profitable.[8] The Willamette, which had been sending some wheat and flour to California since 1847, started in the crop year 1855–1856 to make shipments to San Francisco that were substantial and regular.

With the opening of the new interior mining regions in the 1860s, some of the flour began to go directly "to the mining camps of the mountains," as the surveyor general expressed it, while the rest continued to go to San Francisco, "from where it is sent to Nevada and the vast interior at great speculation, or shipped abroad to different parts of the world."[9]

An English visitor protested at the neglect of fruit and dairying that this "exclusive devotion to wheat" was causing, and yet acknowledged:

But the temptation to grow wheat is very strong. It is the staple product of the State, and hardly ever fails in quality. The farmers understand it; their system of life is organized with a view to it. A thousand bushels of wheat in the warehouse is as good as money in the bank and is in reality a substitute for it. There is a clear understanding of what it costs to plant, harvest, and warehouse, and it involves the lowest amount of trouble and anxiety.[10]

So the Willamette landowners went heavily into wheat, often with an extensive use of migratory crews and equipment. Contractors who brought their own horses and machinery made agreements to plow and sow in the early spring, while other contractors came in the summer to harvest and sack the grain. Crews of transient workers accompanied them. Smaller farmers pressed the whole family into service during the peak season, with wives and daughters working alongside the menfolk.[11]

In part this development of large-scale wheat growing was made possible by Congress' generosity in passing the Donation Land Law of 1850, which granted not the customary 160 acres but rather twice that to each pioneer, and a like amount to his wife. Subsequent amendments extended the privilege to those who came to Oregon as late as 1855, although on the reduced basis of 160 acres to each settler or 320 to a family. These initial grants were often enlarged when Donation Land holders bought out their neighbors' claims.

While big tracts are necessary to large-scale wheat growing, probably this early concentration of landownership helps to explain both the appearance of sharecropper tenancy in a region where one would not expect it, and the frequent reports that through making themselves "land poor," Willamette farmers worked their land badly and were careless about the upkeep of their farms.[12]

California followed much the same course, save on a bigger scale. Quite aside from what the missions had proved, there were old hands who had come before the gold rush and were well aware of what could be grown. John Bidwell, once an impecunious schoolteacher and land claimant in Ohio and on the Missouri River frontier, was a famous example. Arriving in California in 1841, he served as John A. Sutter's ablest assistant before the gold discovery. With money he made in the mines, he acquired from the holders of a Mexican grant a ranch that ultimately totaled almost twenty-six thousand acres at Chico, in the upper Sacramento Valley. He chose well, for he obtained a lovely site on the Sacramento River, where water transportation was possible, and being that far north, the rainfall was twenty-four inches a year, which for California is good indeed.

There Bidwell began raising wheat on what became an imperial scale. To give balance to his operations, he put in fruit trees, vines, vegetables, and melons, irrigating them with water diverted from Chico Creek. By 1878 his wheat was of such a quality as to win a gold medal at the International Exposition in Paris. Distinguished naturalists such as Asa Gray, Sir Joseph Hooker, Joseph LeConte, C. C. Parry, and John Muir visited Bidwell's magnificent farm and stayed in the Italianate Victorian mansion that he built for his bride in 1868. He had met his bride in Washington, D.C., whither he had gone to serve a term in Congress.[13]

There were less-famous examples also. John M. Horner, from New Jersey, had come to California in 1846 with a shipload of Mormons. After trying the mines, he settled at Mission San Jose, near another pre-gold-rush arrival, E. L. Beard, whose varied career included milling, pork packing, stone quarrying, and government contracts. In choosing Mission San Jose, the two men were beginning at a site where even though the padres' old orchards, vineyards, crop fields, and irrigation works had been neglected, their presence was a guide to what had been possible in a place that had a local rainfall of only fifteen inches, because of its position in the shadow of the Coast Range.

Both Horner and Beard raised grain, potatoes, and vegetables. Beard developed a vineyard and became a partner of the Luellings and Meek when they extended their orchard enterprises to California. Horner became famous for his vigorous attempts to develop laborsaving machinery to harvest the wheat crop in this land of high labor costs. By 1867–1868 he and his son were demonstrating a combined harvester-thresher of their own design. It's a pity to spoil a success story by pointing out that Beard went bankrupt through speculating in land, while Horner lost heavily in San Francisco real estate. But that, too, was characteristic of California; farmers were as speculatively minded as miners.[14]

Finally there are the examples of Jean Louis Vignes and William Wolfskill. In the 1840s and 1850s the center of grape culture, wine making, and orange growing was at Los Angeles, where, with a rainfall of sixteen inches, irrigation was considered a necessity. Los Angeles was then an isolated, backward place that could reach the chief market at San Francisco only by none-too-reliable coastal shipping.

Vignes, born near the great Bordeaux wine region, was the leading vineyardist. He and his French nephews developed during the 1830s and 1840s a grape and wine business that became highly profitable during the 1850s and 1860s. Vignes' success attracted the attention of an incongruous recruit, William Wolfskill, a Kentucky-born fur trapper—a "mountain man"—who had wandered over the southwest before settling in Los Angeles, where his brother joined him. There he learned from Vignes how to cultivate grapes and make wine and brandy. Later he shifted part of his grape growing northward to the Sacramento and Napa valleys, from which shipment to San Francisco was far easier. Wolfskill also copied Vignes in transplanting oranges from the old Mission San Gabriel to his own land. When his trees flourished in the warm, dry, sunny atmosphere, Wolfskill expanded his grove into the first commercial-sized citrus enterprise in California. By the 1870s he claimed that he was making a profit of one thousand dollars an acre.[15]

With these veterans of the older California proving that California was capable of a remarkably varied agriculture, it is interesting to discover that even more than in the Willamette Valley, economic pressures pushed farmers toward the customary pioneer obsession with grain growing. Newcomers of the 1850s and 1860s had greater faith in grain as a crop for lands of relatively low rainfall than in other types of agriculture, and they were driven by the realization that grain would give a return at the first harvest and after a minimum initial investment per acre, whereas fruit trees and vines required years to mature. A San Francisco mercantile journal summed up the situation in 1862:

The necessity of quick returns has made the production of the cereal crops almost the sole agricultural employment of California; the vineyard and orchard investments as yet afford employment to but a small minority of our population, and have not reached the point of steady return on the investment.[16]

A rush into grain raising thus characterized the era from the 1850s to the 1890s. Operations were on a large scale—thousands or even tens of thousands of acres to a farm—and were carried on by an extensive use of machinery of increasingly large and sophisticated design, sometimes built in California, sometimes imported from the east. By the late 1880s, "combines" that cut, threshed, and sacked the grain in a single laborsaving operation were in widespread use, and were so big that steam-powered tractors were being used to haul them. As in the Willamette, contractors and migratory crews served many of the ranches. There was much hiring of seasonal labor, in which ethnic minorities such as the Chinese bulked large.[17] Level valley land in big tracts, well suited to machine cultivation and harvesting, could be bought or leased from successful claimants to "Spanish" (really Mexican) grants, or could be obtained through speculators who specialized in putting together estates through exploiting flaws in the congressional and state land laws that controlled disposition of the public domain. A distinguished modern scholar has asserted that "land monopoly or concentration of ownership almost unexampled for the United States" characterized California.[18]

Because of several poor crop years in the late 1850s and early 1860s, and because of the rising demand of California and the mining empire in the interior, really large crops that required heavy exportation overseas did not come into the San Francisco market until the late 1860s. From that date production soared. The federal census, which must always be used with caution, ranked California eighth among the states in wheat production by 1869, seventh by 1879, and second by 1889, at which time only Minnesota exceeded California. The census director pointed out that "practically one-fifth of the total wheat crop of the country in 1889 was raised in the states of Minnesota and California."[19]

The principal foreign market for these huge crops was Liverpool, whose great Corn Exchange attracted grain from all over the world. Liverpool wheat prices came very largely to control California and Oregon prices. British merchants, insurance and shipping men, and the American agents of British firms and banks crowded the business streets of San Francisco. Sailing vessels, predominantly of British registry, carried away the crop on the sixteen-thousand-mile voyage to the United Kingdom. Since the grain exports demanded far more shipping than was required for California's imports, incoming vessels searched the world for inbound cargoes. Some brought coal, pig iron, tin, cement, or general merchandise from British or European ports. Others carried merchandise from Britain or Europe to Australia, and there took on coal for San Francisco, or carried coal or general merchandise from Britain to Calcutta, Bombay, or Hong Kong, and from one of those Oriental ports sailed to San Francisco with light cargoes or in ballast. American ships brought iron, coal, or merchandise from American Atlantic ports.[20]

The grain trade of California and the Pacific Northwest, which marketed much of its crop through San Francisco, thus came to involve a large part of the world. In the record season of 1881–1882, docks on San Francisco Bay or waters immediately tributary to it loaded 559 ships with wheat and flour, while the smaller exports through Portland filled eighty-one ships in 1879–1880 and a hundred or more in the later 1890s, when new railroads had fully opened the interior grain lands. Seattle and Tacoma, sharing a gradually rising export from Puget Sound, cleared a total that ranged from twenty-three to seventy-four ships a year during the decade 1892–1901.[21]

This huge increase of export cargoes was made possible in California by the opening of large new acreages as railroad construction supplemented water transport by building into the Sacramento and San Joaquin valleys and penetrating the Salinas Valley, while in Oregon the filling up of the Willamette Valley forced settlers eastward across the Cascades, into the plains, benchlands, and rolling hills of eastern Oregon and Washington, where the soil was rich and deep but the precipitation far less than on the seaward side of the Cascades. Here settlement was slow at first because of inadequate access to markets. Until the railroads came, the only outlet was down the Snake and Columbia rivers, where, because of successive unloadings and reloadings at each portage, the cost of transportation was equal to the amount the farmer received. Like the Sacramento and the San Joaquin, this was a region suited to laborsaving machinery and large-scale production. The Walla Walla and Palouse-Spokane districts were destined to rank among the richest agricultural regions in the nation, but through railroad service came only in the 1880s and 1890s.[22]

During the first decade of the grain trade the key figure was a man whom the California farmers denounced as a speculator and monopolist. Isaac Friedlander, said to have been six feet seven inches tall and three hundred pounds in weight, was the son of German-Jewish immigrant parents. He had grown up in South Carolina, where he married a lady who later became famous for her lavish San Francisco dinners, which kept her guests at table for hours as they struggled to down a cornucopia of foods. A Forty-Niner, Friedlander soon abandoned the mines for San Francisco and the highly speculative grain, flour, and shipping business.

Friedlander recognized that it was going to be difficult to attract enough grain ships each year to so remote a port as San Francisco. By building up an unrivaled intelligence service to report the probable size of the prospective crop throughout the Pacific Coast, and creating an equally good system for discovering what shipping was available throughout the world, Friedlander performed an essential service, but like any entrepreneur in the cutthroat business atmosphere of San Francisco, he exacted his price. He released to would-be exporters the shipping he had chartered and the grain his agents had contracted for at as great an increase in rate as he could get away with.

In the period when the national Order of Patrons of Husbandry, better known as the Grangers, was at its height, the angry Californians formed a State Grange and tried to unite the farmers in an effort to throw the export business to a rival firm in 1873 and 1874. They failed dramatically because they underestimated Friedlander's shrewdness, but Friedlander, too, had his limits. In 1877 he misjudged the balance between the size of the crop and number of ships needed and went into bankruptcy. He died before he could reestablish his business.[23]

The Granger episode revealed how unusual California farmers could be. The first Master of the State Grange was a Princeton graduate and former Confederate officer, then engaged in cultivating four thousand acres of grain. The Overseer was a large landowner who had studied medicine and law, had operated a quicksilver mine, and had subdivided land grants. The Lecturer was a Yale graduate who had practiced law and served in the legislature. A well-informed contemporary said of the men he saw around him in the San Joaquin that by education and experience they were better suited to "managing general business" than to "tilling the soil."[24] The San Francisco *Alta California* declared, "The great difficulty with our agriculturists . . . is that they all want to own enormous bodies of land and raise tremendous crops of wheat."[25]

As a recent scholar has suggested,[26] being a wheat baron was more than just an occupation; it was a badge of distinction, of social and political status, rather like that of the South Texas cattle kings, the New Mexican sheep grandees, or the southern California rancheros. The greatest of the grain barons was Hugh J. Glenn, called "doctor" because he had studied medicine at St. Louis before the Mexican War and the California gold rush drew him away. Virginia-born, and the son of a merchant, he crisscrossed the west many times as drover, freighter, livestock raiser, and trader before he bought his first seven thousand acres of "Spanish" grant land in 1867, for $1.60 an acre. This he persistently enlarged until he ruled a kingdom of perhaps fifty-five thousand acres along the upper Sacramento River. Like other wheat growers, he depended on an army of migratory workers, and was accused of preferring Chinese and Mexicans to Americans. He bought the biggest and best labor-saving machinery, built barns, shops, bunkhouses, a brick warehouse, miles of fence, and, for himself and his family, a mansion on the farm and another in Oakland. On the side he backed Missouri-born Peter French in what became a large cattle-grazing operation on the pastures of southeastern Oregon. Always a speculator and borrower as well as a builder, Glenn left a long list of anxious creditors when a recently discharged employee blasted him to death with a shotgun.[27]

Meantime, the heedlessness of growers caused the soil to lose its richness through "our slovenly methods of farming,"[28] by which "the land has been exhausted by a succession of crops and poor cultivation, with no other object than the reaping of immediate reward."[29] There was no provision for crop rotation or fertilization. Specialization was so extreme that farmers bought the food they put on their tables, instead of setting aside the land and time to have kitchen gardens.[30] Much land was leased to tenants, often on a shares basis, and on rented property there was little more than "a shanty for cooking and sleeping . . . absolutely nothing to make life endurable or pleasant."[31]

Even as the wheat trade reached its peak in the 1880s and 1890s, a permanent change was beginning. On longer-used lands the yield per acre was declining. The world price was weakening because countries as varied as India, Argentina, Russia, Canada, Australia, and Rumania were joining the American Middle West and North Central states in sending huge surpluses to Britain. Big landowners were being offered attractive terms to convert their holdings into small tracts suitable for irrigation or other types of intensive farming. As the *Pacific Rural Press* expressed it, "Wheat decreases because other more profitable uses are found for the land,"[32] now that more people, capital, and transportation were available. Just at the turn of the century an extraordinarily rapid shift took place. If the census is to be trusted, wheat acreage in California declined about 83 percent between 1899 and 1909. By 1903–1904 California was not growing enough wheat to feed itself, and was making up the deficit by increased importation from the Pacific Northwest, and later from Idaho.[33]

Meanwhile, nearly half a continent away the rush into the Great Plains was carrying another group of agrarian speculators out into lands that were climatically more variable and dangerous than even the southern part of California's San Joaquin. Despite the check during the depression of 1873, all of the Great Plains states and territories save the Dakotas had won an extensive railroad mileage by the end of the 1870s. In 1879 Kansas claimed 3,000 miles, Texas 2,500, Nebraska 1,600, and Colorado 1,200.[34] Land was more available and at lower cost than in much of California and Oregon.

A temporary increase in rainfall, starting in 1878, seemed to disprove the earnest warnings of a dedicated government scientist, John Wesley Powell, whose famous *Report on the Lands of the Arid*

Region of the United States was published in that very year. Powell argued that beyond the hundredth meridian farming of the traditional kind must give way to two types better suited to the climate: small, irrigated farms based on cooperatively built irrigation systems of the Mormon kind, or large grazing farms that would include small irrigable tracts on which to raise food and forage.[35]

Modern research and a century of additional experience have shown the wisdom of Powell's advice. Mary W. M. Hargreaves, a careful historian whose focus has been on the western Dakotas and eastern Montana, has found that "the margin between success and failure in dry-land agriculture is very narrow." An inch less than the essential minimum means "complete failure," and a couple of inches more still means only a light crop. Maps of the United States Department of Agriculture verify the danger by showing that the percentage of years with inadequate rainfall is appallingly high.[36]

With railroads reaching out now into these new lands, few restless westward-looking farmers were willing to listen to gloomy warnings. Hamlin Garland later recalled the excitement among his Iowa neighbors. Speaking of 1881 he said:

The movement of settlers toward Dakota had now become an exodus, a stampede. Hardly anything else was talked about as neighbors met one another on the road or at the Burr Oak school-house on Sundays. Every man who could sell out had gone west or was going. . . . Farmer after farmer joined the march to Kansas, Nebraska, and Dakota. "We are wheat raisers," they said, "and we intend to keep in the wheat belt."[37]

In Kansas and Nebraska, farmers were already beyond the hundredth meridian, despite crop failures in 1879 and 1880, and with the return of better rain and crops in 1883 and 1884, the boom carried settlers out toward the 102d. In the Dakotas, exaggerated reports of the success of the great bonanza farms in the Red River Valley, on the Minnesota-Dakota border east of the Great Plains, misled eager land seekers into thinking that farms further west would be equally good, with the result that in the 1880s the population of the Dakotas increased about three and three quarters times and the number of farms five and a half times. Eastern Colorado, hitherto regarded as unsuited to farming, now began to receive grain raisers.[38]

Texas and Oklahoma had been held back by the Civil War, by the

big Indian reservations in Oklahoma, and by competition with cattlemen once the Plains Indians had been brought under control.
Now in Texas "nesters" began to push determinedly into the cattlemen's domain north of the unassailable cattle baronies of South
Texas. Avaricious eyes turned toward the reservation lands of Oklahoma. White pressure for Oklahoma land became incessant during
the 1870s and 1880s, and between 1889 and 1901 most of Oklahoma fell under white control.[39]

Terrible droughts struck in the late 1880s and early 1890s, sometimes locally, sometimes throughout the plains. Crop failures, the
same sagging world grain prices from which the Pacific Coast was
suffering, and the national depression of 1893 combined to send
some of the recently arrived settlers reeling back eastward whence
they had come, abandoning new homes and whole new towns, while
others grimly hung on and were joined by still newer settlers who
hurried in when better crops and prices returned in the late 1890s.[40]
James Malin, the historian of the Kansas wheat belt, summed up the
two decades 1883–1902 with the terse remark that the era opened
and closed well, but "between these termini was a period of extremes of climate, accompanied by a disastrous world-wide economic depression."[41]

A historian has summarized the grim side of Kansas farm life.
Farm life, he found, was characterized by "hard, physically exhausting, and often unrewarding toil." Farm homes tended to be small
and cramped, "sanitary conditions" were lacking, insect pests were
a problem, drinking water was often polluted, and isolation from
neighbors was common. Upon the overworked housewife fell
"never-ending household and farm drudgery."[42] No wonder that
Kansas rural populations tended to be highly mobile![43]

At a cost, success was possible, as John Ise's intensely personal
recollections demonstrate. His parents, Henry and Rosie, both of
tenacious German stock, were dominated by an exhausting, anxious
struggle in which there was never more than a slim margin between
success and failure. Nevertheless they made their farm in north-
central Kansas support a large family through the children's growing
years and even managed to send the children to college and still have
the farm as a property that could be rented to tenants when Rosie—
old, widowed, and careworn—was persuaded by her daughters to
retire to Lawrence, where they were attending the university.[44]

Those who stayed in the Great Plains had to learn by trial and error that they must be more flexible in their farming, because there was no single crop or formula that would ensure survival in a region of "great variability of rainfall from season to season," of recurrent droughts, "excessively high and low temperatures," and "hazards of hail, frost, and hot winds."[45] Before that essential lesson had been learned, a self-trained exponent of a "system of scientific soil culture" for dry-land farms came forward and won a large following.

A hardy Vermonter, Webster Campbell, homesteaded in South Dakota in 1879 and lost several grain crops before he began to think out the successive steps that became his "system." Campbell proved to be a persuasive advocate who published a magazine about his scheme for dry farming, wrote numerous editions of his "how-to-do-it" manual, organized "congresses" (conventions) to discuss his ideas, and won the railroads' support for demonstration farms.

For a time many accepted his argument that moisture could be stored up in the soil and made available to plants by the right tillage practices, but over a period of years scientists in the new Federal and state agricultural research bureaus became increasingly skeptical, until ultimately most of Campbell's procedures were rejected as damaging to the soil or unnecessarily expensive.[46]

Campbell was curiously uninterested in the much more promising approach of mixing wheat raising with forage crops, corn, and livestock feeding, instead of relying on a single source of income.[47] In the 1880s and 1890s farmers were trying drought-resistant forage crops, often from abroad, such as sorghum, kafir corn, millet, and Australian saltbush. As early as the 1870s a kind of hard winter wheat that became known as Turkey Red was being raised in Kansas by German Mennonites who had formerly lived in the Russian Crimea. Research by Kansas State Agricultural College in the 1880s and the United States Department of Agriculture in the later 1890s confirmed what practical experience was demonstrating: Turkey Red had an unusual winter-hardiness that peculiarly fitted it for this difficult environment.[48]

Great Plains farmers were not unique in trying to find ways to make a crop on lands that were neither safely humid nor so decisively arid as to be unthinkable without irrigation. Long before the term dry farming had come into common usage, Utah Mormons of the 1860s had stumbled upon some of the techniques of that art,[49] and Californians, struggling to overcome the droughts of the 1860s and 1870s, had argued about "summer fallowing," deep versus shallow plowing, and maintaining a "soil mulch," very much as if they had been Campbell's followers. Dry farming in the Columbia Basin of eastern Washington began later but became extensive.[50]

A safer, more certain approach was through irrigation, which had the further advantage of making possible a wide range of crops, including fruits and vegetables. The Mormons, of course, were the example always cited to prove what could be done. In retrospect it is clear that they constituted a special case. Their great accomplishment was to use irrigation for the social and religious purpose of creating self-sustaining, cohesive, small-farm villages whose problems were smoothed out by church leadership and aid.

By the late nineteenth century their irrigation systems were being criticized for inefficiency and waste of water. Their canals and diversion dams had been built in relatively crude fashion, there was much seepage, and the individual canals were rarely more than a few miles long. No attempt to build large reservoirs, so as to retain water that would otherwise be lost in flood season, was made until the 1870s, and as population increased, it became necessary to irrigate additional lands by building costly "highline" canals that tapped the streams well above earlier diversions.[51] Equally disturbing, the much vaunted Mormon ability to settle water disputes was breaking down under the pressure of too many users on each stream, too little coordination between groups of users, and too little observance of the several territorial statues that had been passed to lessen these ills.[52]

A more sophisticated version of the Mormon communal values was sought in Colorado when Nathan C. Meeker of Greeley's New York *Tribune* was sent west on a reportorial assignment.[53] Meeker was a restless soul who had been converted to the teachings of Fourier, the French social philosopher, and in the 1840s had lived in a Fourierist "phalanx" in Meeker's native Ohio. The failure of that experiment did not weaken his convictions about the virtues of communal living. The possibilities that he sensed in Colorado so excited him that upon returning to New York he enlisted his employer's support in organizing the "Union Colony," which soon named its town "Greeley."

The colony, as planned in 1869, was to be restricted to people of good moral character who were believers in temperance. Neither saloons, nor billiard halls, nor gambling houses were to be permitted, and the Sabbath was to be strictly observed. Intellectual life was to be furthered by a school, library, lyceum, dramatic society, and farmers' discussion club. As with the Mormons, social values were to be encouraged by concentrating the residential lots in the town, while leaving the farm tracts outside. This consciously moral, intellectual, and social stance proved to be a uniting influence during the difficult early days of the colony, for the colonists were proud of being different.

William Byers, the journalist, ever alert to promotional opportunities, helped steer the colonists to the purchase of land within the Denver Pacific Railroad grant, in the valley of the Cache la Poudre River, north of Denver. A Denver newspaper reported in June of 1870 that most of the early arrivals were from the east, but "a few from California and Montana, one family from Utah, and about 25 from Colorado."[54] The presence of a western minority was not enough to keep the majority from serious initial errors: at first they failed to provide for water rights, they grossly underestimated the cost of digging an irrigation system, their intended canals were too small and were badly engineered, and they never were able to build two of the four canals anticipated. After one false start, the segments of the canals were built by contractors and workers who were members of the colony.

Harsh reality forced the colonists to abandon their original dream of vineyards and orchards and go into a more general type of farming, which sometimes led to bigger farms than had been intended, and hard necessity, again, led to the development of the famous "Greeley potato" as a reliable and exportable cash crop. Through all this travail the intellectual vitality of the colony was so well maintained that in the judgment of a modern reclamation engineer, "much of the present-day knowledge of the requirements of irrigation in the Western states was learned from the experiments of the Greeley Colony."[55]

Greeley's success inspired many imitators in Colorado in the 1870s. Some were genuine colonies, based on pooling funds to finance the large "start-up" costs of irrigation. Some began as colonies but fell into the control of promoters and speculators. Others were nothing but land-selling schemes masquerading as "colonies."

The successful ones formed a chain of irrigation towns along the eastern base of the Rockies, from Fort Collins to South Pueblo, so that the new Anglo settlements just about linked up with the old Hispano communities and the individual pioneer farms of southern Colorado. Sugar beets, potatoes, and a wide variety of fruits came to characterize these flourishing towns.

The weakness in the Colorado boom was the tendency of developers to project more canals and ditches than there was water to fill them, and for the irrigators to repeat the Mormons' mistake of diverting all the water to lands close to rivers or creeks, without allowing for the eventual costly need to build "highline" canals that could bring water to the far larger amount of land that was "back from the stream" and on benches above it.[56]

California was the most complicated of all the irrigation states and territories, because within it even adjacent localities differed significantly in such critical factors as amount of precipitation, temperature, wind, fog, soil, and nearness to river seepage. In central and northern California it was so hard to tell where or whether irrigation might be necessary that little use of that art was made until after 1870.

By contrast, the plains near Los Angeles, in addition to raising grain, forage, and garden produce for local consumption, used irrigation (as practiced by Wolfskill, Vignes, and others) to supply a modest seaborne export to San Francisco of specialty products such as wine, brandy, table grapes, oranges, and lemons. But foreign wines and brandy continued to be imported at San Francisco, and until well into the 1870s oranges came in from Mexico, the Hawaiian Islands, Tahiti, and China.[57] No major change favorable to southern California could be expected until there was an improvement in transportation, in quality of oranges, grapes, and wine, and in the ability of farmers to irrigate more of southern California's ample acreage.

Transportation improved as local rail service spread during the 1870s and the Southern Pacific connected Los Angeles to the outer world in 1876, the Santa Fe in 1885. Better oranges came with the introduction of two key species: navels in 1873 and Valencias in 1876, the former maturing in winter, the latter in summer.

A pioneer attempt to make irrigated agriculture possible for settlers of limited means started in the later 1850s.[58] Under the intellectual and business leadership of four prominent Germans from San Francisco and Los Angeles, fifty city folk of German origin were persuaded to form the Los Angeles Vineyard Society in 1857. Most of the subscribers were mechanics, artisans, storekeepers, or teamsters—though, being Germans, they included a poet, several musicians, a bookbinder, and a schoolteacher! Nearly all were poor, ignorant of agriculture, and uninformed about the grapes and wine making that were to be their new preoccupation.

They retained George Hansen of Los Angeles, "a German lawyer and civil engineer, a man of culture," to do the preliminaries, which included buying the land, surveying it into twenty-acre vineyard lots and a cluster of small residential lots, putting in an irrigation system based on diverting water from the Santa Ana River, and planting grapevines and some fruit trees. By staying at their city jobs, the subscribers earned the money to send Hansen monthly payments.

Through employing "Spaniards and Indians," Hansen got the ditch digging and planting done on this barren-looking plain where little grew save cactus, wild mustard, and coarse grass, although the presence of willows suggested a high water table. When disagreements broke up the cooperative character of the enterprise in 1859, the members had the good sense to incorporate a communal water company and insist that all landowners must be shareholders and must contribute labor for maintenance. This may have been the inspiration for the mutual water companies that became one of the most frequent and successful patterns for irrigation systems in the west.

Although the first decade proved a time of poverty and uncertainty, in which everything had to be learned by trial and error, nevertheless "Anaheim," as the colonists named their village, finally succeeded, and by the opening of the 1870s was being touted as the pattern for group settlement by small farmers of limited means. Publicity about Anaheim had the greater effect because it coincided with news about Greeley.

What is more, that first decade was not all hardship. When Charles Nordhoff visited Anaheim in 1872, the settlers told him that they had enough to eat, a school for their children, and the satisfaction of being their own boss. One man said: "We had music and dancing in those days; and, though we were very poor, I look back to those times as the happiest in all our lives."

I.   People: The rich variety of ethnic backgrounds and ways of earning one's living in the West are suggested by this first group of photographs.

1.   Spanish-Californian girls at Santa Barbara, c. 1880. (Huntington Library)

2.   One of a group of photographs entitled "Views of Pasadena and San Gabriel Valley," this shows impromptu horseplay among Spanish-Californians. Especially interesting because it shows all ages and several families. (Huntington Library)

3. "Farm House in Kern County," California, photographed by Carleton E. Watkins, a leading photographer, and published in his *Photographic Views of Kern County, California* [San Francisco, 1889?]. (Huntington Library)

4. The steam engine operator and his assistant are black from the dust thrown out by the thresher their engine has been powering. (California State Library, California Section)

5. Idaho miners at work underground. Note power drill. (Idaho State Historical Society)

6. Cheerful skiers at the mining town of Atlanta, Idaho, where deep snow made any other form of travel impossible in winter. (Idaho State Historical Society)

7. *Harper's Weekly*, September 25, 1875, tells the story of the apparent suicide of William Chapman Ralston when the Bank of California failed and brought down Ralston's empire with it. (Huntington Library)

8. A Chinese merchant family. The Saisun family, from Thomas Houseworth Co., *Pacific Coast Scenery* [San Francisco, 1872]. (Huntington Library)

9.   Crow chiefs, from William Henry Jackson, *Photographs of Yellowstone National Park, Utah, Montana, Idaho, Colorado and of Indians* [Washington, 1870–1875]. Part of Jackson's excellent work for the Hayden Survey. (Huntington Library)

10.   Bannock Indian family group, another of Jackson's photographs for the Hayden Survey. (Huntington Library)

II. Their Cities: The few cities were essential. They directed the flow of supplies and equipment and were the recreational and cultural centers. San Francisco was the greatest of them.

11. Instead of the disorderly gold rush town of half a dozen years earlier, this and the following picture show that San Francisco had grown into a well-built commercial and financial center. The two pictures are from G. R. Fardon, *San Francisco Album: Photographs of the Most Beautiful Views and Public Buildings of San Francisco* [San Francisco, 1856]. (Huntington Library)

12. From Fardon, *San Francisco Album.* (Huntington Library)

13. With the constant growth of population, the city thrust its way outward to occupy all of San Francisco's famous hills. (Huntington Library)

14. With new wealth pouring into the bank accounts of railroad builders and mining magnates, ostentatious mansions like this Crocker one were built. (Huntington Library)

15. But wealth also brought culture to San Francisco, as this theater program of 1853 suggests, with its proud boast that it had attracted two of the most famous stage personalities of the day. (Huntington Library)

16. Denver was a decade younger than San Francisco but grew rapidly after railroads reached it. "Panorama of Denver," from William Henry Jackson's album *Centennial State, 1876–1882: A Memorial Offering of the Business Men and Pioneers of Denver, Colorado* [Denver, 1882]. (Huntington Library)

17. To show off his newly acquired wealth, H. A. W. Tabor built the "Tabor Grand Opera House" in Denver in 1880–1881. From Jackson's *Centennial State*. (Huntington Library)

18. "Virginia City from Water Flume," c. 1880, shows how large a mining community could become. In the 1860s and 1870s Virginia City was the queen of the silver mines. (Huntington Library)

19. The city's whole existence depended on the mines. This contemporary photograph of "Gould and Curry Works, General View" shows how elaborate mine buildings could become. (Huntington Library)

20. "The Tunnel, Gould and Curry Mine." (Huntington Library)

21. Between big regional centers like Denver and big mining towns like Virginia City, stood small cities or large towns that served their sub-regions. Main Street of Boise, Idaho, c. 1866. (Idaho State Historical Society)

22. Freighting over Ute Pass, Colorado. The empty trailers and wagon boxes show that the train has delivered its cargo. (Denver Public Library, Western History Department)

23. A photograph by C. E. Watkins shows the Central Pacific Railroad under construction. Note the Chinese workmen. The railroad was completed in 1869. (Huntington Library)

24. L. A. Huffman, a well-known western photographer, took this picture of "Round-up Outfit on the Move, Powder River, 1888." (Huntington Library)

25. Another Huffman photograph, of "Harris Lamb Band, 1888," eastern Montana. Note sheep herder with dog and gun. (Montana Historical Society)

26.   This and the following photograph show how the massive size of the California grain fields forced a use of correspondingly large labor-saving machinery. The "combines" shown here could cut, thresh, and sack the grain in a single sweep. The cutter bar on the left side cut the heads off the standing wheat, an elevator lifted it up to the thresher, where the grain was sacked and tossed onto wagons alongside. (California State Library, California Section)

27.   The number of animals required to haul the combines was so large that farmers resorted to steam power. Note the scope of the operation. (California State Library, California Section)

28 & 29.   These two photographs show the violence that resulted when management and absentee owners refused to negotiate with miners. As militancy grew, the miners blew up the Frisco mill in 1892. This was one of several bitter strikes in which Regular Army and National Guard troops were brought in. (Idaho State Historical Society)

The good reports from Anaheim and Greeley convinced promoters and farmers that a way had been found to open the arid west to small proprietors. In their optimism and inexperience few realized how much capital would be needed to see an irrigation project through its initial phase, before crop raising could begin. Few understood the new profession of irrigation engineering, or appreciated the need for ascertaining carefully what flow of water could be counted on at the critical periods in the growing season. Nor did they anticipate the expensive, obstructive litigation that would result from rival users seeking water from a common source in an era when legal precedents were uncertain and contradictory. The benefits of tying landownership to a right to use water, and of having communal water systems, were reasonably clear, but since promoters were more likely than prospective settlers to have access to the money needed to create an irrigation system, many water companies were sure to be privately owned corporations, at least at first. Many promoters of such corporations did not envisage the gulf that would open between them and the users if they tried to operate an irrigation system as a public utility.

The history of Riverside, farther east than Anaheim but still dependent on Santa Ana River water,[59] illustrates these problems but also shows how a major orange-growing center could arise on bleak ranchland so dry that local wits alleged the coyotes carried canteens. The project was the inspiration of two experienced promoters, Judge John Wesley North and Dr. James Porter Greves; both had come originally from New York State but had served in Nevada during the early mining boom, had been town promoters in the Great Lakes states, and carpetbaggers in the South after the Civil War.

Arriving in California by the new Union Pacific–Central Pacific train, the pair formed the Southern California Colony Association in 1870, with the majority of the stock subscribed by a San Franciscan and lesser amounts by men in Los Angeles, San Bernardino, and from within the colony. While eager families began camping on the dusty desert site to await water, the company built its ditch so badly that the work had to be done over again, and in the meantime two neighboring colony schemes had discovered that their ditches would have to go through the Southern California Colony property. Representing mostly San Francisco money, although with one Indianan, these rival companies bought out the Southern California Colony and consolidated all conflicting projects into one new corporation, whose subsidiary, the Riverside Canal Company, was to own and operate the ditches and water rights separately from the land that the promoters were hawking.

By sheer good luck, the navel orange was first planted in Riverside in 1873 and first fruited there in 1878. The resulting favorable publicity partially hid a growing controversy between the users of the water—the irrigators—and the canal company over the rates to be charged and over the question of whether landowners, once served by a water company, had an inherent right to require the all-important service to be continued, and if so, in view of the finite supply of water in the Santa Ana basin, whether there was a limit to the number of acres that the company could be permitted to contract to serve.

With no public regulatory body to help them, the angry irrigators first sought help from the state legislature and the county board of supervisors, then got Riverside incorporated as a city with power to regulate local water supplies. The company retaliated by neglecting to maintain its canals; crops suffered, lawsuits and counter-suits flew, and land sales dwindled, until in 1884–1885 the canal company agreed to sell out "to the citizens as a water company," with the citizens floating bonds to finance the purchase and put the canals into proper condition.

Once freed of this acute uncertainty, Riverside soon stood forth as a prosperous community of small landholders (average holding, 16.2 acres) that boasted of rising land values, high income per capita, and the beauty of its shady streets and comfortable homes. Riverside became the embodiment of a new California dream of small proprietors living in irrigated oases reclaimed from cattle ranges, wheat fields, or deserts. Its image helped to attract a massive influx of newcomers who took advantage of special railroad rates to pour into southern California.

Curiously, small orange growers proved to be as single-minded as big grain growers had been. A writer hired by the Riverside Board of Trade acknowledged:

The six thousand people now here are non-producers of the ordinary necessaries of life. The butter, eggs and poultry we use are mostly brought from Iowa, Illinois and San Francisco, and the potatoes from Utah and Oregon.

He added that the thousand laborers who cultivated Riverside's soil were "largely Chinese."[60]

In stressing the community control of water that ultimately emerged at Riverside, it is important not to overlook the twenty-one irrigation colonies that developed near Fresno, in the dry part of the San Joaquin Valley, by 1886. Most of these were commercial or even blatantly speculative ventures by owners of big tracts of land, and most were served by privately owned water companies. Finding themselves in competition with one another for settlers to buy their land, these companies resorted to offering attractive terms, including an orderly, planned growth and assured right to water, amenities such as tree-lined roads, and help to inexperienced newcomers. Land monopolies, in other words, were capable of devising appealing and constructive approaches.[61]

The successful efforts in California, Colorado, and the Mormon settlements might seem to indicate that the arid west had turned decisively to a type of agriculture suited to settlers of moderate means. But for the censuses of both 1890 and 1900 the census bureau hired Frederick H. Newell, one of Powell's assistants and later head of the reclamation service, to discover what in fact was being done with irrigation. The results were surprising. Newell reported that in 1890 nearly two thirds of the irrigated acreage was used by livestock ranchers, who gave "large areas of hay land" a crude flooding. This was especially true of Nevada and Wyoming, with their predominant cattle and sheep interests, somewhat less true of Montana and Colorado. Where irrigation was chiefly for forage, irrigated holdings tended to be large. Many had begun planting alfalfa, which by the turn of the century became the most extensively grown of all irrigated crops.[62]

Newell also pointed out that while the amount of land being irrigated seemed large—he estimated it at nearly 3.7 million acres in 1889 and over 7.5 million in 1899—the total for 1889 was actually only four tenths of 1 percent of the land west of the hundredth meridian. What's more, in 1889 he could find only 52,584 irrigators or irrigated farm holdings from the Rockies to the Pacific, plus 1,552 in the Great Plains. California easily led, with 13,732 irrigators and over a million acres, as compared to the next two, Colorado and Utah, which had approximately 9,700 irrigators each; but where Colorado irrigated 890,735 acres, Utah's total was only 263,473. (By 1899 the number of irrigators in the arid states had nearly doubled, to 102,819, and in the semiarid states had tripled, to 4,970.)[63]

Expressed differently, less than 26 percent of California's immense farm acreage in 1889 used any irrigation, whereas in Utah over 92 percent, in New Mexico nearly 70 percent, and in Colorado nearly 59 percent were at least partially irrigated. The same was true of relative newcomers such as Arizona (over 75 percent) and Idaho (over 65 percent). This means that while building a far larger agricultural enterprise than any other western state, up to 1890 California had made proportionately a much less frequent use of irrigation, primarily because wheat and barley were still favored, and secondarily because there were alternative crops that did not need irrigation, especially in the bay and coastal counties of central California.[64]

In that central part of California a remarkably cosmopolitan set of entrepreneurs were developing crops that seemed to offer the most contradictory evidence about the necessity for irrigation. The task of raising vegetables and berries for San Francisco and other urban markets was left to Portuguese, Italians, Germans, and Chinese, whose gardens were picturesquely irrigated by windmills. At San Jose French horticulturists and vineyardists had imported cuttings, seeds, and seedlings from their native country and were irrigating them from artesian wells.[65]

Near Marysville G. G. Briggs, who was the quintessential resourceful Yankee, was showing what could be done with fruit—without irrigation. Born in Ontario County, New York, and raised on a farm, he did a stint in Ohio before catching the gold fever in 1849. With money made not from mining but from raising watermelons to sell to miners, he started a peach orchard on bottomland alongside the Yuba River, where seepage kept the soil moist. By 1858 he was credited with having the largest orchard in bearing in California, and from it was sending off ten thousand pounds of fresh peaches daily to San Francisco and the mines. Soon afterward Briggs and his competitors found themselves producing far more perishable fruit than could be disposed of in markets within their reach. Even the opening of railroad service did not quickly solve their problem of overproduction.[66]

The embryonic northern vineyard and wine industry had especially picturesque pioneers. By great good fortune the European grape *(Vitis vinifera)*, from which all of the world's great wines are made, flourishes in California, whereas it is ill-suited to the cold winters and humid summers of most of America. The Spanish and Mexican "Mission" grape was an inferior but cheap and prolific species of *Vitis vinifera.*

Most flamboyant of the new leaders was the man who is now hailed as the "Father of California Wine," Agoston Haraszthy.[67] Late of the Hungarian landed class and the Royal Hungarian Body Guard, but exiled for liberal political views, Haraszthy had tried Wisconsin before asthma and the gold rush had brought him to California, where false starts at San Diego and San Francisco preceded his finding the warm and sunny Sonoma Valley, already proven by the vineyard planted by Mariano Guadalupe Vallejo, one of the best liked of the California leaders.

Here Haraszthy began in 1857 to develop his Buena Vista vineyard and winery. In 1861 he returned to Europe long enough to select and bring back nearly two hundred thousand cuttings and rooted vines from France, Germany, Italy, Spain, Portugal, and Hungary. He distributed the cuttings and vines among vineyardists and reported the findings of his tour in a widely used handbook.[68]

Haraszthy made Buena Vista his demonstration farm and pulpit. He proved and preached two points that were of major importance: that at least in coastal valleys like Sonoma, a better quality of wine could be made from grapes that had not been irrigated; and that the lighter, better-drained soils of the hillsides were better for wine than the richer, heavier lands of the valley floors.

Publicity generated by leaders like Haraszthy caused the first of many ill-justified rushes into vineyard planting and wine making. By 1863 John S. Hittell, himself a victim of the "wine fever," was warning, "We make more wine than the State consumes, and have not yet established a large export trade."[69] Two German musicians, Charles Kohler and John Frohling, respectively a violinist and a flutist, quixotically went into the wine business, successfully, and vigorously exported California wine to New York, Europe, Australia, Japan, and China.

Like Briggs with his peaches and Haraszthy with his wine, the fruit, table-grape, wine-grape, and wine industries that had expanded so rapidly from small beginnings soon found that it was easier to produce than to market. The big central distributing market at San Francisco and the smaller ones at Sacramento, Stockton, and the California and Nevada mining towns were easily filled. With perishables such as table grapes, peaches, and pears the problem of overproduction became so acute that sometimes crops were left to rot unharvested or were fed to pigs.[70]

A modest percentage of the loss was avoided by developing canning, drying, and preserving plants, but inexperience and high labor cost caused many failures before a successful industry emerged. The development of a raisin industry, centering in the irrigation colonies at Fresno, proved one of the better results of this turning to preserved products. Fresno and its neighbors in the San Joaquin were soon putting up half the state's crop.[71]

The difficulties were the more acute because so many of the growers were inexperienced or careless about selecting and packing crops for wholesalers, with the result that many boxes of fruit were rejected and became sheer loss.[72] In southern California the orange crop was at first sold to jobbers while it was still on the trees, so that the grower lost control over the way his crop would be handled thereafter.[73] Table grapes, a favorite in northern California and many eastern cities, proved a risky item to ship.

Wine had the most disheartening history of all. Too rapid a succession of booms and busts, too many investors ignorant of so delicate and arcane a business, too much money spent on newly designed machines intended to replace expensive human labor—all these built up an unstable industry in which inexperienced wine makers, finding themselves pressed to meet their debts, kept forcing their badly made young wines onto the market for whatever price they could get. California wines thereby acquired a nationwide reputation for poor quality, despite the really good wines that a few leaders were beginning to put on sale.[74]

When railroad transportation opened, vistas of the big markets at Chicago, New York, and elsewhere aroused high expectations. But early reports were disappointing. Californians did not know how to prepare their products for long-distance rail travel. Refrigerator cars and special fast-moving fruit trains were slow in appearing, and shippers complained that the unsympathetic railroads charged so much that shipments were unremunerative. Further, when California produce reached Chicago or New York, the middlemen handled matters in a way that embittered the Californians.[75]

The uncomfortable lesson seemed to be that having moved from local and regional sales into national distribution, the Californians, like other westerners, must now study national marketing. Further, they must unite in a cooperative effort to improve their own standards and to increase their power in bargaining with railroads and middlemen. Finally, better refrigerator cars and ventilated fruit cars must be developed, and the railroads must be persuaded to provide fast service for perishable shipments.

As if to emphasize this need for common action, the Pacific Coast was struck by plant diseases and blights introduced by imported nursery stock or seedlings, or transmitted by the unwise reuse of boxes that had once been sent east. The most disastrous of these pests was the phylloxera that ravaged the vineyards in the 1870s and 1880s, and the mysterious "Anaheim" or "Pierce's" disease that wiped out Anaheim's prosperous vineyards in the 1880s, compelling a shift to oranges and other crops.[76]

In each segment of the fruit, grape, and wine industry worried men turned variously to self-constituted trade associations, to the California State Agricultural Society, and the Grange in the hope of exchanging information and securing united action. Despite the stubborn opposition of skeptics, they sought the scientific services of Eugene Waldemar Hilgard, the German-trained scholar who had already begun his great career at the University of California. The wine men went furthest of all. They organized, sent lobbyists to Washington to fight for protective tariffs against foreign wines and for relief from the revenue tax on brandy, and formed cartels to fix prices at home. When they asked the state legislature for help, they obtained the California State Board of Viticultural Commissioners (1880) that for fifteen years sought quarantines around infested areas, bought foreign books on plant diseases, and made itself a clearinghouse for information.[77]

The southern Californian citrus men of the 1880s, 1890s, and early 1900s, with especial leadership from Riverside, were the first to conceive of a network in which associations of local growers' cooperatives were linked together through district exchanges that, in turn, reported to a powerful central exchange that provided daily reports on prices throughout the nation, set standards, bargained with railroads, supervised sales in distant markets, and promoted their products nationally, until eventually they put a glass of orange juice on every American breakfast table. The central and northern California fruit growers, wracked by internal dissension, followed suit, only after considerable initial difficulties.[78]

While Californians struggled to make a profit out of what seemed to less fortunate westerners to be a superabundance of opportunities, the west turned in piecemeal fashion to the needs of irrigation. Newell's reports proved how important irrigated agriculture and stock raising had become. Newell estimated that the total cost of building the systems in operation in 1899 exceeded $67.7 million, while the value of irrigated crops in the arid states was over $84.4 million, and in the semiarid states about $2 million.[79]

But his earlier survey, in 1889, had warned that the west had about exhausted its supply of lands that could be watered at relatively low cost; indeed, the demands upon many streams had already passed the point where the stream could be counted upon to deliver sufficient water in all critical periods. Less wasteful uses of the water might relieve the need temporarily, but for the long term there must be high-cost, professionally engineered solutions.

How were major projects to be financed and managed? The popular mutual water companies could not raise the money needed for major projects. The few individuals who suggested that only the Federal government could meet the need were ahead of their time; the National Reclamation Act was not to be passed until 1902, and only then because Theodore Roosevelt was in the White House and the national Progressive movement had come to power.

For the moment corporations or commercial companies took on the job, frequently with British or eastern capital. For example, in the 1880s British investors put $650,000 into building the Northern Colorado Irrigation Company's High Line Canal, eighty-five miles long. The British expected to charge farmers a basic fee, uncomfortably reminiscent of a quit rent, for a "perpetual right" to use the water, plus an annual rental to finance maintenance and operation. The Coloradans bitterly denounced the "perpetual right" fee as a "royalty" demanded by a foreign "monopoly," and persuaded the legislature to declare it illegal and the state supreme court to concur. Further, under the state constitution county governments could be empowered to regulate water rentals, if the state legislature should so authorize, which the legislature proceeded to do. The discouraged British ultimately surrendered and sold the canal to the city of Denver.[80]

Most of the corporate ventures made the same unpleasant discovery: that their customers were voters, litigants, and action-prone individuals. Other corporate systems failed because their engineers underestimated costs and could not raise enough money to complete the project. A classic example was Arthur D. Foote's excessively ambitious engineering conception for southern Idaho.[81] By 1900, 90 percent of the corporate schemes were believed to be in financial trouble. Most discovered that they had no alternative but to sell to the water users.[82]

A Federal statute, the Carey Act of 1894 (named for its sponsoring Wyoming senator), helped to only a limited degree. Western states and territories were to be granted up to a million acres each of public lands if they could get them irrigated and sold to settlers in 160-acre pieces. The states and territories were to contract with development corporations to carry out the projects. Only Wyoming and Idaho made extensive and sometimes successful use of the opportunity, and everywhere the development corporations tended to underestimate costs and overestimate available water.[83]

When none of these solutions proved adequate, California put forward an alternative that proved to be widely influential throughout the west, even though its early years were a sad tale of errors and failures. California had had experience with special-purpose districts organized for swampland reclamation, and had made attempts to authorize irrigation districts. Now a young lawyer, C. C. Wright, was elected to the legislature for the express purpose of lobbying his carefully drawn, detailed, and conservative bill through that body.

The Wright Act of 1887 provided that upon receiving a two-thirds vote of a local electorate, a "district" could be formed, to be governed by a board of directors and to be empowered to vote bonds and levy annual assessments. The district could condemn rights of way and condemn or buy existing water rights or irrigation systems, in addition to building new systems. The water was to belong to the district, not to the individual users, to whom the directors were responsible for distributing water at cost.[84]

In providing for local ownership, control, and bonding and assessment power, the Wright Act looked back to long-established American rural prejudices, but it failed to balance local authority with a state supervision that could assure the soundness of the projects and of the bonds issued to finance them. Nor was it reasonable to expect rural districts to produce, overnight, men with the training and experience necessary to plan and guide large and complex systems. Further, the widespread conviction that the Wright Act would break up land and water monopolies by squeezing big landowners between the attraction of rising land prices for subdivided land and the discouragement of rising local taxes did not always prove justified. Some big landowners hired lawyers to obstruct the fledgling districts at every point, even though the California Supreme Court upheld the statute.

Only a small proportion of the districts could be called even a partial success. Of the forty-nine formed from 1887 through 1895, only eight were still in business in 1915.[85] Some never really got started, others were ill-conceived or speculative or lacked support by major landowners. Their bonds sold badly if at all. Repeated amendments by the legislature corrected some of the weaknesses in the original act, including the need for state supervision. The Bridgeford Act of 1897 revised the basic statute so drastically that only six districts were formed from 1895 to 1914. Yet the ideal of combining local ownership and control under some state supervision, with a chance for the moderate-sized proprietor, was so appealing that, with safeguarding modifications, the Wright district was copied throughout much of the west before the First World War and regained its reputation in California in a new enthusiasm that began in 1915.[86]

Looming menacingly over the expansion of irrigation was an exhausting and expensive legal battle to determine who owned the right to use water. Disputes originated not, as one might expect, in differences between Anglo-American practices and the Spanish-Mexican heritage, although the cities of Los Angeles and San Diego won classic battles for their Mexican "pueblo right" to the waters of the Los Angeles and San Diego rivers, while for years the New

Mexicans continued to do as they had always done. Rather the fight was between two patterns of Anglo-American thinking. To quote a solicitor in the United States Department of Agriculture:

The Western law of water rights embraces two diametrically opposite principles—the common-law doctrine of riparian rights, and the statutory doctrine of prior appropriation.[87]

The latter of these two "originated among the miners of California in the earliest days of that State, whence it has been copied in all the Western States and Territories."[88] Simply stated, just as the miners created their own local rules to determine ownership of mining claims, so they also declared that on the public domain water could be diverted from streams to make placer mining possible, and the first person to so "appropriate" a stated amount of water took priority over later appropriators.

The common-law doctrine of riparian rights, by contrast, was put into well-articulated form in the first half of the nineteenth century by eastern and English judges, although it had behind it centuries of English experience in a humid environment. Strictly interpreted, the riparian doctrine meant that "the owner of land contiguous to a watercourse is entitled to have the stream flow by or through his land, undiminished in quantity and unpolluted in quality," save for the very limited use that other riparian proprietors were entitled to make for household purposes or watering domestic animals.[89]

Very little imagination is needed to perceive that in its pure form the doctrine of riparian rights would make irrigation impossible, whereas under prior appropriation, provided it was put to beneficial use the diverted water could be allowed to disappear into the soil. The showdown between the two concepts came when the richest men in California formed rival alliances to gain control of the dry end of the San Joaquin Valley and its neighbor, the Tulare Basin.[90]

Henry Miller and Charles Lux started buying land heavily after the drought of the 1860s had proved their need for vast amounts of pasture. Miller acquired numerous "Spanish" grant ranches, exploited the Swamp Land Act of 1850 to gain control of a block of land one hundred miles long beside the San Joaquin River, and extended his acquisitions into Kern County and up to Tulare Lake. Miller and Lux were already "silent partners" in a huge, incomplete project, the San Joaquin and Kings River Canal Company, which was backed by the biggest names in San Francisco: John Bensley of the California Steam Navigation Company; Isaac Friedlander the grain king; William S. Chapman, a land speculator on a massive scale; William C. Ralston of the Bank of California; and Lloyd Tevis of many activities, including Wells Fargo.

Tevis' partner, James Ben Ali Haggin, recognized the same opportunity that Miller and Lux had seen in the San Joaquin. Although a person of some refinement himself, Haggin now employed the coarse and devious political boss Billy Carr to acquire an empire. This Carr accomplished partly by purchase, partly by misusing the Federal land laws, partly by sharp practices, and partly by forcing out uncooperative farmers. Haggin posed as a public-spirited owner of land that he intended to irrigate someday and sell off in small tracts; Miller appeared as a stock raiser with an insatiable appetite for pastureland, some of which he irrigated.

Miller and Haggin collided in the early 1880s when Haggin's extension of an irrigation canal appropriated water that would otherwise have flowed to Miller and Lux's downstream riparian pasturelands. When appealed to the California Supreme Court, in 1886 that body handed down a decision that was two hundred pages long. *Lux* v. *Haggin* has been termed "probably the most important water case decided in the nineteenth-century West."[91]

The court decided that the doctrine of prior appropriation applied to land that was still in the public domain and to appropriations already established, but as land passed into private ownership, it fell under the common law, meaning the doctrine of riparian rights. California was thus decreed a double system composed of two opposed concepts. This became known as the California Doctrine.[92] To make it work, subsequent courts had to amend and blur it at many points.

The decision caused an uproar throughout the west. Many refused to accept what they regarded as the imposition of a humid-land dictum upon an arid or semiarid region. Colorado, through legislation, through a series of court decisions, and through its state constitution, created an alternative: the Colorado Doctrine, which specifically rejected riparian rights as unsuited to the "physical laws of nature" in Colorado, and accepted prior appropriation. But Colorado went further. Despite a reluctant, balky judiciary and legal profession, Colorado's irrigators made a start toward a logical administration of water rights. Upon petition of the irrigators, districts were to be formed, each with a commissioner, and the local judge was to appoint a referee who would collect the information necessary to prepare for each irrigator a certificate showing the date and amount of his appropriation. A state hydraulic engineer was to be appointed, and future appropriations of water would be more carefully handled.[93]

The Coloradans had hoped to establish an essentially administrative system managed by experienced people, instead of leaving so much to the uncertainties of judicial knowledge, but for the moment they were checked. Wyoming went further still. They hired away from Colorado an able young engineer, Elwood Mead, who guided Wyoming into what has been termed "distributive administration," which meant a system headed by a state engineer who, with a board of control, would decide the use of water in quasi-judicial proceedings. This Wyoming System subordinated the interest of the individual to the welfare of the state. With many revisions to suit different legislatures, it was widely copied throughout the west.[94]

While this administrative approach to law matured, the west completed its battle over the two basic conflicting doctrines. In 1911 the distinguished authority Samuel C. Wiel calculated that ten states and territories had upheld the California Doctrine, as against eight and parts of three others that had adhered to the Colorado Doctrine. A more recent scholar agrees on the ten California Doctrine states but limits the Colorado Doctrine to seven and points out that the California Doctrine adherents tend to be states that have both humid and arid areas.[95]

Hidden behind these statistics is the tragedy of millions of dollars drained from agriculture and stock raising by litigation. Henry Miller was doubtless exaggerating when he said that he had acquired $100 million in property but had had to spend $25 million in defending it in the courts.[96] There is an important point here: learning to cope with the western environment and its dangers, learning to earn a living from it and to build homes in it, was only a part of the task. The rest was the product of our litigious nature and our carelessness in using natural resources and in staffing the legislatures and courts that pass judgment upon our practices.

CHAPTER 12

The Later Days of Mining

TO a contemporary observer of the western scene, it must have appeared that western mining had reached its zenith when Nevada's Virginia City achieved a population of twenty thousand. If measured by the size of operations at individual Comstock mines, the amount of investment, number of workers, dimensions and complexity of machinery, and degree of expertness required, then mining had indeed advanced by light-years in the quarter of a century since the pan, rocker, and sluice had sufficed for the California Forty-Niners.

But in fact the accomplishment symbolized by the Comstock was only the beginning. In the next quarter century, while continuing to extract gold and silver on a large scale and by far more effective methods, western mining would turn to the base metals—copper, lead, zinc—and in so doing would draw far more heavily upon an elite of trained engineers, metallurgists, chemists, and geologists. Base metals and the smelting and refining that they required would become financially feasible because of railroad transportation and because western coal mines were now supplying fuel. Electricity and laborsaving inventions such as the power drills and dynamite already in use on the Comstock would revolutionize the conditions of mining. The size of operations, and thus the amount invested, would far overshadow the Comstock and would attract funds from both experienced and unwary investors on the Atlantic Coast, in the

Middle West, Britain, and Continental Europe as well as from newly rich local men.

There would be social costs for these gains. Labor unions had already been organized on a permanent basis on the Comstock. They were destined to spread across the mining west and become increasingly militant, in response to the great power in the hands of management, the growing size of company labor rosters, and the impersonality of corporate and absentee ownership. While the unions were in part mutual benevolent associations, they were also ways of uniting the scant bargaining power of individuals into a force capable of standing up to employers not only on questions of wages and hours but also to protest the danger, discomfort, and unhealthiness that resulted from the greater depth of mines and from precisely the technological innovations that made the big new operations possible. Where isolation caused mining corporations to build company towns, a further source of potential friction entered the equation of employer-employee relations, for in an age that exalted the rights of property, the company towns could grow all too easily into paternalistic fiefdoms.

The later nineteenth century, then, revolutionized conditions in what had been a relatively individualistic and opportunistic industry. Yet the changes were never accepted by all of the immensely varied individuals who called themselves miners. As late as 1890 the Federal census reported that "an army of prospectors is scattered over the mountains of the western states and territories every year, who explore every canon and river bottom by digging and panning, and when 'pay gravel' is found will remain working until the gold or water supply fails or the frosts of winter drive them back toward the abodes of civilization." The individual earnings of such men were small, the census concluded, but "the aggregate amount is considerable."[1]

Nor were these prospectors and seasonal miners the only westerners who still "kept a hand" in the older types of mining. Conrad Kohrs, the Montana cattle king and butcher, had been a miner in California, British Columbia, and Montana in his earlier days, and now he still invested in modest-sized gold mines and a mining water company.[2] Irving Howbert, at a time when he was preoccupied with getting the First National Bank of Colorado Springs into better financial condition, persuaded two of his banking friends to join him in buying into a dubious Leadville mine that unexpectedly proved rich.[3] Judge Bentley, once the Federal commissioner of patents but now on the bench in Colorado, owned a small gold mine above Boulder that his son managed.[4] All over the west men who had made money grubstaked prospectors. Mining was more than a business; it was a state of mind, a way of life.

Veterans and greenhorns alike felt its allure, as the continuance of rushes demonstrated. The appeal of the distant prize, the vision of sudden wealth in a newly publicized land, persisted throughout the century. Something more than an exclusive desire for gain was involved. Restlessness, boredom with society's restraints, the excitement of a challenge in far places, flight from failure or criticism, mass hysteria—all these impulses added recruits every time the grapevine, personal letters, newspapers, and the telegraph brought reports of a new discovery. "Old Californians" or men they had trained in Idaho, Montana, or Nevada were always on hand to provide leadership.

The great gold and silver rushes that started with the Comstock Lode and Colorado ("Pikes Peak") in 1859 shifted to Idaho and Montana in the early and middle 1860s; to White Pine, Nevada, in the late 1860s; to the Black Hills of South Dakota, Tombstone, Arizona, and Leadville, Colorado, in the later 1870s; to the Coeur d'Alene of northern Idaho in the early 1880s; and to Cripple Creek, Colorado, at the opening of the 1890s. Just before the century ended, rushes started to that most remote and difficult part of North America, Alaska and northwestern Canada, where names like Skagway, Klondike, Yukon, Fortymile, Tanana, and Nome suddenly became familiar words. Like its predecessors, this last romantic thrust of the nineteenth century was, as one departing gold seeker cheerfully declared in 1898, a rush which, "being infectious, attacks all grades and conditions of men. . . . Our hearts, our hopes, ourselves, are on board [our ship] for better or worse."[5]

The leading San Francisco mining journal viewed such performances severely. "Hundreds of lives were sacrificed," it asserted, "and many millions more of money spent than has been realized in these wild hunts after wealth." Ultimately "the remnant of this great army" came straggling back, "poor in pocket, with shattered constitutions and wrecked hopes," to see what prospects there might be in the older regions from which they had departed on their various odysseys.[6]

Opportunities were good for those who were willing to find a niche in the new capitalized mining. Surprisingly, the oldest form of western effort, gold placer mining, was proving to be one of the most exciting because it was well into a new era of mechanized production, and California, the original home of gold seeking, was leading the nation in gold produced. The source of the new wealth was the deeply buried gravels laid down in ancient times by rivers that had long since been obliterated during subsequent tectonic activity and erosion.

Some sought these deep gravels by "drift mining," which was the slow, labor-intensive, patience-demanding process of cutting tunnels from the side of a mountain or ravine through thick layers of overlying material, often capped by lava, to reach the rich "pay streak" at bedrock level. From there the gravel had to be hauled out of the tunnel in handcars.[7]

Others turned to the immense possibilities inherent in hydraulic mining. After a temporary sag when money and men were diverted to the Comstock Lode and other new areas, hydraulic operations forged ahead rapidly as mechanics in the Sierra mining towns, especially in the highly inventive Nevada County, devised successively improved iron nozzles through which the fiercely powerful stream of water could be aimed at whatever hill or mountainside had been chosen for disintegration.

Foundrymen in San Francisco and inland cities such as Marysville supplemented the local mechanics' contributions by turning out iron pipe that was strong enough to stand up under the extremely high pressure used. Soon the reputation of California-made equipment was so high that exports were being shipped to Idaho, Montana, Colorado, Oregon, South Dakota, and later even to the Yukon, as men who had seen what was done in the Sierras introduced hydraulicking into their own areas.

Hydraulicking—or "hydraulicing" (with the c pronounced as an s)—achieved much greater size and results in California than elsewhere because conditions were ideal: thick beds of deep gravels, abundant water that could be dammed high up in the Sierras, and ridges or mountain slopes along which the water could be conducted through canals, flumes, or pipes to a point well above the gravels. There the water flowed into a pressure box, and thence plunged down through pipes to the nozzles, variously known by their trade names as Monitors, Little Giants, or Dictators.[8]

So immensely powerful was the hydraulic that whole hills or mountain slopes disintegrated under its continuing high-pressure bombardment, which was often preceded by a preparatory blast of ground-loosening explosives. Hydraulicking was essentially a mass-production, laborsaving, low-cost-per-unit method of washing tons of gravel out of the sites where nature had placed them and into long lines of sluices, where the gold was supposed to be caught, although critics claimed that there was a greater loss of gold than company managers would admit.[9]

Opening a major hydraulic operation required extensive preliminary work. The promoters had to buy up existing placer claims, consolidate them into a single large property, build reservoirs, canals, and flumes, cut costly tunnels down to the bedrock for drainage, buy expensive equipment, purchase huge quantities of lumber, build workshops, barracks, and mess halls, and provide electricity to illuminate night operations and telephones to make possible instant communication with all parts of the extensive system. By the early 1880s California had nearly six thousand miles of ditches and flumes, plus an additional thousand miles of subsidiary branches and an unknown length of small distributors, the whole said to represent an investment of $30 million out of the $100 million alleged to have been invested in the hydraulic industry.[10]

The history of a single company, the famous North Bloomfield Gravel Mining Company, reveals how one of the biggest of hydraulic corporations came into being, faced repeated demands for more money for capital expenditures, and in the very moment of long-delayed victory suddenly had to face something new in the mining west: an outraged public that for the first time challenged a mine owner's right to operate. Originally conceived by a North Bloomfield promoter who took out options on hundreds of acres, the company was organized in 1866 under the leadership of a small group of wealthy San Franciscans.

Like other companies realizing big schemes, the North Bloomfield operation recruited the name and help of the banker William Chapman Ralston, along with such prominent figures as Lester L. Robinson, the builder of the little Sacramento Valley Railroad, that first of all far western railroads, S. F. Butterworth of the New Almaden quicksilver mine near San Jose, and F. L. A. Pioche, the investment banker who had a mining town in Nevada named after him in return for his heavy involvement in a venture there.[11]

The company went into business at a time when the size of hydraulic operations was increasing rapidly, as promoters sought economies of scale. By 1871, when Hamilton Smith, Jr., a respected engineer, was hired to run the property, the corporation had already acquired nearly sixteen hundred acres (later increased to twenty-five hundred) and had spent $725,000 on construction. Ahead of them lay such big further expenses that the controlling group was debating whether to lower their ambitions or take the big gamble of digging an unusually long and costly tunnel "to bottom the deep and rich gravel," as Smith expressed it. They decided to go for broke, and under Smith's direction spent nearly half a million dollars on the tunnel during 1872–1874. While so engaged they had to raise an additional fifty-two thousand dollars to rebuild their new dam, which burned before it could be filled with water.[12]

Meantime the officers decided to acquire a half interest in two nearby mines that they felt they should control. When added to their own holdings, this gave them possession of two "enormous" reservoirs and over a hundred miles of canals or ditches. In 1878 the company was finally able to run its mines steadily throughout the year, both during daylight hours and under electric lights at night. In that year it began to pay dividends. According to the company's statement, by the end of 1879 the total spent from all sources exceeded $5 million, some of which was in the form of large outstanding debts.[13]

But with the mine now paying large dividends, all this effort seemed justified, and it might have been had no other people than wealthy San Franciscans and working miners been affected by hydraulicking. The contrary was true. Huge masses of gravel, rocks, sand, and finely ground material were accumulating below the North Bloomfield and other mines. All that was needed to create disaster was a few weeks of California's famous wintertime torrential downpours. When that happened, the waste material broke loose and thundered down the canyons and rivers to inundate cities and suffocate farmland under thick layers of life-choking debris, while at the same time the debris raised the level of the river bottoms so drastically that rivers now ran through new channels that were higher than the towns and farms they passed. Private citizens and city councils desperately built higher and yet higher levees in a futile attempt to keep out the mud-laden floods.[14]

After years of complacently letting the mines do whatever they wanted, suddenly Californians realized that there was no governmental authority—Federal, state, or local—that could regulate the mines, or control the use of the rivers, or protect the low-lying valley lands, unless perhaps the Federal government might step in if the Sacramento and Feather rivers became too silted up to be navigable, as the Yuba River had already become. Angry farmers went to the state courts to seek injunctions against further hydraulicking. The city dwellers were divided, because the mines were their best customers.

A kind of populist crusade swept through the rural lower valleys where the damage was being done. Rural anger coincided with a general spirit of revolt symbolized by Kearney's Working Men's party and the radical state constitution of 1879. An Anti-Debris Association was formed to press suits against the mines. In 1879 Judge Phil W. Keyser of the state courts issued an injunction against the mines, only to have the state supreme court invalidate Keyser's action. When the legislature passed a Drainage Act in 1880, and sought to establish a Debris Commission, the state supreme court invalidated that too, and in 1881 ruled that Judge Keyser could not issue an injunction that was sought against the North Bloomfield Company.[15]

Finally, a citizen of New York who owned property in the badly battered Marysville area entered a suit in the Federal courts against the North Bloomfield Company specifically and a list of other mines as well. In the United States Circuit Court in San Francisco the case was heard before Judge Lorenzo Sawyer, who had been a miner in the gold rush before turning to a distinguished legal career that led him first to the state and then to the Federal bench. So vitally important was the case that it went on for a year and a half, took thousands of pages of testimony and reports, and caused Judge Sawyer to visit the scenes of devastation. In January 1884 Judge Sawyer found the North Bloomfield and other mines to be a "public and private nuisance" unauthorized by law, and perpetually enjoined them from hydraulic mining.[16]

Victory was not total immediately, because miners evaded the injunction and harassed marshals sent to enforce it. But by 1890 most of the mines were shut down. In 1893 a Federal statute, the Caminetti Act, seeking to encourage a supervised and controlled resumption, created a California Debris Commission composed of three Army engineers, who were to be "the supreme authority in all matters" relating to hydraulic mining in the main theater, which was the watershed of the Sacramento and San Joaquin valleys. From being the freest of exploiters, suddenly miners would have to petition a military board, have their plans approved, build expensive retaining works, and obtain a license that could be revoked at any time for failure to toe the line.[17] Truly a revolution! Few mines found the new terms appealing.

The Sawyer decision and the creation of the California Debris Commission seem precursors of the national conservation movement that flowered during the presidency of Theodore Roosevelt. Present were some of the key elements characteristic of the Rooseveltian era: well-publicized protest by an organized group, articulate and dedicated leaders, and a turning to the Federal government when powerful business interests declared their profits more important than preventing damage to the community.

The significance of the Anti-Debris crusade was not lost on the placer industry. Almost as soon as the "Monitors" and "Little Giants" were relegated to remote California areas or to other states, the new technique of dredging for gold appeared. First developed in New Zealand and first used successfully in this country in Montana in 1895, the dredges, which were mounted on a floating hull and used an endless chain of digging buckets, comprised another mass-production method of working what were often low-paying gravels. While some operated on rivers, most created their own ponds in the low-lying plains and agricultural lands back from the river—where it was relatively simple to impound the debris they created—so as to avoid the disastrous floods of hydraulicking.[18]

Yet the purpose of dredging was to turn the earth upside down, so as to reach the richest part of the gravel, which usually lay on the bottom. Thus any dredging operation left a wasteland behind it, with the topsoil now covered by rocks, sand, and gravel. Contemporary manuals and reports on dredging usually included a defensive chapter on the damage they were doing.[19] Their chief argument was that it was vastly more profitable to strip the soil than to raise crops on it. In California the Anti-Debris Association was revived and sent committees to harass the dredgers into taking measures to prevent floods.

Although not invented in California, dredge mining was improved so rapidly by Californians, from 1898 onward, that the phrase "California-type" dredge passed into widespread usage. Equipment made in California was exported to all parts of the world, while at the same time California's output of dredge gold "far exceeded the combined output in all of the other States and, for that matter, in any foreign country," even though big-scale operations were mounted in Idaho, Montana, Colorado, British Columbia, the Klondike, and Alaska.[20]

Although mass production made possible a surprisingly high latter-day placer output, interest for the majority had already shifted to the extraordinary range of mining and smelting opportunities that opened during the 1870s and 1880s and, despite the worldwide decline in value of silver and erratic fluctuations in prices for base metals, continued into the new century. The Comstock set the example, by the immense wealth it spewed forth as it emerged from its depression.

Three famous groups won Comstock superwealth in the 1870s, and it was out of their huge profits and massive orders for supplies and services that San Francisco rebuilt itself into a truly great city.[21] The omnipresent Ralston of the Bank of California headed the first group, with the backing of some of the "biggest names" of San Francisco finance and business.

For his manager at Virginia City Ralston chose William Sharon, a reserved and cynical man, trained in law and business, whose recent failure in a mining-stock speculation makes one wonder why he was selected. Taking advantage of the declining value of Comstock property in the 1860s, Sharon gained for the Bank of California a predominant position by lending money to struggling companies and then foreclosing when payments could not be met.

Once Sharon had won command, he set out to reorganize the Comstock's confused affairs. In 1867 he persuaded the bank's reluctant directors to throw all of the milling properties they had acquired into a single Union Milling Company, which would have a near-monopoly on treating the ores. To increase the Union Company's efficiency, Sharon moved operations to a new site on the Carson River, where there would be waterpower, and built a short railroad to haul ores from mines to mill. Later he extended the little railroad, famous for its tortuous, twisting route, to connect with the Central Pacific at Reno. Costs for hauling ores and bringing in supplies and equipment dropped sharply, and the cost of living was reduced. To strengthen his monopolistic position, Sharon bought an interest in the water company that served the mills and mines and the lumber company that supplied them.

Angry Comstockers denounced Sharon's consolidation as a monopoly, but without Ralston's funds and Sharon's reorganization, revival would have been delayed. Furthermore, when revival did come, a high perentage of the profits went to outsiders. John P. Jones, a British-born miner and politician, was a popular figure in California and Nevada. Having failed of election as lieutenant governor of California, he became a mine superintendent on the Comstock, and while managing the Crown Point mine became famous for the courage he displayed when fighting a major fire in his mine.

At a time when the Crown Point's future seemed so poor that its stock could scarcely find buyers, Jones spotted a highly encouraging change in the ore body and hurried off to San Francisco, where he seems to have talked with several of the principal owners. Alvinza Hayward, a veteran of Mother Lode quartz mining and owner of one of the richest mines on that lode, decided to back him. Originally close to Ralston's "bank crowd," Hayward now followed Jones' confidential advice and bought heavily in the Crown Point's depreciated stock, while apparently helping Jones to do the same.

Before Sharon was aware of what was happening, the two had bought control of the company—a mine that Sharon had regarded as one of "his." Always a cold-blooded realist, Sharon quickly agreed to sell the shares of Crown Point stock that he held as agent for the "bank crowd," if Hayward would sell to him his holding in the Crown Point's next-door neighbor, the Belcher, whose boundaries were likely to contain the extension of whatever ore the Crown Point possessed.

Both the Crown Point and Belcher did find bonanzas, and Virginia City and San Francisco went wild with excitement, but Hayward and Jones broke with Sharon's monopoly by building their own milling company and transferring their banking to a bank of which Hayward became president.

A similar independence characterized the next breakthrough on the Comstock, that of the "four Irishmen," all of whom came of essentially penniless origins. John W. Mackay, formerly a California placer man, was without funds when he started to learn silver mining, but by sheer ability he rose to be superintendent of one mine and then chief owner of another. James G. Fair had been more successful in California, where he had operated a gold-quartz mine and mill before crossing to Washoe. James C. Flood, although once a placer man, had turned to unsuccessful small businesses in San Francisco, along with William S. O'Brien, before the two went into partnership as saloon keepers in that city. From that humble start they moved up into stockbroking and speculation. Mackay was the attractive one of the four, a quiet, truthful, generous person with notable ability as a mine operator. Fair was an able, proven mining professional, but his enemies called him "Slippery Jim." Flood developed enough talent for business to handle the four men's San Francisco affairs. O'Brien seems to have contributed little after his fortunate initial participation in the scheme.

This time it was the Hale and Norcross mine that surprised Sharon. The "four Irishmen" had concluded that there were rich possibilities in what seemed an unpromising property whose stock was badly depreciated on the San Francisco market. They bought up a controlling number of shares before Sharon was alerted, developed the mine into a very profitable concern, and like Hayward and Jones acquired their own milling plant and other essential services.

This success enabled them to buy up a piece of ground, the Consolidated Virginia, upon which previous owners had spent thousands of dollars without profit. This they developed carefully and at great cost throughout 1872, 1873, and 1874. No dividends were declared until May of 1874, which may suggest how fallacious is the notion that successful mines produce rich ore quickly and require miraculously low initial investment. But the long, expensive, well-directed effort was worth it. In December 1874 the well-informed San Francisco *Mining and Scientific Press* declared that the Consolidated Virginia and probably its immediate neighbor, the California Mining Company, were opening a "body of ore absolutely immense and beyond all comparison superior in every respect to anything ever before seen on the Comstock lode."[22]

Shares in both corporations soared. The Consolidated Virginia went from $1 a share in 1870 to $700 early in 1875; the California from $37 in 1874 to $780 early in 1875. This was the famous Big Bonanza, forever enshrined in western history, which was said to have produced $105,168,859 from 1873–1882, with $74,250,000 being paid as dividends from 1874–1881.[23] The "four Irishmen" joined the Central Pacific Railroad builders, Alvinza Hayward, John P. Jones, George Hearst, Haggin and Tevis, Miller and Lux, Hugh Glenn, and a few others as the new plutocracy that dominated San Francisco, much of California, as much of Nevada as they wanted, and spread its influence over the Far West as a whole. Hearst, Jones, Sharon, Fair, and Leland Stanford obtained seats in the United States Senate, variously from California and Nevada, along with the mining lawyer and political arranger who served them so well, William M. Stewart. Like the ornate mansions they built for themselves, they contributed to the Senate more display of wealth than statesmanship. Mackay, when offered his turn at the Senate, declined.

The Big Bonanza ended all too soon. By 1877 its future was in doubt, and by 1878 an exodus from Virginia City had begun. From a record output of perhaps $38 million in 1876 the Comstock dropped to $1.4 million in 1881.[24] In the resulting crash in mining stocks, thousands of men and women of every economic level lost everything. Lloyd Tevis asserted that "the spirit of gambling" had "spread through the whole fabric of society." He gave the American Bankers' Association his own terse summary of the disaster:

> Aggregate value of mining stocks on S.F. Board,
> January, 1875 . . . $282,305,404
> Aggregate value of mining stocks on S.F. Board,
> July, 1881, . . . $17,902,700
> Shrinkage . . . $264,402,704[25]

Expressed differently, a student who resurveyed the scene sixty years later concluded that from 1859 to 1882 the total Comstock yield was $292,726,310, of which $125,335,925 was paid out in dividends, chiefly from the four bonanza mines, the Consolidated Virginia, California, Crown Point, and Belcher. But while few mines paid dividends, nearly all levied assessments on their stockholders, and the Comstock assessments totaled $73,929,355.[26]

These generalized figures do not bring out the unevenness with which the Comstock spread its brief blessings. As in other districts where the device of the incorporated mine was used, the "inside" few who controlled the operation of the mines and mills could manipulate profits and the price of shares on the exchange, and could make fortunes while outsiders and the little folk who played the market became losers.

While Comstock mining did not cease, it fell to so reduced a level that superintendents, foremen, engine operators, mechanics, and miners trained on the Comstock scattered throughout the mining west in the late 1870s and the 1880s. Just as the Old Californians had contributed so much to mining in the interior after California had declined, so now the Comstock veterans took their skills to new mines and new districts, while San Francisco manufacturers found new markets for their equipment and San Francisco millionaires new outlets for investment. Thus the west benefited even as many individuals lost.

The moment was peculiarly opportune. Veteran observers were aware of the possibilities that would exist if a way could be found to work ores whose precious metals were in intimate association with base metals—such as lead, zinc, or copper—or were made difficult by the "sulphurets" that were so troublesome in Colorado. In short, the age of smelting had come.

Smelting means converting ores into a fluid state by means of heat and chemicals, as an essential step in separating the metallic content from worthless materials. For success in smelting, promoters had to find men with knowledge based on practical experience and with formal training in chemistry, metallurgy, and mineralogy. Because the west was not rich in such people, many of the early smelters were built or managed on principles inappropriate to the particular ores to be worked, or were too dependent on ores from one or two erratically operated mines, with the result that the western landscape became cluttered with the abandoned buildings and equipment of costly failures.

This later age demanded science, professionalism, and careful management. Colorado showed the way when Nathaniel P. Hill, then a science teacher at Brown University and a consultant to New

England industrialists, accepted an assignment to go out to Colorado to inspect potential mining properties. What he saw in Clear Creek Canyon, Gilpin County, Colorado, caused him to take himself to Britain and continental Europe to study well-established smelting techniques and to send a shipment of Colorado ores all the way to the great smelting center of Swansea, Wales, for experimental treatment under Hill's personal observation.

Upon his return to America, a group of Boston businessmen formed the Boston and Colorado Smelting Company in 1867, with Hill as manager of Colorado operations. When Hill built his first smelter at Black Hawk, up in the canyon, he hired as his metallurgist Hermann Beeger, a German who had studied at the famous academy of mining and metallurgy at Freiberg, Saxony, and had worked at Swansea. Later Hill added to his staff one of the great figures of Colorado mining, Richard Pearce, who had worked in the Cornish mines as a boy, had studied at the Royal School of Mines, London, and had worked at Swansea and visited Freiberg.[27]

Despite immense difficulties, Hill's smelter achieved technological success, but the location in that narrow canyon proved awkward. As Hill expanded the plant's operations, the site became badly cramped, the air unbearably polluted, and fuel increasingly scarce and expensive. Ultimately Hill made the crucial decision to move down to the open plains outside Denver, where there was ample space, more chance to scatter the acrid fumes, and, above all, access to Denver's growing network of railroads. The railroads could bring him Colorado coal and coke and could enable him to buy ores from widely separated mines, both in Colorado and throughout the west, so as to get the right mix of types of ores and the right quantity necessary for large-scale smelting. When other companies followed his example, Denver became a major smelting center and an expanding city. More than a hundred miles south of Denver, Pueblo, situated at the point where the Arkansas River emerges from the mountains, proved to be comparably well situated for smelting, with good rail connections and access to coking coals.[28]

Hill's smelters treated silver as well as gold, and produced copper as a by-product. Now a new prospect opened. At an altitude of ten thousand feet, at the head of the Arkansas Valley, was the decaying placer camp of California Gulch. Here, in the middle 1870s, August R. Meyer, a metallurgist trained at Freiberg, proved that ores that had puzzled and irritated placer miners were silver-lead carbonates. With the backing of his St. Louis employers, in 1877 Meyer built a smelter in a log cabin hamlet that became known as Leadville. Other smelters followed quickly as Meyer's success became known. In particular, a smelter was built by James B. Grant, whose well-to-do Iowa uncle had enabled him to attend college in Iowa before going to Cornell and Freiberg to prepare himself in mining and smelting. With his uncle's continued financial backing, Grant proved brilliantly successful. He was one of those who later moved his smelting headquarters to the plains outside Denver.[29]

From a few log huts in 1877, Leadville boomed into a city of 14,820 people in 1880, with gaslights, a waterworks, schools, churches, hospitals, and, of crucial importance, railroad service to the outer world. Like most "hard-rock" centers, its labor force included Irish, Cornish, Canadians, and Germans. More than a third of its population was of foreign birth. Its silver output, while not the equal of the Comstock's bonanza years, was large and came into production just in time to compensate for the loss of the Comstock's big yield. Lead began to be an important supplementary product in 1879, copper in 1884, and zinc in 1885.[30]

So rapid a development in so new a setting would not have been possible without the presence of a remarkably large number of graduates of the best mining schools in Europe and America. In the rough setting of this raw new mountain town, an elite of well-educated specialists, some from American upper-class backgrounds, some from Germany, added an incongruous element to the brawny Cornishmen and Irishmen who formed the underground crews. Together they tramped the crowded, windy, snowy streets and tried the noisy, convivial bars.[31]

Some of this elite, sent in by the newly formed United States Geological Survey, did the mining fraternity the enormous service of explaining the origin of the Leadville ore deposits. Instead of being veins, the latter were "replacement deposits," which means that hot ore-bearing solutions had penetrated solid rock, dissolved it, and substituted new minerals for the original material. This process was especially common with limestone, and an understanding of it immensely improved the superintendents' ability to locate silver-lead ores.

Just as the Comstock sent its millionaires and their lawyer to the

United States Senate, so Colorado sent as its first two senators Henry M. Teller, the highly successful mining lawyer from Gilpin County and future "Free Silver" leader, and Jerome B. Chaffee, the Denver banker-politician and manipulator of mines at Leadville and elsewhere. When Chaffee retired, Nathaniel Hill, by then a wealthy and respected figure, succeeded him, while James B. Grant became governor.

For one month Colorado was represented by the flamboyant Horace A. W. Tabor, Leadville's storekeeper, postmaster, promoter, opera house proprietor, and first mayor. Tabor had the incredible good luck to buy into two of Leadville's richest mines for a trifle, in the one case by grubstaking two prospectors, in the other by buying a very dubious claim from an even more dubious discoverer. When more money poured in than he could manage, Tabor spent it in all directions and dumped his stern-willed New England wife in favor of scandalous affairs with glamorous young women, one of whom, the famous "Baby Doe," he married. He got himself elected lieutenant governor, but when he tried for the Senate, even his generous bribes won for him only the consolation prize of filling out the remaining thirty days of another man's unexpired term.[32]

In several major respects Leadville represented a transition in western mining. It was forward-looking in its production by smelting of not only silver but also an important base metal, lead, and in its use of well-developed technology and well-trained technologists. Despite its mountainous, lofty setting, Leadville was surprisingly quick to attract railroads that linked it to the regional and national markets so essential to feeding smelters and marketing their product. It went far beyond the Comstock in drawing investment capital not only from successful regional capitalists but also from investors throughout the United States and abroad—even if loose ethics led to sensational scandals in the promotion and manipulation of mining properties. Leadville's broad range of investors contrasted sharply with the domination of the Comstock by San Franciscans. Yet in the large number of separately owned mines and smelters, many of them undercapitalized, Leadville resembled the older camps. The west's future lay with local and regional corporations that gained enough strength to make them attractive targets for absorption into huge national concerns put together by New York capital through the skilled maneuvers of experienced financiers and the corporate and mining lawyers that they employed.

The importance of the mining lawyers must not be overlooked. The relatively simple codes adopted by the California pioneers and copied throughout the west served moderately well for the early placers and even the early quartz mines, but when Congress translated these into national legislation in statutes of 1866, 1870, and 1872, it failed to correct the ambiguities, gaps, and carelessness of the local codes, and in the case of quartz mining, it added a magnificent encouragement to costly litigation when it sought, through the so-called apex law, to determine ownership of a vein as it pursued its geologically uncertain course underground.[33]

A necessary cost in opening any ambitious mine was to buy off a swarm of avaricious adjacent claimants who would otherwise sue, and once thousands of dollars had been committed to sinking a shaft and drilling and blasting passageways underground to trace the vein, there was always the danger of finding oneself in subterranean regions which a neighboring mine claimed as its own under the uncertain provisions of the apex law. That was when expensive, often politically well connected lawyers sought evidence from witnesses who would lie if necessary, and offered bribes to jurymen and judges if there was no other way. The west followed such cases with avid interest, and was treated to the uninspiring spectacle of competent mining engineers, presumably men of integrity, testifying against each other as "expert witnesses."[34]

In seeking outside capital, westerners of the later nineteenth century were greatly helped by two circumstances. The first was that as mining passed into complex ores and base metals, treatment in the isolated mining towns became impracticable and expensive, and with railroad transportation now widely available, major smelting plants at St. Louis, Omaha, and Kansas City took over much of the work, while from there the still-unfinished product was shipped to refineries in New Jersey, Baltimore, and other eastern points. In short, western ores had become a part of national and indeed international business.

This was in addition to the smelters being built on valley lands below the mountains, as at Denver, Pueblo, and near Salt Lake City. Leadville, with its strong head start and large quantities of ore too poor to justify railroad shipment, continued for years to be important, and Durango, Colorado, because of its coking coal, became "Smelter City" after the railroad reached it.[35]

The second factor was the rise of western merchants, bankers, and promoters whose business ties and wealth put them in touch with eastern, middle western, and British sources of capital. Examples of such local leaders were Jerome B. Chaffee, David H. Moffat, and Nathaniel Hill in Denver; Simeon G. Reed in Portland; the Walker brothers of Salt Lake City after they broke with Mormonism; and Samuel T. Hauser, Andrew J. Davis, and William Andrews Clark in Montana.

Clark, a shrewd, grim, devious man who was destined to become a multimillionaire and purchase a Senate seat after repeated unsuccessful attempts at it, was unusual in that he recognized that his background in several successful businesses was insufficient for the latter-day mineral industry. He went east to study at Columbia University's new School of Mines, and upon his return successfully gave preliminary treatment to Butte's difficult silver ores, which contained a high copper content. A shipment of his ores to Nathaniel Hill for further treatment impressed Hill so much that he was persuaded to join Clark in creating the Colorado and Montana Company (1879), which began smelting operations at Butte while waiting for the arrival in 1881 of the Utah Northern Railroad that the Mormons had begun ten years before.[36]

Even before the railroad arrived, others were promoting Butte as a silver town that also had copper prospects. Marcus Daly, Irish-born of poor parents and given an absolute minimum of formal education, had learned mining by working in California and on the Comstock, where he caught the attention of John Mackay, who promoted him to foreman and gave him the chance to prove his competence both in mining and as a leader of men. George Hearst was similarly impressed by Daly's rough-hewn talents, and well he might be, for Daly's tip led to Hearst's buying the Ontario silver mine in Utah, which yielded a fortune.

At Salt Lake City the Walker brothers hired Daly to manage their properties, and when their Utah plant received for treatment a very promising shipment of Butte silver ores, they sent Daly north to investigate the source. Together the Walkers and Daly bought Butte silver lodes, and Daly turned one of them, the Alice, into a highly profitable venture. Davis and Hauser, in the meantime, were drawing New England copper and brass merchants into an interest in Butte, and the Lewisohn brothers of New York, German-Jewish immigrants who had made a success as importers, hired another veteran of the California and Utah mines to advise them in buying claims that became the basis for the Montana Copper Company and the smelter it built.

Clearly Butte, formerly a depressed survivor of the gold days, was entering a boom. Daly bought the Anaconda silver mine, and to obtain the capital to develop it turned to the San Francisco team of Hearst, James Ben Ali Haggin, and Lloyd Tevis, who operated as partners in mining ventures. In 1881 Daly persuaded the wealthy San Francisco trio to back him, but after successfully opening the Anaconda for silver, Daly found the silver playing out and copper becoming prevalent. Unexpectedly he had discovered one of the greatest deposits of copper sulphide in the world.[37]

When he hurried off to San Francisco, his three backers were understandably nonplussed. Copper ores were not yet well known to westerners. The incredibly rich Michigan copper mines, dominated by entrenched Boston capital, had monopolized the American market for decades, and even with electricity now providing an expanding market for copper, it was uncertain that inexperienced westerners would be able to sell their product against Michigan opposition and in an industry that had shown a tendency to periodic overproduction.

Millions of dollars would have to be sunk into developing the mine and its ore bodies, building a concentrator, smelter, and other facilities, and learning the unfamiliar processes of treating copper. Railroad transportation to the outer world would be costly because of pooling agreements between the Union Pacific and Northern Pacific.

Despite the odds, the partners agreed to this momentous venture. In the then-beautiful Deer Lodge Valley, well away from burgeoning Butte, a carefully planned company town, Anaconda, was laid out. Here a huge smelter and related reduction works were erected, with a spur of the Utah Northern Railroad to haul ores to the new town. Rumor had it that the partners sank $4 million into the plant before the smelter could be fired in 1884. At first the copper matte[38] it produced had to be shipped to eastern and British refineries for finishing, but despite a price war that the Michigan producers started in 1884, the partners moved quickly to integrate their operations vertically, building refineries in the 1890s and introducing the relatively new process of electrolytic refining.

They had already adopted the Bessemer process to produce high-quality blister copper. Daly was not one to miss opportunities. He kept pushing ahead, acquiring additional mines to supply ore, additional water rights, huge timber stands, the company's own coal mines, and its own local railroad to avoid dependence on the Utah Northern's spur. During the 1890s the Anaconda became a highly integrated corporation noted for efficiency and modern equipment. Right up to his death in 1900 Daly was still expanding his plant into the world's largest smelter with the world's tallest smokestack, the latter's height being an attempt to lessen the pollution of air and vegetation.[39]

To quote the most recent history of the company, "The Anaconda loomed over Butte, and over Montana itself, like a monstrous leviathan whose every twist and lurch became a life and death concern."[40] Hamilton Smith, the well-known mining engineer, once of the North Bloomfield, termed it "the most extensive mining property in the world."[41] When Marcus Daly wielded the company's great political power, he was able to stave off even the millionaire William Andrews Clark when the latter kept trying to buy the distinction of becoming a United States senator.

Anaconda's success, and the death or advancing age of its owners, made it a target for what today would be termed a "takeover." The end of the nineteenth century was a period of industrial mergers leading to massive "trusts," of which the classic model was Rockefeller's Standard Oil. Now members of the Standard Oil group, led by the handsome, often generous and charming but ruthless Henry H. Rogers, and William Rockefeller, the quiet younger brother of John D., began buying stock in the Anaconda corporation that had been formed to handle the problems created by Hearst's death in 1891.

In 1899 the Amalgamated Copper Company was incorporated in New Jersey as a holding company that started its empire with the Anaconda but quickly swept in other large Butte holdings such as Colorado Smelting and Mining, together with the Lewisohns' properties, which included their big metals brokerage firm and New Jersey refinery. New Yorkers and Bostonians as well as Montanans found themselves pushed to one side as Rogers vigorously took command.

The real sufferers were the investing public. With extraordinary skill Rogers and his lieutenants "watered" the stock in the new giant far beyond its true value, sold it on the market at high prices, depressed it, and bought back in at the bottom. With reason, western mining magnates were criticized for their self-aggrandizing manipulation of stocks, but their intrigues seem small-time steals when compared to what sophisticated New York brought forth.[42]

However ruthless Amalgamated's maneuvers may have seemed, they were in fact part of a pattern that most of the west's base-metal mining and smelting was to follow. Even in the middle 1880s the silver-lead men sensed that too many firms were entering the field. Greater unity was needed if they were to bargain effectively with the all-essential railroads, if they were to avoid price competition with each other, and if they were to have any chance of influencing the price of lead and Congress' readiness to maintain protective tariffs.

In part the stronger firms met the situation by absorbing rivals and by integrating vertically through gaining control of mines that could supply the right kinds of ores. In part the industry tried the usual devices of pools, associations, and price-fixing agreements, but with little success; someone always cheated or openly refused cooperation.[43]

Despite their difficulties, the better smelter firms tended to develop into well-integrated companies, and latecomers such as the Guggenheims proved that opportunity was still open to a firm that could command capital and expertise. Meyer Guggenheim, born in a ghetto in Switzerland, a tailor in his youth, a marked success in many enterprises after his emigration to Philadelphia, was determined to build an empire in association with his seven sons. Through loaning money to a friend who was trying to develop a pair of Leadville claims, Guggenheim became part-owner of the mine when the friend could not repay.

Experiencing only indifferent success with his Leadville mine, Meyer Guggenheim began one of his characteristically meticulous studies to determine whether it would be more profitable to build a smelter. In association with two experienced hands, the Guggenheims incorporated a smelting company and sent Benjamin Guggenheim and one of their experienced associates to bargain with the several Colorado towns that seemed possible sites. Pueblo won the honor by offering generous terms. Initial experience with the smelter was disastrous, but the Guggenheims had the capital to stay with the enterprise while the plant was rebuilt by a veteran trouble-shooter and while Benjamin and Simon learned the business. Simon, by the way, was destined to continue Colorado's tradition of rewarding mining barons with a seat in the United States Senate.[44]

By the time that the Guggenheims were firmly established in the later 1890s, they were one of four large integrated corporations that had emerged from the welter of pioneer smelters in Colorado and the Missouri River cities.[45] With both silver and lead at low prices, the smelter owners began negotiations in 1897 and 1898 looking toward formation of a holding company that would embrace all of them. For this they would need capital and guidance. Henry H. Rogers, the Rockefellers, and the Lewisohns were interested, for they had already embarked on a scheme to control the copper market, and since the silver-lead companies produced copper matte as a by-product, it was important to divert this into the hands of the Rockefeller group.

With Rogers providing the leadership, a New York investment banking house and a New York broker did the legal work and collected options on major firms. When the American Smelting and Refining Company was incorporated in 1899, it had about two thirds of the nation's smelting and refining capacity within its grasp. Nathaniel Hill had tried to sell his company to the syndicate, but failed. The Guggenheims and the few Pacific Coast firms chose to remain outside temporarily.[46]

Familiar and trusted names such as August R. Meyer and James B. Grant appeared prominently in the affairs of ASARCO, as the new "Smelting Trust" was nicknamed. Common and preferred stock was issued liberally. Meantime the Guggenheims were building an organization that was too strong for ASARCO to leave outside the trust. In one of those intricate, Byzantine negotiations that saw huge industrial plants exchanged and millions of dollars of "paper" capital created, the Guggenheims, Rogers, Lewisohn, and other powerful insiders worked out a deal by which the Guggenheims sold their plants to ASARCO, but took control of ASARCO with money obtained from Rogers, and agreed to market their copper through an agency that Rogers' group had created! Daniel Guggenheim became chairman of the board and the leader of the reorganized trust for the next twenty years, while his brothers Simon, Morris, Isaac, and Solomon became directors.[47]

That left one major group still to be dealt with. In the 1880s the lovely narrow valleys of the Coeur d'Alene district of northern Idaho were discovered to be rich in silver-lead ores. Despite violent labor wars in the 1890s, the area boomed into prominence as a major mining region. Its most important mine, the Bunker Hill and Sullivan, was bought by Simeon G. Reed of Oregon Steam Navigation Company fame, but after an exhausting struggle to make the mine pay for its needed development work, while fighting off unusually bitter lawsuits from neighboring claims, Reed sold out, at a loss.[48]

The chief opponent of the Bunker Hill and Sullivan was a fluent-talking promoter, Charles Sweeny, of mixed Irish and English parentage. Sweeny had tried every kind of job, with mixed success, but experience in California and on the Comstock Lode had made mining his real enthusiasm, although his enemies alleged that his "mining" was conducted in the law courts and through smart ploys at others' expense. He was famous for harassing his neighbors with injunctions and lawsuits.

Yet by the opening of the new century Sweeny had become a powerful figure in the Coeur d'Alene and took the lead in a scheme to merge the principal mines under a single holding company. The central weakness of the Coeur d'Alene was its mines' dependence on ASARCO, which was the only smelting combine big enough to treat the district's ores.[49]

Sweeny had the successful effrontery to go to New York and spend ten days seeking an appointment with John D. Rockefeller, Sr. Failing to see Rockefeller himself, he did have a session with Rockefeller's associate, Frederick T. Gates, whom he persuaded to view the idea favorably. Somewhat reluctantly, John D. Rockefeller, Senior, gave his consent. George J. Gould, manager of the Gould fortune, was to join in the venture. Hiring United States Senator George W. Turner of Spokane as a less controversial negotiator than himself, Sweeny obtained options on the chief Coeur d'Alene mines, except the Bunker Hill and Sullivan, and an independent-minded local group that owned the Hercules mine.

The Federal Mining and Smelting Company was formed in 1903, with Sweeny as president and Rockefeller, Gates, Gould, and some well-known bankers and industrialists on the board. Two years later, after much deliberately deceptive bluster from Sweeny about plans for Federal to build its own smelters, the Guggenheims cut off that danger by buying control of Federal, as the Rockefellers and Gates may well have foreseen that they would have to do. Sweeny then negotiated a contract by which ASARCO would buy Federal's ores for the next twenty-five years, while Daniel Guggenheim signed a comparable contract with the Bunker Hill and Sullivan. Thus ASARCO and the Guggenheims reigned supreme and Sweeny and the Rockefeller-Gould group had profited handsomely.[50]

While copper and lead-silver mines and the reduction plants that served them tumbled into combines that the Populists and Progressives denounced as "trusts," events in faraway southeastern Arizona revealed a variant on this pattern of consolidation. Because of its aridity, remoteness from railroads, and Indian danger, Arizona came later into prominence, but the advance of the Southern Pacific Railroad across southern Arizona between 1878 and 1881, and the completion across northern Arizona by 1883 of a line that was later absorbed into the Santa Fe system, materially lessened isolation, while the discovery of rich silver deposits at Tombstone, in the southeast corner of the territory, led to a gaudy boom that made that hitherto unpromising region a national sensation that has been supplying copy for movies and novels ever since.

Arizona's real future lay with copper, not silver. After the usual halting, undercapitalized, overpromoted false starts, serious development of copper began about 1880.[51] In distant New York, the firm of Phelps Dodge, an old, well-established export-import house founded by New Englanders, retained Dr. James Douglas to advise them on copper matters. Douglas was a Canadian who had started to be a minister, had shifted to medicine, but had found his real career in working with a distinguished chemist, Thomas Sterry Hunt, on the chemistry of copper ores. The two men did pioneering work in the electrolytic refining of copper.[52]

Phelps Dodge already had before them an unsolicited plea for investment in a promising but undercapitalized copper property at Morenci, in southeastern Arizona. Douglas told them of another mine, the Copper Queen, in a hamlet named Bisbee, just north of the Mexican border. Douglas had been greatly impressed by Copper Queen ores that had been sent east to him for treatment. The current owners of the Copper Queen were San Francisco investors, but the mine and attached smelter were being developed under the direction of a highly experienced professional, John Williams, originally from Swansea, Wales, more recently from Michigan and Utah. Williams' sons, Louis and Ben, worked with him, and Louis had been sent to develop the Copper Queen.

When Phelps Dodge, which had handled metals for many years, decided to send Douglas to Arizona in 1881 to investigate, Douglas telegraphed back enthusiastically, urging his employers to invest in the Morenci property and to buy a claim called the Atlanta that was adjacent to the Copper Queen—even though the district was sixty miles from the nearest railroad point. Douglas was a man whose integrity, pleasant personality, and high technical qualifications inspired trust. He was put in charge of the Atlanta. He needed every bit of his new employers' trust, for after two years and eighty thousand dollars spent on sinking shafts, he had nothing to show for his efforts, and it took argument to win continued backing. To their intense relief, a little more investment brought Douglas and his Cornish foreman to an exceedingly rich ore body.

Realizing that this was probably the same ore body as the Copper Queen's, Douglas persuaded his backers to buy out the Copper Queen's owners, even though this put the new consolidated Copper Queen–Atlanta heavily into debt at just the time that a bigger and more efficient smelter was needed. Phelps Dodge must have had faith, for by 1887 a new smelter was blown in and the consolidated operation was able to pay off its three-hundred-thousand-dollar debt and begin buying adjacent claims to ward off legal troubles and increase reserves.

Making the most of the great local influence he had won, Douglas led the neighboring mines into a remarkably constructive legal step. He persuaded all owners to suspend the costly apex law so far as Bisbee was concerned, and abide by the much older common-law definition of underground boundaries. To ensure fair play, he induced the owners to make their underground workings open to inspection. The precedent for this seems to have been a similar suspension of the apex law in the twin camps of Morenci and Clifton, starting apparently in 1881. Everyone save the lawyers profited by this sensible solution to one of the west's most costly problems.

For the rest of the century and on into the 1900s the Copper Queen was so astonishingly profitable that Phelps Dodge sanctioned Douglas' introduction of major improvements, such as the Bessemer process that Butte had already tried, a network of local railroads that included a connection to the big national lines so as to be able to bargain, a huge new smelter in 1904, and a model town named Douglas. A chain of Phelps Dodge stores served every town in which the company operated. A newspaper was subsidized.

"The Company," as Arizona came to call Phelps Dodge, took over the Morenci operations in which it had invested earlier. It ran rail lines down into Mexico to reach new sources of ores. "The Company" loomed high in Arizona, as the Anaconda did in Montana, even though in Arizona other major copper companies developed, notably William Andrews Clark's highly profitable venture at Jerome and Clarkdale.[53] In a thinly populated state or territory a rich and closely controlled major enterprise could wield decisive power that the elected or appointed public officials were reluctant to oppose.

Douglas was a kind and generous person with humanitarian instincts, but his rule and that of his son who succeeded him was the essence of paternalism. Cultural and recreational amenities were provided in each town, and vigorous attempts were made to persuade the miners to improve their sanitary standards so as to reduce the typhoid and smallpox epidemics that cursed Bisbee for years. Bisbee was a "white man's camp," with no Chinese allowed in town after nightfall and Spanish-speaking workers confined to jobs that "white men" did not want. An ethnic pecking order was observed: Cornishmen, Welshmen, Irishmen, and Americans were the underground miners; Finns, Italians, Serbs, Poles, and Montenegrins were the muckers and trammers who loaded and pushed the cars underground; Mexicans worked in the smelters and in the railroad construction gangs. It is almost superfluous to add that unions were not permitted.[54]

So stratified and ethnically complex a work force was characteristic of the later, not the earlier, days of western mining. When hardrock mining began to go deep, starting with the Comstock and California, most miners of the older American stocks abandoned the field fairly quickly to Cornishmen and Irishmen. It's not hard to see why. Underground mining was difficult, dangerous, and unhealthy. The chances of being killed, maimed, or subjected to diseases such as silicosis or lead poisoning were high.

The deeper mining went, the more disagreeable working conditions became. While willing to spend heavily on machinery that promised profits, mine owners were slow and miserly when it came to paying for their workers' comfort, health, and safety underground. Even paternalistic owners seemed to consider human lives cheaper than the high cost of adequate safeguards.

The air deep underground was all too often a foul combination of fumes left by the last blast of black powder or dynamite, the smell of rotting timbers, and the stench of human excrement (no toilet facilities provided). Many mines became exceedingly hot as greater depth was reached, and underground water kept getting into the working areas despite continuous pumping. Careful timbering was essential to prevent cave-ins, but at mines where it was difficult to maintain a cash flow, costly replacement of rotting timbers tended to be postponed.

Even the new technology, helpful though it was, created new hazards. Electricity was a boon unless a miner with a steel tool carelessly touched the bare, high-voltage copper wires. The power drills that the richer mines were using extensively spun off sharp-edged granitic dust that settled in men's lungs and caused the growth of an enveloping tissue that ultimately made breathing impossible ("the miners' con," or consumption). The power-operated hoists or cages, used for lifting ores and men, became death traps if the operator was careless for a moment, or was inadequately trained, or if a tired, groggy miner wearily slumped outward and was smashed against the rocky sides of the shaft. The new dynamite could create nausea-causing fumes, and carelessness in dealing with charges that had failed to fire could blow to pieces the next miner who unwarily worked on that rock face.[55]

Machines and dynamite also altered the nature of the working population, because by reducing the need for highly skilled hand drillers, they encouraged mine owners of the later decades to import new ethnic groups of cheaper laborers from eastern and southern Europe. After first sneering at "dagos," "bohunks," and "Polacks," the English-speaking miners ended by accepting them, as they never accepted Chinese or Mexicans. Italians, Poles, Finns, and Yugoslavs were among the newcomers.

Two questions rise quickly to mind. First, why were the mine owners slow to improve conditions underground? The pioneer student of labor in the mines, Vernon H. Jensen, harshly concluded that the basic factor was "greed—shortsighted self-interest," grounded in "the prevailing western frontier attitudes toward property, its use and management."[56] More recent scholars have pointed to the prevalence of similar unsatisfactory conditions in eastern coal mines, smelters, and industrial plants, which suggests that a limited concern for employees' welfare was a national, not solely a western, attitude.

One might add that by the 1890s, when the worst labor warfare broke out, easterners in fact controlled many western mining and smelting operations. What was different about the west was the isolation of so many mines, the dependence of so many towns on a single unstable industry—often on the will of a single company—and therefore the absence of an independent middle group of local business and professional men who might have exercised a moderating influence. To this could be added the footloose character of the unmarried miners, who constituted most of the labor force. Frank Crampton, one of the few miners to write an autobiography, said that his friends among the "mining stiffs" told him never to stay too long on one job—three months was about right.[57] This left little chance to build a coherent community.

The other obvious question is why were men willing to work under such conditions? Look at the foreign past of so many of them, and at the appeal of high American western wages compared to pay in Britain, Europe, or even eastern America. In Cornwall a boy followed his father into the mines when he was less than ten years old, learned his trade by working alongside his father in the ill-ventilated rabbit warrens that had been blasted out of the rock, and at the end of the shift had to climb up endless ladders to get back to the surface—and all that for pay little higher than that of a local day laborer.[58]

The Irishmen's poverty in their homeland was proverbial, and the same could be said for the eastern and southern Europeans. Such men were desperate for a job and in no position to bargain.

Unions, as a means of partially ameliorating working hardships, had their beginning on the Comstock Lode, and with so transient a membership as miners, the Comstock precedents and even the precise wording of the pioneer Comstock union charter were soon carried to camps and towns throughout the west. After the Comstock's big mines had failed, the leadership of unionism passed to Butte, the new capital of western mining, and for years Butte was hailed as "the Gibraltar of unionism."[59]

Both the Comstock and Butte helped form local unions elsewhere and sent them aid in time of strikes. At Butte the Western Federation of Miners was formed in 1893 as the direct result of the violent strike in the Coeur d'Alene mines during the previous year. That strike, which was broken after months of escalating bitterness by bringing in the Idaho National Guard and the United States Army, convinced the more militant of the Butte leaders that greater unity was needed than could be achieved by ad hoc cooperation between local unions. Shortly after the turn of the century the Western Federation of Miners went a step further when it played a brief but important role in founding the radical Industrial Workers of the World, better known as the I.W.W. or "Wobblies."

This means that the obduracy of the mine owners and superintendents unwittingly inspired the rise of an organized, militant, and at times radical and violent labor movement that became a major factor in its own day and preserved for later generations bitter memories that poisoned western thinking for decades. Ultimately out of the political activity to which these unions gave rise came corrective state and Federal legislation that mandated minimum safety and health standards and inspections, but such reforms became a reality only after stubborn fights in legislatures and courts.

It is easy to use the unquestioned violence of the strikes of the 1890s to create an impression of universal conflict, whereas in fact recent research has shown that many a district and individual mine had a far more peaceful experience because of wiser local leadership on both sides. Yet the tumult was possible because it took place within a stratified society that had recently emerged in what had once been a reasonably equalitarian mining west. In his excellent case study of Grass Valley and Nevada City, California—two adjacent but quite different towns, the one based on quartz, the other on hydraulicking and general business—Ralph Mann has shown that as early as the late 1860s stratification based on wealth, occupational status, and ethnicity had developed. The change was pronounced in Grass Valley, which drew in Cornishmen to do its underground quartz work. Ownership of the mines passed to absentee investors, while the resident superintendents joined with the local business and professional class to form an upper segment of society that was remote from the immigrant miners.[60]

Several decades later Frank Crampton gave an even bleaker picture of mining towns as he saw them when he was a mere "working stiff." Crampton was unique. He had run away from his parents' Fifth Avenue home and from the Ivy League college that had flunked him. As he experienced the towns, they had "narrow streets with a few stores, eating places run by Chinese . . . sometimes a bank, not often an 'opera house,' but always saloons and gambling places . . . always the 'line' or 'stockade' with its dance halls, parlor houses, and cribs." For living arrangements there was a drab bunkhouse and mess hall, or room and board in one of the few homes. "Of mining engineers, real and self-designated, there were many, but most of them were too far up in the clouds to have truck with ordinary hard-rock stiffs."[61]

As Crampton remarked, "life at the mines was tough." He felt that the Western Federation of Miners and the I.W.W. "did a fine job for the working stiffs," because "mine owners were hard, calloused, almost ruthless, and organized," and an individual had no chance against them.[62]

The unions developed within this unbalanced society for two reasons. First, as benevolent societies. Following Comstock precedents, unions used their members' monthly dues and occasional assessments to help miners who became sick or injured, to help with the all-too-frequent funerals, and to aid widows and children. At times they were able to win support for building local hospitals and getting medical treatment independently of the distrusted company doctors. Their union halls provided an alternative to the saloons and brothels by serving as social and entertainment centers and maintaining the only public library and reading room in most towns.[63]

But they were also fighting organizations that crusaded for a standard four-dollar daily wage for all underground workers, for an eight-hour day instead of the much more common ten, for greater safety precautions. There they collided with the owners and super-intendents, whose basic philosophy was that no one was going to tell them how to run their mines—their property—least of all unions, which they regarded as dangerously radical intrusions between em-ployer and employee.

The mine owners formed their own "protective" associations to counter the unions. They hired private detectives to infiltrate the unions so that the owners could learn which men were leaders and thus should be fired; they recruited strikebreakers ("scabs") and hired armed guards. Their best source of scabs proved to be the native-born American population of the Missouri-Kansas lead re-gion, and by importing them in large numbers the owners changed the ethnic composition of some embattled towns.[64]

When the miners resorted to violence, including blowing up property with dynamite stolen from the mines, the mine owners successfully demanded the protection of the state militia and the intervention of the United States Army. By then the strikes had become class warfare. Strikers were thrown into stockades or run out of town, without regard for constitutional rights. Union men found themselves blacklisted and the lists circulated throughout the west, so as to deny them jobs anywhere.[65]

It was a curious outcome for an industry and a region whose original appeal had been a bright new opportunity for all.

CHAPTER 13

Other Opportunities

A T the start of this book the Prologue stressed the extraordinarily varied nature of the west, and the equally varied kinds of human beings who moved restlessly into the west during the last four decades of the century. Out of such a multiplicity of types one would expect a considerable number of industries and occupations to emerge. Such was indeed the case.

To borrow a concept from Leonard Arrington, the "basic industries"—meaning the major industries that produced for export beyond the west, attracted capital from outside, and built up centers of trade and service—were mining, livestock, and agriculture. To these Arrington added a somewhat surprising fourth: the military.[1] Another scholar has not only concurred with this last but has extended the category to include Federal agencies generally. "Consistently for over a century the federal government was the largest single employer in the Dakotas, Arizona, Utah and New Mexico."[2] Even in the more populated, more economically developed western states and territories, Federal expenditures in the nineteenth century were an important source of incoming revenue, and the network of officials—Federal, state, and local—and contractors through which this largess was distributed was an influential force in both politics and economics.

While sufficient for the Mormon country that was Arrington's chief concern, this categorization is not comprehensive enough for the west as a whole. To it must be added the comments that have already been presented on the rise of regional capitals such as San Francisco, Denver, Salt Lake City, and Portland, together with a discussion that might well be added on the later appearance of Los Angeles, Seattle, and Spokane as railroads and regional markets reached them, or some consideration of the decline in relative importance of old communities such as Santa Fe and Tucson. It was in these cities that substantial mercantile houses developed, that banking split off from its early involvement with traders or with express companies, and that the professions became significant.

One profession was especially important. Lawyers were omnipresent in western life just as in the rest of the nation. Lawyers wrote the contracts by which clients closed deals, they foreclosed mortgages, collected debts, drew up wills, sought injunctions and writs, defended their clients, initiated suits, and argued in flowing Victorian rhetoric when cases came to trial.

This was their private function. They were equally important in public life. As judges, members of their profession presided over the courts; as legislators, they devised the statutes; as state-makers, they drafted constitutions when territories were applying for statehood; and in each new territory or state they drew up codes of civil and criminal procedure. Many of them were deep in politics, sometimes as elected or appointed officeholders, sometimes as wire-pullers who preferred to work quietly behind the scenes. The contributions of Judge Matthew P. Deady of Portland, Oregon, suggest how constructive and influential a lawyer could be in a new country.

The lawyers' role is the more interesting because it challenges the late Walter Prescott Webb's thesis that when Americans moved out of the humid east, they crossed a "cultural fault line" similar to a geological fault, where new environmental conditions forced changes in basic institutions.[3] The fact is that inaugural legislatures, assembling with little preparation and under pressure to meet immediate needs, usually adopted the English common law because it was what they knew and it promised continuity. Lawrence Friedman, the historian of American law, melodramatically expressed this when he asserted that the central "theme of American law, East and West, in the last half of the 19th century was 'organize or die.' "[4] The common law was an obvious body of precedents and procedures around which to organize, although the west's isolation and special conditions inspired subsequent piecemeal modifications. The innovations in mining and water law were the most drastic, although in the Hispanic southwest, land titles and community property (to protect wives' interests) were of great importance. Eastern influence, bringing with it the common law, was the greater since this was the period in which David Dudley Field's famous code of civil procedure, prepared for New York, was being widely adopted throughout the west, and western supreme courts were showing a keen awareness of eastern decisions, especially those of New York.[5]

As in other parts of the nation, lawyers had a modest and informal training. Jackson A. Graves, who became one of Los Angeles' most successful attorneys, took a clerical job in a San Francisco law office so that after completing his day's work he could use the partners' law library to study, "frequently until 11 o'clock."[6] His future partner, Henry W. O'Melveney, obtained a position as tutor to two boys in the Hawaiian Islands, and took with him a trunkload of lawbooks to study. Both men passed the bar examination, which was an oral questioning by the judges of the California Supreme Court.[7]

This was a more thorough preparation and examination than most fledgling lawyers received. A large percentage of the west's lawyers were young men who claimed prior experience in the east or Middle West. Some, such as Henry M. Teller of Colorado, proved by their superior performance in their new homes that they were indeed qualified. There were always some who were "sloppy, tardy, or incompetent,"[8] as their clients learned by sad experience.

Federal territorial judges had an especially burdensome task, because an economy-minded Congress required the three judges to sit separately as district judges, and then to sit together as a supreme court to hear appeals from the decisions that they had handed down at the lower level. A further appeal to the United States Supreme Court was possible.[9] In contrast to the condescending criticism with which historians have traditionally treated the judiciary of the territories, recent scholars have stressed that the western judges were underpaid, given miserly expense accounts in a land of high living costs, and assigned to districts too big to be covered reasonably by the limited transportation available. To quote a study of the Rocky Mountain bench, "they played a major part in establishing law and order; they brought American society to the West—society as it was envisioned by the majority to the east."[10]

Perhaps it was the very omnipresence of lawyers in city and town that has caused historians to give insufficient attention to their role. Somewhat the same could be said of an utterly different economic activity that on the Pacific Coast deserves to rank as one of Arrington's "basic industries": lumber. Lumber was America's universal building material, and despite the success of adobe in the southwest and the resort to brick and iron in an attempt to reduce susceptibility to fire, wood was still the first structural material. As a leading Californian writer remarked in 1863, "our houses are built of lumber, our streets are planked with lumber, our fields are fenced with lumber, and our flumes and sluices are made of lumber."[11]

Initial needs at boom towns were met locally by what were essentially transient mills, small units that stripped the trees off the public domain without so much as a by-your-leave, and stayed in business as long as the timber lasted and was within ox-team hauling distance of the local market. A much more enduring operation was possible in the Pacific Coast strip that began at Santa Cruz, below San Francisco, and extended up through northwestern California, through Oregon and Washington west of the Cascades, and up into British Columbia.

Here, where the Coast Ranges and the Cascades catch the moisture coming in from the ocean, were some of the most magnificent dense stands of coniferous trees in the world: Douglas fir ("Oregon pine"), redwood, Port Orford cedar, and western red cedar. In addition to yielding a remarkable number of board feet per acre, these coastal forests had the great attraction of growing down to the edge of salt water, so that transportation to markets was possible decades before railroads were built.

When the California gold rush created a huge demand, San Francisco emerged as the biggest single consumer and as the central market that attracted lumber and then redirected much of it into the interior via the river system, or down the coast by sea. It was true that there were vast forests in the Sierras and lesser ones in the Coast Ranges, but getting timber out of those mountains and into some form of water transportation was so difficult that by 1863 San Francisco's leading newspaper was reporting that "this mart is furnished with very little lumber from the State of which it is the emporium."[12]

That was too good an opportunity to be missed by a country that developed a major lumber industry in Maine, New York, Pennsylvania, and eastern Canada, and had subsequently moved whole units of that industry—the entrepreneurs, skilled workers, equipment, techniques, and capital—out to Michigan, Wisconsin, and Minnesota. First to try out the rich coastal regions between San Francisco and British Columbia were "Down East" veterans of the New England lumber and shipping trade, but other experienced hands followed, until John S. Hittell could say thirty years later:

Whatever had been learned in the forests of Europe, Maine, Michigan, and Canada was transferred in all its completeness by experienced men to California soon after the gold discovery, and combined and applied in the construction and management of the sawmills of the Sierra Nevada, the redwood regions, and Oregon, Washington, and British Columbia.[13]

Particularly influential and successful were the Maine men who initiated some of the most important sawmilling ventures of the 1850s and 1860s, and the Great Lakes veterans who seized leadership in the late nineteenth century, starting in the later 1880s. With them came the lumberjacks, who brought their established habits and attitudes, just as they brought their Paul Bunyan legends and their special vocabulary. As the lumberjacks had been a migratory, isolated, "homeless, womanless" breed farther east, so were they now in the Far West. To quote the leading student of lumber labor:

It was in the eastern states, particularly in Maine, where was set the pattern which, with only a few notable exceptions, was to go with the industry across the continent.[14]

Western lumbering, unlike mining or cattle raising, was thus a transplant from a great national industry, but it was an isolated one. Until the completion of railroad service to the Pacific Northwest in the decade 1883–1893, it was impracticable to ship western lumber across the space barrier of the Great Plains. The opening of rail service to California in 1869 is deceptive. That pioneer road, together with its early connections to Salt Lake City and Denver, brought in more lumber from the Great Lakes than it ever carried out from local sources. The special forest census of 1880 reported that Colorado, Utah, and New Mexico were drawing supplies from the great national lumber market at Chicago.[15]

The turning point that began to open the major interior markets to Pacific Coast lumber did not come until 1893, when James J. Hill's Great Northern Railroad granted a more reasonable rate than his grasping rivals had been willing to allow. By then signs of impending exhaustion of the northeastern and Great Lakes forests had made the issue one of crucial importance.

In the meantime, throughout the 1850s, 1860s, and 1870s men from the northeastern corner of North America, including both Canada and the United States, went vigorously to work to develop a major industry that could survive on trade by sea, which meant primary reliance on the big San Francisco market and secondary shipments to harbors throughout the islands and shores of the Pacific. Hawaii, for example, was a favorite export market for the great firm of Pope and Talbot, which was founded by lumber and shipping men from East Machias, Maine, established its headquarters at San Francisco, and pioneered in building a sawmill, docks, workshops, and living quarters on Puget Sound, whence they derived their lumber.[16]

Such firms were about as much in the shipping business as in lumber. Their captains were constantly seeking markets in exotic places such as Australia, Tahiti, China, Central and South America, later Japan and South Africa and Alaska of the gold-rush era.

Those same captains were sent north to explore the coast for sites that had passable harbors in the midst of the thick forests. The Pacific Coast is dangerous, characterized by sandbars across many otherwise promising openings, many rocks and reefs, heavy fogs, currents, and winter storms. Puget Sound was by far the best site, for coves and good landing places abounded along its sheltered waters. Company mill towns sprang up all around its shores. One of the most startling, to westerners, was the white-painted, picket-fenced New England town that Pope and Talbot built to house the workers that they imported from East Machias, Maine, their old home base.[17]

The lower Columbia might have been expected to be a major competitor, but the heavy surf and fearsome bar across the entrance to the river was a severe impediment. But Grays Harbor and Willapa Bay in Washington, Coos Bay in Oregon, and Humboldt Bay in

California each became the site of large lumbering operations. Elsewhere seamen and lumbermen showed extraordinary daring in
loading boards down chutes into little schooners bobbing up and
down in rock-surrounded "dog-holes."[18]

Until late in the century most of these isolated coastal lumber
camps owed their beginnings to pioneer lumbermen who were not
concerned at all about cutting timber from the public domain. It is
illuminating to find one of the Pope and Talbot partners remarking
in November 1861 that although the company had been sawing
there since September 1853, they "have never had any lands here
until they purchased of University Commiss's this year."[19] His reference was to lands bought out of the grant voted by Congress for a
state university. When, during Lincoln's administration, the district
attorney tried to prosecute for cutting on the public domain, he
found it an unpopular and difficult business, for the citizenry of
Washington Territory were not ready to support interference with
their principal industry.[20] Much of the fault was Congress', for as
John Ise has remarked in speaking of conditions in 1878, there was
"no general legal and honest way of acquiring public timber lands,
or the timber itself," in most of the west. Hence "timber which
could not be secured honestly was secured by fraud."[21]

Because of the enormous size of Douglas fir and redwood trees,
considerable ingenuity was required to handle the logs. Small mov-
able steam engines (the Dolbeer "steam donkey," a western inven-
tion) came into universal use as a means of pulling and loading the
logs, while short, steam-powered logging railroads were thrust into
the woods to increase the area within economical reach of the mill.
Until band saws became available, Pacific Coast millmen used an
ingenious arrangement of multiple circular saws that simultaneously cut and sliced the thick logs from several directions, since no
one circular saw could cut through logs of such great diameter.[22]

The lumber so cut and sent off by sea was known as the "cargo
trade," to distinguish it from local small-scale output and the later
national distribution by railroad.[23] San Francisco was the headquarters of the cargo trade and of the fleet of oceangoing and coastal
ships and tugboats that the great firms came to operate—and sometimes to build themselves. When Hittell tried reworking the figures
published in the census of 1880, he concluded that exclusive of
shipping, the lumber industry of California, Oregon, Washington,

and British Columbia probably represented an investment of $10 million, employed ten thousand men, and produced lumber of all types worth about $12 million.[24]

Despite their great strength, the big San Francisco firms could never bring order into an industry that was chronically guilty of overproduction, price cutting, and frequent financial failures. They tried and failed to enforce price-fixing and production-fixing agreements.[25] Meantime, as railroads reached the California interior, the market had to absorb the output of new and sometimes large firms that were now able to exploit the Sierra forests.[26]

Finally, starting in the 1880s and continuing until the national financial depression of 1907, veterans of the Great Lakes forests began acquiring large tracts of the farther west's timber lands, through such devices as buying from the huge railroad land grants. The most famous instance was the news that the greatest firm of the upper Mississippi Valley, the Weyerhaeuser interests, had formed a consortium to buy nine hundred thousand acres from the Northern Pacific Railroad, in one of the greatest land transactions in American history. This proved to be only the beginning of continuing Weyerhaeuser acquisitions. By the outbreak of the First World War, the Weyerhaeuser direct ownerships totaled nearly 2 million acres, three fourths of which were in Washington.[27]

Washington Territory went into a boom as middle western money and veteran middle western leadership began a campaign to bring discipline into the industry and to beat the railroads into lower rates to the middle western markets that they knew so well. They crusaded for more efficient cutting that would use a higher percentage of the tree, and when the states delayed appropriating for fire protection, they used their own money to start patrols. They even reached partial agreement with Gifford Pinchot about conservation practices. In short, despite a bad record for gutting the Mississippi Valley, in their new western home the transplanted middle westerners showed the beginnings of a more responsible attitude toward the nation's forest resources.

The number of men from New England and the Canadian Maritime Provinces who sailed to the Pacific Coast for the express purpose of mixing lumbering and seafaring, just as they had in their home country, should be sufficient proof that the west attracted many people who had no intention of becoming miners, cowboys, wheat kings, irrigation farmers, or freighters or railroad men—the most visible occupations.

The modest but vigorous fishing industry illustrated the same point. Commercial fishing started during the California gold rush when the salmon ran abundantly on the Sacramento. Subsequently mining debris polluted the water, steamboat traffic became heavy, and too much fishing depleted the breeding stock.[28] By the spring of 1860 an observer who had followed the industry since 1849 was reporting a "rapid" disappearance of the salmon. Hitherto salmon had been sold fresh or had been dried, smoked, or salted for export.[29]

As the Sacramento trade was dwindling, a determined young Maine man, with his brothers and a fellow Down East partner, arrived on the Sacramento to begin the difficult task of canning salmon. According to R. D. Hume's own account, he and his partners lost half of their first output before discovering how to keep the cans from leaking, and Hume found it difficult to persuade San Francisco merchants to buy his new product. After two discouraging years he had the good sense to move his operation to the Columbia River, and there in the early 1870s the foundations were laid for the American salmon-canning industry.[30]

While on the Columbia, Hume found that his best market was in far-off Great Britain, and he also learned that Chinese made ideal cannery workers. Personal affairs presently caused him to sell out his Columbia investment and to move to the much smaller Rogue River of southern Oregon. Here he made himself king: for years he controlled fishing on the Rogue, even though it was a public river. He ran a company town and newspaper, owned the boats and nets that the local men rented from him in order to earn their living, and employed Chinese to work in the cannery. He owned his own ships to take the product away and to bring in supplies. Opposition he crushed.[31]

Salmon remained for years the most important fish caught in the North Pacific. As if the Columbia were not rich enough, fishermen received the great boon of discovering that the Alaskan Purchase opened the way to rich grounds that extended clear to Russia. In a wasteful, exploitative fashion typical of the west, big companies took over much of the business, fitted out large ships as floating canneries, hired Chinese cannery workers, dismissed the angry local natives who wanted the jobs, and made themselves an economic and political power.[32]

Meantime New Englanders were coming west in search of halibut and cod. While some began the struggle as early as the late 1880s and the 1890s, the main effort had to wait for halibut to become increasingly scarce in the Atlantic. Presently they began to transfer their best ships and their headquarters to the northwest, where Seattle rather than San Francisco tended to become their new base. Like so many promising new industries, the New Englanders had to battle the railroads for lower rates, better refrigeration service, and special fast express trains.[33]

To westerners who wanted an opportunity that was as exciting, as speculatively appealing as precious-metal mining in its wildest days, there was the possibility of oil. Ever since "Colonel" Drake had drilled his successful well in northwestern Pennsylvania in 1859, men by the thousands had been seeking petroleum at promising places, such as oil seepages, and had been learning how to drill wells and how to refine the raw product into something useful such as kerosene and lubricants. The main center of activity had been the Appalachian region and an extension from there across the mountains into Ohio, and down through Ohio to the Lima (Ohio)–Indiana fields. In 1899 nearly 93 percent of the total output of crude petroleum was derived from those few major fields.[34] Needless to say, by then Rockefeller's Standard Oil combine dominated the industry.

But this eastern focus did not discourage oil seeking elsewhere in the Middle West, on the Gulf Coast, in Texas, and in California. Veterans of the Pennsylvania fields took the lead, just as "Old Californians" had in so many new precious-metal regions. Because California was so remote, operations there tended to be separate from the other regions but surprisingly lively considering the difficulties encountered and the fact that real gushers did not flow in until the opening of the Los Angeles field in the 1890s.

Meantime, speculators, drillers, and "wildcatters" (men who drilled in districts removed from proven fields) were eagerly approaching from the east. In Kansas, oil springs and wells were being investigated as early as the 1860s, but commercial production did not begin until 1892.[35] Oklahoma, which was of course Indian Territory, went through intricate negotiations to gain permission, but its first commercial well was brought in only in 1897.[36] The real beginning of a new era came in Texas, and it came by sheer accident. The city of Corsicana, south of Dallas, had contracted to have three water wells drilled in 1894, but the drilling produced oil, and local enthusiasts promptly contracted with experienced Pennsylvanians to drill more wells. By 1896–1897 a wide-open boom was transforming what had been a quiet country town into a crowded, boisterous city that soon had its own large refinery.[37]

Soon afterward came the event that forever changed Texas, the oil industry, and the domination of Standard Oil. A determined engineer and salt dome prospector, A. F. Lucas, once an Austrian naval officer, decided to try again where others had failed, at Spindletop, Beaumont, Texas. Obtaining financial backing from a Pennsylvania firm of wildcatters, on January 10, 1901, Lucas brought in the most famous gusher in American history. It spewed forth more oil than anyone had seen before and led to a frantic drilling of wells both at Beaumont and at many other points in Texas. From being a poor state with huge areas of cattle range and cotton fields, suddenly Texas was thrust into modern industry. Its output probably did more than the United States Supreme Court's 1911 decision to break up the Standard Oil trust, for that huge organization simply could not readjust quickly enough to handle so much oil; instead, a whole series of strong new companies arose to offer real competition. Railroads hastily converted to oil in place of the expensive coal, tank cars and seagoing tankers were built to move the new product, big refineries and large storage tanks were constructed, pipelines were laid in key directions. Truly it was a revolution, not only for Texas but for Louisiana, Oklahoma, Kansas, and Arkansas.[38]

Meantime in California both Californians and recruits from Pennsylvania were struggling to make a success of the numerous modest-sized oil discoveries. The chief money-maker in those days was kerosene, but California's crudes, because of relatively low gravity and excessive carbon, yielded a poor quality of illuminant that could not compete with imported eastern kerosene. Nor did California's crudes provide a good quality of lubricant. Energetic attempts to sell the crudes for fuel, in a state singularly lacking in good coal, produced considerable results prior to the 1890s. California oil men succeeded in selling crude oil for making illuminating gas and for use in breweries, iron and steel plants, cement companies, and brick companies.[39]

Then the whole picture changed when E. L. Doheny, who was essentially a mining prospector, discovered the great Los Angeles field in 1892, soon followed by major discoveries in the Coalinga and Kern River fields in the interior. Railroads, steamships, and other major consumers quickly shifted to the abundant new fuel. Pipelines, storage tanks, and big refineries were built. The Federal census attributed much of Los Angeles's rapid growth in the 1890s to the fact that suddenly it had access to ample supplies of fuel. With more oil than could be used locally, shipments were made to the Arizona copper mines.[40]

It's worth noting that during the experimental years prior to the 1890s, familiar names appeared among the backers of the numerous oil companies. Lloyd Tevis became and remained a major figure in oil. His partner James Ben Ali Haggin joined him. Alvinza Hayward, the mining tycoon, invested. In other words, local capital was often, though not invariably, available. By 1900 the future seemed bright enough to attract a major Standard Oil investment.[41]

Taking the west as a whole, it is clear that opportunities were numerous, but that outside the managerial class the jobs were often laborious, disagreeable, and dangerous. Opportunities in manufacturing were notably scant. The west was still primarily a producer of raw materials and processed raw materials. San Francisco was exceptional in the degree of heavy industry it had developed, and on a much smaller scale Denver had done the same. Stockton was well known for its farm machinery, and Levi Strauss of San Francisco had won something close to immortality when he invented tough, riveted work clothes. It is significant that unionization and labor strife tended to focus in San Francisco and the mining and smelting towns—in other words, only the highly industrialized communities.

CHAPTER 14

If Horace Greeley Could See It Now

I T'S a pity that Horace Greeley died halfway through the immense changes that this book has been chronicling. With his perceptive reporting, his enthusiasm, and his eccentricities he would have been an intriguing critic of the west that emerged by 1900. Lacking his presence, we will have to make do with guidebooks and travel accounts that were published at the turn of the century.

One of the indications of change in the west was its appearance as a tourist attraction by 1900. The west could be reached now in comfort in a Pullman car, and the unadventurous tourist could see much out of the railroad car's broad windows.[1] But with a little greater effort a rich variety of sights awaited the traveler. There were the famous natural wonders; glimpses of "quaint" inhabitants such as Indians, Hispanic Americans, cowboys, and miners; a few fine old buildings such as Santa Barbara Mission; and dramatic new cities and resorts with their self-proclaimed "first-class hotels." The west had come a long way from the painful, primitive accommodations that Greeley had faced in 1859.

To James F. Muirhead, who had been sent to the United States to prepare the first Baedeker guide to America, his assignment seemed almost impossible. "The process of change in the United States goes on so rapidly that an attempt of a guidebook . . . becomes almost futile. The speed with which Denver metamorphosed her outward appearance has already been commented on. . . . [Or again,] the rough horse-trail of today becomes the stage-road of tomorrow and the railroad of the day after."[2]

The key point, Muirhead concluded, was that Americans were optimistic expansionists. "Denver . . . is an excellent example, both in theory and practice, of the confident expectation of growth with which American cities are founded. The necessary public buildings are not huddled together as a nucleus from which the municipal infant may grow outwards; but a large and generous view is taken of the possibilities of expansion." In similar fashion, the capitol of Bismarck, North Dakota, was built a mile from the city, but already it was being surrounded by houses.[3]

Change and optimism, then, were external characteristics, but what about the private lives and attitudes of individuals? Muirhead reported that "[n]o more fundamental contrast can well be imagined than that between the noisy, rough, crude, and callous street-life of some Western towns and the quiet, reticence, delicacy, spirituality, and refinement of many of the adjacent interiors."[4] This contrast, he suspected, might be part of "the fermenting process of life-in-the-making on the frontier."[5] But on the whole, Muirhead concluded, "there is a distinct tendency for the stamp of the Eastern States to be applied to the inhabitants of the cities, at least, of the West."[6]

Muirhead's cautious limitation "to the cities, at least" was a wise one, for the usual visitor by rail had little basis for judging the presumably less "refined" life of ranch, farm, or mine. But like all English travelers Muirhead heard constant western boasting about how well they treated their wives. The westerners were not speaking of anything as dramatic as the beginning of woman's suffrage, where Wyoming and Utah had led the way in 1869 and 1870 and a growing number of other western states were following as the new century began.[7]

Rather the westerners were speaking of ordinary life at home. It would be pleasant to accept their boasting at face value, but modern research suggests the obvious: that family relationships varied widely and were affected by economic and class differences.[8] A study of families and divorce in California suggests that in the later nineteenth century wives were challenging the hierarchical concept of marriage, which left authority in the husband's hands, in favor of the companionate marriage, "predicated on the notion of domestic equality between husband and wife."[9]

As a sophisticated observer, Muirhead brushed aside as a thing of the past "the almost theatrical romance of frontier life," but he still found himself fascinated to watch settlers of European descent adjusting themselves to new conditions. Perhaps, he meditated, "the nineteenth century is the most romantic of all."

Just consider, he suggested, the picturesqueness "in the long thin lines of gleaming steel, thrown across the countless miles of desert sand and alkali plain, and in the mighty mass of metal with its glare of cyclopean eye and its banner of fire-illumined smoke, that bears the conquerors of stubborn nature from side to side of the great continent."[10]

Most travelers on these impressive new trains found almost more dramatic scenes than they could absorb. A popular guidebook gushed that the visitor would journey from

the boundless prairie to the rugged grandeur of the American Alps, from the picturesque quaintness of New Mexico and the nomadic wildness of the Indian reservations to the polished civilization of metropolitan cities.

These are the lands of gold, of silver, of coal, of agriculture, of all fruits known to the temperate and sub-tropical zones.

At times travelers would see "hardy pioneers . . . turning the buffalo sod" preparatory to planting grain. An occasional antelope, colonies of prairie dogs, and fast-running jackrabbits would show that all wildlife had not disappeared when the buffalo were slaughtered.[11]

Denver was the first city reached by many travelers. Remembering the crude hamlet of tents, hovels, and cottonwood-log cabins that Greeley saw in 1859, it's worth quoting the rhapsody with which a guidebook greeted Denver:

A beautiful city, beautifully situated, is Denver, with broad, tree-shaded streets, with public buildings of massive proportions and attractive architecture, with residences erected in accordance with the canons of good taste, with innumerable lawns of shaven grass, ornamented with shrubs and flowers.[12]

An Englishman, sent over as correspondent for the *Daily Mail,* was far less impressed. Acidly he commented that "the Queen City of the Plains is more plain than queenly." Granted that the city was well built and well laid out, nevertheless it was "undistinguished."[13]

San Francisco was the magnet for most visitors. The guidebook promised that the initial impression would be pleasant and that this happy beginning would be strengthened by each day's experiences. But Muirhead, the sophisticated observer, added a sour note. As the cable car carried him up to where he could see the millionaires' mansions on Nob Hill, he "bemoaned . . . the misdirected efforts of their architects, who instead of availing themselves of the unique chance of producing monuments of characteristically developed timber architecture, have known no better than to slavishly imitate the incongruous features of stone houses in the style of the Renaissance."

Muirhead's revulsion was a part of his general distaste for the way newly rich western millionaires had spent their money. "The result is often as appalling in its hideousness as it is startling in its costliness."[14]

Visitors tended to cluster at the great resort hotels that had sprung up on the California coast. The Hotel del Coronado, opposite San Diego, was already famous; so were the Del Monte at Monterey, the Arlington and Potter hotels at Santa Barbara, and the Cliff House looming above Seal Rocks outside San Francisco. It was an interesting insight into their reputations that when the leaders of the middle western lumber industry wanted to scrutinize the possibility of buying timberlands in the Far West, they brought their families out for a California vacation while the men of the family went searching.[15]

All visitors, of course, regarded it as a "must" to see Yosemite and the Big Trees, the Grand Canyon, and Yellowstone. Some were intrigued by the cactus, Joshua trees, and desert succulents. A sturdy few—a very few—realized that in this rapidly changing west it was still possible to hire horses, pack animals, and an Indian guide to visit the relatively unchanged Colorado Plateau, where they could see the impressive stone buildings of a prehistoric civilization, the humble hogans of modern Navajos, and the adobe apartment houses of modern Pueblo Indians.[16]

Few travelers had significant contact with the rank-and-file of westerners. But G. W. Steevens of the *Daily Mail,* goaded by a reporter's instinct to be where the action was, first visited the Argo Smelting Works outside Denver, then went up to Leadville, where a bitter, major strike was taking place. His information seems to have come partly from the local newspaper editor and partly from management and from the National Guard that had been called in to impose martial law.

Steevens' conclusions after visiting Leadville were extreme. "Every American," he pontificated, "is at heart an Anarchist. He hates constraint, he hates regulation, he hates law." And yet on one point the American was more conservative than the czar of Russia: "He will have no tampering with the rights of property. He may have nothing himself, but he will guard the havings of others. . . . In a land where you may be a pauper to-day and a millionaire to-morrow," there must be no attack on wealth.[17]

Was there truth in Steevens' unflattering conclusion? The ruthless pursuit of private gain was the driving force behind most western enterprises. Look at the railroad scandals, the mining frauds, the refusal to accept any obligation for the safety and welfare of the underground miners, the deceit in obtaining Federal and state lands. The minority groups—the Mormons, Hispano-Americans, and Native American Indians—were more apt than the conquering Anglo-Europeans to show a real concern for the community welfare. This does not mean that city builders did not have pride in the cities they were creating, but often that pride was bolstered by the realization of how much new business and banking would come into a boom city, and how greatly their speculatively held lands would increase in value.

Then there is Steevens' accusation that Americans were anarchists at heart, in that they hated regulation or law. Such a charge was far more true of 1859, when the gunman and vigilante were real problems, than of 1900. By 1900 regular courts were functioning, the common law, as amended, was established, and very rich men were finding it to their advantage to settle cases out of court to avoid high litigation fees. By 1900 the Progressive era was beginning and would receive its first national leader in Theodore Roosevelt a year later. Words like "conservation," "reclamation," and "regulation" would become commonplace.

That the over-rapid development of the west in the later nineteenth century was hard on the landscape, the resources, and the lives of the people is unquestionable, but what else would be expected of a people as optimistically expansionist as Muirhead found them to be? A people as uncontrollably resourceful, versatile, and energetic?

Source Notes

Prologue

1. Emerson Hough, *The Story of the Cowboy* (New York, 1897), p. viii.
2. Stephan Thernstrom and Peter R. Knights, "Men in Motion: Some Data and Speculations about Urban Population Mobility in Nineteenth-Century America," *Journal of Interdisciplinary History*, I (1970–1971), 7–35.
3. Rodman W. Paul, *Mining Frontiers of the Far West, 1848–1880* (New York, 1963), pp. 115–16.
4. Alfred Doten, *The Journals of Alfred Doten, 1849–1903*, Walter Van Tilburg Clark, ed., 3 vols. (Reno, Nevada, 1973).
5. *The National Atlas of the United States of America* (Washington, 1970), p. 97; O. E. Baker, ed., *Atlas of American Agriculture* (Washington, 1936), incorporating section on "Precipitation and Humidity" (originally published Washington, 1922), pp. 6–7.
6. *Climate and Man: Yearbook of Agriculture, 1941* (Washington, 1941), p. 179.
7. *Ibid.*, p. 199.
8. *Soils and Men: Yearbook of Agriculture, 1938* (Washington, 1938), p. 680.
9. *Climate and Man*, p. 189.

Chapter 1: Horace Greeley Goes West

1. Glyndon G. Van Deusen, *Horace Greeley: Nineteenth Century Crusader* (Philadelphia, 1953), p. 230.
2. Mark Twain, *Roughing It*, Rodman W. Paul, ed. (New York, 1953), p. 106.
3. Horace Greeley, *An Overland Journey, From New York to San Francisco, in the Summer of 1859* (New York, 1860), pp. 100, 112, 272. Subsequent page references will appear in the text.
4. Save where otherwise indicated, population statistics in this chapter are from U. S. Bureau of the Census, *Eighth Census, 1860: Population* (Washington, 1864).

5. Van Deusen, *Horace Greeley*, p. 231.

6. Leslie M. Scott, "The Pioneer Stimulus of Gold," *Oregon Historical Society Quarterly*, XVIII (September 1917), 147.

7. *Ibid.*

8. Dorothy O. Johansen and Charles M. Gates, *Empire of the Columbia: A History of the Pacific Northwest* (New York, 1957), p. 341.

9. J. P. Keller, Teekalet (Port Gamble), Washington Territory, to Charles Foster, January 2, 1856, Coe Collection, Yale University.

10. Johansen and Gates, *Empire of the Columbia*, pp. 313, 322–23; Hubert H. Bancroft, *Works*, 39 vols. (San Francisco, 1882–1890), XXX, 465, footnote 9; XXXI, 1–67, 198–200.

11. Raphael Pumpelly, *Across America and Asia: Notes of a Five Years' Journey around the World and of Residence in Arizona, Japan and China* (New York, 1870), pp. 3–5.

12. *Ibid.*, pp. 30, 34.

13. Rodman W. Paul, "The Spanish-Americans in the Southwest, 1848–1900," in John G. Clark, ed., *The Frontier Challenge: Responses to the Trans-Mississippi West* (Lawrence, Kans., 1971), pp. 31–54.

14. W. W. H. Davis, *El Gringo; or, New Mexico and Her People* (New York, 1857), pp. 164–65, 177, 234.

15. *Ibid.*, p. 193.

16. *Ibid.*, pp. 180–84, 216–17.

17. Some modern scholars have argued that existing figures for Spanish-speaking Americans have been consistently too low. Oscar J. Martínez, "On the Size of the Chicano Population: New Estimates, 1850–1900," *Aztlan*, VI (1975), pp. 43–67.

18. Commissioner of Indian Affairs, *Report for the Year 1858* (Washington, 1858), p. 5.

Chapter 2: The Mining Advance into the Interior

1. In general, see Rodman W. Paul, *Mining Frontiers of the Far West, 1848–1880* (New York, 1963; reprinted Albuquerque, N.M., 1974), especially pp. 3–7, 37–48.

2. *Ibid.*, pp. 27–46.

3. Sacramento *Daily Union*, May 28, 1858.

4. Paul, *Mining Frontiers*, pp. 62–63.

5. Eliot Lord, *Comstock Mining and Miners*, U.S. Geological Survey, *Monographs*, IV (Washington, 1883), pp. 74–75.

6. Paul, *Mining Frontiers*, p. 62.

7. Elma Dill Russell Spencer, *Green Russell and Gold* (Austin, Texas, 1966).

8. Paul, *Mining Frontiers*, pp. 42–48; William J. Trimble, *The Mining Advance into the Inland Empire*, reprint edition, Rodman W. Paul, ed. (New York, 1972), pp. 141, 154.

9. Merrill D. Beal and Merle W. Wells, *History of Idaho*, 3 vols. (New York, 1959), I, pp. 282–85; Trimble, *Mining Advance*, pp. 65–66; Herman F. Rheinhart, *The*

Golden Frontier: The Recollections of Herman Francis Reinhart, 1851–1869. Doyce B. Nunis, Jr., ed. (Austin, Tex., 1962), p. 184.

10. William A. Goulder, *Reminiscences: Incidents in the Life of a Pioneer in Oregon and Idaho* (Boise, Idaho, 1909), p. 241.

11. John Hailey, *The History of Idaho* (Boise, Idaho, 1910), p. 30. Having lived in Oregon since 1853, Hailey came to Idaho in 1862.

12. Bancroft, *Works*, XXXI, pp. 406, 427–28. Merle W. Wells, "Territorial Government in the Inland Empire," *Pacific Northwest Quarterly*, XLIV (April 1953), 80, footnote 1, summarizes the special census. Hailey, *History of Idaho*, p. 62, gives the estimate for 1863.

13. C. Aubrey Angelo (Chaos, pseud.), *Idaho: A Descriptive Tour, and Review of its Resources and Route* (San Francisco, 1865), p. 26.

14. Granville Stuart, *Forty Years on the Frontier, as Seen in the Journals and Reminiscences of Granville Stuart, Gold-Miner, Trader, Merchant, Rancher and Politician*, Paul C. Phillips, ed. 2 vols. (Cleveland, Ohio, 1925), I, pp. 105, 133–211.

15. Merrill G. Burlingame and K. Ross Toole, *A History of Montana*, 3 vols. (New York, 1957), I, pp. 119–30; Rossiter W. Raymond, *Statistics of Mines and Mining in the States and Territories West of the Rocky Mountains* (Washington, 1870), 2d report, covering 1869, p. 253; Trimble, *Mining Advance*, pp. 79–82.

16. Hailey, *History of Idaho*, pp. 92, 116.

17. Merrill G. Burlingame, *The Montana Frontier* (Helena, Mont., 1942), p. 85.

18. Paul, *Mining Frontiers*, p. 144.

19. *Ibid.*, pp. 40, 115–16. Duane A. Smith, *Colorado Mining: A Photographic History* (Albuquerque, N.M., 1977), especially pp. 13–14.

20. Rufus K. Wyllys, *Arizona: The History of a Frontier State* (Phoenix, Ariz., 1950), pp. 117–22, 219. Fayette A. Jones, *New Mexico Mines and Minerals. . . . Being an Epitome of the Early Mining History* (Santa Fe, N.M., 1904), pp. 47–48. Bancroft, *Works*, XVII, pp. 649, 748.

21. Frank Fossett, *Colorado: Its Gold and Silver Mines, Farms and Stock Ranges, and Health and Pleasure Resorts* (New York, 1879), p. 120.

22. Joseph H. Boyd, "Reminiscences," William S. Lewis, recorder and editor, *Washington Historical Quarterly*, XV (1924), 243–62.

23. *Mining and Scientific Press*, December 14, 1861.

24. Walter W. De Lacy, "A Trip up the South Snake River in 1863," Historical Society of Montana, *Contributions*, I (1876; republished 1902), p. 100.

25. Charles R. Hubbard, *A Survey of the Mineral Resources of Idaho*, Idaho Bureau of Mines and Geology, *Pamphlet* no. 105 (Moscow, Idaho, 1955), p. 1.

26. Samuel F. Emmons, "Geological Sketch of the Rocky Mountain Division," in Samuel F. Emmons and George F. Becker, eds., *Statistics and Technology of the Precious Metals*, in *Tenth Census, 1880*, XIII (Washington, 1885), p. 96. J. Ross Browne, *Report on the Mineral Resources of the States and Territories West of the Rocky Mountains* (Washington, 1868), 2d report, covering 1867, pp. 506–11. Rossiter W. Raymond, *Mineral Resources of the States and Territories West of the Rocky Mountains* (Washington, 1869), 1st report, covering 1868, p. 143. J. T. Pardee and F. C. Schrader, *Metalliferous Deposits of the Greater Helena Mining*

Region, Montana, U.S. Geological Survey, *Bulletin* 842 (Washington, 1933), p. 120.

27. *Mining and Scientific Press,* January 19, 1863.
28. Except where otherwise noted, the remainder of this chapter is based on the present writer's *Mining Frontiers.*
29. Browne, *Report on the Mineral Resources,* 2d report, covering 1867, p. 9.
30. *Ibid.,* p. 509.
31. Paul, *Mining Frontiers,* pp. 30–32.
32. Beal and Wells, *History of Idaho,* I, pp. 359–67.
33. Burlingame and Toole, *History of Montana,* I, p. 130.
34. This sketch of Virginia City is based on Eliot Lord's *Comstock Mining and Miners;* upon the present writer's *Mining Frontiers of the Far West,* pp. 56–86; Russell R. Elliott, *History of Nevada* (Lincoln, Nebr., 1973), pp. 123–51; George D. Lyman, *The Saga of the Comstock Lode: Boom Days in Virginia City* (New York, 1934); Harry M. Gorham, *My Memories of the Comstock* (Los Angeles, 1939); Richard G. Lillard, *Desert Challenge: An Interpretation of Nevada* (New York, 1942); and upon the admirably illustrated study by John W. Reps, *Cities of the American West: A History of Frontier Urban Planning* (Princeton, 1979), pp. 227–31.
35. Elliott, *History of Nevada,* p. 149.
36. Lord, *Comstock Mining,* p. 210.
37. This comment and the reference to elegant wives' luncheons are from Louise M. Palmer, "How We Live in Nevada," *Overland Monthly,* II (1869), 457–62.
38. Elliott, *History of Nevada,* p. 147.
39. Excerpts from Galloway's diary are printed in John D. Galloway, *Early Engineering Works Contributory to the Comstock,* University of Nevada, *Bulletin,* XLI, no. 5, Geology and Mining Series no. 45 (Reno, 1947), pp. 13–21.
40. Elliott, *History of Nevada,* pp. 148–49.

Chapter 3: The Response to the Mining Boom: I. From the East

1. Bureau of the Census, *Historical Statistics of the United States, Colonial Times to 1957* (Washington, D.C., 1960), p. 13.
2. John D. Unruh, *The Plains Across: The Overland Emigrants and the Trans-Mississippi West, 1840–60* (Urbana, Ill., 1979), p. 120.
3. *Ibid.,* p. 298.
4. Robert M. Utley, *Frontiersmen in Blue: The United States Army and the Indian, 1848–1865* (New York, 1967), pp. 6–9, 15–19, 80–84, 108–12; Robert M. Utley, *Frontier Regulars: The United State Army and the Indian, 1866–1891* (New York, 1973), pp. 98–107, 257–62.
5. *Report of the Secretary of War,* 35th Cong., 2d sess., House Exec. Doc. no. 2 (Washington, December 6, 1858), p. 3.
6. Endpaper map, "The Military West in 1860," in Utley, *Frontiersmen in Blue.*
7. *Ibid.,* pp. 215–18.
8. Utley, *Frontier Regulars,* pp. 10–17.
9. Henry Pickering Walker, *The Wagonmasters: High Plains Freighting from the Earliest Days of the Santa Fe Trail to 1880* (Norman, Okla., 1966), pp. 227–38.

10. *Report of the Secretary of War, 1865*, 39th Cong., 1st sess. (Washington, November 22, 1865), I, 113–14.

11. Walker, *Wagonmasters*, pp. 249–54.

12. William E. Lass, *From the Missouri to the Great Salt Lake: An Account of Overland Freighting* (Lincoln, Nebr., 1972), passim; Walker, *Wagonmasters*, pp. 53–64; Samuel Bowles, *Across the Continent: A Summer's Journey to the Rocky Mountains, the Mormons, and the Pacific States* . . . (Springfield, Mass., and New York, 1865), pp. 4–5.

13. Walker, *Wagonmasters*, pp. 45–46.

14. Bowles, *Across the Continent*, p. 5.

15. Lass, *From the Missouri to the Great Salt Lake*, p. 53.

16. Alexander Majors, *Seventy Years on the Frontier: Alexander Majors' Memoirs of a Lifetime on the Border*, Col. Prentiss Ingraham, ed. (Chicago and New York, 1893); see also the sketch by Stella M. Drumm in *Dictionary of American Biography*, 20 vols. plus supplements (New York, 1928–), XII, 214–15, hereinafter cited as *DAB*. And note W. F. "Buffalo Bill" Cody's preface to Majors' book.

17. Majors, *Seventy Years*, p. 145; Lass, *From the Missouri*, pp. 4–10.

18. Majors, *Seventy Years*, pp. 103–5; Lass, *From the Missouri*, pp. 3–25.

19. Henry Villard, *Memoirs of Henry Villard, Journalist and Financier, 1835–1900*, 2 vols. (Boston and New York, 1904), II, 273.

20. John Doniphan to the St. Joseph *Catholic Tribune*, June 22, 1895, as printed in Frank A. Root and William E. Connelley, *The Overland Stage to California: Personal Reminiscences and Authentic History* . . . (Topeka, Kans., 1901), p. 448.

21. James V. Frederick, *Ben Holladay the Stagecoach King: A Chapter in the Development of Transcontinental Transportation* (Glendale, Calif., 1940), pp. 19–42.

22. *Ibid.*, pp. 54–60; Walker, *Wagonmasters*, pp. 68–72.

23. Walker, *Wagonmasters*, pp. 70–75.

24. Lass, *From the Missouri*, pp. 93–100.

25. LeRoy R. Hafen, *The Overland Mail, 1849–1869, Promoter of Settlement, Precursor of Railroads* (Cleveland, 1926), passim; Roscoe P. Conkling and Margaret B. Conkling, *The Butterfield Overland Mail, 1857–1869*, 3 vols. (Glendale, 1947), I, 85–120.

26. For Butterfield's career, see Conkling and Conkling, *Butterfield Overland Mail*, I, 27–41, and LeRoy R. Hafen's sketch in *DAB*, III, 374–75. Throughout this discussion of stagecoaching and express companies I have made use of the excellent sketches by W. Turrentine Jackson in Howard R. Lamar, ed., *The Reader's Encyclopedia of the American West* (New York, 1977).

27. *DAB*, IV, 271–72; XIX, 639–40.

28. W. Turrentine Jackson, "A New Look at Wells Fargo, Stagecoaches and the Pony Express," *California Historical Society Quarterly*, XLV (1966), 295.

29. Conkling and Conkling, *Butterfield Overland Mail*, I, p. 123–49.

30. Jackson, "A New Look," *California Historical Society Quarterly*, XLV, 301.

31. *Ibid.*, p. 303. See also the same writer's "Wells Fargo's Pony Expresses," *Journal of the West*, XI (1972), 412–17.

32. Frederick, *Ben Holladay*, pp. 63–262. The approach of the railroad, discussed later, was a further pressure.

33. Robert L. Thompson, *Wiring a Continent: The History of the Telegraph Industry in the United States, 1832–1866* (Princeton, 1947), pp. 348–73; *DAB*, IV, 534–35; XXVII, 145–46.

34. William E. Lass, *A History of Steamboating on the Upper Missouri River* (Lincoln, 1962), pp. 1–39 (quotation is from p. 39).

35. Hiram M. Chittenden, *History of Early Steamboat Navigation on the Missouri River*, 2 vols. (New York, 1902), II, 273.

36. Lass, *History of Steamboating*, pp. 56–57, 75–89.

37. *Ibid.*, pp. 44, 77–111.

38. Lass, *From the Missouri*, p. 184.

39. Robert W. Fogel, *The Union Pacific Railroad: A Case in Premature Enterprise* (Baltimore, 1960), esp. pp. 74–90.

40. Henry V. Poor, "The Pacific Railroad," *North American Review*, CXXVIII (1879), 667.

41. *Ibid.*, 677.

42. Commissioner of Railroads, *Annual Report Made to the Secretary of the Interior, for the Year Ending June 30, 1883* (Washington, 1883), p. 116, gives a convenient summary, including the passage quoted.

43. For a detailed discussion of the Credit Mobilier and a sturdy defense of his ancestors, see Charles E. Ames, *Pioneering the Union Pacific: A Reappraisal of the Builders of the Railroad* (New York, 1969), esp. pp. 46–61, 197–215, on Credit Mobilier. But also Nelson Trottman, *History of the Union Pacific: A Financial and Economic Survey* (New York, 1923), pp. 23–25; Fogel, *Union Pacific*, pp. 59–73.

44. Trottman, *History of the Union Pacific*, p. 25.

45. *Ibid.*, pp. 62–64. Fogel, *Union Pacific*, pp. 80–81, points out that this burst of construction speed so altered the public readiness to buy Union Pacific bonds that it "saved the road from collapse for want of funds." For an admirable picture of the Union Pacific's inability to pay the construction workers and contractors, see Robert G. Athearn, *Union Pacific Country* (Chicago, 1971).

46. Grenville M. Dodge, *How We Built the Union Pacific Railway, and Other Railway Papers and Addresses* (Washington, 1910), p. 43. The Chicago and North Western's tracks reached Council Bluffs on January 17, 1867, but spring floods on the Missouri damaged the new line so severely as to cause "a long suspension and delay of business upon it." Chicago and North Western Railway Company, *Report for the Seventh and Eighth Fiscal Years Ending May 31st, 1866, and May 31st, 1867* (New York, 1867), pp. 11, 14, 17.

47. Dodge, *How We Built the Union Pacific*, pp. 13–14.

48. *Ibid.*, p. 14.

49. Dodge's career as a builder is studied in Jacob R. Perkins, *Trails, Rails and War: The Life of General G. M. Dodge* (Indianapolis, 1929). The more recent biography of Stanley P. Hirshson, *Grenville M. Dodge: Soldier, Politician, Railroad Pioneer* (Bloomington, Ind., 1967) concentrates on his less savory activities as a wirepuller, to the neglect of Dodge the builder.

50. As quoted by Dodge, *How We Built the Union Pacific*, p. 39.

51. Perkins, *Trails, Rails and War*, pp. 243–44.

Chapter 4: The Response to the Mining Boom: II. From the West

1. Frank Soule, John H. Gihon, and James Nisbet, *The Annals of San Francisco; Containing a Summary of the . . .* (New York and San Francisco, 1855), pp. 544, 548.
2. *Ibid.*, p. 546.
3. The statistics are assembled and analyzed in Rodman W. Paul, *California Gold: The Beginning of Mining in the Far West* (Cambridge, Mass., 1947; reprinted, Lincoln, Nebr., 1965 et seq.), pp. 345–46, 349–50.
4. Rodman W. Paul, "After the Gold Rush: San Francisco and Portland," *Pacific Historical Review*, LI (1982), 7–8.
5. *Ibid.*, pp. 9–10, discusses these conflicting interpretations.
6. John S. Hittell, *The Resources of California, Comprising . . .* (San Francisco, 1863), pp. 333–34.
7. Cf. Stephan Thernstrom, *The Other Bostonians: Poverty and Progress in the American Metropolis, 1880–1970* (Cambridge, Mass., 1973), pp. 220–61, on "the American Pattern," and table of persistence, p. 222, which shows a "persistence rate" of 48 percent for San Francisco for 1870–1880. See also Howard P. Chudacoff, *Mobile Americans: Residential and Social Mobility in Omaha, 1880–1920* (New York, 1972).
8. Peter R. Decker, *Fortunes and Failures: White-Collar Mobility in Nineteenth-Century San Francisco* (Cambridge, Mass., 1978), pp. 86, 92, 170. Also Thomas Bender, *Toward an Urban Vision: Ideas and Institutions in Nineteenth-Century America* (Lexington, Ky., 1975), pp. 177–78, on the turnover in the mercantile class in San Francisco.
9. Henry G. Langley, comp., *The San Francisco Directory for the Year Commencing July 1860: Embracing . . .* (San Francisco, 1860), p. 41.
10. John S. Hittell, *The Commerce and Industries of the Pacific Coast of North America, Comprising . . .* (San Francisco, 1882), p. 197.
11. "From San Francisco to Sacramento City," *Hutchings' Illustrated California Magazine*, IV (1859), 2.
12. Soule, Gihon, and Nisbet, *Annals of San Francisco*, p. 626.
13. Hittell, *Resources of California* (1863 ed.), p. 336.
14. Hittell, *Commerce and Industries*, p. 195. On the Panama steamers, see John H. Kemble, *The Panama Route, 1848–1869* (Berkeley and Los Angeles, 1943).
15. Roger W. Lotchin, *San Francisco 1846–1856: From Hamlet to City* (New York, 1974), pp. 17, 65–66; Hittell, *Resources of California* (1863 ed.), p. 325; Paul, *Mining Frontiers*, p. 50.
16. Hittell, *Resources of California* (1863 ed.), p. 305; Decker, *Fortunes and Failures*, p. 65.
17. Biographical sketches are given in Alonzo Phelps, *Contemporary Biography of California's Representative Men*, 2 vols. (San Francisco, 1881–1882), II, 370–74, and Oscar T. Shuck, *Sketches of Leading and Representative Men of San Francisco: Being Original Sketches . . .* (San Francisco, 1875), pp. 855–60.
18. For examples of such newspaper complaints, cf. *Napa County Reporter*, July 14, 1860; Columbia *Tuolumne Courier*, October 10, 1863; *Napa County Reporter*, Octo-

ber 27, 1866; (San Francisco) *Scientific Press,* June 25, 1870; San Francisco *Daily Evening Bulletin,* May 11, 1871.

19. *Scientific Press,* May 24, 1860. This is the San Francisco publication that soon changed its name to *Mining and Scientific Press.*
20. *Napa County Reporter,* January 19, 1867.
21. Henry George, Jr., *The Life of Henry George,* 2 vols. (New York, 1911), I, 148–49.
22. A vivid picture of this unprincipled competition is given in David Lavender's *Nothing Seemed Impossible: William C. Ralston and Early San Francisco* (Palo Alto, Calif., 1975), esp. pp. 39–96. Against this should be set Wheaton J. Lane's *Commodore Vanderbilt, an Epic of the Steam Age* (New York, 1942), and John H. Kemble's *Panama Route.*
23. Hittell, *Commerce and Industries,* pp. 195–96, 200, and note his comment on resentment at rates (p. 163). Kemble, *Panama Route,* p. 45, states that when the Pacific Mail increased its capital, only a minority of the new shares were made "available to Californians"; most were subscribed in New York. The San Francisco *Daily Alta California,* October 10, 1860, spoke of the Pacific Mail as "this odious monopoly."
24. Sacramento *Daily Union,* November 12, 1857.
25. San Francisco *Daily Alta California,* January 7, June 13, 1852; Sacramento *Weekly Union,* February 7, May 29, June 5, June 19, 1852; February 5, 1853.
26. Sacramento *Weekly Union,* March 11, 1854, gives the story. See also San Francisco *Daily Alta California,* March 1, 1854, and *California Farmer,* March 9, 1854.
27. "Men We Know: William Norris," *California Mail Bag,* IX (July 1876), 69. Norris was an official of the company from its beginning.
28. San Francisco *Daily Evening Bulletin,* February 24, 1860.
29. *Ibid.,* January 5, 1867, January 9, 1868, January 13, 1869, January 4, 1870, January 10, 1871.
30. The elusive history of this little railroad can be pieced together. See Sacramento *Weekly Union,* November 12, 1853, February 17, 1855, January 3, 1857, November 13, 1858, January 7, 1860; Sacramento *Daily Union,* October 28, 1854, February 9, October 18, 1855, February 2, 23, 1856, November 11, 1857; San Francisco *Daily Alta California,* July 30, October 18, 1855. See also Sacramento Valley Railroad Company, *Articles of Association and By-Laws . . .* (New York, 1853), and its *Report of Committee of Board of Directors . . . Made August 7th, A.D., 1855* (San Francisco, 1855), together with reports of the board of directors printed in the Sacramento *Weekly Union,* January 24, 1857 and November 13, 1858.
31. Sacramento *Daily Union,* June 16, July 8, 1858. Note that two and a half years after the Sacramento Valley Railroad had opened, the stubborn teamsters were hauling more freight than the railroad, because they cut their rates to compete. *Ibid.,* May 26, June 4, 1858.
32. *Ibid.,* October 12 and 17, November 9, 1855, June 5, 1865, January 1, 1866.
33. Lord, *Comstock Mining and Miners,* pp. 191–95.
34. Oscar O. Winther, *Express and Stagecoach Days in California* (Stanford, Calif., 1936), pp. 87–96; William Banning and George H. Banning, *Six Horses* (New York, 1930).

35. Samuel Colville, comp., *Colville's Sacramento Directory . . . for the Year Commencing May, 1856* (San Francisco, 1856), p. xvii.
36. Winther, *Express and Stagecoach Days*, pp. 152–53; Banning and Banning, *Six Horses*, p. 47.
37. Winther, *Express and Stagecoach Days*, pp. 127–35.
38. Alexander L. Stimson, *History of the Express Business, Including the Origin of the Railway System in America* (New York, 1881), p. 260.
39. Winther, *Express and Stagecoach Days*, pp. 142–50.
40. Jackson, "A New Look at Wells Fargo," *California Historical Society Quarterly,* XLV, 293–94.
41. W. Turrentine Jackson, "Wells Fargo Staging over the Sierra," *California Historical Society Quarterly,* XLIX (1970), 99–133, gives an excellent account and has a good map. And see the same author's "Wells Fargo: Symbol of the Wild West?" *Western Historical Quarterly,* III (1972), 179–96.
42. Jackson, "Wells Fargo Staging over the Sierra," XLIX, 115–16.
43. *Ibid.,* pp. 111, 113, 122.
44. Detailed contemporary sketches of Louis McLane, Lloyd Tevis, and James Ben Ali Haggin are given in Phelps, *Contemporary Biography of California's Representative Men,* I, 27–31, 43–46, 325–28. The *DAB,* VIII, 83–84, and XVIII, 384–85, leans heavily on these sketches.
45. The quotations are from Oscar T. Shuck, *Bench and Bar in California: History, Anecdotes, Reminiscences* (San Francisco, 1889), p. 247.
46. Hubert Howe Bancroft, *Retrospection* (New York, 1912), p. 112.
47. George T. Marye, Jr., *From '49 to '83 in California and Nevada: Chapters from the Life of George Thomas Marye, a Pioneer of '49* (San Francisco, 1923), pp. 115–20. See also Edward Hungerford, *Wells Fargo: Advancing the American Frontier* (New York, 1949), pp. 110–18, and Noel M. Loomis, *Wells Fargo* (New York, 1968), pp. 202–5, 240. As prominent stockbrokers in San Francisco and Virginia City, Marye and his father were in a good position to observe.
48. Sacramento *Weekly Union,* October 29, 1853.
49. There are two accounts: Thompson, *Wiring a Continent,* p. 343–72, 400–1, 432; and Alice L. Bates, "The History of the Telegraph in California," *Historical Society of Southern California, Annual Publications,* IX (1912–1914), 181–87. The quotation is from Thompson, p. 369.
50. Based on a study of the annual city directories for San Francisco and Sacramento, which give the boards of directors of the important corporations. Henry G. Langley, comp., *The San Francisco Directory for the Year Commencing September, 1862* (San Francisco, 1862), p. 580, lists Tevis, and the same compiler's *San Francisco Directory for the Year Commencing September, 1867* (San Francisco, 1867), pp. 693–94, explains the leasing and operation by Western Union.
51. San Francisco *Chronicle,* July 25, 1899. The latter part of this long article draws heavily upon Phelps, *Contemporary Biography,* I, 27–31. See also comments in the column "Etc.," *Overland Monthly,* 2d ser., XXVIII (1896), 713.
52. George E. Waring, Jr., comp., "Report on the Social Statistics of Cities," parts I and II, *Tenth Census, 1880* (Washington, 1887), part II, pp. 813–15, and cf. pp. 772–835.

53. Ralston has been the subject of four full-length biographies. The best is David Lavender's *Nothing Seemed Impossible: William C. Ralston and Early San Francisco* (Palo Alto, 1975). But see also Cecil G. Tilton, *William Chapman Ralston, Courageous Builder* (Boston, 1935); George D. Lyman, *Ralston's Ring: California Plunders the Comstock Lode* (New York, 1937); and Julian Dana, *The Man Who Built San Francisco: A Study of Ralston's Journey with Banners* (New York, 1936). The account that follows leans heavily on Lavender's excellent study.

54. The fullest and the best account of the Central Pacific group is David Lavender's *The Great Persuader* (New York, 1970), a biography of Huntington; but see also Oscar Lewis, *The Big Four: The Story of Huntington, Stanford, Hopkins, and Crocker, and of the Building of the Central Pacific* (New York, 1938), and Stuart Daggett, *Chapters on the History of the Southern Pacific* (New York, 1922).

55. Lewis, *Big Four*, p. 211.

56. Lavender, *Great Persuader*, p. 157.

57. *Ibid.*, pp. 292–93.

58. *Ibid.*, pp. 136–37.

59. *Ibid.*, pp. 168.

60. Caspar T. Hopkins, *Business versus Speculation: A Lecture Delivered before the Students of the University of California, Sept. 1st, 1876* (San Francisco, 1876), p. 15.

61. Sacramento *Daily Union*, April 15, 1871.

Chapter 5: Build Thee More Stately Mansions: Leadership in Three Western Cities

1. Earl Pomeroy, *The Pacific Slope: A History of California, Oregon, Washington, Idaho, Utah, and Nevada* (New York, 1965), p. 120.

2. Charles N. Glaab and A. Theodore Brown, *A History of Urban America* (New York, 1967), pp. 108–9.

3. *Tenth Census, 1880: Statistics of the Population*, pp. 670–71.

4. Glaab and Brown, *History of Urban America*, p. 118.

5. Lyle W. Dorsett, *The Queen City: A History of Denver* (Boulder, Colo., 1977), pp. 1–6; and see, in general, Robert L. Perkin, *The First Hundred Years: An Informal History of Denver and the Rocky Mountain News* (New York, 1959), including comments on Mrs. Byers, p. 171.

6. Jerome C. Smiley, *History of Denver, with Outlines of the Earlier History of the Rocky Mountain Country* (Denver, 1901), pp. 248, 251, 295, 303.

7. *Ibid.*, pp. 338–50; quotation is from p. 349.

8. Howard R. Lamar, *The Far Southwest, 1846–1912, a Territorial History* (New Haven, 1966), pp. 213–25, 228–40.

9. Harry E. Kelsey, Jr., *Frontier Capitalist: The Life of John Evans* (Denver and Boulder, 1969).

10. See especially Kenneth N. Owens, "Pattern and Structure in Western Territorial Politics," *Western Historical Quarterly*, I (1970), 373–92; John D. W. Guice, *The Rocky Mountain Bench: The Territorial Supreme Courts of Colorado, Montana, and Wyoming, 1861–1890* (New Haven, 1972); Lewis L. Gould, *Wyoming: A Political History, 1868–1896* (New Haven, 1968); and Lamar, *Far Southwest*.

11. Earl S. Pomeroy, *The Territories of the United States, 1861–1890: Studies in Colonial Administration* (Philadelphia, 1947; new ed., Seattle, 1969) is the basic analysis. For a recent study of the territorial system in action, see Thomas G. Alexander, *A Clash of Interests: Interior Department and Mountain West, 1863–1896* (Provo, Utah, 1977).

12. Kelsey, *Frontier Capitalist*, p. 118.

13. Smiley, *History of Denver*, p. 369.

14. *Ibid.*, pp. 402–15.

15. *Ibid.*, p. 426.

16. Paul, *Mining Frontiers*, pp. 114–21.

17. Elmer Ellis, *Henry Moore Teller: Defender of the West* (Caldwell, Idaho, 1941). Golden's rivalry with Denver is further discussed in Reps, *Cities of the American West*, p. 477.

18. Ellis, *Teller*, pp. 41, 51–53.

19. Owens, "Pattern and Structure," *Western Historical Quarterly*, I, 377.

20. Lamar, *Far Southwest*, pp. 253–64, 297–301.

21. *Ibid.*, pp. 235–36, 273–77; Dorsett, *Queen City*, pp. 1–21; Lass, *From the Missouri to the Great Salt Lake*, pp. 238–39. Real estate speculation was a common activity among urban businessmen. Blake McKelvey, *The Urbanization of America (1860–1915)* (New Brunswick, N.J., 1963), p. 12. For a bluntly candid modern appraisal of the dubious tactics of Moffat, Chaffee and the "Denver crowd," see Steven F. Mehls, "Success on the Mining Frontier: David H. Moffat and Eben Smith: A Case Study," *Essays in Colorado History*, no. 1 (Denver, 1983), 91–105.

22. Smiley, *History of Denver*, pp. 427–32.

23. *Ibid.*, p. 433. For a similar modern conclusion, see Athearn, *Union Pacific Country*, pp. 46–50.

24. Lamar, *Far Southwest*, pp. 283–84; Athearn, *Union Pacific Country*, pp. 214–24.

25. Athearn, *Union Pacific Country*, pp. 130–33; Kelsey, *Frontier Capitalist*, pp. 172–79; Dorsett, *Queen City*, pp. 21–25.

26. Thomas J. Noel, "All Hail the Denver Pacific: Denver's First Railroad," *Colorado Magazine*, L (1973), 91–116, gives the fullest account. But see also Athearn, *Union Pacific Country*, pp. 130–33.

27. S. D. Mock, "The Financing of Early Colorado Railroads," *Colorado Magazine*, XVIII (1941), 208.

28. Kelsey, *Frontier Capitalist*, p. 179.

29. Noel, "All Hail the Denver Pacific," *Colorado Magazine*, L, 105–12. On Palmer, see *DAB*, XIV, 195–96, and Robert G. Athearn's well-written *Rebel of the Rockies: A History of the Denver and Rio Grande Western Railroad* (New Haven, 1962).

30. Athearn, *Union Pacific Country*, pp. 133, 136; Smiley, *History of Denver*, pp. 454–55, 457–59, 481; Perkin, *First Hundred Years*, pp. 308–10. In a suggestive article, Carl Abbott has divided Denver's growth into periods: "(1) frontier town, 1858–early 1860s (2) small city, middle 1860s–late 1870s (3) large city, late 1870s–early 1940s." Carl Abbott, "Boom State and Boom City, Stages in Denver's Growth," *Colorado Magazine*, L (1973), 207–30.

31. Isabella L. Bird, *A Lady's Life in the Rocky Mountains,* 3d ed. (New York, 1879–1880), pp. 161–63. A note to this third edition, dated January 16, 1880, clearly established the date of her visit.

32. Smiley, *History of Denver,* pp. 456–57; Paul, *Mining Frontiers,* pp. 126–27; Waring, "Report on the Social Statistics," part II, *Tenth Census, 1880,* p. 772.

33. Leonard J. Arrington and Davis Bitton, *The Mormon Experience: A History of the Latter-day Saints* (New York, 1979), p. 116.

34. *Ibid.*

35. Richard F. Burton, *The City of the Saints and Across the Rocky Mountains to California* (London, 1861), pp. 244–47.

36. Daniel S. Tuttle, *Reminiscences of a Missionary Bishop* (New York, 1906), p. 107, quoting text of a letter dated Salt Lake City, July 5, 1867.

37. Leonard J. Arrington, *Great Basin Kingdom: An Economic History of the Latter-day Saints, 1830–1900* (Cambridge, Mass., 1958), p. 81. For an apostate's comment on Young's attitude and the paucity of Mormon merchants, see Thomas B. H. Stenhouse, *The Rocky Mountain Saints: A Full and Complete History of the Mormons . . .* (New York, 1873), pp. 622–23. The most recent discussion is that edited by Richard D. Poll, Thomas G. Alexander, and others, *Utah's History* (Provo, Utah, 1978), pp. 193–95, 212.

38. Arrington, *Great Basin Kingdom,* pp. 66–72. Cf. Unruh, *The Plains Across,* pp. 302–37.

39. Arrington, *Great Basin Kingdom,* pp. 196–99.

40. Albert D. Richardson, *Beyond the Mississippi: From the Great River to the Great Ocean. Life and Adventure . . .* (Hartford, Conn., 1867), p. 351; Arrington, *Great Basin Kingdom,* pp. 195–96.

41. Burton, *City of the Saints,* p. 249.

42. Edward W. Tullidge, *History of Salt Lake City* (Salt Lake City, 1886), p. 384.

43. *Ibid.,* "Biographies" section (separate pagination), p. 70.

44. *Ibid.,* p. 381.

45. Arrington, *Great Basin Kingdom,* p. 237.

46. Tullidge, *History of Salt Lake City,* p. 383.

47. Arrington, *Great Basin Kingdom,* pp. 243–56. Stenhouse, *Rocky Mountain Saints,* pp. 630–45, gives an apostate's view of the controversy.

48. Arrington, *Great Basin Kingdom,* p. 306.

49. Stenhouse, *Rocky Mountain Saints,* p. 627; Leon L. Watters, *The Pioneer Jews of Utah* (New York, 1952), p. 58.

50. Tullidge, *History of Salt Lake City,* "Biographies" section (separate pagination), pp. 52–58, describes the Walkers. The apostate quoted here is Stenhouse, *Rocky Mountain Saints,* p. 645.

51. Poll, Alexander, and others, *Utah's History,* pp. 247–49.

52. Leonard J. Arrington, "The Deseret Telegraph—A Church-Owned Public Utility," *Journal of Economic History,* XI (1951), 117–39. The quotations are from this article. On the *Deseret News,* see Monte B. McLaws, *Spokesman for the Kingdom: Early Mormon Journalism and the Deseret News, 1830–1898* (Provo, Utah, 1977), especially pp. 27–30, 50–55, which discuss the church's firm control over its newspaper.

53. Arrington, *Great Basin Kingdom*, pp. 257–92; Poll, Alexander, and others, *Utah's History*, pp. 218–21.

54. In general, see James N. Tattersall, "The Economic Development of the Pacific Northwest to 1920" (Ph.D. diss., University of Washington, 1960).

55. Arthur L. Throckmorton, *Oregon Argonauts: Merchant Adventurers on the Western Frontier* (Portland, Oreg., 1961); William Bowen, "The Oregon Frontiersman: A Demographic View," in Thomas Vaughan, ed., *The Western Shore: Oregon Country Essays Honoring the American Revolution* (Portland, Oreg., 1975?), pp. 181–97.

56. As quoted in Trimble, *Mining Advance*, p. 67.

57. Dorothy O. Johansen, "The Oregon Steam Navigation Company: An Example of Capitalism on the Frontier," *Pacific Historical Review*, X (1941), 179–88, and the same author's comments in *Empire of the Columbia: A History of the Pacific Northwest*, 2d ed. (New York and Evanston, 1967), pp. 279–82, 310. Also Randall V. Mills, *Stern-Wheelers up the Columbia: A Century of Steamboating in the Oregon Country* (Palo Alto, Calif., 1947).

58. See Oregon Steam Navigation Company business correspondence edited in Dorothy O. Johansen and Frank B. Gill, "A Chapter in the History of the Oregon Steam Navigation Company," *Oregon Historical Quarterly*, XXXVIII (1937), 1–43, 300–322, 398–410; XXXIX (1938), 50–64.

59. Throckmorton, *Oregon Argonauts*, passim; Paul G. Merriam, "Portland, Oregon, 1840–1890: A Social and Economic History" (Ph.D. diss., University of Oregon, 1971); Harvey W. Scott, ed., *History of Portland, Oregon* (Syracuse, N.Y., 1890).

60. Samuel Bowles, *Across the Continent: A Summer's Journey to the Rocky Mountains, the Mormons, and the Pacific States, with Speaker Colfax* (Springfield, Mass., and New York, 1865), p. 183.

61. *Ninth Census, 1870: Population*, pp. 242, 369, 634, 653. Multnomah County's total population was 8,425, of which 8,293 lived in Portland.

62. Matthew P. Deady, "Portland-on-Wallamet," *Overland Monthly*, 1st ser., I (1868), 39–40.

63. As shown by his diaries. Malcolm Clark, Jr., ed., *Pharisee among Philistines: The Diary of Judge Matthew P. Deady, 1871–1892*, 2 vols. (Portland, Oreg., 1975).

64. E. Kimbark MacColl, *The Shaping of a City: Business and Politics in Portland, Oregon, 1885–1915* (Portland, Oreg., 1976).

65. Lawrence H. Larsen, *The Urban West at the End of the Frontier* (Lawrence, Kans., 1978), pp. xi, 48.

66. Tuttle, *Reminiscences of a Missionary Bishop*, p. 77.

67. Fossett, *Colorado: Its Gold and Silver Mines, Farms and Stock Ranges, and Health and Pleasure Resorts*, p. 33.

Chapter 6: Many Peoples: I. White Immigrants, Black Americans, and Red Indians

1. See Frederick C. Luebke, "Ethnic Group Settlement in the Great Plains," *Western Historical Quarterly*, VIII (1977), 405–30; Arrington, *Great Basin Kingdom*, pp. 99, 382; Leonard Dinnerstein and David M. Reimers, *Ethnic Americans: A History*

of Immigration and Assimilation (New York, 1975), pp. 24, 27; Doris M. Wright, "The Making of Cosmopolitan California: An Analysis of Immigration, 1848–1870," *California Historical Society Quarterly*, XX (1941), 65–79. Census data from *Eleventh Census, 1890: Population*, part I (Washington, 1895) and *Twelfth Census, 1900*, part I (Washington, 1901).

2. Ray Allen Billington, *The Protestant Crusade, 1800–1860: A Study of the Origins of American Nativism* (New York, 1938).

3. Leonard Pitt, "The Beginning of Nativism in California," *Pacific Historical Review*, XXX (1961), 36–37. Jay Monaghan, *Chile, Peru, and the California Gold Rush of 1849* (Berkeley and Los Angeles, 1973), gives a vivid picture of the fate of South Americans.

4. R. A. Burchell, *The San Francisco Irish, 1848–1880* (Berkeley and Los Angeles, 1980), p. 178. For extremes of point of view, see Hugh Quigley, *The Irish Race in California, and on The Pacific Coast* . . . (San Francisco, 1878), which compiles biographies of successful Irishmen; and John B. Duff, *The Irish in the United States* (Belmont, Calif., 1971), which stresses discrimination against them.

5. Robert E. Levinson, "American Jews in the West," *Western Historical Quarterly*, V (1974), 285–94; Peter R. Decker, "Jewish Merchants in San Francisco: Social Mobility on the Urban Frontier," in Moses Rischin, ed., *The Jews of the West: The Metropolitan Years* (Waltham, Mass., and Berkeley, 1979), 13–22; and Mitchell Gelfand, "Progress and Prosperity: Jewish Social Mobility in Los Angeles in the Booming Eighties," *ibid.*, 28–48; William Toll, "Fraternalism and Community Structure on the Urban Frontier: The Jews of Portland, Oregon—A Case Study," *Pacific Historical Review*, XLVII (1978), 369–403.

6. For an optimistic appraisal of the European experience in one state, see Moses Rischin, "Immigration, Migration, and Minorities in California: A Reassessment," *Pacific Historical Review*, XLI (1972), 71–90.

7. Andrew F. Rolle, *The Immigrant Upraised: Italian Adventurers and Colonists in an Expanding America* (Norman, Okla., 1968); Kenneth O. Bjork, *West of the Great Divide: Norwegian Migration to the Pacific Coast, 1847–1893* (Northfield, Minn., 1958).

8. Frederick C. Luebke, *Immigrants and Politics: The Germans of Nebraska, 1880–1900* (Lincoln, Nebr., 1969), p. 33.

9. *Ibid.*

10. Moses Rischin, "Beyond the Great Divide: Immigration and the Last Frontier," *Journal of American History*, LV (1968), 46.

11. Roger Daniels and Harry H. L. Kitano, *American Racism: Exploration of the Nature of Prejudice* (Englewood Cliffs, N.J., 1970), p. 2.

12. W. Sherman Savage, *Blacks in the West* (Westport, Conn., 1976), pp. 4–19, and statistical appendix p. 201.

13. Eugene H. Berwanger, *The Frontier Against Slavery: Western Anti-Negro Prejudice and the Slavery Extension Controversy* (Urbana, Ill., 1967), pp. 3, 5, 78, 85; Eugene H. Berwanger, *The West and Reconstruction* (Urbana, Ill., 1981), pp. 130–58, 188. And cf. Leon F. Litwack, *North of Slavery: The Negro in the Free State, 1790–1860* (Chicago, 1961).

14. Berwanger, *The West and Reconstruction*, pp. 9, 24–25; Douglas H. Daniels, *Pioneer Urbanites: A Social and Cultural History of Black San Francisco* (Philadelphia, 1980), pp. 15–17; Rudolph M. Lapp, *Blacks in Gold Rush California* (New Haven, Conn., 1977), pp. 95–96, 99.

15. Daniels, *Pioneer Urbanites*, pp. 107–10; Charles Wollenberg, *All Deliberate Speed: Segregation and Exclusion in California Schools, 1855–1975* (Berkeley and Los Angeles, 1976), especially pp. 8–9, 25.

16. Savage, *Blacks in the West*, pp. 48–64, 76–95, William H. Leckie, *The Buffalo Soldiers: A Narrative of the Negro Cavalry in the West* (Norman, Okla., 1967).

17. Note the contrasting appraisals in Savage, *Blacks in the West*, p. 87, and Kenneth W. Porter, *The Negro on the American Frontier* (New York, 1971), pp. 493–523.

18. Robert G. Athearn, *In Search of Canaan: Black Migration to Kansas 1879–80* (Lawrence, Kans., 1978); Nell Irvin Painter, *Exodusters: Black Migration to Kansas after Reconstruction* (New York, 1977).

19. Monroe E. Price, *Law and the American Indian: Readings, Notes and Cases* (Indianapolis, 1973), pp. 33–35.

20. John C. Ewers, "When Red and White Men Met," *Western Historical Quarterly*, II (1971), 134.

21. John C. Ewers, "Intertribal Warfare as the Precursor of Indian-White Warfare on the Northern Great Plains," *Western Historical Quarterly*, VI (1975), 402; Harold E. Driver, *Indians of North America*, 2d ed., rev. (Chicago, 1969), p. 309.

22. For a case study, see Clyde C. Dollar, "The High Plains Smallpox Epidemic of 1837–38," *Western Historical Quarterly*, VIII (1977), 15–38.

23. Alfred W. Crosby, Jr., *The Columbian Exchange: Biological and Cultural Consequences of 1492* (Westport, Conn., 1972), pp. 122–64.

24. "Whiskey everywhere seems to possess for the Indian an irresistible attraction." Commissioner of Indian Affairs, *Report for the Year 1861* (Washington, 1861), p. 16. Cf. Robert M. Utley, *The Indian Frontier of the American West, 1846–1890* (Albuquerque, 1984), p. 17.

25. Richard White, *The Roots of Dependency: Subsistence, Environment, and Social Change among the Choctaws, Pawnees and Navajos* (Lincoln, Nebr., 1983), passim.

26. Driver, *Indians of North America*, 2d ed., rev., p. 63 (exclusive of Alaska and Hawaii). This figure would be inflated perhaps up to 9 million if one accepts the methodology of Henry F. Dobyns, "Estimating Aboriginal Population: An Appraisal of Techniques with a New Hemispheric Estimate," *Current Anthropology*, VII (1966), 395–416, and comments, pp. 425–49. But see criticism by William Petersen, "A Demographer's View of Prehistoric Demography," *ibid.*, XVI (1975), 227–45, and William M. Denevan, ed., *The Native Population of the Americas in 1492* (Madison, Wis., 1976).

27. *Eleventh Census, 1890: Report on Indians Taxed and Indians not Taxed in the United States (Except Alaska)* (Washington, 1894), pp. 17–18, 24–25, 81. This massive study reviews all preceding estimates and census reports.

28. Wilcomb E. Washburn, *The Indian in America* (New York, Evanston, etc., 1975), pp. 197–202; William T. Hagan, *American Indians* (Chicago, 1961), pp. 100–104; H. Craig Miner and William E. Unrau, *The End of Indian Kansas: A Study in Cultural Revolution, 1854–1871* (Lawrence, Kans., 1978).

29. Albert L. Hurtado, " 'Hardly a Farm House—A Kitchen without Them': Indian and White Households on the California Borderland Frontier in 1860," *Western Historical Quarterly*, XIII (1982), 245–70; quotation is from Commissioner of Indian Affairs, *Report for the Year 1862* (Washington, 1863), p. 39 (italics in text); cf. Sherburne F. Cook, "The California Indian and Anglo-American Culture," Charles Wollenberg, ed., *Ethnic Conflict in California History* (Los Angeles, 1970), pp. 23–42.

30. J. W. Nesmith, Superintendent for Oregon and Washington, to the Commissioner, Salem, Oregon, August 20, 1858, in Commissioner of Indian Affairs, *Report for the Year 1858* (Washington, 1858), p. 214.

31. Washburn, *Indian in America*, pp. 173–80; Utley, *Indian Frontier* pp. 56, 113.

32. Portland *Oregonian*, July 12, 1866, July 9, 1867, as reprinted in Harvey W. Scott, *History of the Oregon Country*, Leslie M. Scott, comp., 6 vols, (Cambridge, Mass., 1924), II, 102, 119.

33. U.S. Congress, 38th Cong., 2d sess., Joint Special Committee to Inquire into the Condition of the Indian Tribes, Appointed under Joint Resolution of March 3, 1865, *Report, with an Appendix* (Washington, 1867), pp. 93, 96 of appendix. Usually known as the Doolittle Report.

34. *Ibid.*, p. 70 of appendix.

35. Charles A. Huntington, memoir written for his children, completed April 1899, typescript, Coe Collection, Yale University.

36. For example, Commissioner of Indian Affairs, *Report for the Year 1858*, pp. 8–10, 214–15, 305; *Report for the Year 1860*, p. 249; *Report for the Year 1861*, pp. 73, 78, 88–89. Note the comment of Robert A. Trennert, Jr., that even "the period between 1846 and 1851 was largely one of policy formulation and experimentation, not implementation," in his *Alternative to Extinction: Federal Indian Policy and the Beginning of the Reservation System, 1846–1851* (Philadelphia, 1975), p. 195.

37. Francis A. Walker, *The Indian Question* (Boston, 1874), pp. 38–39, 144.

38. Clark Wissler, Foreword to *The Changing Culture of an Indian Tribe*, by Margaret Mead (New York, 1932), p. vii. For an admirable picture of the reservation experience, see Utley, *Indian Frontier*, pp. 227–52.

39. William T. Hagan, "The Reservation Policy: Too Little and Too Late," in Jane F. Smith and Robert M. Kvasnicka, eds., *Indian-White Relations: A Persistent Paradox* (Washington, 1976), pp. 157–69 (quotation is from p. 161); Washburn, *Indian in America*, pp. 209–32; Henry E. Fritz, *The Movement for Indian Assimilation, 1860–1880* (Philadelphia, 1963), pp. 19–30; Clark Wissler, *Indians of the United States: Four Centuries of Their History and Culture* (New York, 1941), p. 282.

40. Robert F. Berkhofer, Jr., *The White Man's Indian: Images of the American Indian from Columbus to the Present* (New York, 1978), especially pp. 29, 55–56, 154–55.

41. Commissioner of Indian Affairs, *Report for the Year 1861*, pp. 73, 88.

42. Robert W. Mardock, *The Reformers and the American Indian* (Columbia, Mo., 1971), p. 1.

43. *Ibid.*, pp. 2–14; Francis Paul Prucha, *Indian Policy in the United States: Historical Essays* (Lincoln, Nebr., 1981), pp. 26–39, 229–51; Francis Paul Prucha, ed., *Americanizing the American Indians: Writings by the "Friends of the Indian," 1880–1900*, repr. ed. (Lincoln, Nebr., 1978).

44. Paul Bohannan and Fred Plog, eds., *Beyond the Frontier: Social Process and Cultural Change* (New York, 1967), p. 121.

45. Loring B. Priest, *Uncle Sam's Stepchildren: The Reformation of United States Indian Policy, 1865–1887* (New Brunswick, N.J., 1942), pp. 28–53; Henry E. Fritz, "The Board of Indian Commissioners and Ethnocentric Reform, 1878–1893," in Smith and Kvasnicka, *Indian-White Relations*, pp. 57–78; Utley, *Indian Frontier*, pp. 203–26.

46. Hagan, *American Indians*, p. 141.

47. *Ibid.*, pp. 141–46; Prucha, *Indian Policy in the United States*, pp. 198–213; Priest, *Uncle Sam's Stepchildren*, pp. 188–98.

48. Hagan, *American Indians*, p. 134.

49. Washburn, *Indian in America*, p. 241; cf. Robert A. Trennert, "Educating Indian Girls at Nonreservation Boarding Schools, 1878–1920," *Western Historical Quarterly*, XIII (1982), 271–90.

50. Donald J. Berthrong, *The Cheyenne and Arapaho Ordeal: Reservation and Agency Life in the Indian Territory, 1875–1907* (Norman, Okla., 1976), p. 99.

51. William T. Hagan, *Indian Police and Judges: Experiments in Acculturation and Control* (New Haven, 1966), passim.

52. For an intriguing case study of the contradictory results of comparing such variables as agricultural success, educational achievement, and adjustment to white ways, see Clyde A. Milner II, "Off the White Road: Seven Nebraska Indian Societies in the 1870s—A Statistical Analysis of Assimilation, Population, and Prosperity," *Western Historical Quarterly*, XII (1981), 37–52.

53. Clark Wissler, *Indian Cavalcade, or Life on the Old-Time Indian Reservations* (New York, 1938), p. 58.

Chapter 7: Many Peoples: II. The Spanish-Speaking and the Chinese

1. David J. Weber, *The Mexican Frontier, 1821–1846: The American Southwest under Mexico* (Albuquerque, 1982).

2. D. W. Meinig, *Southwest: Three Peoples in Geographical Change, 1600–1970* (New York, 1971), pp. 27–37.

3. Joyce Carter Vickery, *Defending Eden: New Mexican Pioneers in Southern California, 1830–1890* (Riverside, Calif., 1977).

4. Cf. Frances Leon Swadesh, *Los Primeros Pobladores: Hispanic Americans of the Ute Frontier* (Notre Dame, Ind., 1974); William B. Taylor and Elliott West, "Patrón Leadership at the Crossroads: Southern Colorado in the Late Nineteenth Century," *Pacific Historical Review*, XLII (1973), 335–57.

5. Nathaniel Alston Taylor, *The Coming Empire, or Two Thousand Miles in Texas on Horseback*, rev. ed., ed. Natalie Taylor Carlisle (Houston, 1936), p. 107 (original edition 1877).

6. Miguel Antonio Otero, *My Life on the Frontier, 1864–1882: Incidents and Characters of the Period when Kansas, Colorado, and New Mexico Were Passing through the Last of Their Wild and Romantic Years* (New York, 1935), pp. 1–12, 34–37, 57–60; Arnold L. Rodríguez, "New Mexico in Transition," *New Mexico Historical Review*, XXIV (1949), 275.

7. Floyd S. Fierman, "The Spiegelbergs: Pioneer Merchants and Bankers in the Southwest," *American Jewish Historical Quarterly*, LVI (1967), 371–451; William J. Parish, *The Charles Ilfeld Company: A Study of the Rise and Decline of Mercantile Capitalism in New Mexico* (Cambridge, Mass., 1961). Poles also were pioneer merchants. Cf. Francis C. Kajencki, "Alexander Grzelachowski, Pioneer Merchant of Puerto De Luna, New Mexico," *Arizona and the West*, XXVI (1984), 243–60.

8. Dianna Everett, "The Public School Debate in New Mexico, 1850–1891," *Arizona and the West*, XXVI (1984), 107–34.

9. Aurelio M. Espinosa, *The Spanish Language in New Mexico and Southern Colorado*, History Society of New Mexico, *Publications*, no. 16 (Santa Fe, 1911), pp. 17–18.

10. Howard R. Lamar, *The Far Southwest, 1846–1912: A Territorial History* (New Haven, 1966), pp. 136–70.

11. Victor Westphall, *Thomas Benton Catron and His Era* (Tucson, 1973).

12. This account is based on Robert W. Larson, "The White Caps of New Mexico: A Study of Ethnic Militancy in the Southwest," *Pacific Historical Review*, XLIV (1975), 171–85, and Robert J. Rosenbaum, *Mexicano Resistance in the Southwest: The Sacred Right of Self-Preservation* (Austin, Tex., 1981), pp. 99–147.

13. Frederick Law Olmsted, *A Journey through Texas; or, A Saddle-Trip on the Southwestern Frontier* (New York, 1857), pp. 455–56.

14. D. W. Meinig, *Imperial Texas: An Interpretive Essay in Cultural Geography*, paperback ed. (Austin, 1975), pp. 54–55.

15. Arnoldo De León, *The Tejano Community, 1836–1900* (Albuquerque, 1982), pp. 10–22; Paul S. Taylor, *An American-Mexican Frontier: Nueces County, Texas* (Chapel Hill, N.C., 1934), pp. 15–67; Arnoldo De León and Kenneth L. Stewart, "Lost Dreams and Found Fortunes: Mexican and Anglo Immigrants in South Texas, 1850–1900," *Western Historical Quarterly*, XIV (1983), 294–97.

16. De León and Stewart, "Lost Dreams and Found Fortunes," *Western Historical Quarterly*, XIV, 297.

17. Evan Anders, *Boss Rule in South Texas: The Progressive Era* (Austin, 1982), p. xii.

18. *Ibid.;* Taylor and West, "Patrón Leadership at the Crossroads," *Pacific Historical Review*, XLII, 337–40.

19. Anders, *Boss Rule*, pp. 3–25.

20. De León, *Tejano Community*, pp. 50–86, 90, 105–12; Mario T. García, *Desert Immigrants: The Mexicans of El Paso, 1880–1920* (New Haven, 1981), pp. 1–35. Cf. Joan W. Moore, with Alfredo Cuéllar, *Mexican Americans* (Englewood Cliffs, N.J., 1970), p. 14.

21. García, *Desert Immigrants*, pp. 127–71; De León, *Tejano Community*, pp. 23–49.

22. Bancroft, *Works*, XXI, 617, 649; XXII, 643.

23. Robert Glass Cleland, *The Cattle on a Thousand Hills: Southern California, 1850–1870* (San Marino, Calif., 1941), pp. 26–33.

24. Paul Wallace Gates, *History of Public Land Law Development* (Washington, 1968), p. 115.

25. Albert Camarillo, *Chicanos in a Changing Society: From Mexican Pueblos to American Barrios in Santa Barbara and Southern California, 1848–1930* (Cambridge, Mass., 1979), pp. 10–13, 101–4; Leonard Pitt, *The Decline of the Californios: A Social*

History of the Spanish-Speaking Californians, 1846–1890 (Berkeley and Los Angeles, 1966), pp. 9–12.

26. Cf. Oscar J. Martínez, "On the Size of the Chicano Population: New Estimates, 1850–1900," *Aztlan*, VI (1975), 43–67; Richard Griswold del Castillo, *La Familia: Chicano Families in the Urban Southwest, 1848 to the Present* (Notre Dame, Ind., 1984), p. 60.

27. Camarillo, *Chicanos in a Changing Society*, p. 118, has calculated a somewhat higher figure for 1850 than has Richard Griswold del Castillo, *The Los Angeles Barrio, 1850–1890: A Social History* (Berkeley and Los Angeles, 1979), p. 35.

28. Pitt, *Decline of the Californios*, pp. 130–47, 195–213, 229–42; del Castillo, *Los Angeles Barrio*, pp. 153–60; Ricardo Romo, *East Los Angeles: History of a Barrio* (Austin, Tex., 1983), pp. 5, 25–26; Mario T. García, "The Californios of San Diego and the Politics of Accommodation, 1846–1860," *Aztlan*, VI (1975), 69–81.

29. Camarillo, *Chicanos in a Changing Society*, pp. 22–25, 41–46, 71–76.

30. Cleland, *Cattle on a Thousand Hills*, p. 142.

31. *Ibid.*, p. 147.

32. Horace Bell, *Reminiscences of a Ranger or, Early Times in Southern California* (Los Angeles, 1881), p. 449.

33. Jackson A. Graves, *My Seventy Years in California, 1857–1927* (Los Angeles, 1927), pp. 135–37.

34. Gates, *History of Public Land Law Development*, pp. 89, 115.

35. *Ibid.*; pp. 115–17, 427; Pitt, *Decline of the Californios*, pp. 85–95. See also Gates' two articles: "Adjudication of Spanish-Mexican Land Claims in California," *Huntington Library Quarterly*, XXI (1957–1958), 213–36, and "California's Embattled Settlers," *California Historical Society Quarterly*, XLI (1962), 99–130.

36. Graves, *My Seventy Years*, p. 137; and cf. Robert C. Gillingham, *The Rancho San Pedro: The Story of a Famous Rancho in Los Angeles County and of its Owners, the Dominguez Family*, rev. ed. (n.p., 1983).

37. C. A. Caufield to the Monterey *Gazette*, May 20, 1864, as reprinted in Sacramento *Weekly Union*, June 4, 1864.

38. Report of Monterey County Assessor, September 12, 1865, in State Surveyor General, *Annual Report for the Year 1865* (Sacramento, c. 1865), p. 161.

39. Cleland, *Cattle on a Thousand Hills*, pp. 182–83.

40. Camarillo, *Chicanos in a Changing Society*, pp. 86, 139. As partial confirmation, the *Directory of Los Angeles for 1875* (Los Angeles, 1875) shows Spanish-surnamed people scattered thinly over a wide variety of jobs, but with a heavy concentration under "laborer."

41. A modern historian has entitled the years 1828–1856 "Hanging On." John L. Kessell, *Friars, Soldiers, and Reformers: Hispanic Arizona and the Sonora Mission Frontier, 1767–1856* (Tucson, Ariz., 1976), pp. 275–319.

42. W. Clement Eaton, "Frontier Life in Southern Arizona, 1858–1861," *Southwestern Historical Quarterly*, XXXVI (1933), 189.

43. Diane North, " 'A Real Class of People' in Arizona: A Biographical Analysis of the Sonora Exploring and Mining Company, 1856–1863," *Arizona and the West*, XXVI (1984), 261–74, quotation on p. 269.

44. James Officer, "Historical Factors in Interethnic Relations in the Community of Tucson," *Arizoniana,* I (1960), 13–14.
45. Elizabeth Albrecht, "Estévan Ochoa: Mexican-American Businessman," *Arizoniana,* IV (1963), 35–40; Charles L. Sonnichsen, *Tucson: The Life and Times of an American City* (Norman, Okla., 1982), pp. 47, 53, 94; Frank C. Lockwood, *Pioneer Days in Arizona: From the Spanish Occupation to Statehood* (New York, 1932), pp. 142–44.
46. Officer, "Historical Factors in Interethnic Relations," *Arizoniana,* I, 14.
47. Richard Griswold del Castillo, "Tucsonenses and Angelenos: A Socio-Economic Study of Two Mexican-American Barrios, 1860–1880," *Journal of the West,* XVIII (1979), 58–66.
48. W. C. Disturnell, comp., *Arizona Business Directory and Gazetteer; Containing the Names and Post-Office Addresses of all Merchants, Manufacturers and Professional Men . . .* (San Francisco, 1881).
49. Ronald C. Brown, *Hard-Rock Miners: The Intermountain West, 1860–1920* (College Station, Tex., 1979), pp. 9, 134; Richard E. Lingenfelter, *The Hardrock Miners: A History of the Mining Labor Movement in the American West, 1863–1893* (Berkeley and Los Angeles, 1974), pp. 5–7.
50. Dane Coolidge, *Old California Cowboys* (New York, 1939), pp. 53–113.
51. Lockwood, *Pioneer Days,* pp. 273–75; Roger L. Nichols, "A Miniature Venice: Florence, Arizona, 1866–1910," *Journal of Arizona History,* XVI (1975), 335–56.
52. The Federal census recorded 63,199 in 1870, 105,465 in 1880, and 107,475 in 1890. As with other racial minorities in the west, these figures probably report less than were actually present, and there was a temporary bulge as Chinese crowded in just before the Exclusion Act of 1882 took effect. Mary Roberts Coolidge, *Chinese Immigration* (New York, 1909), p. 498, estimated the total at 132,300 in 1882. The Chinese Six Companies claimed very much higher numbers (150,130 in 1876, and a Chinese official's estimate of 160,000). Shi-shan Henry Tsai, *China and the Overseas Chinese in the United States, 1868–1911* (Fayetteville, Ark., 1983), p. 34.
53. John Higham, *Strangers in the Land: Patterns of American Nativism, 1860–1925,* corrected 2d ed., paperback (New York, 1963), p. 25.
54. Coolidge, *Chinese Immigration,* pp. 100–3, 337–56, 391–400.
55. By a decision of the state supreme court in 1854, Chinese could not testify against whites. Elmer C. Sandmeyer, *The Anti-Chinese Movement in California* (Urbana, Ill., 1939), pp. 34, 45.
56. Gunther Barth, *Bitter Strength: A History of the Chinese in the United States, 1850–1870* (Cambridge, Mass., 1964).
57. Stuart C. Miller, *The Unwelcome Immigrant: The American Image of the Chinese, 1785–1882* (Berkeley and Los Angeles, 1969).
58. Alexander Saxton, *The Indispensable Enemy: Labor and the Anti-Chinese Movement in California* (Berkeley and Los Angeles, 1971).
59. Tsai, *China and the Overseas Chinese,* pp. 37–87.
60. J. D. Borthwick, *Three Years in California* (Edinburgh and London, 1857), pp. 55.
61. *Ibid.,* p. 75–76, 79.

62. William Perkins, *Three Years in California: William Perkins' Journal of Life at Sonora, 1849–1852*, Dale L. Morgan and James R. Scobie, eds. (Berkeley and Los Angeles, 1964), p. 338.

63. *Sacramento Transcript*, July 10, 1850.

64. Borthwick, *Three Years*, p. 51; cf. Perkins, *Three Years*, p. 319.

65. Perkins, *Three Years*, p. 281.

66. San Francisco *Daily Alta California*, February 17, 1852.

67. Custom House figures in Coolidge, *Chinese Immigration*, p. 498.

68. San Francisco *Daily Alta California*, March 8, 10, April 5, 12, 26, May 3, 4, 1852; Sacramento *Weekly Union*, March 13, April 17, May 1, July 3, 1852.

69. California State Legislature, Senate, 3d sess., *Journal* (April 23, 1852), p. 373.

70. California State Legislature, Assembly, 3d sess., *Journal* (April 16, 1852), "Report of the Committee on Mines," p. 835. Both Mexican and Chilean entrepreneurs had imported gangs of peons to work mining claims for them.

71. Barth, *Bitter Strength*, pp. 55–57, 67–68.

72. Tsai, *China and the Overseas Chinese*, p. 16.

73. *Ibid.*, 31–38; Stanford M. Lyman, "Strangers in the City: The Chinese on the Urban Frontier," in Charles Wollenberg, ed., *Ethnic Conflict in California History* (Los Angeles, 1970), pp. 69–70, 78–83; Fong Kum Ngon (Walter N. Fong), "The Chinese Six Companies," *Overland Monthly*, 2d ser., XXIII (1894), 518–26.

74. Herman Francis Reinhart, *The Golden Frontier: The Recollections of Herman Francis Reinhart, 1851–1869*, Doyce B. Nunis, ed. (Austin, Tex., 1962), p. 104.

75. Joint Special Committee to Investigate Chinese Immigration, 44th Cong., 2d sess., *Senate Report* no. 689 (February 27, 1877), 667–83.

76. *Ibid.*, 436–42, 626–30.

77. Rossiter W. Raymond, U.S. Commissioner of Mining Statistics, "Mining Statistics West of the Rocky Mountains," 42d Cong., 1st sess., *House Executive Document* no. 10 (serial 1470), (March 21, 1871), 4.

78. Sucheng Chan, "Chinese Livelihood in Rural California: The Impact of Economic Change, 1860–1880," *Pacific Historical Review*, LIII (1984), 273–307.

79. Ping Chiu, *Chinese Labor in California, 1850–1880: An Economic Study* (Madison, Wis., 1963), p. 81.

80. See editorial, *California Farmer*, January 17, 1889, and the extensive survey by an ex-missionary, Rev. Augustus W. Loomis, "How our Chinamen are Employed," *Overland Monthly*, 1st ser., II (1869), 231–40.

81. Ira B. Cross, *A History of the Labor Movement in California* (Berkeley and Los Angeles, 1935), pp. 60–72.

82. Stuart Daggett, *Chapters on the History of the Southern Pacific* (New York, 1922), p. 70, shows that in 1866 and 1867 the Central Pacific employed 11,000 Chinese and 2,500–3,000 whites, but by 1869 this had dropped to 5,000 Chinese and 1,500–1,600 whites.

83. Cross, *History of the Labor Movement*, pp. 56–58, 78–79; Saxton, *Indispensable Enemy*, pp. 6, 71–77.

84. Cross, *History of the Labor Movement*, p. 84; Lucile Eaves, *A History of California Labor Legislation, with an Introductory Sketch of the San Francisco Labor Movement* (Berkeley, 1910), pp. 6, 14.
85. Cross, *History of the Labor Movement*, pp. 66, 83.
86. For a convenient summary of the Kearney episode, see *ibid.*, pp. 88–129.
87. John R. Wunder, "The Chinese and the Courts in the Pacific Northwest: Justice Denied," *Pacific Historical Review*, LII (1983), 191–211.
88. Paul Crane and T. Alfred Larson, "The Chinese Massacre," *Annals of Wyoming*, XII (1940), 47–55, 153–61. Quotation from p. 48.
89. Jules Alexander Karlin, "The Anti-Chinese Outbreak in Tacoma, 1885." *Pacific Historical Review*, XXIII (1954), 271–83.
90. Jules Alexander Karlin, "The Anti-Chinese Outbreaks in Seattle, 1885–1886," *Pacific Northwest Quarterly*, XXXIX (1948), 103–30.
91. Patricia K. Ourada, "The Chinese in Colorado," *Colorado Magazine*, XXIX (1952), 273–84; Betty Derig, "Celestials in the Diggings," *Idaho Yesterdays*, XVI (1972), 2–23; Larry D. Quinn, "Chink Chink Chinaman: The Beginning of Nativism in Montana," *Pacific Northwest Quarterly*, LVII (1967), 82–89.
92. Saxton, *Indispensable Enemy*, pp. 148–50.

Chapter 8: Self-Proclaimed "Peculiar People"

1. Cf. Thomas F. O'Dea, *The Mormons* (Chicago, 1957), especially pp. 113–17, and Donald W. Meinig, "The Mormon Culture Region: Strategies and Patterns in the Geography of the American West, 1847–1964," *Annals of the Association of American Geographers*, LV (1965), 191–220.
2. The most recent interpretation is by Jan Shipps, *Mormonism: The Story of a New Religious Tradition* (Urbana and Chicago, 1985); but see also O'Dea, *The Mormons*, pp. 19–75.
3. Leonard J. Arrington, *Brigham Young: American Moses* (New York, 1985). p. xvi.
4. Austin Fife and Alta Fife, *Saints of Sage and Saddle* (Bloomington, Ind., 1956), p. 105.
5. Arrington, *Brigham Young*, pp. 153–58, 164, 178.
6. Arrington, *Great Basin Kingdom*, p. 34.
7. The classic account is by Lowry Nelson, *The Mormon Village: A Pattern and Technique of Land Settlement* (Salt Lake City, 1952).
8. George Thomas, *The Development of Institutions under Irrigation, with Special Reference to Early Utah Conditions* (New York, 1920), pp. 17–28.
9. *Ibid.*, pp. 27, 61.
10. Elwood Mead, *Irrigation Institutions: A Discussion of the Economic and Legal Questions Created by the Growth of Irrigated Agriculture in the West* (New York, 1903), p. 232.
11. Hosea Stout, *On the Mormon Frontier: The Diary of Hosea Stout, 1844–1861*, Juanita Brooks, ed., 2 vols. (Salt Lake City, 1964), II, 720–38 (despite the title page, Stout's diary for 1869 is included); Charles L. Walker, *Diary*, A. Karl Larson and Katharine M. Larson, eds., 2 vols. (Logan, Utah, 1980), I, 325.

12. Frederick S. Dellenbaugh, *Breaking the Wilderness: The Story of the Conquest of the Far West* (New York, 1905), p. 307. Dellenbaugh had known the southwest since the early 1870s.

13. Charles S. Peterson, *Take Up Your Mission: Mormon Colonizing along the Little Colorado River, 1870–1900* (Tucson, 1973), p. 155.

14. Juanita Brooks, *John Doyle Lee: Zealot-Pioneer-Builder-Scapegoat* (Glendale, Calif., 1961), p. 154.

15. Milton R. Hunter, *Brigham Young the Colonizer*, 2d ed. (Salt Lake City, 1941) pp. 366–74. Arrington and Bitton, *Mormon Experience*, pp. 117–20; Arrington, *Great Basin Kingdom*, pp. 88–95.

16. For a vivid description of Bernard De Voto's grandfather—an English mechanic converted to Mormonism, struggling to make a farm on barren, alkaline soil—see De Voto's "The Life of Jonathan Dyer: A Paragraph in the History of the West," *Forays and Rebuttals* (Boston, 1936), pp. 3–24.

17. Nelson, *The Mormon Village*, p. 137.

18. Meinig, "Mormon Culture Region," *Annals*, LV, 209, 213–18.

19. William Mulder, *Homeward to Zion: The Mormon Migration from Scandinavia* (Minneapolis, 1957), p. 190.

20. Richard Sherlock, "Mormon Migration and Settlement after 1875," *Journal of Mormon History*, II (1975), 53–68; Peterson, *Take Up Your Mission*, pp. 160–88; Nelson, *Mormon Village*, p. 137.

21. Nelson, *Mormon Village*, pp. 89, 144–48.

22. Cf. Arrington and Bitton, *Mormon Experience*, pp. 161–62, 185; James B. Allen and Glen M. Leonard, *The Story of the Latter-day Saints* (Salt Lake City, 1976), pp. 296, 300, 303, 331.

23. Arrington and Bitton, *Mormon Experience*, pp. 195–99.

24. *Ibid.*, pp. 204–5, quoted phrase p. 204.

25. Stanley S. Ivins, "Notes on Mormon Polygamy," *Western Humanities Review*, X (1956), 229–39; Larry Logue, "A Time of Marriage: Monogamy and Polygamy in a Utah Town," *Journal of Mormon History*, XI (1984), 3–26; and Lowell Bennion, "The Incidence of Mormon Polygamy in 1880: 'Dixie' versus Davis Stake," *ibid.*, 27–42.

26. Leonard J. Arrington, Feramorz Y. Fox, and Dean L. May, *Building the City of God: Community and Cooperation among the Mormons* (Salt Lake City, 1976).

27. Mark P. Leone, *Roots of Modern Mormonism* (Cambridge, Mass., 1979), pp. 53–66.

28. J. H. Beadle, *Life in Utah, or, the Mysteries and Crimes of Mormonism, Being an Exposé of the Secret Rites and Ceremonies of the Latter-day Saints* (Philadelphia, Chicago, etc., 1870), p. 9.

29. E. Leo Lyman, "A Mormon Transition in Idaho Politics," *Idaho Yesterdays*, XX (1977), 2–11, 24–29; same author, "Elimination of the Mormon Issue from Arizona Politics, 1889–1894," *Arizona and the West*, XXIV (1982), 205–28; Grenville H. Gibbs, "Mormonism in Idaho Politics, 1880–1890," *Utah Historical Quarterly*, XXI (1953), 285–305; Merle W. Wells, *Anti-Mormonism in Idaho, 1872–92* (Provo, Utah, 1978).

30. Norman F. Furniss, *The Mormon Conflict, 1850–1859*, reprint ed. (New Haven, 1960).

31. Gustive O. Larson, *The "Americanization" of Utah for Statehood* (San Marino, Calif., 1971), pp. 58–63, 77–78.
32. *Ibid.*, pp. 69, 210–17; Allen and Leonard, *Story of the Latter-day Saints,* pp. 404–13.
33. Arrington and Bitton, *Mormon Experience,* pp. 183–84; Allen and Leonard, *Story of the Latter-day Saints,* pp. 412–16.
34. Leone, *Roots of Modern Mormonism,* p. 1, for quoted phrase, and see the book as a whole for the change in Mormonism. See also Allen and Leonard, *Story of the Latter-day Saints,* pp. 416–19, and Jan Shipps, "The Principle Revoked: A Close Look at the Demise of Plural Marriage," *Journal of Mormon History,* XI (1984), 65–77.

Chapter 9: Into the Pasturelands: I. Cattlemen Occupy the Ranges

1. Allen's career is sketched in *DAB,* I, 201, and Liberty H. Bailey, ed., *Cyclopedia of American Agriculture,* 4 vols. (New York, 1910), III, 375.
2. Lewis F. Allen, "Improvement of Native Cattle," Commissioner of Agriculture, *Report for the Year 1866* (Washington, 1867), pp. 299–300.
3. John S. Hittell, "Notes on Amador Valley," *Hutchings' Illustrated California Magazine,* V (1860), 162, 163, 166. For a much later rodeo, and again near San Francisco Bay, see *Pacific Rural Press,* October 4, 1873.
4. J. Orin Oliphant, *On the Cattle Ranges of the Oregon Country* (Seattle, 1968), p. 31.
5. *Eighth Census, 1860: Agriculture* (Washington, 1864), p. cxvii.
6. *Ibid.,* p. clxxi.
7. Josiah Gregg, *Commerce of the Prairies,* Max L. Moorhead, ed. (Norman, Okla., 1954), p. 134.
8. The census statistics, which were primarily lists of livestock "on farms," were unavoidably incomplete, since there was no way for the census takers to count the thousands of cattle and sheep that were scattered over distant ranges, their numbers unknown to their owners or claimants. For 1860 the census sought estimates of unenumerated livestock. Figures given here are the totals of enumerated plus estimated unenumerated stock, with the probability that these results are below the actual fact. They are derived from the volume *Eighth Census, 1860: Agriculture.*
9. Walter Prescott Webb, ed., *The Handbook of Texas,* 2 vols. (Austin, 1852, plus supplement, Austin, 1976), I, 807. Hereafter cited simply as *Handbook of Texas.*
10. Edward N. Wentworth, *America's Sheep Trails: History, Personalities* (Ames, Iowa, 1948), pp. 112–14.
11. Ralph P. Bieber, Introduction to *Historic Sketches of the Cattle Trade of the West and Southwest,* by Joseph G. McCoy (Glendale, Calif., 1940), pp. 25–27.
12. Clarence W. Gordon, "Report on Cattle, Sheep, and Swine, Supplementary to Enumeration of Live Stock on Farms in 1880," part III, *Tenth Census, 1880: Report on the Production of Agriculture* (Washington, 1883), p. 81; Wentworth, *America's Sheep Trails,* pp. 135, 165–69.
13. Oliphant, *On the Cattle Ranges of the Oregon Country,* pp. 41–44; Wentworth, *America's Sheep Trails,* pp. 181–82.

14. *California Farmer*, January 5, September 21, October 19, 1854, October 5, 1855, December 26, 1856; April 17, June 19, 1857; Sacramento *Weekly Union*, October 1, 1853, July 14, 1860; Sacramento *Weekly Union* (supplement), March 3, March 10, 1860; Thomas F. McConnell, "A Half-Century on California Livestock Trails," *Pacific Rural Press*, January 1, 1921.

15. *California Farmer*, October 26, 1860; *Eighth Census, 1860: Agriculture*, p. clxxi.

16. Cleland, *The Cattle on a Thousand Hills*, passim; James M. Guinn, "The Passing of the Cattle Barons of California," Historical Society of Southern California, *Annual Publications*, VIII (1909–1911), 51–60.

17. Sacramento *Weekly Union*, October 15, 1864, clipping Pajaro *Times*.

18. James M. Guinn, "From Cattle Range to Orange Grove," Historical Society of Southern California, *Annual Publications*, VIII (1909–1911), 145–57.

19. " 'Men We Know,' Messrs. Lux & Miller," *California Mail Bag*, IX (1876), 84; Lux's obituary in San Francisco *Call*, March 20, 1887; *Pacific Rural Press*, November 11, 1871; *Reader's Encyclopedia of the American West*, p. 732. For a semifictional account, see Edward F. Treadwell, *The Cattle King: A Dramatized Biography* (New York, 1931).

20. John Clay, *My Life on the Range*, new ed., introduction by Edward E. Dale (New York, 1961), p. 27.

21. *Ibid.*

22. San Francisco *Weekly Alta California*, March 18, 1871.

23. Gordon, "Report on Cattle, Sheep," *Tenth Census, 1880*, III, 83, 76 for origins of cattle driven into California in 1880.

24. Tom Lea, *The King Ranch*, 2 vols. (Boston, 1957), I, 2–10, 35, 58, 100–110; *Handbook of Texas*, I, 946–47, 959.

25. J. R. Dodge, ed., "The Texas Cattle Trade," Commissioner of Agriculture, *Report for the Year 1870* (Washington, 1871), p. 347.

26. Chris Emmett, *Shanghai Pierce: A Fair Likeness* (Norman, Okla., 1953), pp. 12–59; *Handbook of Texas*, II, 376.

27. J. Evetts Haley, *Charles Goodnight, Cowboy and Plainsman* (Boston and New York, 1936), pp. 2–20; *Handbook of Texas*, I, 709, II, p. 87.

28. Lea, *King Ranch*, I, 153; Emmett, *Shanghai Pierce*, p. 29; Haley, *Charles Goodnight*, pp. 20–21; *Handbook of Texas*, II, 87.

29. David Galenson, "Origins of the Long Drive," *Journal of the West*, XIV (1975), 4–12.

30. Bieber, Introduction to *Historic Sketches*, by McCoy, pp. 27–32, 39–43.

31. Gordon, "Report on Cattle, Sheep," *Tenth Census, 1880*, III, 12.

32. Bieber, Introduction to *Historic Sketches*, by McCoy, pp. 32–38.

33. Haley, *Charles Goodnight*, pp. 121–216, 241–43; Agnes Wright Spring, " 'A Genius for Handling Cattle': John W. Iliff," in Maurice Frink, W. Turrentine Jackson, and Agnes Wright Spring, *When Grass Was King* (Boulder, Colo., 1956), pp. 333–450.

34. Joseph G. McCoy, *Historic Sketches of the Cattle Trade of the West and Southwest* (Kansas City, Mo., 1874; facsimile reprint, Washington, 1932), pp. 20–39, 70–71.

35. Ernest Staples Osgood, *The Day of the Cattleman* (Minneapolis, Minn., 1929), pp. 32–38. On the role of the drover, see Jimmy M. Skaggs, *The Cattle-Trailing Industry: Between Supply and Demand, 1860–1890* (Lawrence Kans., 1973).
36. Robert R. Dykstra, *The Cattle Towns* (New York, 1968), pp. 17–21.
37. McCoy, *Historic Sketches*, p. 44. For a sketch of McCoy, see *DAB*, XI, 618–19.
38. Dykstra, *Cattle Towns*, pp. 21–30.
39. Dodge, "Texas Cattle Trade," Commissioner of Agriculture, *Report for 1870*, p. 349.
40. Dykstra, *Cattle Towns*, passim.
41. Joseph Nimmo, Jr., "The Range and Ranch Cattle Business of the United States," *Report on the Internal Commerce of the United States*, part 3 (Washington, 1885), p. 122.
42. Edward Everett Dale, *The Range Cattle Industry: Ranching on the Great Plains from 1865 to 1925*, new ed. (Norman, Okla., 1960), pp. 43–46, 147–49.
43. Nimmo, "Range and Ranch Cattle Business," *Report on Internal Commerce*, part 3, p. 95.
44. Oliphant, *On the Cattle Ranges of the Oregon Country*, pp. 63–114.
45. Theodore Roosevelt, *Hunting Trips of a Ranchman: Sketches of Sport on the Northern Cattle Plains* (New York and London, 1885), pp. 2–4, 9.
46. Theodore Roosevelt, *An Autobiography* (New York, 1913), pp. 103, 107, 109.
47. Roosevelt, *Hunting Trips of a Ranchman*, pp. 6–7.
48. *Ibid.*, p. 7. For an admirable appraisal of the cowboy, see Joe B. Frantz and Julian E. Choate, Jr., *The American Cowboy: The Myth and the Reality* (Norman, Okla., 1955).
49. Gordon, "Report on Cattle, Sheep," III, *Tenth Census, 1880*, pp. 17–18. Dale, *Range Cattle Industry*, pp. 49–50, gives the higher range of twenty-five to forty dollars. McCoy was one of Gordon's principal informants on Texas.
50. Dale, *Range Cattle Industry*, p. 77; Osgood, *Day of the Cattleman*, pp. 98–99.
51. W. Turrentine Jackson, *The Enterprising Scot: Investors in the American West after 1873* (Edinburgh, 1968), p. 75.
52. Haley, *Charles Goodnight*, pp. 260–333.
53. Harmon R. Mothershead, *The Swan Land and Cattle Company, Ltd.* (Norman, Okla., 1971), esp. pp. 19, 22, 45–50.
54. Lincoln A. Lang, *Ranching with Roosevelt* (Philadelphia, 1926), pp. 14, 169, 177, 179, 182.
55. Osgood, *Day of the Cattleman*, pp. 114–17. The adjective *unsocial* is Osgood's (p. 115).
56. *Ibid.*, p. 125.
57. Clay, *My Life on the Range*, p. 67.
58. *Ibid.*, pp. 66, 68. In some areas, cattlemen formed "pools," in which each member retained ownership of his cattle but ran them together with other members' stock. Louis Pelzer, *The Cattlemen's Frontier: A Record of the Trans-Mississippi Cattle Industry from Oxen Trains to Pooling Companies, 1850–1890* (Glendale, Calif., 1936), p. 76.
59. Osgood, *Day of the Cattleman*, pp. 125–28; Pelzer, *Cattlemen's Frontier*, pp. 81–82.
60. Lang, *Ranching with Roosevelt*, pp. 222–24.

61. Dale, *Range Cattle Industry*, pp. 90–96; Osgood, *Day of the Cattleman*, pp. 94–95, 105.
62. Lang, *Ranching with Roosevelt*, pp. 234–51.
63. Clay, *My Life on the Range*, pp. 178–79.
64. Mothershead, *Swan Land and Cattle Company*, p. 111.
65. W. M. Pearce, *The Matador Land and Cattle Company* (Norman, Okla., 1964), esp. pp. 3–24, 28, 42–43, 54, 58, 73, 99, 113. Pearce's figure for the cattle count is at odds with Jackson, *The Enterprising Scot*, p. 129, which I have followed here.
66. Osgood, *Day of the Cattleman*, p. 106.
67. Gene M. Gressley, *Bankers and Cattlemen* (New York, 1966), pp. 109–11.
68. Clay, *My Life on the Range*, pp. 146–49. On the transition to a new type of cattle raising, see Dale, *Range Cattle Industry*, pp. 147–85; Osgood, *Day of the Cattleman*, pp. 216–58; John T. Schlebecker, *Cattle Raising on the Plains, 1900–1961* (Lincoln, Nebr., 1963), pp. 1–27; Maurice Frink, "When Grass Was King," in Frink, Jackson, and Spring, *When Grass Was King*, pp. 99–123.
69. Lewis Atherton, *The Cattle Kings* (Bloomington, Ind., 1961), pp. 186, 219–40.
70. McCoy, *Historic Sketches*, pp. 145, 146.

Chapter 10: Into the Pasturelands: II. Sheep Men Also Enter the Ranges

1. D. A. Spencer, M. C. Hall, and others, "The Sheep Industry," in U.S. Department of Agriculture, *Agriculture Yearbook, 1923* (Washington, 1924), p. 229. On the tendency to look disparagingly at sheep men, see Alexander Campbell McGregor, *Counting Sheep: Farm Open Range to Agribusiness on the Columbia Plateau* (Seattle, 1982), p. 25.
2. For a very attractive appreciation, see Winifred Kupper, *The Golden Hoof: The Story of the Sheep of the Southwest* (New York, 1945).
3. Spencer, Hall, et al., "The Sheep Industry," U.S.D.A., *Agriculture Yearbook, 1923*, p. 232.
4. Gregg, *Commerce of the Prairies*, Moorhead edition, p. 133.
5. Gordon, "Report on Cattle, Sheep," *Tenth Census, 1880*, III, 26–27, 83; Spencer, Hall, et al., U.S.D.A., *Agriculture Yearbook, 1923*, p. 251; U.S. Tariff Commission, *The Wool-Growing Industry* (Washington, 1921), p. 22; Paul H. Carlson, *Texas Woolybacks: The Range Sheep and Goat Industry* (College Station, Tex., 1982) pp. 52–56; Charles M. Sypolt, "Keepers of the Rocky Mountain Flocks: A History of the Sheep Industry in Colorado, New Mexico, Utah and Wyoming to 1900" (Ph.D. diss., University of Wyoming, 1974), pp. 32–33.
6. Gordon, "Report on Cattle, Sheep," *Tenth Census, 1880*, III, 82, says that at times only 30 to 40 percent of the stock survived. J. H. Hollister started from Ohio in 1857 with four thousand sheep, spent twenty-seven months in reaching Los Angeles, and lost nearly half his original stock plus all the lambs born en route. Sacramento *Weekly Union*, February 11, 1860.
7. Gordon, "Report on Cattle, Sheep," *Tenth Census, 1880*, III, 73.
8. Spencer, Hall, et al., U.S.D.A., *Agriculture Yearbook, 1923*, p. 275.

9. *Ibid.*, pp. 232, 289; John Hayes, "Sheep-Farming in California," *Overland Monthly*, 1st ser., VIII (1872), 492–93; San Francisco *Daily Alta California*, January 31, 1872.

10. U.S. Tariff Commission, *The Wool-Growing Industry*, pp. 24–25, 34–35, 55–56; McGregor, *Counting Sheep*, pp. 79–83.

11. Arthur H. Cole, *The American Wool Manufacture*, 2 vols. (Cambridge, Mass., 1926), I, 273, II, 73–76.

12. Gordon, "Report on Cattle, Sheep," *Tenth Census, 1880*, III, 26; Hayes, "Sheep-Farming in California," *Overland Monthly*, VIII, 491. But note Gordon's later comment (p. 37 of his report) that to run five thousand sheep, more nearly the equivalent of one thousand cows, would require an investment of twelve thousand dollars.

13. Gordon, "Report on Cattle, Sheep," *Tenth Census*, III, 25, 82; Kupper, *Golden Hoof*, pp. 19–20; Spencer, Hall, et al., U.S.D.A., *Agriculture Yearbook, 1923*, pp. 234, 244; U.S. Tariff Commission, *The Wool-Growing Industry*, pp. 29–30; Bureau of Statistics, U.S. Treasury Department, *Wool and Manufactures of Wool, Special Report . . .* , Treasury Department Document no. 1025 (Washington, 1887), p. xxxviii.

14. For example, the Santa Barbara *Gazette*, March 10, 1859, was quoted as saying that within ten days forty thousand sheep from New Mexico had passed through that town, and that the total from New Mexico that spring was nearly one hundred thousand. Sacramento *Weekly Union*, April 2, 1859. On Texas sheep breeding in this era, see Carlson, *Texas Woolybacks*, pp. 23–47.

15. *Napa County Reporter*, April 30, 1859.

16. See repeated reports of importations of Spanish and French merino and some English stock in *California Farmer*, March 13, July 24, 31, August 7, 21, October 16, 1857; August 13, 1858; September 2, December 2, 23, 1859; June 8, 29, 1860.

17. Wilson Flint, "Textile Fibres of the Pacific States," California State Agricultural Society, *Transactions during the Years 1864 and 1865* (Sacramento, 1866), pp. 217–89, reviews the beginnings of wool and wool exports. On the careless and almost "fraudulent" manner in which the wool clip was prepared, see San Francisco *Daily Alta California*, April 13, 1872.

18. *California Farmer*, October 14, November 11, 1859. The first mill burned down but a second one had been built in the meantime. *Ibid.*, March 14, 1862. By 1872 local consumption of wool was said to have totaled about 15 percent of the whole output of the preceding dozen years. San Francisco *Daily Alta California*, January 31, 1872.

19. The deficiencies of nineteenth-century sheep statistics in the census, especially for 1870, are reviewed in *Twelfth Census, 1900: Agriculture*, part I (Washington, 1902), pp. ccxiii–ccxiv. Statistics for both sheep and wool, 1850–1900, in all states and territories, are given on pp. 708–9 and are the source for figures quoted in the present chapter. Note that the reports of the U.S. Department of Agriculture differ sharply from the census and in 1880 credit California with almost 2 million more sheep than counted by the census. Worthington C. Ford,

Wool and Manufactures of Wool (Washington, 1894), pp. 36–41 (a report to the Treasury Department).

20. Gordon, "Report on Cattle, Sheep," *Tenth Census, 1880,* III, 82.

21. See, for example, George Robertson, "Statistical Summary of the Production and Resources of California," California State Board of Agriculture, *Report for the Year 1911* (Sacramento, 1912), p. 81; *California Patron,* August 17, 1878, and *Pacific Rural Press,* January 8, 1881, both citing the books of E. Grisar Co., and specifically excluding Oregon and foreign wool shipped through San Francisco; and San Francisco *Daily Alta California,* January 31, 1872. The 1880 census seems to have excluded the fall clip and the wool from range sheep.

22. San Francisco *Daily Alta California,* September 2, 1872; *Pacific Rural Press,* April 6, 1872.

23. Gordon, "Report on Cattle, Sheep," *Tenth Census, 1880,* III, 17.

24. Wentworth, *America's Sheep Trails,* pp. 190–206; L. T. Burcham, *California Range Land: An Historico-Ecological Study of the Range Resource of California* (Sacramento, 1957), pp. 159–75.

25. *Pacific Rural Press,* April 6, 1872.

26. Gordon, "Report on Cattle, Sheep," *Tenth Census, 1880,* III, 38–39, 82, 91.

27. Carman, Heath, and Minto, *Special Report,* pp. 897, 903, 907; Carlson, *Texas Woolybacks,* pp. 60–78; L. G. Connor, *A Brief History of the Sheep Industry in the United States,* in American Historical Association, *Annual Report for the Year 1918* (Washington, 1921), I, 138; Wentworth, *America's Sheep Trails,* pp. 383–87, 619–20.

28. Carman, Heath, and Minto, *Special Report,* p. 926; Alvar W. Carlson, "New Mexico's Sheep Industry, 1850–1900: Its Role in the History of the Territory," *New Mexico Historical Review,* XLIV (1969), 25–49; Erna Fergusson, *New Mexico: A Pageant of Three Peoples* (New York, 1951), pp. 316–23.

29. Carman, Heath, and Minto, *Special Report,* pp. 914–29; Carlson, *Texas Woolybacks,* pp. 85–108; Sypolt, "Keepers," pp. 35–41; William R. Palmer, "The Early Sheep Industry in Southern Utah," *Utah Historical Quarterly,* XLII (1974), 178–88; Arrington, *Great Basin Kingdom,* pp. 122, 310, 365.

30. John Minto, "Sheep Husbandry in Oregon," *Quarterly of the Oregon Historical Society,* III (1902), 219–47; Frederick V. Coville, "Forest Growth and Sheep Grazing," U.S. Department of Agriculture, Division of Forestry, *Bulletin* no. 15 (Washington, D.C., 1898). Minto was a pioneer sheep man in Oregon. For a vivid account of sheep raising and sheep wars, see Phil F. Brogan, *East of the Cascades* (Portland, Oreg., 1964), pp. 106–21.

31. Carman, Heath, and Minto, *Special Report,* pp. 771–80. Cf. Harold E. Briggs, "The Early Development of Sheep Ranching in the Northwest," *Agricultural History,* XI (1937), 168–69; Gordon, "Report on Cattle, Sheep," *Tenth Census, 1880,* III, 51–52, Sypolt, "Keepers," pp. 103–35.

32. Paul S. Richards, "The Golden Fleece," *Forum,* XLVII (1912), 546.

33. Connor, *Brief History of Sheep,* p. 138; Bert Haskett, "History of the Sheep Industry in Arizona," *Arizona Historical Review,* VII (1936), 24; Sypolt, "Keepers," pp. 75–101.

34. Carman, Heath, and Minto, *Special Report,* pp. 736–52, 835–44, 872–79.

35. *Ibid.*, p. 711.
36. Richards, "Golden Fleece,"; *Forum*, XLVII, 546.
37. *Ibid.*, p. 548.
38. Carman, Heath, and Minto, *Special Report*, p. 714.
39. Stephen Powers (Mr. Socrates Hyacinth, pseud.), "A Flock of Wool," *Overland Monthly*, 1st ser., IV (1870), 141–42.
40. Gordon, "Report on Cattle, Sheep," *Tenth Census, 1880*, III, 26–27, 38–39.
41. Harris Newmark, *Sixty Years in Southern California, 1853–1913*, Maurice H. and Marco R. Newmark, eds., 3d ed. (Boston and New York, 1930), p. 310.
42. Carman, Heath, and Minto, *Special Report*, pp. 972–73.
43. *Ibid.*, p. 773. Cf. James Withycombe, "Sheep Husbandry in the Pacific Northwest," U.S. Department of Agriculture, *Farmers' Bulletin* no. 117 (Washington, 1900). For an excellent case study of one family's transition to leased or owned land, and the profits this led to, see Alexander Campbell McGregor's *Counting Sheep.*
44. Carmen, Heath, and Minto, *Special Report*, p. 791.
45. Sarah Bixby Smith, *Adobe Days, Being the Truthful Narrative . . . of a California Girl on a Sheep Ranch . . .* 3d ed. (Los Angeles, 1931), p. 85.

Chapter 11: Farming in a Land of Limited Rain

1. Bureau of the Census, *Statistical Atlas of the United States* (Washington, 1914), pp. 12–13, 19–25. Quotations from pp. 19, 20; maps are plates 10–15, inclusive.
2. Arrington, *Great Basin Kingdom*, p. 148.
3. "Ogden and its Representative Men," *Tullidge's Quarterly Magazine*, II (1882), 306–9; Arrington and Bitton, *The Mormon Experience*, pp. 111, 116.
4. Alvin T. Steinel and Daniel W. Working, *History of Agriculture in Colorado: A Chronological Record of Progress . . . 1858 to 1926* (Fort Collins, Colo., 1926), pp. 47–54; Robert G. Dunbar, "The Significance of the Colorado Agricultural Frontier," *Agricultural History*, XXXIV (1960), 119–25; same author, "Water Conflicts and Controls in Colorado," *Agricultural History*, XXII (1948), 181.
5. Gilbert C. Fite, *The Farmers' Frontier, 1865–1900* (New York, Chicago, etc., 1966), pp. 13–14, 94–136.
6. J. R. Dodge, "Report of the Statistician," in Secretary of Agriculture, *Report, 1890* (Washington, 1890), p. 310.
7. Thomas C. McClintock, "Henderson Luelling, Seth Lewelling and the Birth of the Pacific Coast Fruit Industry," *Oregon Historical Quarterly*, LXVIII (1967), 153–74.
8. Wallis Nash, *Oregon: There and Back in 1877* (London, 1878), pp. 115, 187.
9. Commissioner of the General Land Office, *Report for the Year 1868* (Washington, 1868), p. 319.
10. Wallis Nash, *Two Years in Oregon* (New York, 1882), p. 35.
11. *Ibid.*, pp. 63–66; Nash, *Oregon: There and Back*, pp. 112–14.
12. State Board of Immigration, *Oregon As It Is* (Portland, Oreg., 1886), p. 16; William L. Adams, *Oregon As It Is: Its Present and Future, by a Resident of Twenty-Five*

Years (Portland, Oreg., 1873), p. 17; Wallis Nash, *The Settler's Handbook to Oregon* (Portland, Oreg., 1904), pp. 25, 45, 77–78.

13. Rockwell D. Hunt, *John Bidwell, Prince of California Pioneers* (Caldwell, Idaho, 1942).

14. Information on Horner and Beard is scattered through *California Farmer:* January 26, February 2, July 20, November 16, 1854, April 4, 1867, March 12, August 13, 27, November 19, 1868, July 22, 1869; San Francisco *Daily Alta California*, May 31, 1853; *Mining and Scientific Press*, July 31, 1869.

15. Iris Higbie Wilson, *William Wolfskill, 1798–1866: Frontier Trapper to California Ranchero* (Glendale, Calif., 1965); Vincent P. Carosso, *The California Wine Industry, 1830–1895: A Study of the Formative Years* (Berkeley and Los Angeles, 1951), pp. 7–12; Rahno M. MacCurdy, *The History of the California Fruit Growers Exchange* (Los Angeles, 1925), pp. 2–6; Irving McKee, "Jean Paul [*sic*] Vignes, California's First Professional Winegrower," *Agricultural History*, XXII (1948), 176–80.

16. Sacramento *Weekly Union*, April 12, 1862.

17. *Wheat: An Illustrated Description of California's Leading Industry* (San Francisco, 1887); Nathan A. Cobb, *The California Wheat Industry*, Department of Agriculture, New South Wales, *Miscellaneous Publication* no. 519 (Sydney, 1901); Leo Rogin, *The Introduction of Farm Machinery in Its Relation to the Productivity of Labor* . . . vol. IX, *University of California Publications in Economics* (Berkeley, 1931).

18. Paul Wallace Gates, *History of Public Land Law Development* (Washington, 1968), p. 412.

19. *Eleventh Census, 1890: Agriculture* (Washington, 1895), p. 16.

20. Rodman W. Paul, "The Wheat Trade between California and the United Kingdom," *Mississippi Valley Historical Review*, XLV (1958), 394–400.

21. Joseph Nimmo, Jr., *Report on the Internal Commerce of the United States, Submitted May 6, 1885* (Washington, 1885), pp. 24–43; Edwin S. Holmes, Jr., "Wheat Ports of the Pacific Coast," U.S. Department of Agriculture, *Yearbook, 1901* (Washington, 1902), pp. 567–80.

22. Meinig, *Great Columbia Plain*, pp. 220–83, 294–320; Robert C. Nesbit and Charles M. Gates, "Agriculture in Eastern Washington, 1890–1910," *Pacific Northwest Quarterly*, XXXVIII (1946), 279–95.

23. Rodman W. Paul, "The Great California Grain War: The Grangers Challenge the Wheat King," *Pacific Historical Review*, XXVII (1958), 331–49.

24. Letter from E. S. Holden, former president of the San Joaquin Valley Agricultural Society, Stockton, February 21, 1871, to *Pacific Rural Press*, March 11, 1871.

25. San Francisco *Weekly Alta California*, October 29, 1870. For a contrary point of view, see Gerald L. Prescott, "Farm Gentry vs. the Grangers: Conflict in Rural America," *California Historical Quarterly*, LVI (1977–1978), 328–45.

26. Donald J. Pisani, *From the Family Farm to Agribusiness: The Irrigation Crusade in California and the West, 1850–1931* (Berkeley and Los Angeles, 1984), p. 260.

27. San Francisco *Call*, February 18, 1883 (obituary); Mrs. Rebecca T. Lambert, "History of Glenn County," in *History of Colusa and Glenn Counties, California* . . . (Los Angeles, 1918), pp. 208–11, 441–45; Giles French, *Cattle Country of Peter*

French (Portland, Oreg., 1965); *Pacific Rural Press*, August 15, 1885; Hittell, *Commerce and Industries*, p. 281.

28. Horace Davis, "Wheat in California," *Overland Monthly*, 1st ser., I (1868), 451. Davis, Harvard Class of 1849, was president of the San Francisco Produce Exchange, owner of a large flour mill, and a major figure in the trade.

29. *Santa Cruz County Times*, March 21, 1868. cf. Henry F. Blanchard, "Improvement of the Wheat Crop in California," U.S. Department of Agriculture, Bureau of Plant Industry, *Bulletin* no. 178 (Washington, 1910), and G. W. Shaw, "How to Increase the Yield of Wheat in California," University of California Agricultural Experiment Station *Bulletin* no. 211 (Berkeley, 1911).

30. *Napa County Reporter*, January 12, 26, March 2, 30, 1867; Isaac N. Hoag, "Farmers' Gardens," California State Agricultural Society, *Transactions 1870–71* (Sacramento, 1871), 328–37.

31. Charles Nordhoff, *California: for Health, Pleasure, and Residence* (New York, 1873), p. 187. For other complaints against tenancy's ill effects on farms, see *Pacific Rural Press*, February 11, 25, 1871.

32. *Pacific Rural Press*, April 16, 1887.

33. T. Carey Friedlander, "Cereal Crop of California, 1910," in California State Agricultural Society, *Report for the Year 1910* (Sacramento, 1911), p. 16.

34. Joseph Nimmo, Jr., *Report on the Internal Commerce of the United States, 1880*, part 2 (Washington, 1881), pp. 184–87.

35. John Wesley Powell, *Report on the Lands of the Arid Region of the United States, with a More Detailed Account of the Lands of Utah*, 2d ed. (Washington, 1879). This second edition contains revisions and corrections of the original 1878 printing.

36. Mary Wilma M. Hargreaves, *Dry Farming in the Northern Great Plains, 1900–1925* (Cambridge, Mass., 1957), pp. 8–10. Hargreaves found that about fifteen inches was the minimum for grain, although factors of timing and relative humidity would cause variation. Another student feels that fourteen to sixteen inches is the usual minimum. Edward Higbee, *American Agriculture: Geography, Resources, Conservation* (New York, 1958), p. 54.

37. Hamlin Garland, *A Son of the Middle Border* (New York, 1917), p. 234.

38. Fite, *Farmer's Frontier*, pp. 94, 97–100, 116–26; Robert G. Dunbar, "Agricultural Adjustments in Eastern Colorado in the Eighteen-Nineties," *Agricultural History*, XVIII (1944), 41–52. See also Hiram M. Drache, *The Day of the Bonanza: A History of Bonanza Farming in the Red River of the North* (Fargo, N.D., 1964).

39. Fite, *Farmer's Frontier*, pp. 193–214.

40. *Ibid.*, pp. 126–31. For a case study of boom and bust, see James C. Malin, "The Kinsley Boom of the Late Eighties," *Kansas Historical Quarterly*, IV (1935), 23–49, 164–87.

41. James C. Malin, *Winter Wheat in the Golden Belt of Kansas: A Study in Adaptation to Subhumid Geographical Environment* (Lawrence, Kans., 1944), p. 141.

42. Homer E. Socolofsky, "Kansas in 1876," *Kansas Historical Quarterly*, XLIII (1977), p. 4.

43. Malin, *Winter Wheat*, pp. 131–34, and the same author's "The Turnover of Farm Population in Kansas," *Kansas Historical Quarterly*, IV (1935), 339–72.

44. John Ise, *Sod and Stubble: The Story of a Kansas Homestead* (New York, 1936; reprint, 1938). See also Howard Ruede, *Sod-House Days: Letters from a Kansas Homesteader, 1877–78,* John Ise, ed. (New York, 1937).

45. U.S.D.A., *Climate and Man,* pp. 178–80.

46. For modern verdicts on Campbell's procedures, see U.S.D.A., *Soils and Men,* pp. 679–92, and Mary W. M. Hargreaves, "The Dry-Farming Movement in Retrospect," in Thomas R. Wessel, ed., "Agriculture in the Great Plains, 1876–1936," *Agricultural History,* LI (1977), 149–65. See also Campbell's autobiographical account in Bailey, ed., *Cyclopedia of American Agriculture,* I, 398–402.

47. Carl F. Kraenzel, *The Great Plains in Transition* (Norman, Okla., 1955), pp. 162, 283. See also E. Lloyd Barber, "Summer Fallowing to Meet Weather Risks in Wheat Farming," U.S. Department of Agriculture, *Agricultural Economics Research,* III, no. 4 (1951), 118–23.

48. Karl S. Quisenberry and L. P. Reitz, "Turkey Wheat: The Cornerstone of an Empire," in James W. Whitaker, ed., "Farming in the Midwest, 1840–1900: A Symposium," *Agricultural History,* XLVIII (1974), 98–110; and Robert G. Dunbar, "Turkey Wheat: A Comment," *ibid.,* 111–14.

49. John A. Widtsoe, *Dry-Farming: A System of Agriculture for Countries under a Low Rainfall* (New York, 1911), pp. 354–60. Widtsoe was president of Utah Agricultural College.

50. Board of Directors, "Annual Report," California State Agricultural Society, *Transactions, 1864 and 1865,* pp. 35–36, and the same, *Transactions, 1866 and 1867,* p. 47. *California Farmer,* March 7, October 17, 1867, April 9, May 21, 1868; *Pacific Rural Press,* August 12, 1871, November 2, 1872, January 18, 1873. Mary W. M. Hargreaves, "Dry Farming alias Scientific Farming," *Agricultural History,* XXII (1948), 39–56.

51. Leonard J. Arrington and Dean May, " 'A Different Mode of Life': Irrigation and Society in Nineteenth-Century Utah," in James H. Shideler, ed., *Agriculture in the Development of the Far West* (Washington, 1975), 3–20; George L. Strebel, "Irrigation as a Factor in Western History, 1847–1900" (Ph.D. diss., University of California, Berkeley, 1965), pp. 135–36.

52. Ray P. Teele, "General Discussion of Irrigation in Utah," in Elwood Mead, chief, *Report of Irrigation Investigations in Utah,* U.S. Department of Agriculture, Office of Experiment Stations, *Bulletin* no. 124 (Washington, 1903), pp. 21–27.

53. The discussion that follows is based upon James F. Willard, ed., *The Union Colony at Greeley, Colorado, 1869–1871* (Boulder, Colo., 1918); James F. Willard and Colin B. Goodykoontz, eds., *Experiments in Colorado Colonization, 1869–1872* (Boulder, Colo., 1926); Carl Ubbelohde, Maxine Benson, and Duane A. Smith, *A Colorado History,* 3d ed. (Boulder, Colo., 1972), pp. 123–31; William E. Smythe, *The Conquest of Arid America,* rev. ed. (New York, 1905), pp. 79–91.

54. Denver *Daily Rocky Mountain News,* June 21, 1870, as quoted in Willard, *Union Colony,* p. 268.

55. Alfred R. Golzé, *Reclamation in the United States* (Caldwell, Idaho, 1961), p. 10.

56. Frederick H. Newell, *Report on Agriculture by Irrigation in the Western Part of the United States at the Eleventh Census: 1890, vol. V of Eleventh Census, 1890* (Washington, 1894), p. 132.

57. Taliesin Evans, "Orange Culture in California," *Overland Monthly*, 1st ser., XII (1874), 239; Cronise, *Natural Wealth of California*, p. 363; Hittell, *Commerce and Industries*, p. 243.

58. The discussion that follows is based on Hallock F. Raup, "The German Colonization of Anaheim, California," *University of California Publications in Geography*, VI (1932), 123–46; Charles Nordhoff, *The Communistic Societies of the United States; From Personal Visit and Observation* . . . (New York, 1875), pp. 361–66; Mildred Yorba MacArthur, *Anaheim, "The Mother Colony"* (Los Angeles, 1959).

59. The discussion that follows is based upon Smythe, *Conquest of Arid America*, pp. 97–105; H. J. Rudisill, *Riverside Illustrated; A City Among the Orange Groves* (Riverside, 1889); *A General Historical, Statistical and Descriptive Review of Riverside, California, and Riverside County* (Riverside, c. 1893); William Hammond Hall, *Irrigation in California (Southern)* (Sacramento, 1888), II, 198–244; Merlin Stonehouse, "The Michigan Excursion for the Founding of Riverside, California," *Michigan History*, XLV (1961), 193–209.

60. Rudisill, *Riverside Illustrated*, pp. 49–51. The "to the citizens as a water company" is from Hall, *Irrigation in California*, II, 232, and the average acreage figure is from the same source, p. 221.

61. Pisani, *From the Family Farm to Agribusiness*, pp. 121–27; Virginia E. Thickens, "Pioneer Agricultural Colonies of Fresno County," *California Historical Society Quarterly*, XXV (1946), 17–38, 169–77.

62. Newell, *Report on Agriculture by Irrigation* (1890), pp. 1, 6; Ray P. Teele, *Irrigation in the United States: A Discussion of Its Legal, Economic and Financial Aspects* (New York, 1915), pp. 34–41.

63. Newell, *Report on Agriculture by Irrigation* (1890), pp. vii, 1; same author, "Section IX. Irrigation," *Twelfth Census, 1900: Agriculture*, part II (Washington, 1902), 819.

64. Newell, *Report on Agriculture by Irrigation* (1890), pp. 2–4.

65. San Francisco *Weekly Alta California*, May 13, 1871; *Pacific Rural Press*, May 27, 1871; "Strawberry Growing in California," *California Horticulturist*, VII (1877), 139–40; Board of Directors, "Report for 1868 and 1869," California State Agriculture Society, *Transactions for 1868 and 1869*, p. 24; *California Farmer*, April 25 and 30, 1856.

66. G. G. Briggs, "Fruit Culture," California State Agricultural Society, *Transactions during the Year 1881* (Sacramento, 1881), pp. 181–89; Sacramento *Daily Union*, September 3, 1858; *California Farmer*, August 17, 1860; *Mining and Scientific Press*, September 18, 1869.

67. Theodore Schoenman, ed., *Father of California Wine: Agoston Haraszthy; Including "Grape Culture, Wines and Wine-Making"* (Santa Barbara, 1979); Joan Marie Donohue, "Agostin Haraszthy: A Study in Creativity," *California Historical Quarterly*, LIV (1975), 139–74.

68. Agoston Haraszthy, *Grape Culture, Wines and Wine-Making; with Notes Upon Agriculture and Horticulture* (New York, 1862).

69. John S. Hittell, "The Wines of California," *Pacific Monthly*, X (1863), 203.

70. *Pacific Rural Press*, July 29, October 14, 1871; Henry De Groot, "Fruit Growing and Curing in California," *California Horticulturist*, IV (1874), 274–76.

71. San Francisco *Daily Alta California,* November 18, 1872; De Groot, "Fruit Growing and Curing," *California Horticulturist,* IV (1874), 274–76; *Pacific Rural Press,* March 11, July 29, 1882, March 31, 1883; *California Patron,* May 16, 1877; George C. Husmann, "Grape, Raisin, and Wine Production in the United States," U.S. Department of Agriculture, *Yearbook,* 1902 (Washington, 1903), pp. 407–20.

72. *Pacific Rural Press,* March 5, 1881; *California Horticulturist,* III (1873), 253, IV (1874), 176–78.

73. Rahno M. MacCurdy, *The History of the California Fruit Growers Exchange* (Los Angeles, 1925), p. 7.

74. Vincent P. Carosso, *The California Wine Industry, 1830–1895,* passim; George Husmann, "The Present Condition of Grape Culture in California," U.S. Department of Agriculture, *Yearbook, 1898* (Washington, 1899), pp. 551–62; Arpad Haraszthy, "Wine-Making in California," *Overland Monthly,* 1st ser. VII (1871), 489–97, VIII (1872), 34–41, 105–9, 393–98.

75. *California Farmer,* April 7, 21, May 5, 26, July 7, 1870; *California Horticulturist,* I (1870–1871), 23, 330–31, V (1875), 20–21; *Pacific Rural Press,* July 8, August 12, 1871, July 27, 1872, January 6, 1883, June 21, 1884, January 31, 1885, April 26, 1890; *California Patron,* August 16, 1876, April 18, 1877.

76. *Pacific Rural Press,* January 7, 1882, November 17, 1883; *California Horticulturist,* VIII (1878), 287–88; Carosso, *California Wine Industry,* pp. 109–19, 128–29.

77. Carosso, *California Wine Industry,* pp. 120–59.

78. Mansel G. Blackford, *The Politics of Business in California, 1890–1920* (Columbus, Ohio, 1977), pp. 13–29; MacCurdy, *History of the California Fruit Growers Exchange,* pp. 16–35; *Pacific Rural Press,* March 15, 1884, August 1, 1885, April 17, 1886; Erich Kraemer and H. E. Erdman, *History of Cooperation in the Marketing of California Deciduous Fruits,* California Agricultural Experiment Station, *Bulletin* no. 557 (Berkeley, 1933); John W. Lloyd, *Cooperative and Other Organized Methods of Marketing California Horticultural Products* (Urbana, Ill., 1919).

79. Newell, "Section IX. Irrigation," *Twelfth Census, 1900: Agriculture,* p. 819.

80. Robert G. Dunbar, *Forging New Rights in Western Waters* (Lincoln, Nebr., 1983), pp. 23–26.

81. Mary Hallock Foote, *A Victorian Gentlewoman in the Far West,* Rodman W. Paul, ed. (San Marino, Calif., 1972), pp. 263–330. Mrs. Foote's reminiscences reveal severe tensions that developed within the family as they waited helplessly for funds.

82. Dunbar, *Forging New Rights,* p. 27.

83. *Ibid.,* pp. 39–42.

84. Frank Adams, *Irrigation Districts in California, 1887–1915,* California Department of Engineering, *Bulletin* no. 2 (Sacramento, 1916). For an excellent modern appraisal of the Wright Act, see Pisani, *From the Family Farm to Agribusiness,* p. 250–82.

85. Adams, *Irrigation Districts,* p. 9.

86. Pisani, *From the Family Farm to Agribusiness,* p. 281.

87. Wells A. Hutchins, *Selected Problems in the Law of Water Rights in the West*, U.S. Department of Agriculture, *Miscellaneous Publication* no. 418 (Washington, 1942), p. 30.
88. Samuel C. Wiel, *Water Rights in the Western States: The Law of Prior Appropriation of Water as Applied Alone in Some Jurisdictions, and as, in Others, Confined to the Public Domain, with the Common Law of Rights for Waters upon Private Lands* . . . 3d ed., 2 vols. (San Francisco, 1911), I, 66.
89. Hutchins, *Selected Problems*, p. 39.
90. Donald Pisani gives an excellent account in *From the Family Farm to Agribusiness*, pp. 18, 105–27, 191–249.
91. *Ibid.*, p. 191.
92. Wiel, *Water Rights in the Western States*, I, 135–37.
93. Dunbar, *Forging New Rights*, pp. 74–98. The quotation is from Chief Justice Hallett's decision, as quoted on p. 78.
94. *Ibid.*, pp. 99–132. The phrase "distributive administration" is from Gordon M. Bakken, "The English Common Law in the Rocky Mountain West," *Arizona and the West*, XI (1969), 121–22.
95. Wiel, *Water Rights in the Western States*, I, 137–44; Pisani, *From the Family Farm to Agribusiness*, p. 248.
96. Pisani, *From the Family Farm to Agribusiness*, p. 243.

Chapter 12: The Later Days of Mining

1. Richard P. Rothwell, "Gold and Silver," in David T. Day, special agent, *Report on Mineral Industries in the United States*, in *Eleventh Census, 1890*, vol. VII (Washington, 1892), p. 36.
2. Conrad Kohrs, *Autobiography*, Conrad Kohrs Warren, ed. (Deer Lodge, Mont., 1977), pp. 89–90.
3. Irving Howbert, *Memories of a Lifetime in the Pike's Peak Region* (New York and London, 1925), pp. 244–53.
4. Henry C. Morris, *The Mining West at the Turn of the Century*, C. S. Rice, ed. (Washington, 1962), pp. 1–5. Reminiscences of a mining engineer.
5. Joseph Grinnell, *Gold Hunting in Alaska*, Elizabeth Grinnell, ed. (Elgin and Chicago, 1901), pp. 3–4. The book was "Dedicated to disappointed gold-hunters the world over."
6. *Mining and Scientific Press*, June 27, 1874.
7. Henry De Groot, "Hydraulic and Drift Mining," in California State Mineralogist, *Second Report, from December 1, 1880, to October 1, 1882* (Sacramento, 1882), pp. 172–90; Samuel F. Emmons and George F. Becker, *Statistics and Technology of the Precious Metals*, in *Tenth Census, 1880*, vol. XIII (Washington, 1895), pp. 203–4.
8. The classic contemporary manual, whose early pages trace the evolution of hydraulicking, is Augustus J. Bowie's *A Practical Treatise on Hydraulicking in California. With Description of the Use and Construction of Ditches, Flumes, Wrought-Iron Pipes, and Dams* . . . (New York, 1885).

9. Cf. F. W. Robinson, "Notes on Hydraulic Mining," in California State Mineralogist, *Second Report*, p. 128, and Emmons and Becker, *Statistics and Technology*, p. 200.

10. Such high estimates, although often quoted, are suspect. Cf. Emmons and Becker, *Statistics and Technology*, pp. 184–85.

11. Robert L. Kelley, *Gold vs. Grain: The Hydraulic Mining Controversy in California's Sacramento Valley, a Chapter in the Decline of Laissez Faire* (Glendale, Calif. 1959), passim; *Mining and Scientific Press*, February 29, 1868, October 22, 1870.

12. Hamilton Smith, Jr., *An Account of the Operations of the North Bloomfield Gravel Mining Co. from 1871 to 1875; also, a Statement Showing Present Condition of the Various Properties of the Company* (1875).

13. *General Statement Concerning the Property of the North Bloomfield Gravel Mining Company, Organized August 7, 1866* (1880).

14. For a contemporary description, see Judson Farley, "The Yuba," *Overland Monthly*, 1st ser., V (1870), 444–48.

15. Kelley, *Gold vs. Grain*, pp. 79–215.

16. Woodruff v. North Bloomfield Gravel Mining Company and others, 18 Fed. 753–813, Sawyer, J., Deady concurring. Circuit Court for the District of California, January 7, 1884. The Huntington Library has two briefs filed for the complainant.

17. Joseph J. Hagwood, Jr., *The California Debris Commission: A History of the Hydraulic Mining Industry in the Western Sierra of California, and of the Governmental Agency Charged with Its Regulation* (Sacramento, 1981), p. 31. An official history commissioned by the U.S. Army Corps of Engineers.

18. Clark C. Spence, "The Golden Age of Dredging: The Development of an Industry and Its Environmental Impact," *Western Historical Quarterly*, XI (1980), 401–14; Charles Janin, *Gold Dredging in the United States*, U.S. Bureau of Mines, *Bulletin* 127 (Washington, 1918); Lewis E. Aubry, *Gold Dredging in California*, California State Mining Bureau, *Bulletin* no. 36 (Sacramento, 1905), and enlarged edition, *Bulletin* no. 57 (Sacramento, 1910); Hennen Jennings, *The History and Development of Gold Dredging in Montana*, U.S. Bureau of Mines, *Bulletin* 121 (Washington, 1916).

19. Cf. D'Arcy Weatherbe, *Dredging for Gold in California* (San Francisco, 1907), pp. 164–68; Aubury, *Gold Dredging in California* (1905 ed.), pp. 17–18; Aubury, *Gold Dredging in California* (1910 ed.), pp. xiii–xiv; Janin, *Gold Dredging*, pp. 198–203.

20. Janin, *Gold Dredging*, p. 7.

21. The discussion that follows is based on Paul, *Mining Frontiers*, pp. 75–86.

22. *Mining and Scientific Press*, December 26, 1874.

23. Grant H. Smith, *The History of the Comstock Lode, 1850–1920*, University of Nevada, *Bulletin*, XXXVII, no. 3, Geology and Mining Series no. 37 (Reno, 1943), p. 259.

24. Bertrand F. Couch and Jay A. Carpenter, *Nevada's Metal and Mineral Production (1859–1940, Inclusive)*, University of Nevada, *Bulletin*, XXXVII, no. 4, Geology and Mining Series no. 38 (Reno, 1943), p. 133.

25. Lloyd Tevis, *California and the Pacific Coast: Address of Mr. Lloyd Tevis, President of Wells, Fargo & Company, San Francisco, before the American Bankers' Association at Niagara Falls, August 10, 1881* (pamphlet, San Francisco, 1881).

26. Smith, *History of the Comstock Lode*, pp. 292–93.

27. James E. Fell, Jr., *Ores to Metals: The Rocky Mountain Smelting Industry* (Lincoln, Nebr., 1979), pp. 11–47.

28. *Ibid.*, pp. 49–54, 166–76.

29. *Ibid.*, pp. 78–94, 142–43; Don L. Griswold and Jean Harvey Griswold, *The Carbonate Camp Called Leadville* (Denver, 1951), pp. 61–63.

30. Paul, *Mining Frontiers*, pp. 127–31.

31. For a vivid picture of this elite and the men of the geological survey, see Mary Hallock Foote, *A Victorian Gentlewoman in the Far West*.

32. Duane A. Smith, *Horace Tabor: His Life and the Legend* (Boulder, Colo., 1973).

33. For an illustrated discussion of veins and lodes and the apex law, see A. H. Ricketts, *American Mining Law, with Forms and Precedents*, 4th ed., 2 vols., California Division of Mines, *Bulletin* 123 (Sacramento, 1948), I, 114–329, especially the diagrammatic illustrations on pp. 323–26. See also Paul, *Mining Frontiers*, pp. 172–75.

34. For an excellent, brief case-study of how far a leading western entrepreneur and his professionally well-trained superintendent were prepared to go, see Richard H. Peterson, "Simeon Gannett Reed and the Bunker Hill and Sullivan: The Frustrations of a Mining Investor," *Idaho Yesterdays*, XXIII (1979), 5–8.

35. Duane A. Smith, *Rocky Mountain Boom Town: A History of Durango* (Albuquerque, 1980).

36. Fell, *Ores to Metals*, pp. 140–41; James High, "William Andrews Clark, Westerner: An Interpretative Vignette," *Arizona and the West*, II (1960), 245–64; Michael P. Malone, *The Battle for Butte: Mining and Politics on the Northern Frontier, 1864–1906* (Seattle, 1981), pp. 12–16, 21–22.

37. Malone, *Battle for Butte*, pp. 18–28.

38. Matte is "the small residue of metallic sulphides which . . . encloses . . . all of the copper, gold, and silver" after the worthless materials have been driven off. Edward D. Peters, *The Principles of Copper Smelting* (New York, 1907), p. 429.

39. Malone, *Battle for Butte*, pp. 28–45.

40. *Ibid.*, p. 45.

41. As quoted *ibid.*, p. 46.

42. *Ibid.*, pp. 131–40, 161–87. The colorful stories of Amalgamated's long fight with the daring and unprincipled young F. Augustus Heinze and Marcus Daly's feud with William Andrews Clark are told in detail in Malone's book.

43. Fell, *Ores to Metals*, pp. 118–27.

44. *Ibid.*, pp. 178–88.

45. *Ibid.*, pp. 218–19.

46. *Ibid.*, pp. 218–24.

47. *Ibid.*, pp. 232–40.

48. Peterson, "Simeon Gannett Reed and the Bunker Hill and Sullivan," *Idaho Yesterdays*, XXIII, 2–8; Henry L. Day, "Mining Highlights of the Coeur d'Alene

District," *ibid.*, VII (1963–1964), 2–9; Dallas E. Livingston Little, "The Bunker Hill and Sullivan," *ibid.*, VII (1963), 34–43.

49. John Fahey, *The Ballyhoo Bonanza: Charles Sweeny and the Idaho Mines* (Seattle, 1971), pp. 3–67, 144–69.

50. *Ibid.*, pp. 170–201; Fell, *Ores to Metals*, pp. 244–48.

51. Robert L. Spude, "Mineral Frontier in Transition: Copper Mining in Arizona, 1880–1885," *New Mexico Historical Review*, LI (1976), 19–34.

52. This account is based primarily on Lynn R. Bailey, *Bisbee: Queen of the Copper Camps* (Tucson, 1983), but with use also of Robert Glass Cleland, *A History of Phelps Dodge, 1834–1950* (New York, 1952), and Arthur L. Walker, "Recollections of Early Day Mining in Arizona," *Arizona Historical Review*, VI (1935), 14–43.

53. James W. Brewer, *Jerome: A Story of Mines, Men and Money*, 12th ed. (Globe, Ariz., 1970); Russell Wahman, "A Centennial Commemorative: United Verde Copper Company, 1882–1982," *Journal of Arizona History*, XXIII (1982), 249–66; E. M. J. Alenius, *A Brief History of the United Verde Open Pit, Jerome, Arizona*, Arizona Bureau of Mines, *Bulletin* 178 (Tucson, 1968).

54. Bailey, *Bisbee*, pp. 49–84, 111.

55. Mark Wyman, *Hard Rock Epic: Western Miners and the Industrial Revolution, 1860–1910* (Berkeley and Los Angeles, 1979), passim; Richard E. Lingenfelter, *The Hardrock Miners*, pp. 12–30; Ronald C. Brown, *Hard-Rock Miners: The Intermountain West*, passim.

56. Vernon H. Jensen, *Heritage of Conflict: Labor Relations in the Nonferous Metals Industry up to 1930* (Ithaca, N.Y., 1950), p. ix.

57. Frank Crampton, *Deep Enough: A Working Stiff in the Western Mine Camps* (Denver, 1956), p. 47.

58. D. B. Barton, *Essays in Cornish Mining History* (Truro, Cornwall), I, 14–37. For a general survey, see Bryan Earl, *Cornish Mining: The Techniques of Metal Mining in the West of England, Past and Present* (Truro, Cornwall, 1968).

59. This account is based primarily on Lingenfelter, *The Hardrock Miners*, passim.

60. Ralph Mann, *After the Gold Rush: Society in Grass Valley and Nevada City, California, 1849–1870* (Stanford, 1982).

61. Crampton, *Deep Enough*, preface (no pagination). See also the autobiography of the well-known labor leader William D. Haywood, *Bill Haywood's Book* (New York, 1929).

62. Crampton, *Deep Enough*, preface. For an analytical study of employers, see Richard H. Peterson, *The Bonanza Kings: The Social Origins and Business Behavior of Western Mining Entrepreneurs, 1870–1900* (Lincoln, Nebr., 1977).

63. Lingenfelter, *The Hardrock Miners*, pp. 27, 51–54, 133.

64. *Ibid.*, 46–63, 157–81; Wyman, *Hard Rock Epic*, pp. 53–57.

65. Cf. Robert Wayne Smith, *The Coeur d'Alene Mining War of 1892* (Corvallis, Oreg., 1961).

Chapter 13: Other Opportunities

1. Leonard J. Arrington, *The Changing Economic Structure of the Mountain West, 1850–1950* (Logan, Utah, 1963), especially pp. 9–21.

2. Gerald D. Nash, "Bureaucracy and Reform in the West: Notes on the Influence of a Neglected Interest Group," *Western Historical Quarterly*, II (1971), 295–96.

3. Walter Prescott Webb, *The Great Plains* (Boston, New York, etc., 1931), pp. 8–9, 432–52.

4. Lawrence M. Friedman, *A History of American Law* (New York, 1973), p. 322.

5. *Ibid.*, p. 343; Gordon M. Bakken, *The Development of Law on the Rocky Mountain Frontier: Civil Law and Society, 1850–1912* (Westport, Conn., 1983), pp. 25, 42; same author, *The Development of Law in Frontier California: Civil Law and Society, 1850–1890* (Westport, Conn., 1985), pp. 27, 70, 75, 87, 93.

6. Jackson A. Graves, *My Seventy Years in California, 1857–1927* (Los Angeles, 1927), p. 85.

7. William W. Clary, *History of the Law Firm of O'Melveney and Myers, 1885–1965*, 2 vols. (Los Angeles, 1966), I, 36–38.

8. Bakken, *Development of Law in Frontier California*, p. 64.

9. Earl S. Pomeroy, *The Territories and the United States, 1861–1890: Studies in Colonial Administration*, new ed. (Seattle, 1969), p. 51. Cf. Richard E. Sloan, *Memories of an Arizona Judge* (Stanford, Calif., 1932), pp. 78–79.

10. John D. W. Guice, *The Rocky Mountain Bench: The Territorial Supreme Courts of Colorado, Montana, and Wyoming, 1861–1890* (New Haven, 1972), p. 150; cf. Kermit L. Hall, "Hacks and Derelicts Revisited: American Territorial Judiciary, 1789–1959," *Western Historical Quarterly*, XII (1981), 272–89.

11. John S. Hittell, *The Resources of California, Comprising Agriculture, Mining, Geography, Climate, Commerce, etc.* (San Francisco, 1863), p. 306.

12. San Francisco *Daily Alta California*, October 17, 1863.

13. John S. Hittell, *The Commerce and Industries of the Pacific Coast of North America; Comprising . . .* (San Francisco, 1882).

14. Vernon H. Jenson, *Lumber and Labor* (New York, 1945), p. 21.

15. Charles S. Sargent, *Report on the Forests of North America, Tenth Census, 1880*, vol. IX (Washington, 1884), pp. 567–69. Cf. Franklin B. Hough, *Report upon Forestry* (Washington, 1878), p. 595, which points to the rivalry in Utah between lumber from California and from the Great Lakes.

16. Thomas R. Cox, *Mills and Markets: A History of the Pacific Coast Lumber Industry to 1900* (Seattle, 1974), pp. 49–52, 61–62, 80, 119–20.

17. Pope and Talbot's history has been reported in Edwin T. Coman, Jr., and Helen M. Gibbs, *Time, Tide and Timber: A Century of Pope and Talbot* (Stanford, 1949). For a rival firm, see Richard C. Berner, "The Port Blakely Mill Company, 1876–89," *Pacific Northwest Quarterly*, LVII (1966), 158–71.

18. For superb photographs, plus text, see Karl Kortum and Roger Olmsted, *". . . it is a dangerous-looking place": Sailing Days on the Redwood Coast* (San Francisco, 1971).

19. Captain J. P. Keller, Teekalet, Washington Territory, to Charles Foster, November 26, 1861, Keller correspondence, Yale Western Americana collection, New Haven.

20. Ivan Doig, "John J. McGilvra and Timber Trespass," *Forest History*, XIII (1970), 10.

21. John Ise, *The United States Forest Policy* (New Haven, 1920), pp. 56, 79.

22. Edmond S. Meany, Jr., "The History of the Lumber Industry in the Pacific Northwest to 1917" (Ph.D. diss., Harvard University, 1935), especially pp. 249–51; Cox, *Mills and Markets*, pp. 231–37.

23. Cox, *Mills and Markets*, p. 101.

24. Hittell, *Commerce and Industries*, p. 582.

25. Cox, *Mills and Markets*, pp. 255–83.

26. William H. Hutchinson, *California Heritage: A History of Northern California Lumbering*, rev. ed. (Santa Cruz, Calif., 1974).

27. Ralph Hidy, Frank E. Hill, and Allan Nevins, *Timber and Men: The Weyerhaeuser Story* (New York, 1963), pp. 207–25; Bureau of Corporations, *The Lumber Industry*, (parts I–IV (Washington, 1913–1914), I, 237; II, 6.

28. Sacramento *Transcript*, April 3, 1850; San Francisco *Daily Alta California*, November 2, 1851; Sacramento *Weekly Union*, April 16, 1853, May 14, 1853, January 3, 1857, January 8, 1859; Sacramento *Daily Union*, June 6, 1854.

29. C. A. Kirkpatrick, "Salmon Fishing on the Sacramento River," *Hutchings' Illustrated California Magazine*, IV (1860), 529–34.

30. R. D. Hume, *Salmon of the Pacific Coast; with Engravings, Showing the Apparatus Used for their Artificial Propagation, and the Operations of Salmon Fishing and Canning* . . . (n. p., 1893).

31. Gordon B. Dodds, *The Salmon King of Oregon: R. D. Hume and the Pacific Fisheries* (Chapel Hill, N.C., 1959), and see R. D. Hume, *A Pygmy Monopolist: The Life and Doings of R. D. Hume, Written by Himself and Dedicated to His Neighbors*, Gordon B. Dodds, ed. (Madison, Wis., 1961), especially pp. v, 1.

32. Ted C. Hinckley, *The Americanization of Alaska, 1869–1897* (Palo Alto, Calif., 1972), pp. 121–28, 185–95.

33. Edmund T. Peckham, "The Halibut Fishery of the Pacific Northwest" (Ph.D. diss., Harvard University, 1954). For a comparison of fisheries in 1880 and 1890, of Pacific Coast and New England conditions, see David Starr Jordan, "The Fisheries of California," *Overland Monthly*, 2d ser., XX (1892), 469–78. The Federal government published extensive studies.

34. Harold Williamson, Ralph L. Andreano, Arnold R. Daum, and Gilbert C. Klose, *The American Petroleum Industry: The Age of Energy, 1899–1959* (Evanston, Ill., 1963), p. 17.

35. Samuel W. Tait, Jr., *The Wildcatters: An Informal History of Oil-Hunting in America* (Princeton, 1946).

36. Carl C. Rister, *Oil! Titan of the Southwest* (Norman, Okla., 1949), p. 31.

37. *Ibid.*, p. 21.

38. *Ibid.*, pp. 43–49; John S. Spratt, *The Road to Spindletop: Economic Change in Texas, 1875–1901*, reprint ed. (Austin, 1970), pp. 272–73.

39. Rister, *Oil!*, pp. 50–79; Spratt, *Road to Spindletop*, pp. 273–76, 282–83.

40. Gerald T. White, "California's Other Mineral," *Pacific Historical Review*, XXXIX (1970), 138–42.

41. Gerald T. White, *Formative Years in the Far West: A History of Standard Oil Company of California and Predecessors through 1919* (New York, 1962), pp. 25, 59, 67, 134.

Chapter 14: If Horace Greeley Could See It Now

1. Richard Harding Davis, *The West from a Car-Window* (New York, 1892).
2. James F. Muirhead, *The Land of Contrasts: A Briton's View of his American Kin* (Boston, New York, and London, 1898), pp. 220–21.
3. *Ibid.*, pp. 213–14.
4. *Ibid.*, p. 23.
5. *Ibid.*, p. 6.
6. *Ibid.*, p. 37.
7. T. A. Larson, "Dolls, Vassals, and Drudges—Pioneer Women in the West," *Western Historical Quarterly*, III (1972), 5–16.
8. Sandra L. Myres, *Westering Women and the Frontier Experience, 1800–1915* (Albuquerque, 1982).
9. Robert L. Griswold, *Family and Divorce in California, 1850–1890: Victorian Illusions and Everyday Realities* (Albany, N.Y., 1982), pp. 4–5.
10. Muirhead, *Land of Contrasts*, pp. 37–38.
11. Stanley Wood, *Over the Range to the Golden Gate: A Complete Tourist's Guide*, revised to 1904 by C. E. Hooper (Chicago, 1904), pp. 5, 9.
12. *Ibid.*, p. 13.
13. G. W. Steevens, *The Land of the Dollar* (Edinburgh and London, 1900), p. 199.
14. Muirhead, *Land of Contrasts*, pp. 96, 210–11.
15. *American Lumberman*, May 2, 1903.
16. T. Mitchell Prudden, *On the Great American Plateau: Wanderings among Canyons and Buttes, in the Land of the Cliff-Dweller, and the Indian of To-day* (New York and London, 1906).
17. Steevens, *The Land of the Dollar*, p. 204.

Bibliographical Essay

General

In the New American Nation Series, the present volume occupies the space between Ray A. Billington's *The Far Western Frontier, 1836–1860* and Earl Pomeroy's forthcoming study of the west in the twentieth century. Those who wish to study this period against the whole sweep of earlier frontiers and "wests" should consult Ray A. Billington and Martin Ridge, *Westward Expansion: A History of the American Frontier*, 5th ed. (New York and London, 1982). For this fifth edition Martin Ridge has carried out a meticulously careful revision that preserves the felicities of Billington's style while introducing new material and making any needed corrections.

The Billington and Ridge volume has a massive bibliography of 159 double-columned pages. A shorter bibliography (three thousand items) has been published by Rodman W. Paul and Richard W. Etulain, *The Frontier and the American West* (Golden Tree Bibliographies, Arlington Heights, Ill., 1977). The Paul and Etulain bibliography includes unpublished doctoral dissertations.

Recent years have brought a heartening improvement in the quality of monographs dealing with the west and a vast increase in the number of significant books and articles. Scholarly journals such as the *Western Historical Quarterly, Pacific Historical Review, Journal of American History,* and *Arizona and the West* bulge with worthwhile essays. Subjects that had received inadequate attention are now taken up in new books. Examples are studies of women, of Mormons, and of Spanish-speaking Americans. At the same time the long-neglected field of state history has produced competent, informative, up-to-date books.

343

An essential aid to anyone reading in western history is the volume edited by Howard R. Lamar, *The Reader's Encyclopedia of the American West* (New York, 1977). A comparably good historical atlas is not available. *The American Heritage Pictorial Atlas of the United States* (New York, 1966) does only a part of the job. It should be supplemented by James T. Adams and Roy V. Coleman, eds., *Atlas of American History* (New York, 1943). Fortunately, parallel to the new interest in state histories has been an increasing publication of state historical atlases.

Because the physical environment is so important in western history, much use can be made of the United States Geological Survey's excellent *National Atlas of the United States of America* (Washington, 1970), which shows climatic and soil factors, physical resources, Indian affairs, governmental activities, and economic and social factors. The United States Bureau of the Census has assembled a useful volume, *Historical Statistics of the United States: Colonial Times to 1970* (Washington, 1975), but this modern reworking of the statistics fails to reach down to the state and territorial level where the most revealing figures are needed.

The Mining Advance into the Interior

The present writer has discussed this in detail in *Mining Frontiers of the Far West* (New York, 1963; repr. Albuquerque, 1974). T. H. Watkins has published a handsomely illustrated big volume entitled *Gold and Silver in the West: The Illustrated History of an American Dream* (Palo Alto, Calif., 1971). The pioneer study of the northern part of this advance was William J. Trimble's doctoral dissertation, *The Mining Advance into the Inland Empire: A Comparative Study of the Beginnings of the Mining Industry in Idaho and Montana, Eastern Washington and Oregon* . . . (Madison, Wis., 1914; repr. with introduction by Rodman W. Paul, New York, 1972).

An equally important pioneer history of the Comstock Lode was written by Eliot Lord, *Comstock Mining and Miners*, U.S. Geological Survey, *Monographs*, IV (Washington, 1883; repr. with introduction by David F. Myrick, Berkeley, 1959). Grant H. Smith brought Lord's findings up to date with *The History of the Comstock Lode, 1850–1920*, University of Nevada *Bulletin*, XXXVII, no. 3, (Reno, 1943).

The classic contemporary accounts of the Comstock are Mark Twain's *Roughing It* (Hartford, 1872; repr. many times) and the history by Mark Twain's friend William Wright, better known as Dan De Quille, *History of the Big Bonanza: An Authentic Account of the Discovery, History, and Working of the World Renowned Comstock Silver Lode* (Hartford, 1876; repr. with introduction by Oscar Lewis, New York, 1947). Oscar Lewis has written a collective biography of the Four Irishmen in *Silver Kings, the Lives and Times of Mackay,*

Fair, Flood, and O'Brien, Lords of the Nevada Comstock Lode (New York, 1947).

For other mining regions, major contemporary accounts include: Granville Stuart, *Forty Years on the Frontier, as Seen in the Journals and Reminiscences of Granville Stuart, Gold-Miner, Trader, Merchant, Rancher and Politician*, Paul C. Phillips, ed., 2 vols. (Cleveland, 1925); John Hailey, *The History of Idaho* (Boise, 1910); and Frank Fossett, *Colorado: Its Gold and Silver Mines, Farms and Stock Ranges, and Health and Pleasure Resorts* (New York, 1879).

The Federal government made available a rich store of information about mining in the 1860s and 1870s. In connection with the census of 1880 a group of able mining engineers and geologists contributed to Samuel F. Emmons and George F. Becker, eds., *Statistics and Technology of the Precious Metals* (*Tenth Census, 1880*, XIII, Washington, 1885). James D. Hague, a well-qualified mining engineer, wrote *Mining Industry* for Clarence King's Fortieth Parallel Survey, which published it as volume III of their reports (Washington, 1870). In 1866 the office of Commissioner of Mining Statistics was created. The first two reports, filled with both general and local information, were prepared by J. Ross Browne, published in 1867 and 1868; the remaining reports were by Rossiter W. Raymond, a distinguished figure, until the office was discontinued after the report covering 1875.

Response to the Mining Boom: I. From the East

An excellent way to start is with John D. Unruh's *The Plains Across: The Overland Emigrants and the Trans-Mississippi West, 1840–1860* (Urbana, Ill., 1979). The story of freighting is best told in William E. Lass' *From the Missouri to the Great Salt Lake: An Account of Overland Freighting* (Lincoln, Nebr., 1972), but it should be supplemented by Henry Pickering Walker's good study, *The Wagonmasters: High Plains Freighting from the Earliest Days of the Santa Fe Trail to 1880* (Norman, Okla., 1966). An essential contemporary book is Alexander Majors, *Seventy Years on the Frontier: Alexander Majors' Memoirs of a Lifetime on the Border*, Prentiss Ingraham, ed. (Chicago and New York, 1893).

The Overland Mail and its stagecoaches have been discussed many times. James V. Frederick wrote *Ben Holladay the Stagecoach King: A Chapter in the Development of Transcontinental Transportation* (Glendale, Calif., 1940). Roscoe P. Conkling and Margaret B. Conkling contributed *The Butterfield Overland Mail, 1857–1869*, 3 vols. (Glendale, 1947) and LeRoy R. Hafen *The Overland Mail, 1849–1869, Promoter of Settlement, Precursor of Railroads* (Cleveland, 1926). Raymond W. and Mary L. Settle have written several histories of the famous firm of Russell, Majors and Waddell, the most recent being *War Drums and Wagon Wheels: The Story of Russell, Majors and Waddell* (Lincoln, 1966). W. Turrentine Jackson has written the history of Wells Fargo in many informative essays, of which the most important probably are: "Wells Fargo: Symbol of the Wild West?" *Western Historical Quarterly*, III (1972), 179–96, and "A New Look at Wells Fargo, Stagecoaches and the Pony Express," *California Historical Society Quarterly*, XLV (1966), 291–324.

The most famous contemporary account of stagecoach travel across the plains is Mark Twain's *Roughing It*, previously cited, but see also Samuel Bowles, *Across the Continent: A Summer's Journey to the Rocky Mountains, the Mormons, and the Pacific States . . .* (Springfield, Mass., and New York, 1865).

The alternative to freighting and stagecoaching is well described by William E. Lass, *A History of Steamboating on the Upper Missouri River* (Lincoln, 1962), which largely supersedes Hiram Chittenden's classic *History of Early Steamboat Navigation on the Missouri River*, 2 vols. (New York, 1902).

The story of the Army, which was charged with safeguarding all this travel, has been very well told by Robert M. Utley in two books: *Frontiersmen in Blue: The United States Army and the Indian, 1848–1865* (New York, 1967) and *Frontier Regulars: The United States Army and the Indian, 1866–1891* (New York, 1973).

Robert L. Thompson has written what has become the standard history of the telegraph: *Wiring a Continent: The History of the Telegraph Industry in the United States, 1832–1866* (Princeton, 1947).

An old but still helpful general survey of the building of the Union Pacific and other early railroads that approached from the east is Robert E. Riegel's *The Story of the Western Railroads* (New York, 1926). Robert G. Athearn's *Union Pacific Country* (Chicago, 1971) is the best study we have of the complex problem of the construction of the Union Pacific and its effect on the country it was traversing. To understand the financial difficulties and the scandals they led to, one should study Nelson Trottman's *History of the Union Pacific: A Financial and Economic Survey* (New York, 1923); Robert W. Fogel's *The Union Pacific Railroad: A Case in Premature Enterprise* (Baltimore, 1960); and Charles E. Ames' defense of his family's role, in *Pioneering the Union Pacific: A Reappraisal of the Builders of the Railroad* (New York, 1969).

The engineer in charge of western construction, Grenville M. Dodge, has given his own version in *How We Built the Union Pacific Railway, and Other Railway Papers and Addresses* (Washington, 1910), but two biographers differ sharply in their estimate of him: Jacob R. Perkins, *Trails, Rails and War: The Life of General G. M. Dodge* (Indianapolis, 1929) and Stanley P. Hirshson, *Grenville M. Dodge: Soldier, Politician, Railroad Pioneer* (Bloomington, Ind., 1967).

To try to hold together the facts concerning these quite different forms of western transportation, and the problems to which they gave rise, is extremely difficult. The only person who has attempted a comprehensive survey is Oscar O. Winther in *The Transportation Frontier: Trans-Mississippi West, 1865–1890* (New York, Chicago, etc., 1964).

The Response to the Mining Boom: II. From the West

In writing of the response from the west, and indeed in describing Pacific Coast development in general, frequent use has been made of the work of John S. Hittell, a San Francisco journalist, historian, and essayist. Hittell was remarkably well informed about the economic and social events transpiring around him. Through the courtesy of the Hittell family, the present writer has been able to go through the elaborate set of scrapbooks in which Hittell pasted pertinent clippings from contemporary publications and in which he collected and identified his own writings for newspapers. He was especially well known for his *The Resources of California*, which was first published in 1863 and went through several later editions, for his *The Commerce and Industries of the Pacific Coast . . .* (San Francisco, 1882), for his descriptive survey, *Mining in the Pacific States of North America* (San Francisco, 1861), and his annalistic *History of the City of San Francisco and Incidentally of the State of California* (San Francisco, 1878). Quotations and citations from Hittell occur throughout the present volume.

In studying the development of San Francisco it is important to keep in mind what was happening in other, quite different, cities. Particularly illuminating is Stephan Thernstrom's *The Other Bostonians: Poverty and Progress in the American Metropolis, 1880–1970* (Cambridge, 1973). Three major studies of San Francisco tell the story from different points of view: Roger W. Lotchin, *San Francisco 1846–1856: From Hamlet to City* (New York, 1974); Peter R. Decker, *Fortunes and Failures: White-Collar Mobility in Nineteenth-Century San Francisco* (Cambridge, 1978); and Gunther Barth, *Instant Cities: Urbanization and the Rise of San Francisco and Denver* (New York, 1975).

The key figure in much San Francisco development has been well studied in David Lavender's *Nothing Seemed Impossible: William C. Ralston and Early San Francisco* (Palo Alto, 1975), but see also the older biography by Cecil G. Tilton, *William Chapman Ralston, Courageous Builder* (Boston, 1935).

On transportation, John H. Kemble's *The Panama Route, 1848–1869* (Berkeley and Los Angeles, 1943) has long been the standard book on the steamer route, and Oscar O. Winther's *Express and Stagecoach Days in California, From the Gold Rush to the Civil War* (Stanford, 1936) on land travel. Winther covered the northern area in *The Old Oregon Country: A History of Frontier Trade, Transportation, and Travel* (Bloomington, 1950). W. Turrentine Jackson made a major addition with "Wells Fargo Staging over the Sierras," *California Historical Society Quarterly*, XLIV (1970), 99–133, which includes a good map.

✳

For the building of the Central Pacific Railroad, the most important book is David Lavender's biography of Collis P. Huntington, *The Great Persuader* (New York, 1970). Oscar Lewis has written a group biography: *The Big Four: The Story of Huntington, Stanford, Hopkins, and Crocker, and of the Building of the Central Pacific* (New York, 1938). There is much value in Stuart Daggett's *Chapters on the History of the Southern Pacific* (New York, 1922). Many insights into the intricate way in which these men operated can be found in George T. Marye, Jr., *From '49 to '83 in California and Nevada: Chapters from the Life of George Thomas Marye, a Pioneer of '49* (San Francisco, 1923).

Build Thee More Stately Mansions

Recent historical writing has been characterized by a growing realization of the importance of cities in western life. Earl Pomeroy pointed in this direction in his *The Pacific Slope: A History of California, Oregon, Washington, Idaho, Utah, and Nevada* (New York, 1965). A general discussion of cities in America is available in Charles N. Glaab and A. Theodore Brown, *A History of Urban America* (New York, 1967) and Blake McKelvey, *The Urbanization of America (1860–1915)* (New Brunswick, N.J., 1963). John W. Reps has published a handsomely illustrated volume, *Cities of the American West: A History of Frontier Urban Planning* (Princeton, 1979). Lawrence H. Larsen used the material in the census of 1880 to write *The Urban West at the End of the Frontier* (Lawrence, 1978).

On individual cities, Lyle W. Dorsett has written the most recent history of Denver: *The Queen City: A History of Denver* (Boulder, 1977), but this does not lessen the value of Jerome C. Smiley's *History of Denver, with Outlines of the Earlier History of the Rocky Mountain Country* (Denver, 1901). Robert L. Perkin's book is just what the title promises: *The First Hundred Years: An Informal History of Denver and the Rocky Mountain News* (New York, 1959).

Harry E. Kelsey, Jr., has written the biography of an early governor and capitalist of Colorado in *Frontier Capitalist: The Life of John Evans* (Denver and Boulder, 1969), while Elmer Ellis has reported on *Henry Moore Teller: Defender of the West* (Caldwell, Idaho, 1941).

On the complexities of government and politics in the west, leading sources include Earl Pomeroy, *The Territories of the United States, 1861–1890: Studies in Colonial Administration* (Philadelphia, 1947); Howard R. Lamar, *The Far Southwest, 1846–1912, a Territorial History* (New Haven, 1966); Kenneth N. Owens, "Pattern and Structure in Western Territorial Politics," *Western Historical Quarterly*, I (1970), 373–92; John D. W. Guice, *The Rocky Mountain Bench: The Territorial Supreme Courts of Colorado, Montana, and Wyoming, 1861–1890* (New Haven, 1972), and Lewis L. Gould, *Wyoming: A Political History, 1868–1896* (New Haven, 1968).

Building Colorado's railroads involved as much politics and high finance as engineering. The story is told in Robert G. Athearn, *Rebel of the Rockies: A History of the Denver and Rio Grande Western Railroad* (New Haven, 1962); Thomas J. Noel, "All Hail the Denver Pacific: Denver's First Railroad," *Colorado Magazine*, L (1973), 91–116; and S. D. Mock, "The Financing of Early Colorado Railroads," *Colorado Magazine*, XVIII (1940), 201–9.

An unusually interesting contemporary description of Colorado is Isabella L. Bird's *A Lady's Life in the Rocky Mountains*, 3d ed. (New York, 1879–1880).

Salt Lake City's history should be considered against the background supplied by Leonard J. Arrington in his excellent *Great Basin Kingdom: An Economic History of the Latter-day Saints, 1830–1900* (Cambridge, 1958). Edward W. Tullidge, who was cut off from the Mormon church because of questioning its policies, wrote a very useful *History of Salt Lake City* (Salt Lake City, 1886), while another ex-Mormon, who had been a merchant and publisher, wrote a reasonably restrained book, *The Rocky Mountain Saints: A Full and Complete History of the Mormons . . .* (New York, 1873). A dispassionate appraisal by an experienced British traveler helps to balance up the picture of this controversial city: Richard F. Burton, *The City of the Saints and Across the Rocky Mountains to California* (London, 1861). Brigham Young's determination to make Salt Lake City the communications headquarters for "the Kingdom" is illustrated in Leonard J. Arrington's "The Deseret Telegraph—A Church-Owned Public Utility," *Journal of Economic History*, XI (1951), 117–39, and Monte B. McLaws' *Spokesman for the Kingdom: Early Mormon Journalism and the Deseret News, 1830–1898* (Provo, 1977).

The key book for understanding early Portland is Arthur L. Throckmorton's *Oregon Argonauts: Merchant Adventurers on the Western Frontier* (Portland, 1961). Paul G. Merriam has written a doctoral dissertation, "Portland, Oregon, 1840–1890: A Social and Economic History" (University of Oregon, 1971). E. Kimbark MacColl has stressed business control of government in *The Shaping of a City: Business and Politics in Portland, Oregon, 1885–1915* (Portland, 1976).

In placing Portland in its regional context, it is helpful to consult James N. Tattersall's doctoral dissertation, "The Economic Development of the Pacific Northwest to 1920" (University of Washington, 1960). The all-essential steamboat service has been described by Dorothy O. Johansen, "The Oregon Steam Navigation Company: An Example of Capitalism on the Frontier," *Pacific Historical Review*, X (1941), 179–88, and by Johansen and Frank B. Gill, eds., "A Chapter in the History of the Oregon Steam Navigation Company," *Oregon Historical Quarterly*, XXXVIII (1937), 1–43, 300–22, 398–410, XXXIX (1938), 50–64.

Many Peoples

The literature on this subject is so voluminous that no more can be attempted here than to select books or articles that were of especial significance. General surveys include John Higham's *Strangers in the Land: Patterns of American Nativism, 1860–1925*, corrected 2d ed. (New York, 1963), and Leonard Dinnerstein and David M. Reimers, *Ethnic Americans: A History of Immigration and Assimilation* (New York, 1975). Related are Ray A. Billington's *The Protestant Crusade, 1800–1860: A Study of the Origins of American Nativism* (New York, 1938); Charles Wollenberg, ed., *Ethnic Conflict in California History* (Los Angeles, 1970); and Leonard Pitt's "The Beginning of Nativism in California," *Pacific Historical Review*, XXX (1961), 23–38. Moses Rischin has fitted immigration into western history in two essays: "Beyond the Great Divide: Immigration and the Last Frontier," *Journal of American History*, LV (1968), 42–53, and "Immigration, Migration, and Minorities in California: A Reassessment," *Pacific Historical Review*, XLI (1972), 71–90.

Discussions of European immigrants include Frederick Luebke's *Immigrants and Politics: The Germans of Nebraska, 1880–1900* (Lincoln, 1969) and the same author's "Ethnic Group Settlement in the Great Plains," *Western Historical Quarterly*, VIII (1977), 405–30; Terry G. Jordan, *German Seed in Texas Soil: Immigrant Farmers in Nineteenth-Century Texas* (Austin, 1966); and R. A. Burchell, *The San Francisco Irish, 1848–1880* (Berkeley and Los Angeles, 1980). Insights into the important role of the Jews can be found in Robert E. Levinson's article, "American Jews in the West," *Western Historical Quarterly*, V (1974), 285–94; in a volume edited by Moses Rischin, *The Jews of the West: The Metropolitan Years* (Waltham, Mass., and Berkeley, 1979); in Floyd S. Fierman's case study, "The Spiegelbergs: Pioneer Merchants and Bankers in the Southwest," *American Jewish Historical Quarterly*, LVI (1967), 371–451; and in William J. Parish's business study, *The Charles Ilfeld Company: A Study of the Rise and Decline of Mercantile Capitalism in New Mexico* (Cambridge, 1961).

Kenneth O. Bjork has written *West of the Great Divide: Norwegian Migration to the Pacific Coast, 1847–1893* (Northfield, Minn., 1958), and Andrew F. Rolle has given an optimistic picture of immigration in *The Immigrant Upraised: Italian Adventurers and Colonists in an Expanding America* (Norman, 1968).

Treatment of minorities has been a much harsher story. A good beginning can be made by reading Roger Daniels and Harry H. L. Kitano, *American Racism: Exploration of the Nature of Prejudice* (Englewood Cliffs, N.J., 1970). Eugene H. Berwanger has studied western attitudes toward blacks in two books: *The Frontier Against Slavery: Western Anti-Negro Prejudice and the Slavery Extension Controversy* (Urbana, 1967), and *The West and Reconstruction*

(Urbana, 1981). W. Sherman Savage has written *Blacks in the West* (Westport, Conn., 1976), and Douglas H. Daniels has produced an insightful study, *Pioneer Urbanites: A Social and Cultural History of Black San Francisco* (Philadelphia, 1980). Kenneth W. Porter's incomplete *The Negro on the American Frontier* (New York, 1971) has real strengths. Rudolph M. Lapp has focused on a special part of the frontier in *Blacks in Gold Rush California* (New Haven, 1977). Charles Wollenberg has traced the school question in *All Deliberate Speed: Segregation and Exclusion in California Schools, 1855–1975* (Berkeley and Los Angeles, 1976). The often overlooked contribution of black soldiers has received recognition in William H. Leckie's *The Buffalo Soldiers: A Narrative of the Negro Cavalry in the West* (Norman, 1967). A bizarre and tragic episode has been studied by Robert G. Athearn, *In Search of Canaan: Black Migration to Kansas, 1879–80* (Lawrence, 1978) and by Nell Irvin Painter, *Exodusters: Black Migration to Kansas after Reconstruction* (New York, 1977).

An extraordinary amount is written annually about Indians (Native Americans) and their relations with whites. Fortunately Francis Paul Prucha has compiled *A Bibliographical Guide to the History of Indian-White Relations in the United States* (Chicago, 1977), and has supplemented this with *Indian-White Relations in the United States: A Bibliography of Works Published, 1975–1980* (Lincoln, 1982). To these excellent guides Prucha has added a notable study: *The Great Father: The United States Government and the American Indians*, 2 vols. (Lincoln, 1984). He has published many other books, including *Indian Policy in the United States: Historical Essays* (Lincoln, 1981).

The standard anthropological reference book is by Harold E. Driver, *Indians of North America*, 2nd ed., rev. (Chicago, 1969). Relatively brief comprehensive surveys have been published by Wilcomb E. Washburn, *The Indian in America* (New York, 1975) and William T. Hagan, *American Indians* (Chicago, 1961). Clark Wissler, the distinguished anthropologist, wrote *Indians of the United States: Four Centuries of Their History and Culture* (New York, 1941), and he also wrote a reminiscent volume that drew upon recollections of his earliest experiences on reservations: *Indian Cavalcade, or Life on the Old-Time Indian Reservations* (New York, 1938).

Robert M. Utley was the author of an excellent survey of the second half of the nineteenth century, *The Indian Frontier of the American West, 1846–1890* (Albuquerque, 1984). Useful essays presented at a Washington conference were edited by Jane F. Smith and Robert M. Kvasnicka, *Indian-White Relations: A Persistent Paradox* (Washington, 1976).

A fierce dispute has developed over the question of how many Indians there were when they first came into contact with whites, and hence how severe has been the elimination of them. The dispute started when Henry F. Dobyns published "Estimating Aboriginal Population: An Appraisal of

Techniques with a New Hemispheric Estimate," *Current Anthropology*, VII (1966), 395–416, and comments 425–49. William Petersen answered Dobyns with "A Demographer's View of Prehistoric Demography," *Current Anthropology*, XVI (1975), 227–45, and William M. Denevan edited *The Native Population of the Americas in 1492* (Madison, 1976). Meantime the first real United States census of the Indians still stands: *Report on Indians Taxed and Indians Not Taxed in the United States (Except Alaska), Eleventh Census, 1890* (Washington, 1894).

In "When Red and White Men Met," *Western Historical Quarterly*, II (1971), 133–50, John C. Ewers made an important point, while Alfred W. Crosby, Jr., ventured into a complex interdisciplinary debate with *The Columbian Exchange: Biological and Cultural Consequences of 1492* (Westport, 1972). Richard White entered an important field when he published *The Roots of Dependency: Subsistence, Environment, and Social Change among the Choctaws, Pawnees and Navajos* (Lincoln, 1983).

Other studies of cultural change on reservations include: H. Craig Miner and William E. Unrau, *The End of Indian Kansas: A Study in Cultural Revolution, 1854–1871* (Lawrence, 1978); Donald J. Berthrong, *The Cheyenne and Arapaho Ordeal: Reservation and Agency Life in the Indian Territory, 1875–1907* (Norman, 1976); and Clyde A. Milner, II, "Off the White Road: Seven Nebraska Indian Societies in the 1870s—A Statistical Analysis of Assimilation, Population, and Prosperity," *Western Historical Quarterly*, XII (1981), 37–52. William T. Hagan has described a promising experiment in *Indian Police and Judges: Experiments in Acculturation and Control* (New Haven, 1966).

White attitudes and intentions toward Indians are revealed in Robert F. Berkhofer's *The White Man's Indian: Images of the American Indian from Columbus to the Present* (New York, 1978), in Robert W. Mardock's *The Reformers and the American Indian* (Columbia, Mo., 1971), and two books of a somewhat older cast of mind: Henry E. Fritz, *The Movement for Indian Assimilation, 1860–1880* (Philadelphia, 1963) and Loring B. Priest's *Uncle Sam's Stepchildren: The Reformation of United States Indian Policy, 1865–1887* (New Brunswick, N.J., 1942).

In recent years there has been a new recognition of the significance of the Spanish-speaking part of the population. This is partly because writers of Hispanic descent have come forward with major books, partly because Anglo writers have shown a new understanding. The Mexican background has been very well presented in David J. Weber's *The Mexican Frontier, 1821–1846: The American Southwest under Mexico* (Albuquerque, 1982). Donald W. Meinig, an able geographer, has given a new picture in *Southwest: Three Peoples in Geographical Change, 1600–1970* (New York, 1971). Writers of Hispanic descent have insisted that the size of the Spanish-speaking population has been underestimated: Oscar J. Martínez, "On the Size of the

Chicano Population: New Estimates, 1850–1900," *Aztlan*, VI (1975), 43–67. Meinig has also written an important monograph on Texas: *Imperial Texas: An Interpretive Essay in Cultural Geography*, paperback ed. (Austin, 1975). Meinig's interpretation supplements Arnoldo De León's impressive picture, *The Tejano Community, 1836–1900* (Albuquerque, 1982), and an article by De León and Kenneth L. Stewart, "Lost Dreams and Found Fortunes: Mexican and Anglo Immigrants in South Texas, 1850–1900," *Western Historical Quarterly*, XIV (1983), 291–310. Evan Anders, *Boss Rule in South Texas: The Progressive Era* (Austin, 1982) deals with many of the same issues. See also Paul S. Taylor's pioneering study, *An American-Mexican Frontier: Nueces County, Texas* (Chapel Hill, 1934). Mario T. Garcia has done an urban study, *Desert Immigrants: The Mexicans of El Paso, 1880–1920* (New Haven, 1981).

For New Mexico there is a good autobiography by an aristocrat: Miguel Antonio Otero, *My Life on the Frontier, 1864–1882: Incidents and Characters of the Period When Kansas, Colorado, and New Mexico Were Passing through the Last of Their Wild and Romantic Years* (New York, 1935). Lamar's *Far Southwest*, previously cited, has an excellent analysis of New Mexican government. Victor Westphall's *Thomas Benton Catron and his Era* (Tucson, 1973) is a biography of a leading figure in New Mexican politics. Dianna Everett, "The Public School Debate in New Mexico, 1850–1891," *Arizona and the West*, XXVI (1984), 107–34, takes up an issue that illustrates the rivalry between Anglos and Hispanos. Robert W. Larson's "The White Caps of New Mexico: A Study of Ethnic Militancy in the Southwest," *Pacific Historical Review*, XLIV (1975), 171–85, reveals the limits of Hispano tolerance, as does Robert J. Rosenbaum, *Mexicano Resistance in the Southwest: The Sacred Right of Self-Preservation* (Austin, 1981). Frances Leon Swadesh, *Los Primeros Pobladores: Hispanic Americans of the Ute Frontier* (Notre Dame, Ind., 1974) deals with a group that has received inadequate attention. An article by William B. Taylor and Elliott West gives an excellent insight into the working of the patrón system: "Patrón Leadership at the Crossroads: Southern Colorado in the Late Nineteenth Century," *Pacific Historical Review*, XLII (1973), 335–57.

In Arizona, where Tucson was the only center of continuous residence, two articles reveal much about Anglo-Hispano relations: James Officer's "Historical Factors in Interethnic Relations in the Community of Tucson," *Arizoniana*, I (1960), 12–16, and Elizabeth Albrecht's "Estévan Ochoa: Mexican-American Businessman," in the same journal, IV (1963), 35–40.

For California, Albert Camarillo's *Chicanos in a Changing Society: From Mexican Pueblos to American Barrios in Santa Barbara and Southern California, 1848–1930* (Cambridge, 1979) is outstanding. Other books on the same theme include: Leonard Pitt's *The Decline of the Californios: A Social History of the Spanish-Speaking Californians, 1846–1890* (Berkeley and Los Angeles, 1966), Richard Griswold del Castillo's *The Los Angeles Barrio, 1850–1890: A Social History* (Berkeley and Los Angeles, 1979), the same author's *La Familia: Chicano Families in the Urban Southwest, 1848 to the Present* (Notre Dame, 1984), and Ricardo Romo's *East Los Angeles: History of a Barrio* (Austin, 1983).

Mario T. Garcia has written more briefly on this theme in "The Californios of San Diego and the Politics of Accommodation, 1846–1860," *Aztlan*, VI (1975), 68–81. Joyce Carter Vickery has reported on a unique group of California settlers: *Defending Eden: New Mexican Pioneers in Southern California, 1830–1890* (Riverside, Calif., 1977).

The Chinese constitute the most intricate puzzle of all the minorities. Gunther Barth's *Bitter Strength: A History of the Chinese in the United States, 1850–1870* (Cambridge, 1964) stresses the differentness and the fact that they were mostly transients. Alexander Saxton, in *The Indispensable Enemy: Labor and the Anti-Chinese Movement in California* (Berkeley and Los Angeles, 1971), shows how anti-Chinese sentiment was the one point upon which labor could agree. His explanation should be read in conjunction with Ira B. Cross' *A History of the Labor Movement in California* (Berkeley and Los Angeles, 1935). Stuart C. Miller's *The Unwelcome Immigrant: The American Image of the Chinese, 1785–1882* (Berkeley and Los Angeles, 1969) is not entirely convincing. Mary Roberts Coolidge's *Chinese Immigration* (New York, 1909) was the first important study and still deserves attention. So does Elmer C. Sandmeyer's *The Anti-Chinese Movement in California* (Urbana, 1939). A new study that makes use of extensive Chinese material is Shih-shan Henry Tsai, *China and the Overseas Chinese in the United States, 1868–1911* (Fayetteville, Ark., 1983).

Special studies include: Ping Chiu's *Chinese Labor in California, 1850–1880: An Economic Study* (Madison, 1963), Sucheng Chan's "Chinese Livelihood in Rural California: The Impact of Economic Change, 1860–1880," *Pacific Historical Review*, LIII (1984), 273–307, and the elaborate hearings held by the Joint Special Committee to Investigate Chinese Immigration, *Senate Report*, no. 689, 44th Cong., 2d sess. (February 27, 1877).

Self-Proclaimed "Peculiar People"

Two comprehensive studies of the Mormons have been written in recent years, both by partnerships of Mormons. Leonard J. Arrington and Davis Bitton have produced *The Mormon Experience: A History of the Latter-day Saints* (New York, 1979), while James B. Allen and Glen M. Leonard wrote *The Story of the Latter-day Saints* (Salt Lake City, 1976). The latter volume, unfortunately, seems to have been withdrawn from sale because of objections raised by the church. Thomas F. O'Dea, not a Mormon, made an admirable study of the organization and working of the church, *The Mormons* (Chicago, 1957). Donald W. Meinig, the historical geographer, prepared a revealing analysis in "The Mormon Culture Region: Strategies and Patterns in the Geography of the American West, 1847–1964," *Annals of the Association of American Geographers*, LV (1965), 191–220. Jan Shipps, while not a Mormon, has written a book that Mormons hail as at last explaining their faith: *Mormonism: The Story of a New Religious Tradition* (Urbana and Chicago, 1985). A perceptive book essential for understanding Mormonism is Mark P. Leone's *Roots of Modern Mormonism* (Cambridge, 1979). Finally, Leonard J. Arrington has at last given us a full biography of Brigham Young: *Brigham Young: American Moses* (New York, 1985).

More specialized works include Lowry Nelson's classic, *The Mormon Village: A Pattern and Technique of Land Settlement* (Salt Lake City, 1952), and the collaborative study by Leonard J. Arrington, Feramorz Y. Fox, and Dean L. May, *Building the City of God: Community and Cooperation among the Mormons* (Salt Lake City, 1976). Stanley S. Ivins has done a very useful job on a controversial subject with his "Notes on Mormon Polygamy," *Western Humanities Review*, X (1956), 229–39. Juanita Brooks' *John Doyle Lee: Zealot-Pioneer-Builder-Scapegoat* (Glendale, 1961) tells the story of the man who was executed for participating in the murder of a wagon train of emigrants. Norman F. Furniss wrote of the "Mormon War": *The Mormon Conflict, 1850–1859*, repr. ed. (New Haven, 1960). Charles S. Peterson did an outstanding job with *Take Up Your Mission: Mormon Colonizing along the Little Colorado River, 1870–1900* (Tucson, 1973). An older study of colonizing is Milton R. Hunter's *Brigham Young the Colonizer*, 2d ed. (Salt Lake City, 1941). Richard Sherlock, "Mormon Migration and Settlement after 1875," *Journal of Mormon History*, II (1975), 53–68, like Peterson's book, brings colonization well down through the period after Brigham Young's death. Jan Shipps has made an important reappraisal in "The Principle Revoked: A Close Look at the Demise of Plural Marriage," *Journal of Mormon History*, XI (1984), 65–77. Gustive O. Larson has made a major political study in *The "Americanization" of Utah for Statehood* (San Marino, Calif., 1971). An important commentary on the Mormons' early use of irrigation can be found in George Thomas, *The Development of Institutions under Irrigation, with Special Reference to Early Utah Conditions* (New York, 1920).

Into the Pasturelands: I. Cattlemen Occupy the Ranges

Out of the mass of second-rate writing on the cow country west, a few excellent books have emerged. One of the best is by Ernest Staples Osgood, *The Day of the Cattleman* (Minneapolis, 1929; repr. many times). A second good one is by Edward E. Dale, *The Range Cattle Industry: Ranching on the Great Plains from 1865 to 1925*, new ed. (Norman, 1960), and Dale has written more informally in *Cow Country* (Norman, 1945). Louis Pelzer has written *The Cattlemen's Frontier: A Record of the Trans-Mississippi Cattle Industry from Oxen Trains to Pooling Companies, 1850–1890* (Glendale, 1936). Joe B. Frantz and Julian E. Choate, Jr., have brought common sense to the overworked subject of *The American Cowboy: The Myth and the Reality* (Norman, 1955), while Lewis Atherton has shifted the focus to the men in charge: *The Cattle Kings* (Bloomington, 1961). Jimmy M. Skaggs has filled in a gap with *The Cattle-Trailing Industry: Between Supply and Demand* (Lawrence, 1973). Robert R. Dykstra, partly using insights from the social sciences, has given us a dramatically different appraisal of *The Cattle Towns* (New York, 1968).

These are all secondary sources. A classic contemporary account is Joseph G. McCoy's *Historic Sketches of the Cattle Trade of the West and Southwest* (originally published Kansas City, Mo., 1874; repr. several times), and an excellent autobiography is John Clay's *My Life on the Range*, new ed., introduction by Edward E. Dale (New York, 1961).

Two government reports of major importance are Clarence W. Gordon, "Report on Cattle, Sheep, and Swine, Supplementary to Enumeration of Live Stock on Farms in 1880," part III, *Tenth Census, 1880: Report on the Production of Agriculture* (Washington, 1883), and Joseph Nimmo, Jr., "The Range and Ranch Cattle Business of the United States," *Report on the Internal Commerce of the United States*, part 3 (Washington, 1885).

More specialized studies include: J. Orin Oliphant, *On the Cattle Ranges of the Oregon Country* (Seattle, 1968); J. Evetts Haley, *Charles Goodnight, Cowboy and Plainsman* (Boston and New York, 1936); Chris Emmett, *Shanghai Pierce: A Fair Likeness* (Norman, 1953); and Agnes Wright Spring, " 'A Genius for Handling Cattle': John W. Iliff," in Maurice Frink, W. Turrentine Jackson, and Agnes Wright Spring, eds., *When Grass Was King* (Boulder, 1956), 333–450.

Histories of individual ranches can contribute a great deal. Examples are W. M. Pearce, *The Matador Land and Cattle Company* (Norman, 1964); Harmon R. Mothershead, *The Swan Land and Cattle Company, Ltd.* (Norman, 1971); and Tom Lea, *The King Ranch*, 2 vols. (Boston, 1957).

W. Turrentine Jackson has traced foreign investment in *The Enterprising Scot: Investors in the American West after 1873* (Edinburgh, 1968).

Finally, John T. Schlebecker has carried the story forward into the twentieth century: *Cattle Raising on the Plains, 1900–1961* (Lincoln, 1963).

Into the Pasturelands: II. Sheep Men Also Enter the Ranges

Popular accounts include Winifred Kupper, *The Golden Hoof: The Story of the Sheep of the Southwest* (New York, 1945) and Charles W. Towne and Edward N. Wentworth, *Shepherd's Empire* (Norman, 1945). Wentworth has also compiled a thick volume of biographies of sheep men: *America's Sheep Trails: History, Personalities* (Ames, Iowa 1948).

Much information can be found in governmental reports. Ezra A. Carman, H. A. Heath, and John Minto, *Special Report on the History and Present Condition of the Sheep Industry of the United States* (U.S. Department of Agriculture, Bureau of Animal Husbandry, Washington, 1892), and D. A. Spencer, M. C. Hall, and others, "The Sheep Industry," U.S. Department of Agriculture, *Agriculture Yearbook, 1923* (Washington, 1924). See also James Withycombe, "Sheep Husbandry in the Pacific Northwest," in U.S. Department of Agriculture, *Farmers' Bulletin* no. 117 (Washington, 1900), and Clarence Gordon's census report, previously cited.

For the history of individual areas, see Alexander Campbell McGregor, *Counting Sheep: From Open Range to Agribusiness on the Columbia Plateau* (Seattle, 1982); Alvar W. Carlson, "New Mexico's Sheep Industry, 1850–1900: Its Role in the History of the Territory," *New Mexico Historical Review*, XLIV (1969), 25–49; William R. Palmer, "The Early Sheep Industry in Southern Utah," *Utah Historical Quarterly*, XLII (1974), 178–88; Harold E. Briggs, "The Early Development of Sheep Ranching in the Northwest," *Agricultural History*, XI (1937), 161–80; John Minto, "Sheep Husbandry in Oregon," *Quarterly of the Oregon Historical Society*, III (1902), 219–47; Bert Haskett, "History of the Sheep Industry in Arizona," *Arizona Historical Review*, VII (1936), 3–49; and Paul H. Carlson, *Texas Woolybacks: The Range Sheep and Goat Industry* (College Station, Tex., 1982).

Charles M. Sypolt has written an unpublished doctoral dissertation, "Keepers of the Rocky Mountain Flocks: A History of the Sheep Industry in Colorado, New Mexico, Utah and Wyoming to 1900" (University of Wyoming, 1974).

Arthur H. Cole has written a general study of the wool trade: *The American Wool Manufacture*, 2 vols. (Cambridge, 1926). Because of tariff implications, the Treasury Department and the Tariff Commission have published many reports: Bureau of Statistics, U.S. Treasury, *Wool and Manufactures of Wool, Special report . . .* , Treasury Dept. Doc. 1025 (Washington, 1887); Worthington C. Ford, *Wool and Manufactures of Wool*, Treasury report (Washington, 1894); and U.S. Tariff Commission, *The Wool-Growing Industry* (Washington, 1921). All of these include historical and statistical material.

Farming in a Land of Limited Rain

Western agriculture is so varied in its natural conditions and its crops, in its use or nonuse of irrigation, that no one has succeeded in giving a truly comprehensive picture, even though two distinguished historians have tried, with Fred A. Shannon's *The Farmer's Last Frontier, 1865–1900* (New York, 1945) and Gilbert C. Fite's *The Farmers' Frontier, 1865–1900* (New York, Chicago, etc., 1966). But some of the related topics have been well handled. Paul Wallace Gates has covered the land question admirably with his *History of Public Land Law Development* (Washington, 1968). Robert G. Dunbar has written a brief but good overview of the troubled water question in *Forging New Rights in Western Waters* (Lincoln, 1983).

Dunbar had further comments in "Water Conflicts and Controls in Colorado," *Agricultural History*, XXII (1948), 180–86. The great legal classic on water is Samuel C. Wiel's *Water Rights in the Western States: The Law of Prior Appropriation of Water as Applied Alone in Some Jurisdictions, and as, in Others, Confined to the Public Domain, with the Common Law of Rights for Waters upon Private Lands . . .* , 3d ed., 2 vols. (San Francisco, 1911). A convenient and more up-to-date legal treatise is by Wells A. Hutchins, *Selected Problems in the Law of Water Rights in the West*, U.S. Department of Agriculture, *Miscellaneous Publication* no. 418 (Washington, 1942).

John Wesley Powell's great but neglected warning was published as *Report on the Lands of the Arid Region of the United States, with a More Detailed Account of the Lands of Utah*, 2d ed., rev. (Washington, 1879; 1st ed., 1878). One of Powell's staff prepared a major *Report on Agriculture by Irrigation in the Western Part of the United States at the Eleventh Census: 1890*, vol. V of *Eleventh Census, 1890* (Washington, 1894). There is an unpublished doctoral dissertation by George L. Strebel, "Irrigation as a Factor in Western History, 1847–1900" (University of California, Berkeley, 1965). Frank Adams prepared a brief history of *Irrigation Districts in California, 1887–1915*, California Dept. of Engineering, *Bulletin* no. 2, (Sacramento, 1916).

A book very popular in its own day was William E. Smythe, *The Conquest of Arid America*, rev. ed. (New York, 1905). One of the best scholarly books on the Great Plains is Mary W. M. Hargreaves' *Dry Farming in the Northern Great Plains, 1900–1925* (Cambridge, 1957). Carl F. Kraenzel's *The Great Plains in Transition* (Norman, 1955) carries a grim warning that is worth listening to. One of the great scholars of the region was James C. Malin, whose writings did not reach as big an audience as they deserved. Particularly important for present purposes was his *Winter Wheat in the Golden Belt of Kansas: A Study in Adaptation to Subhumid Geographical Environment* (Lawrence, 1944), and his article "The Turnover of Farm Population in Kansas," *Kansas Historical Quarterly*, IV (1935), 339–72. The human story that gives vivid reality to all this is John Ise's *Sod and Stubble: The Story of a Kansas Homestead* (New York, 1936).

The role of plant selection is suggested in an article by Karl S. Quisenberry and L. P. Reitz, "Turkey Wheat: The Cornerstone of an Empire," in James W. Whitaker, ed., "Farming in the Midwest, 1840–1900: A Symposium," *Agricultural History*, XLVIII (1974), 98–110. The great bonanza farms just east of the Great Plains are well described in Hiram M. Drache's *The Day of the Bonanza: A History of Bonanza Farming in the Red River of the North* (Fargo, 1964). Colorado's first irrigation colony is best studied through the papers edited by James F. Willard, *The Union Colony at Greeley, Colorado, 1869–1871* (Boulder, 1918), and by Willard and Colin B. Goodykoontz, *Experiments in Colorado Colonization, 1869–1872* (Boulder, 1926).

Donald W. Meinig made an excellent study of *The Great Columbia Plain: A Historical Geography, 1805–1910* (Seattle, 1968). Robert C. Nesbit and Charles M. Gates contributed a specialized insight in "Agriculture in Eastern Washington, 1890–1910," *Pacific Northwest Quarterly*, XXXVIII (1946), 279–95.

California agriculture has been particularly difficult because so many types of farming have been practiced, often simultaneously. The best single book on California is Donald J. Pisani's *From the Family Farm to Agribusiness: The Irrigation Crusade in California and the West, 1850–1931* (Berkeley and Los Angeles, 1984). While Pisani gives his book cohesion by following the central thread of irrigation, his approach is so comprehensive and well informed that he manages to give a remarkably catholic understanding of the larger whole.

Because Californians have made such an extensive use of machinery, alongside Pisani's book should be placed Leo Rogin's *The Introduction of Farm Machinery in Its Relation to the Productivity of Labor . . .*, University of California Publications in Economics, IX (Berkeley, 1931). Rogin stresses the Pacific Coast. California's great wheat trade has been described by Rodman W. Paul in "The Wheat Trade between California and the United Kingdom," *Mississippi Valley Historical Review*, XLV (1958), 391–412, and in "The Great California Grain War: The Grangers Challenge the Wheat King," *Pacific Historical Review*, XXVII (1958), 331–49. Paul's interpretation of the social status of the Grangers has been challenged in part by Gerald L. Prescott, "Farm Gentry vs. the Grangers: Conflict in Rural America," *California Historical Quarterly*, LVI (1977–1978), 328–45. Edwin S. Holmes, Jr., "Wheat Ports of the Pacific Coast," U.S. Department of Agriculture, *Yearbook*, 1901 (Washington, 1902), 567–80, is filled with useful material. An excellent contemporary pamphlet, author unknown, shows the complex industry at work—*Wheat: An Illustrated Description of California's Leading Industry* (San Francisco, 1887)—while an Australian investigation gives a very full description: Nathan A. Cobb, *The California Wheat Industry,* Department of Agriculture, New South Wales, *Miscellaneous Publication* no. 519 (Sydney, 1901.)

William Hammond Hall, state irrigation engineer, unfortunately completed only the southern part of what was to have been a comprehensive survey: *Irrigation in California (Southern)* (Sacramento, 1888). The pioneer irrigation colony has been studied by Hallock F. Raup, "The German Colonization of Anaheim, California," *University of California Publications in Geography,* VI (1932), 123–46.

The wine industry was the subject of a good monograph: Vincent P. Carosso, *The California Wine Industry, 1830–1895: A Study of the Formative Years* (Berkeley and Los Angeles, 1951). One of its pioneers was the subject of a substantial biography: Iris Higbie Wilson, *William Wolfskill, 1798–1866: Frontier Trapper to California Ranchero* (Glendale, 1965). Another pioneer was discussed in a book that included a reprinting of Haraszthy's classic manual: Theodore Schoenman, ed., *Father of California Wine: Agoston Haraszthy; Including "Grape Culture, Wines and Wine-Making"* (Santa Barbara, 1979).

Two excellent appraisals were made at the turn of the century: George Husmann, "The Present Condition of Grape Culture in California," U.S. Department of Agriculture, *Yearbook, 1898* (Washington, 1899), 551–62, and Husmann's "Grape, Raisin, and Wine Production in the United States," U.S.D.A., *Yearbook, 1902* (Washington, 1903), 407–20.

As troubles began to afflict Utah's irrigation, Elwood Mead's office submitted a *Report of Irrigation Investigations in Utah,* U.S. Department of Agriculture, Office of Experiment Stations, *Bulletin* no. 124, (Washington, 1903). Leonard J. Arrington and Dean May took an objective view of the situation in " 'A Different Mode of Life': Irrigation and Society in Nineteenth-Century Utah," in James H. Shideler, ed., *Agriculture in the Development of the Far West* (Washington, 1975), 3–20. Next door in Colorado Robert G. Dunbar reported his findings in two articles: "The Significance of the Colorado Agricultural Frontier, *Agricultural History,* XXXIV (1960), 119–25, and "Agricultural Adjustments in Eastern Colorado in the Eighteen-Nineties," in the same journal, XVIII (1944), 41–52. An older, ill-organized historical source for Colorado is by Alvin T. Steinel and Daniel W. Working, *History of Agriculture in Colorado: A Chronological Record of Progress . . . 1858 to 1926* (Fort Collins, Colo., 1926).

A fine old California agricultural pioneer was studied by Rockwell D. Hunt in *John Bidwell, Prince of California Pioneers* (Caldwell, 1942), while equally notable Oregon pioneers received attention in Thomas C. McClintock's "Henderson Luelling, Seth Lewelling and the Birth of the Pacific Coast Fruit Industry," *Oregon Historical Quarterly,* LXVIII (1967), 153–74.

The California fruit exchanges have been discussed by Rahno M. Mac-

Curdy, *The History of the California Fruit Growers Exchange* (Los Angeles, 1925); John W. Lloyd, *Cooperative and Other Organized Methods of Marketing California Horticultural Products* (Urbana, 1919); and Erich Kraemer and H. E. Erdman, *History of Cooperation in the Marketing of California Deciduous Fruits*, California Agricultural Experiment Station, *Bulletin* no. 557 (Berkeley, 1933).

The Later Days of Mining

In general, see Emmons and Becker, *Statistics and Technology*, previously cited. On the hydraulic debris question, the two principal books are Robert L. Kelley, *Gold vs. Grain: The Hydraulic Mining Controversy in California's Sacramento Valley, a Chapter in the Decline of Laissez Faire* (Glendale, 1959), and the official history by Joseph J. Hagwood, Jr., *The California Debris Commission: A History of the Hydraulic Mining Industry in the Western Sierra of California, and of the Governmental Agency Charged with Its Regulation* (Sacramento, 1981).

On gold dredging, Clark Spence has written a succinct article, "The Golden Age of Dredging: The Development of an Industry and Its Environmental Impact," *Western Historical Quarterly*, XI (1980), 401–14. The story has been well told by the people who were involved in it: Charles Janin, *Gold Dredging in the United States*, U.S. Bureau of Mines, *Bulletin* 127 (Washington, 1918); Lewis E. Aubry, *Gold Dredging in California*, California State Mining Bureau, *Bulletin* no. 57 (Sacramento, 1910); and Hennen Jennings, *The History and Development of Gold Dredging in Montana*, U.S. Bureau of Mines, *Bulletin* 121 (Washington, 1916).

After years of historical neglect, smelting has been well treated by James E. Fell, Jr.'s *Ores to Metals: The Rocky Mountain Smelting Industry* (Lincoln, 1979). A convenient manual of mining law is A. H. Ricketts's *American Mining Law, with Forms and Precedents*, 4th ed., 2 vols., California Division of Mines, *Bulletin* 123 (Sacramento, 1948).

Duane A. Smith has told a colorful story about *Horace Tabor: His Life and the Legend* (Boulder, 1973), whereas Richard H. Peterson has shown that an able entrepreneur could get into an unprofitable mess: "Simeon Gannett Reed and the Bunker Hill and Sullivan: The Frustrations of a Mining Investor," *Idaho Yesterdays*, XXIII (1979), 2–8. Peterson has also written an important analysis of *The Bonanza Kings: The Social Origins and Business Behavior of Western Mining Entrepreneurs, 1870–1900* (Lincoln, 1977). His book stands with Ralph Mann's excellent *After the Gold Rush: Society in Grass Valley and Nevada City, California, 1849–1870* (Stanford, 1982).

Michael P. Malone, with *The Battle for Butte: Mining and Politics on the Northern Frontier, 1864–1906* (Seattle, 1981) has done an outstanding job of untangling a very complex story. John Fahey's *The Ballyhoo Bonanza: Charles*

Sweeny and the Idaho Mines (Seattle, 1971) tells a different story about the northern region, but it, too, is important. Lynn R. Bailey does a fine job with *Bisbee: Queen of the Copper Camps* (Tucson, 1983).

The position of the mining worker and his attempts to better himself through unions have received much needed attention from a series of recent books. Richard E. Lingenfelter has made a careful study of mining unions in *The Hardrock Miners: A History of the Mining Labor Movement in the American West, 1863–1893* (Berkeley and Los Angeles, 1974). Mark Wyman linked up technological and social change in his excellent *Hard Rock Epic: Western Miners and the Industrial Revolution, 1860–1910* (Berkeley and Los Angeles, 1979). Ronald C. Brown took a somewhat different approach in his *Hard-Rock Miners: The Intermountain West, 1860–1920* (College Station, Tex., 1979).

Note that these recent books find perceptibly less universal anger than was stressed by the older studies, which included Vernon H. Jensen's *Heritage of Conflict: Labor Relations in the Nonferous Metals Industry up to 1930* (Ithaca, 1950) and Robert Wayne Smith's *The Coeur d'Alene Mining War of 1892: A Case Study of an Industrial Dispute,* which was published at Corvallis in 1961, many years after it was written.

Frank Crampton's *Deep Enough: A Working Stiff in the Western Mine Camps* (Denver, 1956) has the unique quality of being an autobiography by a miner literate enough to say exactly what he felt.

Other Opportunities

On Federal largess, see Leonard J. Arrington, *The Changing Economic Structure of the Mountain West, 1850–1900* (Logan, Utah, 1963) and Gerald D. Nash, "Bureaucracy and Reform in the West: Notes on the Influence of a Neglected Interest Group," *Western Historical Quarterly,* II (1971), 295–305.

The courts are discussed in Guice, *Rocky Mountain Bench,* and Pomeroy, *Territories,* previously cited, but see also Gordon M. Bakken's two new monographs, *The Development of Law on the Rocky Mountain Frontier: Civil Law and Society, 1850–1912* (Westport, 1983) and *The Development of Law in Frontier California: Civil Law and Society, 1850–1890* (Westport, 1985).

The best book on the lumber industry is by Thomas R. Cox, *Mills and Markets: A History of the Pacific Coast Lumber Industry to 1900* (Seattle, 1974). See also Edmond S. Meany, Jr.'s unpublished doctoral dissertation, "The History of the Lumber Industry in the Pacific Northwest to 1917" (Harvard University, 1935). John Ise, *The United States Forest Policy* (New Haven, 1920) is important. Vernon H. Jensen, *Lumber and Labor* (New York, 1945) is a well-handled study.

Studies of individual companies include Edwin T. Coman and Helen M. Gibbs, *Time, Tide and Timber: A Century of Pope and Talbot* (Stanford, 1949), and Richard C. Berner, "The Port Blakely Mill Company, 1876–89," *Pacific Northwest Quarterly*, LVII (1966), 158–71.

William H. Hutchinson wrote a useful history of interior lumbering: *California Heritage: A History of Northern California Lumbering*, rev. ed. (Santa Cruz, 1974). On the Weyerhaeusers, see Ralph Hidy, Frank E. Hill, and Allan Nevins, *Timber and Men: The Weyerhaeuser Story* (New York, 1963).

Fisheries are discussed in Gordon B. Dodds, *The Salmon King of Oregon: R. D. Hume and the Pacific Fisheries* (Chapel Hill, 1959), and Dodds has edited Hume's account of himself: *A Pygmy Monopolist: The Life and Doings of R. D. Hume, Written by Himself and Dedicated to His Neighbors* (Madison, 1961). There is much on the fisheries in Ted C. Hinckley's *The Americanization of Alaska, 1869–1897* (Palo Alto, 1972). Edmund T. Peckham has an unpublished doctoral dissertation on "The Halibut Fishery of the Pacific Northwest" (Harvard University, 1954).

Consideration of the oil industry starts with the two volumes in which Harold Williamson was the principal mover: Harold Williamson and Arnold R. Daum, *The American Petroleum Industry: The Age of Illumination, 1859–1899* (Evanston, 1959); and Harold F. Williamson, Ralph L. Andreano, Arnold R. Daum, and Gilbert C. Klose, *The American Petroleum Industry: The Age of Energy, 1899–1959* (Evanston, 1963). Samuuel W. Tait, Jr., *The Wildcatters: An Informal History of Oil-Hunting in America* (Princeton, 1946) adds another insight. The principal history for the southwest is Carl C. Rister's *Oil! Titan of the Southwest* (Norman, 1949). John S. Spratt has written a perceptive short history, *The Road to Spindletop: Economic Change in Texas, 1875–1901*, reprint ed. (Austin, 1970). Gerald T. White has summarized California's role briefly in "California's Other Mineral," *Pacific Historical Review*, XXXIX (1970), 135–54, and at much greater length in *Formative Years in the Far West: A History of Standard Oil Company of California and Predecessors through 1919* (New York, 1962).

Index

Fargo, William G., 56
Farmers: immigrants as, 5, 122–23,
144, 222, 242; markets for, 221–22,
244–45, 283; and sheep raising,
212–13, 216, 217; vs. cattlemen,
146, 188, 189, 192, 195; vs. miners,
257, 258. *See also* Fruit raising;
Irrigation; Wheat growing
Farmers and Merchants Bank, 126
Farming: in Arizona, 155; in
California, 5, 15–16, 146, 162–63,
188, 189, 212–13, 223, 226, 229,
230, 231, 235; in Colorado, 47, 222,
232; dry-land, 3, 4–5, 222, 231–34,
235, 332n.36; and forage crops, 4,
15–16, 204, 223, 234, 241; on Great
Plains, 4, 122–23, 222, 231–34;
Greeley on, 11, 15–16; in New
Mexico, 21, 47, 221, 242, 248; in
Pacific Northwest, 5, 115, 118, 223,
228–29; and share cropping, 224,
231; in Utah, 14, 47, 107, 173–74,
175, 221. *See also* Fruit growing;
Irrigation; Wheat growing
Federal government: Indian policies
of, 11, 129–38, 316n.36; and
railroads, 62–63, 89, 91; and
telegraph, 58, 82; vs. Mormons, 179,
180–81. *See also* Officeholders,
Federal; United States Army; United
States Bureau of Indian Affairs;
United States Congress; United
States Supreme Court
Federal Mining and Smelting
Company, 275
Ferries: Oakland-San Francisco, 94
Fetterman, Capt. William J., 48
Field, David Dudley, 285
Fishing industry, 290–92
Five Civilized Tribes, Okla., 136
Flint family, 213
Flood, James C., 262
Floods, 152, 187, 211. *See also* Rainfall
Florence, Idaho: gold at, 29
Folsom, Calif., 75
Foote, Arthur D., 247, 335n.81
Forests, Pacific coastal, 286, 290. *See
also* Lumber industry
Forts: Benton, 59; Bridger, 13; Hall, 8;
Yuma, 55
Fourier, François Marie Charles, 235
Fraser River, B.C.: gold at, 25–26, 32, 34

Free trade: and wool prices, 209
Freiberg Institute, Saxony, 265, 266
Freighting business: in California,
76–77; eastern termini of, 50–51;
and Federal government, 49–50,
53–54, 61; on Great Plains, 76, 183;
and mines, 42, 50; operations of,
12–13, 51–55, 60; and railroads, 56,
62, 64; vs. steamboats, 51, 59; in
Utah, 106, 109
French, Peter, 230
Friedlander, Isaac, 229–30, 250
Frohling, John, 243
Frontier, eastern: defined (1870), 220,
221, 222
Fruit raising, 15, 105, 223–226, 237,
242–46. *See also* Orange industry
Fur traders, 8, 9, 10, 103

Gadsden Purchase, 153
Galloway, James, 44, 45
Gamble, James, 82–83, 108
Gambling, 13, 44, 65, 95, 158, 161,
175, 198, 281
Game, wild, 130, 133. *See also* Buffalo
Garland, Hamlin, 232
Gates, Frederick T., 274, 275
George, Henry, *Progress and Poverty*, 2,
32, 73, 164
Georgia: miners from, 13, 27, 28, 32
Germans. *See* Immigrants: German
Geronimo, 132
Gila River, Ariz.: gold at, 31
Gila Valley, Ariz., 153
Gilpin, Col. William, 95, 96
Gilpin County, Colo., mining in, 99,
101
Glenn, Hugh J., 230, 263
Godbeite heresy, 110, 112
Gold: export of, 66, 71; production
statistics (1852–1880s), 66–67;
smelting of, 104, 264, 265. *See also*
Miners; Mining; names of specific
mines and gold towns
Gold and silver booms and rushes: 1,
2, 9, 13, 24–31, 35, 61, 104, 116,
155; effect of on local economy, 35,
107, 109, 112, 115–16, 151, 286. *See
also* Miners; Mining; names of
specific mines and gold and silver
towns
Golden, Colo., 98–99, 101